Electronic Collaborators

Learner-Centered Technologies for Literacy, Apprenticeship, and Discourse

Electronic Collaborators

Learner-Centered Technologies for Literacy, Apprenticeship, and Discourse

Edited by

Curtis Jay Bonk

Kira S. King

Indiana University

LEA LAWRENCE ERLBAUM ASSOCIATES, PUBLISHERS

1998 Mahwah, New Jersey London

Lawrence Erlbaum Associates, Inc., Publishers
10 Industrial Avenue
Mahwah, NJ 07430

Permission to use the photograph of the International Artic Project explorers holding up the IU flag at the North Pole was granted by Gordon Wiltsie. Permission to use the other photographs on the front cover was provided by Nick Judy, Lisa Denlinger, Phyllis Taylor, Bob Appelman, Mark Simons, and Indiana University Photographic Services.

Cover design by Kathryn Houghtaling Lacey

Library of Congress Cataloging-in-Publication Data

Electronic collaborators : learner-centered technologies for literacy, apprenticeship, and discourse / edited by Curtis Jay Bonk, Kira S. King.
p. cm.
Includes bibliographical references and indexes.
ISBN 0-8058-2796-X (cloth : alk. paper). —ISBN 0-8058-2797-8 (pbk. : alk. paper)
1. Computer conferencing in Education. 2. Group work in education. 3. Authorship—Collaboration. 4. Instructional systems—Design. 5. Constructivism (Education). 6. Distance education. I. Bonk, Curtis Jay. II. King, Kira S.
LB1044.875.E53 1998
98-9394 371.33'4—dc21
CIP

Books published by Lawrence Erlbaum Associates are printed on acid-free paper, and their bindings are chosen for strength and durability.

Printed in the United States of America
10 9 8 7 6 5 4 3 2 1

This book is dedicated to our parents and in memory of the late Jerome A. Bonk

Contents

About the Contributors

Bob Althauser is a professor in the Sociology Department at Indiana University. Bob's interests are in the sociology of work and the changing workplace. As such, his publications and research have focused on labor markets and how technology reorganizes work. He has additional interests and experience in college teaching and instructional technology. He can be reached via the Internet at althause@indiana.edu.

Charoula Angeli is a recent doctoral graduate of the Department of Instructional Systems Technology at Indiana University. She is involved in research related to critical thinking theory. Charoula also has interests in instructional theories, instructional design, curriculum development, problem-based learning, and the design of computer supported learning environments. She currently is a postdoctoral fellow at the Learning Research and Development Center (LRDC) at the University of Pittsburgh.

Curt Bonk is an associate professor in the Learning, Cognition, and Instruction Program within the Department of Counseling and Educational Psychology at Indiana University. Currently, he is a Faculty Fellow for Research at the Center for Excellence in Education, as well as a core member of the Center for Research on Learning and Technology located at the School of Education at Indiana University. As a former accountant and CPA, Curt is interested in enhancing college and K–12 pedagogy with technological supports, scaffolded instruction, and alternative instructional strategies that he seldom observed in business school. His other professional interests include nontraditional learning and distance education, interactive learning environments, learning in a social context, electronic mentoring, social cognition, writing theory, and collaborative writing technologies. Curt directed or guided many of the research projects reported in this book and is currently teleapprenticing preservice teachers on the World Wide Web. He can be reached via the Internet at cjbonk@indiana.edu. Dr. Bonk's web homepage can be found at http://php.indiana.edu/~cjbonk, and his recent course in undergraduate educational psychology is located at http://www.indiana.edu/~smartweb.

Siat-Moy Chong is presently a consulting project manager and instructional designer for CARA Corporation in Oakbrook, Illinois. During the past year, she has been developing and testing training programs for Andersen Worldwide. Her primary interests are in distance learning and training, distributed education, groupwork strategies, and electronic performance support systems. She can be reached via the Internet at smchong@enteract.com.

Don Cunningham is a professor in the Learning, Cognition, and Instruction Program within the Department of Counseling and Educational Psychology at Indiana University. Don was the founder of the Centre for Research Into Educational Application of Multimedia at the University of New England at Armidale in Australia. He has an active program of research and development in computer-mediated instruction and is a leading contributor to the development of semiotic/constructivist theories of learning and instruction. He is currently Associate Dean for Graduate Studies at Indiana University and is a member of the interdisciplinary cognitive science program as well as the Center for Research on Learning and Technology. He can be reached via the Internet at cunningh@indiana.edu, and his web homepage can be found at http://php.indiana.edu/~cunningh/.

Bill Dueber is a doctoral student in the Department of Instructional Systems Technology at Indiana University. Bill is presenting developing and piloting the *Asynchronous Collaboration Tool* (ACT) with Tom Duffy and Chandra Hawley. His interests are in asynchronous group work, problem-based learning, small group interaction, and artificial intelligence. Bill has also worked as an instructional designer at the Center for Excellence in Education and is currently working in the Center for Research on Learning and Technology at Indiana University. He can be reached via the Internet at wdueber@indiana.edu, and his web homepage is located at http://www.cs.indiana.edu/hyplan/wdueber/.

Thomas Duffy, the Barbara Jacobs Chair in Education and Technology, is currently the Director of the Center for Research on Learning and Technology in the School of Education at Indiana University. Professor Duffy's academic appointment is in the School of Education (Language Education and Instructional Systems Technology), and he is also a member of the Cognitive Science faculty at Indiana University. He has published books on the design of online help systems and the design of constructivist learning environments. Tom is currently directing the development of the *Asynchronous Collaborative Tool* (ACT) with Bill Dueber and Chandra Hawley. His interests are in learning theory, the design of inquiry-based learning environments, and distributed collaborative inquiry. He can be reached via the Internet at duffy@indiana.edu.

Melissa Marie Grabner-Hagen is a doctoral student in the Department of Counseling and Educational Psychology at Indiana University. Melissa is a campus learning disabilities service coordinator who has professional interests in learning disabilities and teacher education. She can be reached via the Internet at mgrabner@indiana.edu.

Edmund Hansen is an assistant professor at Emporia State University in Emporia, Kansas. As Director of the Teaching Enhancement Center, Edmund's interests are in student development, including students' development of cognitive learning skills and their motivational dispositions toward college. He work also focuses on how this development can be facilitated through interactive and learner-centered mediated instruction. He can be reached via the Internet at hansened@esumail.emporia.edu and the homepage of the Teaching Enhancement Center is http://www.emporia.edu/tec/homepage.htm.

Chandra Hawley is doctoral student in the Department of Instructional Systems Technology at Indiana University. Chandra's professional interests include critical thinking, problem solving, constructivism, technology in education, teacher training, and effective learning environments. She can be reached via the Internet at chawley@indiana.edu, and her web homepage is located at http://php.ucs.indiana.edu/~chawley/home.html.

Deborah Hoogstrate-Cooney is the Director of Technology Training at Park Tudor School, a private school in Indianapolis, Indiana. Park Tudor is noted for being one of the most technologically sophisticated schools in Indiana and the nation. Deborah's interests include electronic communication, instructional design and development, electronic web support, and collaborative learning. She can be reached via the Internet at dcooney@parktudor.pvt.k12.in.us, and her web homepage is located at http://www.parktudor.pvt.k12.in.us.

Inae Kang is an assistant professor at Kyung Hee University in Korea. As a result of significant educational changes taking place in Korea today, Inae's interests and experience in teaching and learning using computer-mediated communication, constructivist design of instruction, and problem-based learning are in high demand. She can be reached via the Internet at iakang@chollian.net.

Kira King is a recent doctoral graduate of the Department of Instructional Systems Technology at Indiana University and also has a master's in Computers and Education from Teachers College, Columbia. As a former elementary teacher, Dr. King is interested in designing learning environments that are hands-on, learner-generated, and fun. Her research is focused on bridging informal and formal learning through the creation of a new alternative educational system, the museum school. Kira has also done work in educational systems design, systems thinking, instructional and educational design, and educational software design. She can be reached via the Internet at ksking@iag.net, and her web homepage is located at http://www.iag.net/~ksking/home.html.

Sonny Kirkley is Assistant Director of Research and Development at the Center for Excellence in Education at Indiana University. Sonny has interests in human–computer interface and interaction design, the use of technology to support social-constructivist learning environments, the design of "fun" in learning, and the application of virtual and augmented reality to learning. Sonny can be reached via the Internet at ekirkley@indiana.edu. His web homepage can be found at http://www.wisdomtools.com/staff_sonny.html or find staff listings at http://www.wisdomtools.com.

Shannon Ann Lazar is a doctoral candidate in the Department of Counseling and Educational Psychology at Indiana University. Shannon's interests are in child development, cognitive and social development of children with autism, and teacher education. She can be reached via the Internet at shabrown@indiana.edu.

Julia Matuga is an associate instructor in the Department of Counseling and Educational Psychology. As former art teacher, Julia is interested in the impact of peer interaction and instructional scaffolding on artistic development. Her other interests are in sociocultural theory (especially issues of private speech), sociocultural instructional strategies, simulated technology environments, and creative behavior. Julia can be reached via the Internet at jmatuga@indiana.edu.

Christina Mirabelli is a school counselor at Harlan Elementary School in Indiana. She has interests in academically and emotionally at-risk children. She can be reached via the Internet at cmirabelli@eacs.k12.in.us.

Margaret Riel is an internationally known scholar and pioneer in collaborative learning technology and virtual learning communities. She began her career as a researcher studying interactive learning environments at the University of California, San Diego and is now Associate Director of the Center for Collaborative Research in Education at the University of California, Irvine as well as Director of InterLearn. In the latter role, she has researched and developed various network learning environments for cross-classroom collaboration and electronic travel. Moreover, Dr. Riel designed, coordinated, and evaluated a global networking program for elementary and secondary schools called "*Learning Circles*" initially for the AT&T Learning Network and currently for the International Education And Resource Network (I*EARN). She was also involved in the initial design and evaluation of an electronic fieldtrip called *Passport to Knowledge* which combines live television, electronic networking of scientists and students, online resources, and in-class materials to involve students in the collaborative processes of scientific discovery. Dr. Riel has a number of journal articles and book chapters on research related to these interactive technology environments. She can be reached via the Internet at mriel@uci.edu, and her web office is located at http://www.gse.uci.edu/mriel.html.

John Savery is an adjunct faculty member in the Computer Science and Telecommunications Department at DePaul University. He is also the lead instructional application designer with the Academic Technology Development group. In this role, he is designing faculty training programs to encourage the use of learner-centered instructional principles and the incorporation of instructional technology across teaching/learning settings. John also has published and presented work related to problem-based learning and issues of learning ownership. He can be reached via the Internet at jsavery@condor.depaul.edu, and his web homepage is located at http://www.depaul.edu/~jsavery.

Martin Siegel is currently a professor in the Instructional Systems Technology Department at Indiana University and is the Director of the Laboratory for Research and Development in Teaching and Learning at the Center for Excellence in Education at IU. Also of note, Marty was the first Faculty Fellow at Microsoft Corporation. His interests are in human–computer interface design, the design of digital environments, and the design of Internet-based interactive instructional tools. Recent projects includes work with Jim Spohrer at Apple Computer in the creation of the *WorldBoard*, a planetary augmented reality system, creating "just in place" learning. In addressing the emergence of digital learning environments, Marty has spearheaded the *WisdomTools* project at Indiana University. He can be reached via the Internet at msiegel@indiana.edu, and his web homepage can be found at http://www.wisdomtools.com under the staff listings.

Bill Sugar is an assistant professor in the Department of Library Science and Instructional Technology at Southern Connecticut State University. Bill's interests are in developing suitable usability techniques to ensure user-centered design. He is also intrigued by issues related to the design of effective computer mediated communications environments, democratizing information issues, and facilitating student-centered learning environments. He can be reached via the Internet at sugar@scsu.ctstateu.edu.

Erping Zhu is leading various course and faculty development projects within the Office of Instructional Technology at the newly established Florida Gulf Coast University. She has interests in the design of hypermedia, the development of web-based instruction, and the use of technology in problem-based and distance learning environments. She can be reached via the Internet at ezhu@fgcu.edu.

Foreword: Conceptual Order and Collaborative Tools—Creating Intellectual Identity

Margaret Riel
University of California, Irvine

"I think, therefore I am." This observation about intellectual identity comes to us from Descartes across many centuries by way of communication technology. Thinking may give us our identity, but sharing our ideas offers the possibility of intellectual immortality across time and space. What role does thinking and the sharing of ideas play in our schools? How is learning related to reflection, problem-solving, and writing?

We know from psychology that students learn best when—motivated by interest and empowered by knowledge—they take on a conceptual challenge to solve a problem or accomplish a task that is just out of their reach. Equipped with metacognitive skills, they set goals and work with human and informational resources to assess their progress towards the completion of the task. Once completed, the learner is eager to share this new knowledge with others.

How do we help students develop their interests? How do we give them the power of knowledge? How can we structure these conceptual challenges? Furthermore, what role do schools play in helping students learn to learn and to share what they have learned with others?

In the group settings of schools, it has been difficult to facilitate engaged learning. Instead, most time in school is spent preparing students to learn—empowering them with knowledge. This is done by packaging information into small conceptual units and delivering them to students in an ordered sequence. Students are then responsible for developing a filing system to organize these units so they will be easy to retrieve when they are intellectually challenged. Not surprisingly, most of our current assessment techniques simply check the status of the most recent deliveries. Did the student get the information packet that was sent?

It is difficult to know how students are organizing their minds. Just what happens to these packets of information? Are they empowering students to solve problems or create new knowledge? We cannot see how students arrange mental objects, but we can make inferences from their skills with physical objects—toys, clothes, books, pens, models, and games. Why do adults work so hard to keep the physical world of children ordered? The value of physical objects diminishes if they are all thrown into a disorganized heap. Categorizing toys invites new forms of play, new connections, and generative activities. And so it is with mental objects; organizing one's ideas has the same generative properties. When we order our thoughts, we make them readily available for the creation of entirely new concepts. The effort to order ideas ultimately makes them more powerful.

Well organized play spaces are most often the interactive accomplishment of adults working with children. Children need help understanding the reasons for organization and developing the discipline to accomplish this process. Teachers and parents need to help students understand that keeping materials organized increases their value. It is not something that is done once, but is repeated again and again, with one often finding new ways to organize things as past uses give rise to new ones.

A mind that is filled with experiences, feelings, and information needs order and organization. How do children learn to organize conceptual spaces, mental objects, and these packets of information that are routinely delivered in schools? Does it make sense to expect children to have more skill with mental objects and conceptual information than they exhibit with physical objects? If we could see the internal organization of their minds, we might not be surprised at the difficulty they have at finding what they need, when they need it.

So, what strategies and tools do we have for helping create intellectual order? How can we help students learn what it means to use information in generative ways? Also, perhaps most importantly, what role can teachers play in facilitating the design of these mental systems?

The learner-centered technologies for literacy, apprenticeship, and discourse described in this book are the tools of intellectual identity. They help shape the mind of a student, his or her ability to reflect on what he or she knows, and his or her ability to use what he or she knows to create new knowledge. When used in thoughtful ways by teachers, these tools ask students to take out the packages of information, examine them, and begin to think about how to organize them to create new understandings—knowledge products. It is not enough to just make the deliveries. The organization of information into knowledge is too difficult to leave for students to work out alone. Without help, much of what students need for leaning is hopelessly buried under masses of unexamined information delivered by well-intentioned teachers. Collaborative technologies make it easier to facilitate collective sense-making, an activity that can take place in schools. By making explicit the process of using information to develop new understandings, teachers can help students create intellectual order and generate new mental pathways that define the way they think and learn, thereby authoring their own intellectual identities.

The authors in this book anchor their work in the writings of Piaget, Bruner, and especially the sociocultural work of Vygotsky. Vygotsky describes a developmental sequence in which social exchanges between a child and more competent others in a social and historical environment form the basis of individual thought. Children learn more than language as they repeat what they hear. Gradually these voices of self and other become inner dialogs and are eventually internalized, forming individual thought. The work reported in this book extends this argument. The tools that help build knowledge systems in social settings between students and more knowledgeable adults represent a way to organize information into powerful thinking tools. These intellectual dialogues are internalized as conceptual schemes and models that eventually help students to organize information into conceptual knowledge. The process of collaborative thinking and writing help students to:

- examine their ideas in a social context of different perspectives and develop collective ways to understand issues
- challenge the ideas of others through critical thinking.

Collaborative critical inquiry, such as the research reported in this book, provides students with the tools for self-reflection and knowledge construction. This process creates mental pathways and links between ideas and flexible filing systems, making it possible to use information in new and different organizations.

The contributors to *Electronic Collaborators* describe a range of tools that are available to facilitate collaborative writing, from simple e-mail and writing applications, to more complex environments that combine asynchronous and synchronous communication with interactive use of multimedia applications and databases. Each of the authors in this volume use learner-centered, constructivist, and sociocultural theories to inform the design and research on new technologies. The goal of the authors is to increase our understanding of the effects of different electronic collaboration tools on student learning. As we increase the collaborative learning tools that we have available, we can be more selective in matching such tools to learning outcomes.

This book itself is a reflection of the power of collaborative writing within a community of learners. All of the authors have been a part of research efforts in the School of Education at Indiana University. They are themselves making sense of, and experimenting with, communication technology in both research and instructional contexts. Although most universities extend the reach of face-to-face courses with online replications, few institutions have created the innovative uses of the technology to design new forms of learning that are taking place at Indiana University. The strong coherence across and within the chapters presented in this volume make it closer to a book with multiple authors then an edited anthology. This collective dialog about collaborative work, as well as the work that has been accomplished, helps us understand both the evolving tools and how they can help shape new patterns of education in the future.

The work tools of our society are increasingly mental and our need to use such tools for life-long learning is the path to the future. Those who learn how to create and use mental tools in a space that is ordered and organized will be better prepared to generate the knowledge products that will be the trade of tomorrow. They will also have strong intellectual identities and their ideas will continue to inspire those who follow in the years to come.

Preface

It was a hot August night in 1992 when I arrived at Indiana University (IU) in a rusted-out Honda Civic loaded down with books and journals from my previous post at West Virginia University. Stepping out of my tired car, I gazed up at a magnificent new structure known as the School of Education at IU, a federally supported project intended to promote the use of technology in teaching and learning. This limestone castle seemed to be beckoning all those approaching it to unlock the countless secrets of its technology treasures. Looking back, I was awestruck. Sure, I had read all the hype about the new facility in various journals and press releases and had seen the place when it was in an earlier phase of construction. However, this was a very different feeling, a humbling but exhilarating one, too seldom experienced in life. It was an awareness that I had arrived at the right place.

So, with beads of sweat fogging my glasses and an unwieldy stack of books teetering my balance, I maneuvered through the heavy doors of this technology fortress and tried to find my designated place in one of its towers. Of course, I had little knowledge that the research that would be sparked here during the next 5 years would serve as a basis for a book on electronic collaboration. The research described herein provides a glimpse into the innovations and experimentations that have transpired as a result of this wondrous learning and technology resource. Although some of these projects took place at locations outside the School of Education, all of the chapters in this book were written by individuals who worked in that grand building during those initial years.

Not long after my arrival at Indiana, a cadre of researchers investigating various electronic collaboration and communication tools began to meet informally to discuss their electronic learning ideas, models, and findings. This soon evolved into the loosely connected Computer Conferencing and Collaborative Writing (CCCW) Group at Indiana University which included professors, graduate students, instructional designers, and directors of technology projects. The idea for this book on electronic collaboration emerged when the CCCW group discovered the commonalities of our interests and findings. We recognized the need for a book that detailed the tools for computer conferencing and collaboration, the learning theories grounding their use, and the preliminary results of this merging of theory building with technology tool implementation.

It is our hope that this text will help provide collaborative learning tools and ideas that powerfully transform education with innovative ideas for electronic social interaction and new learning communities in both public school and higher education settings. Consequently, this book provides separate illustrations of electronic collaboration in asynchronous and synchronous environments as well as a several examples wherein both forms of collaboration are employed. In addition, we attempt to document collaborative learning tool use from constructivist, learner-centered, and sociocultural perspectives. This documentation of the diverse environments for computer conferencing and collaborative writing should appeal to a wide range of potential readers.

ADDITIONAL BACKGROUND AND SETTING

Indiana University (IU) was recently ranked as the top public university in the country for its technological support and was in the top 10 overall. Given this access to technology, many faculty across disciplines at IU have become increasingly unsatisfied with teaching in the familiar and routine manner in which they themselves were taught. Fortunately, during the past decade, IU has been at the forefront of innovative teaching and learning by supporting various resources on collaborative learning. During this time, the university has sponsored several major conferences, a listserv, and a sourcebook related to collaborative learning in higher education. In October 1995, in fact, IU hosted the Seventh Annual Hypermedia Conference as well as the first International Conference on Computer Supported Collaborative Learning (CSCL) wherein some of the projects in this book were originally presented.

Like the rest of the university, the School of Education at IU also is a leader in the field of educational technologies (see Fig. P1). It is here that every contributor to this book worked or learned at some point during the past 5 years. In a walk through the W. W. Wright Education Building, one would find extremely talented graduate students from the top-ranked Instructional Systems Technology program in the country, cutting-edge distance-education technologies and classroom suites, extensive educational technology support services, and the Center for Excellence in Education (CEE). The CEE, a national educational technology demonstration and training site, offers valuable support and direction to K–12 schools from across the nation in the use of educational technologies. The Arctic adventure project described in chapters 6 and 14 of this book, in fact, was originally organized by the World School for Adventure Learning division of the CEE. A short walk down the hall from the CEE is the Center for Research on Learning and Technology, whose mission is to support the School of Education's program of research on the linkage between learning theory, pedagogy, and technology.

FIG. P1. The School of Education at Indiana University. From Indiana University Instructional Support Services (Mark Simons, Photographer)., Bloomington, Indiana 47405-5901.

AUDIENCE

Electronic Collaborators is reflective of the editors' and authors' belief that as new tools for collaboration and conferencing are developed, it is essential that we disseminate research findings that document the powerful theoretical foundations and instructional approaches of these educational technologies. As schools and universities are providing increased technological support and infrastructure for distance learning and collaboration, most of us still need practical examples of effective technology for electronic collaboration.

At present, there is surprisingly minimal information on the effects of computer conferencing and collaborative writing tools in either K–12 or collegiate settings. This book, therefore, is intended for use in graduate courses in such areas as educational technology, instructional design, educational psychology, social psychology, curriculum and instruction, language education, and telecommunications. We hope that this text strikes a chord with those interested in such fields as sociocultural theory, process approaches to writing, collaborative writing, cooperative learning, adventure learning, learner-centered instruction, constructivism, distance education, peer conferencing and tutoring, electronic mentoring and collaboration, problem- and project-based learning, and educational reform. In effect, this text should be a useful reference tool on electronic collaboration for a wide range of audiences.

This book is meant to inform teachers, researchers, designers, graduate students, policymakers, and administrators of the importance of the collaborative educational learning tools and techniques for promoting student–student and student–teacher electronic interaction. Teachers will gain insights into unique venues for learning collaboration, opportunities for extending classroom boundaries, and varied experimentations and struggles to embed learning tools in one's instruction. The work in the book should also help other researchers think about useful ways to implement and assess collaborative learning tools. Instructional designers, on the other hand, should find inspiration in the range of collaborative tools employed here and the ways in which they were incorporated to enhance learning. Graduate students should gain some insight into both research and theory related to electronic collaboration as well as the types of electronic learning formats that require additional testing and where they can play a role in furthering this research. Educational policymakers will hopefully be better informed about the theoretical justification for the purchase of collaborative learning tools as well as some of the more promising areas of use. Finally, practitioners and administrators should benefit from windows into the teaching–learning process and from the implications of the electronic collaboration research emanating from the educational technology palace where I work.

ACKNOWLEDGMENTS

My coeditor, Kira King, and I are indebted to Naomi Silverman, Senior Editor at Lawrence Erlbaum Associates (LEA), and her assistant, Kate Graetzer, for their positive feedback and timely editorial advice. Along these same lines, we thank Kathy Dolan, Editorial Associate, as well as all the production staff at LEA for their help and assistance in this process. We recognize LEA reviewers, Jay David Bolter and David Tillyer for their insightful and informative suggestions. In addition, we must thank Mary, Alex, and Nicki Bonk and Christopher King and Nadia Nedzel for their love and encouragement during this project. I am deeply thankful to my late father, Jerome Bonk, who encouraged me to work at Indiana University so that I could work in the most technologically sophisticated school of education in the country, which was significantly funded by his lifetime employer, AT&T. I also want to acknowledge my mother, Joanne Bonk, for her unending encouragement and guidance throughout my life. My high school humanities teacher, Mr. Kim Rhode, is credited here for nurturing my interests in human learning, technology trends, cultural tools, and effective pedagogy; ironically, many of his subtle predictions from more than two decades ago are clearly evident in this book today. Finally, I wish to thank all the contributors to this volume who each have uniquely impacted teaching and learning at Indiana University and are now electronically extending this influence throughout the world.

—*Curtis Jay Bonk*

Introduction to Electronic Collaborators

Curtis Jay Bonk
Kira S. King
Indiana University

PERSPECTIVE

Various technological, instructional, and pedagogical developments have recently converged to dramatically alter conceptions of the teaching and learning process. As innovations in computer technology, instructional design, and learning pedagogy intersect, powerful new collaborative learning tools are beginning to emerge and play a pivotal role in the educational process. Clearly, technology tools for learning are becoming increasingly interactive, distributed, and collaborative. For instance, computer-networking software is supporting our schools with unparalleled access to information resources and instruction. Through the use of the Internet and the World Wide Web (WWW), we now have easy access to highly interactive learning environments that include a wide variety of learning media (text, sound, video, and three-dimensional imaging). Virtual reality appears to be the next phase of these developments.

Not only do such technological breakthroughs offer us opportunities for accessing an overwhelming array of data and resources, but they are also generating new collaborative technologies that alter the way we learn, research, work, and socialize. Additionally, parallel advances in learning theory and in instructional design are helping educational stakeholders transform traditional notions of schooling, while challenging us to redefine the roles of teacher and student. For example, there is increasing pressure to replace the teacher-centered instruction of the Industrial and Information Ages with learner-centered ideas of the Communication Age (e.g., collaborative learning, knowledge as design, and building communities of learners).

During the 1990s, collaborative technologies, both real-time and delayed formats, have begun to augment and redefine most academic learning environments. But as these technologies emerge to facilitate human–human interactions across classrooms, universities, and worldwide learning communities, various instructional design and implementation problems arise. Instructors simply need more guidelines from educational researchers about integrating electronic collaboration and communication tools into their classrooms.

PURPOSE

The goal of the book, therefore, is to display a range of collaborative technology tools, while documenting several representative ways of using them for enhancing human learning and development. All the projects presented in this volume are closely linked to theories of learning that emphasize social interaction and student active knowledge construction. Hence, the sociocultural work of Vygotsky, Wertsch, Cole, and Rogoff inform and underpin many of the works mentioned here (see chap. 2 for key references). The grounding of this work in sociocultural, constructivist, and learner-centered theory, is meant to afford this text a longer shelf life than typical books related to educational technology. This may, in fact, be the first book on electronic conferencing or "online education" directly addressing such perspectives.

We feel that now is the time to combine the technological and pedagogical advancements of the past decade with a text that details unique electronic learning communities now found in both K–12 and collegiate settings. In order to make decisions that productively transform learning environments, however, documentation is needed regarding how schools and teachers are discovering and incorporating new electronic collaboration and communication tools. As such tools have surfaced in schools, the contributors to this book have focused on understanding the effects of various conferencing and collaborative composing formats on social interaction and resulting student learning. Five of the key objectives of this book, therefore, are to:

- Document some of the collaborative learning tools and formats currently employed by teachers in schools and universities.
- Situate these emerging tools within various electronic interaction levels and formats (e.g., synchronous and asynchronous).
- Explore how various learning theories—learner-centered, constructivist, and sociocultural—can be used to structure, analyze, and assess electronic learning environments and social dialogue.
- Examine collaborative dialogue transcripts collected at numerous collaborative tool sites that provide rich documentation of instances wherein collaborative technologies were successfully as well as unsuccessfully used.
- Start a dialogue about the importance of student electronic social interaction and dialogue.

CONTENT OVERVIEW

This volume is divided into five distinct sections. The chapters in each respective section are chronologically sequenced according to the grade level under investigation or intended audience. Part I outlines the foundational theories, concepts, and tools for the remaining portions of this book. Parts II, III, and IV detail research on the social interaction and discourse within electronic conferencing. The second section relates to studies of collaboration in stand-alone computing environments. The more technologically sophisticated third section concerns research on asynchronous collaboration tools. Even more electronically rich is the fourth section, which features a few studies involving both synchronous and asynchronous communication. Although this sequencing of chapters is intended to represent a hierarchy of collaborative tool use, from lower level to more elegant learning tools, the stand-alone and asynchronous ideas of Parts II and III are currently more common and cost effective than the synchronous electronic discussions and multiconferencing work found in the latter chapters of this book. Finally, Part V offers both a retrospective review of these electronic conferencing studies as well as an appeal to future digital environments and networks for social interaction.

PART I: THEORETICAL AND TECHNICAL FOUNDATIONS

The first part of this book establishes key theoretical underpinnings for the use of electronic learning tools. In addition, a number of conferencing and collaboration tools are discussed.

In chapter 1, Bonk and King detail a taxonomy for thinking about computer conferencing and collaborative writing tools. Using this framework, we provide insights into how the various work in this book was initially conceptualized from a collaborative writing perspective. This chapter also surveys the sociocultural variables and instructional methods related to electronic collaboration. Central to this chapter, we describe how various electronic learning tools and approaches can be used for different levels of electronic interaction and collaboration. Tools for collaborative writing, for instance, are categorized into five levels of interaction including: (a) electronic messaging devices, (b) delayed collaboration tools, (c) real-time brainstorming and conversational tools, (d) synchronous text collaborative writing tools, and (e) collaborative multimedia and hypermedia tools. After detailing the taxonomy, electronic dialogue in both academic and informal settings is sampled and discussed. In effect, this chapter is intended to begin a dialogue about student dialogue.

Chapter 2 by Bonk and Cunningham offers three theoretical viewpoints for the work on collaborative tools. This chapter explicates learner-centered, constructivist, and sociocultural beliefs, principles, and approaches that inform the use of electronic conferencing and collaboration media. As such, this chapter builds on the previous one by pointing out that as educators have responded to passive, compartmentalized learning of the past century, new ways for thinking about teaching and learning have emerged. Most important, chapter 2 explains and defines key sociocultural terminology and principles while outlining much of the rationale for the research and ideas presented in the remaining sections of this book.

Whereas chapter 2 surveys learning theories applicable to collaborative tools, chapter 3, by Duffy, Dueber, and Hawley, details how pedagogy merges with computer-based conferencing systems to support critical thinking and learner collaboration. In particular, this group focuses on how their new web-based collaboration tool, Asynchronous Collaboration Tool (i.e., ACT), can be used to support issue-based discussion. The primary focus of this chapter, therefore, is to promote student critical thinking through electronic means. Duffy et al.'s explicit hope is that better understanding of the critical-thinking features and opportunities within computer conferencing and collaboration tools will lead to improved design of these devices and ultimately to better instruction.

PART II: STAND-ALONE SYSTEM COLLABORATION

The tools and methods of electronic interaction presented in Part II involve the most common but least elegant form of computer-supported collaboration: pairs or teams of students working together at a single workstation or sharing a common computer disk of one's work. In this section, one can read about pairs or teams of students working on papers, ideas, and reports in a computer lab or on a single computer workstation.

Chapter 4, by Angeli and Cunningham, for instance, discusses a tool for literacy development, *Bubble Dialogue*, which was tested for a period of 7 months with elementary students to enhance their reading and writing. As a tool to promote literacy among pairs of students, Bubble Dialogue supported student dialogue and role play by engaging them in meaningful, goal-oriented activity wherein word meanings were socially constructed. The authors detail how speech bubbles were used to foster intermental, social behavior, whereas thought bubbles were incorporated to foster intramental, individual behavior. In this particular study, student dialogue transcripts revealed that Bubble Dialogue has great potential as a literacy tool in promoting the articulation and development of young learners' thought processes, the development of word meaning, and the acquisition of sentence structure awareness. Using the learner-centered psychological principles as a guiding framework, the authors develop and evaluate an instructional model based on the design characteristics of this collaborative tool.

In chapter 5, Savery documents how students in an undergraduate business communications course work in five-person collaborative teams to produce written responses to problem situations presented by their teachers. Within the context of an elaborate business simulation, the students planned, drafted, revised, and edited numerous letters and memos. Notice that the teachers here coached, rather than lectured, as student teams worked in a computer lab on their writing assignments. Savery qualitatively examined teams from four classrooms for an entire semester with a focus on: (a) student self-regulation of their learning, (b) the instructional scaffolding and coaching provided by the teachers, (c) the patterns of collaboration in the writing process; (d) the use of computers in the collaborative composing process, (e) the design principles of this learning simulation and other more authentic learning environments, and (f) the intersubjectivity developed within the teams over the semester. Perhaps, most important to the purposes of this text, the development of student ownership within this learner-centered environment was documented and a model of student ownership within such settings was devised. From this study, it can be concluded that even simple word-processing tools offer rich avenues for learning collaboration and self-regulated learning.

PART III: ASYNCHRONOUS ELECTRONIC PROCESSING

The next set of five chapters explores the world of asynchronous conferencing and electronic mail systems (E-mail). Whereas Part II of this text involves the most prevalent form of collaboration, Part III extends this text into the area that most readers would immediately associate with electronic collaboration. Many of us, in fact, could not survive professionally and personally without the E-mail or other asynchronous conferencing tools described in this section.

Chapter 6, by Sugar and Bonk, focuses on middle and high school student use of the Internet to build online "telecommunities." Here, adventure-learning ideas were used to create a novel cognitive apprenticeship that connected students to Internet "pen pals" in an asynchronous telecommunications project of the World School for Adventure Learning known as the World Forum. In this particular World Forum activity, students explored critical environmental issues within a real-life Arctic expedition through discussions, questions, and debates with Arctic explorers, researchers, World Forum mentors, and peers. During the project, students responded to environmental alerts, flash points, and daily explorer journals sent from the Arctic and, in turn, were encouraged to ask questions of the explorers. Sugar and Bonk employ several different measures to understand the frequency of participation, level of questioning, depth of discussion, degree of perspective taking, and forms of mentoring and learning assistance in this unique environment.

The results indicate that this form of computer-mediated communication does enhance student learning when supported by peers, mentors, teachers, and experts.

The application of delayed computer conferencing is also a significant innovation in higher education, especially when compared to conventional classroom settings. As electronic conferencing proliferates in education, studies related to its use as a supplementary tool to traditional higher education experiences seems vital. However, employing computer conferencing as a collaborative learning device in conventional settings is still in the developmental stages.

In chapter 7, Chong examines how computer conferencing may facilitate collaborative learning and enhance social interactions in large-section college classes. She tracks the support provided to a number of instructors at Indiana University as they incorporated asynchronous computer conferencing technology for student collaboration and topical discussion. Her longitudinal work includes a description of how these instructors differentially adopted a university-licensed conferencing tool in undergraduate and graduate college courses in computer science, sociology, recreation and parks administration, education, and library science. To her credit, she selected courses whose high enrollment normally allowed little interaction with the instructor and among students. In qualitatively evaluating this approach, Chong uses interviews, surveys, observations, and journals to determine how computer conferencing supplemented classroom instruction and assignments, while enhancing student discussion and social interaction. Within four basic delayed-collaboration models that Chong discovered, instructors used this electronic classroom to discuss weekly topics, analyze case studies, solve sample exams, and foster collaborative learning communities. Chong's results also indicate that delayed computer conferencing can contribute to building a student-centered learning climate if properly integrated into a course. However, student expectations and previous competitive experiences, software inadequacies, system availability, and conventional pedagogy all interfere with effective use of the medium's interactive potential. As Chong aptly notes, there is an assortment of issues that currently limit asynchronous computer conferencing and collaboration in higher education.

Instead of a longitudinal study of one particular technology, chapter 8 by Althauser and Matuga recounts the variety of electronic tools and activities used by one professor over a span of 5 years in his undergraduate courses. This chapter highlights the pedagogical possibilities facing a professor when he or she becomes interested in how cooperative grouping and computer conferencing can support "active learning." This particular professor's journey included student electronic collaboration on previewed exam questions as well as electronic discussion questions that encouraged students to integrate course content. Within each of these modes, the learning environment is described in terms of student engagement in the learning process as well as pivotal changes in the professor's instructional tactics. The reader should note the unique ideas are discussed for fostering weekly participation, interaction, metacognitive reflection, and group commentary within small, cooperative groups. Pedagogical limits and guidelines also are outlined. Additionally, near the end of the chapter, the authors compare the instructional scaffolding found in electronic conferencing to that modeled in the traditional, lecture-based classroom. As WWW courses and fully asynchronous instruction become more common, this journey raises larger questions about the viability and advisability of electronic instruction absent from the social fabric created by at least some real-time, face-to-face social interaction.

In chapter 9, Kirkley, Savery, and Grabner-Hagen explore the use of E-mail distribution lists for extending classroom discussion in three different graduate courses. In the first instance, the instructors of a team-taught media production course use E-mail to model the feedback of a contemporary business-training setting. By focusing on the means of assistance the instructors provided, a range of pedagogical strategies was discovered.

In contrast to this production course, E-mail dialogue in two doctoral seminars was also analyzed to determine how it extended classroom discussion and coordinated course logistics. In addition to the forms of learning assistance previously studied, other factors investigated here included the content of discussions, the timing of interactions, and the frequency of participation. Interestingly, this later study found that electronic interaction maintained the common gender, status, and ethnicity differences found in the regular classroom. Despite these results, E-mail appears to be an effective resource for helping build cognitive apprenticeships and mentoring graduate students in higher education settings. In the end, the authors caution readers that the overall impact of E-mail on classroom learning environments remains unanswered.

The purpose of chapter 10, by Zhu, was to document patterns of student–teacher and student–student electronic discussions and meaning negotiations in a distance-learning class. This chapter examines: (a) the use of technology in facilitating teaching and learning, (b) the role of instructors in electronic discussions, and (c) weekly changes in student electronic social interaction and discourse. Data collected here revolves around a 15-week graduate seminar on interactive learning technologies that was taught using Picture-tel and CU-SeeMe videoconferencing technologies. Electronic social interaction data were derived from weekly asynchronous computer conferences on the assigned course readings. Electronic transcripts were analyzed in terms of note categories (e.g., comments, questions, scaffolding, and reflections), types of interaction (e.g., horizontal or vertical), and participant roles (e.g., contributor, wanderer, seeker, and mentor). Once these categories were established, the patterns of electronic discussion and meaning negotiation were examined. Zhu's analyses revealed relationships in the nature of student and instructor interaction in delayed conferencing that shed light on how electronic conferences can be efficiently organized to facilitate learning; in particular, how to help students construct new knowledge electronically. Also central to this particular study, a model for understanding the pattern of knowledge construction and zones of engagement in electronic discussion was developed.

PART IV: MULTICONFERENCING: ASYNCHRONOUS AND SYNCHRONOUS CLASSROOMS

Multiple modes of conferencing is the focus of Part IV of this text. These three chapters push this text into the synchronous or real-time conferencing arena. With the exponential growth of electronic computer-conferencing technologies, synchronous communication, such as computer conferencing chat, is emerging as an important tool within collaborative learning environments. In the late 1990s, real-time conferencing and chat tools are becoming increasingly popular on the Internet.

The first study of this section by Cooney (i.e., chap. 11) describes a 10th-grade English teacher who effectively uses *Aspects*, a prominent synchronous conferencing tool, to engage her class in discussing characters and themes, summarize and represent knowledge, and debate "aspects" of the popular but complex American play, T*he Crucible*. The teacher selected this real-time collaboration tool in an attempt to spur classroom discourse and collaboration on common text and graphics products and information. In contrast to the tools mentioned in other chapters of this book, students in this study used multiple tools, including: (a) the free-for-all text mode for writing and reporting, (b) the chat box for brainstorming and discussion, and (c) the draw and paint tools for representing knowledge (e.g., knowledge webs and concept maps). As Cooney points out, on-task behaviors were extremely high when using this tool, while student discussion was raised to new levels of discourse. Additional analyses of communication patterns indicate that social interaction patterns change when students move from a traditional classroom to an electronic setting. Although the relative participation rate was raised significantly for all students during electronic conferencing, some of the traditionally "low contributors" became high contributors when communicating online, whereas a few others remained low contributors. Transcripts, field observations, and teacher interviews all indicate that synchronous communication fostered more depth of thought, peer interaction, and learning ownership than previous semesters. In addition, new connections and skill appeared to transfer, at least in part, to the regular classroom setting.

In contrast to the use of various synchronous communication options by Cooney, chapter 12 by Bonk, Hansen, Grabner-Hagen, Lazar, and Mirabelli evaluates both synchronous and asynchronous collaboration. More specifically, this study investigates how preservice teachers resolved electronically presented case vignettes when working in subject matter-specific teams. In the first classroom studied here, students interacted about brief, one-paragraph cases during class time using real-time brainstorming features of *Connect*, whereas, in a later class, students solved two-page dilemmas at their leisure using a delayed-collaboration tool called *VAX Notes*. Although the differences in case formats and time allotment prohibit direct comparisons between these synchronous or asynchronous options, both qualitative and quantitative analyses indicated that the delayed communication afforded serious and elaborate discussions, whereas the real-time mode encouraged a content focus and brief but frequent student responding.

This chapter also illuminates how cases might be used to support sociocultural ideas about scaffolded learning, zones of proximal development, intersubjectivity, and intermental processing. Electronic transcripts, for instance, reveal that students—within both real-time and delayed formats—quickly took ownership over this communication medium and carefully crafted their words for others to read. Some students, in trying to impress peers with their ideas, were unknowingly operating at the edges of peer zones of proximal development, thereby significantly extending case discussions and debates. Also highlighted in this chapter are issues of group size, participant roles, task requirements, and case length. Equally important, a coding scheme for analyzing student–student interactions in collaborative environments is proposed.

Instead of comparing the results of real-time and delayed conferencing modes, chapter 12 by Kang combines both modes in one graduate classroom in Seoul, Korea. Here, a week of traditional, live classroom instruction was alternated with two weeks of nontraditional, electronic conferencing. The structure of computer-mediated communication activities in this classroom included bulletin boards for posted assignments, faculty and student lounges, asynchronous conferencing, synchronous chatting, question-and-answer forums, assorted learning resources, E-mail, and self-introduction lists. Although most course work and discussions were asynchronously posted, student teams had to meet synchronously at least once per week. In qualitatively exploring the results of these conferencing tools, Kang found various instances of impersonal, interpersonal, and "hyperpersonal" communication. In the end, she concludes that these tools can be used for focused decision making, democratic participation, and task orientation, as well as for fostering self-reflection, mentoring, and team-building consensus. Kang also notes that any affective influence of collaborative technologies is dependent on task assignment, grouping structures, and, most important, the longevity of the experience. As would be expected, semester-long electronic partnerships appear to foster greater shared understandings and concerns than briefer experiences.

PART V: LOOKING BACK AND GLANCING AHEAD

The final section of this text reflects on the work presented here and predicts several possible paths for this research on the horizon. In gleaning information and lessons from previous research projects, these authors suggest a few practical guidelines for educators and developers on how technology can support collaborative learning and the development of electronic learning communities. These chapters push us toward a framework for building integrated learning environments with access to resources, tools, and online learning communities such as the WWW.

Chapter 14, by Siegel and Kirkley, describes projects conducted within the Center for Excellence in Education (CEE) at Indiana University. Since 1991, the CEE has been involved in a series of projects organized around the concept of "adventure learning." The core idea here is to bring the excitement and adventure of the world into the classroom while simultaneously transporting the classroom into that world. Those curious about adventure learning will find program overviews, implementation guidelines, and sample electronic interactions at the beginning of this chapter. In addition, one can also read about delightful electronic field trips offered via *Turner Adventure Learning* to more than 100,000 students across the country. An integral portion of these virtual field trip adventures is the online chat forums and electronic bulletin boards of students, teachers, and experts over America Online. Collaborations from over 10 trips, including one visit to Gettysburg, were used to illustrate how temporary communities can be formed to discuss educationally significant issues and foster ingenious electronic collaborations. Third, Siegel and Kirkley describe the *Wetlands Explorations ThinkShop,* which is a project jointly developed by the CEE and the Wonderlab (a science, technology, and health museum) that extends adventure learning into informal learning settings. The *Wonderlab Community* offers teachers, students, parents, and experts an opportunity to use a variety of electronic tools: electronic discussion forums, interactive exhibits, electronic publications and other online information resources, private forums and chats, Internet audio- and videoconferencing, and expert mentoring. These three projects are part of the CEE's "Digital Learning Environment" vision of developing cutting-edge technology tools and resources that facilitate student and teacher activity in a student-centered, problem-based learning environment.

Chapter 15, by King, is an invitation to participate in the Communication Age with many of the technologies and instructional practices documented in this text. After discussing the new job roles and educational systems required by this new age, King connects systemic educational reform to the emergence of sociocultural learning theory and the parallel rise of collaborative tools and virtual classrooms. Research in this volume informs her discussion of where collaborative media breakthroughs are structuring new social spaces for teaching and learning as well as unique knowledge-building communities. As a precautionary step, however, King compares advances in collaborative technologies to other historical developments in technology that were also predicted to drastically change teaching. Appropriately, King poses critical questions related to possible electronic course formats, learning activities, teacher roles, and assessment techniques. Finally, while recapping the qualitative and quantitative research approaches and schemes discussed in various chapters of this book, King proposes several key ingredients in effective collaborative tool research.

CONCLUSIONS

The purpose of this text is to increase the knowledge base on the benefits and drawbacks of various electronic collaboration formats, in part, by investigating the student dialogue evident in various electronic learning settings. In contrast to researcher-imposed ideas, many of the studies presented here typically did not dictate the use of a particular collaborative tool or task, but, instead, simply observed and recorded existing electronic collaboration practices. These studies focus on how peer interaction and discourse influences group processing, intersubjectivity, and resulting cognitive change. Coding schemes of these diverse activity settings were fine-tuned to better account for the transactions occurring in these interactive environments. Across these studies, it is clear that collaborative technologies can be significant new learning tools. Equally important, questions about the benefits of social interaction and dialogue are beginning to be addressed and answered. As questions about interaction patterns, forms of learning assistance,and electronic settings are confronted and responded to, we see the benefits of recording how schools, teachers, and students are employing and exploiting numerous new electronic learning tasks and tools.

This book serves many purposes. For instance, the works in this book are organized to help: (a) teachers involved in computer conferencing and collaborative writing decisions, (b) schools debating how electronic collaboration can enhance learning, and (c) administrators and policymakers supplying discretional funding for electronic resources and training. Even though many of these audiences are currently captivated by the Internet and other tools for electronic collaboration, this enthusiasm could wane without sufficient theoretical rationale and positive social and cognitive results. We hope that the research and theory presented in this book will serve as a catalyst for future exploration of electronic collaboration related to student learning and educational reform. If this occurs, perhaps teachers will begin to grasp how to marry learning pedagogy with collaborative learning tools to create socially and intellectually rich learning environments.

To assist in this progress, the authors of this book have begun to focus on how different electronic tools and learning formats impact social interaction and student learning. The findings and conclusions across the work featured here point to some commonalities in effective instructional use of these technologies as well as a myriad of procedures for analyzing student discourse processes and meaning making. Before computer-conferencing and electronic collaboration tools can significantly impact educational reform, new approaches are needed to observe and measure the impact of these tools on both social and cognitive functioning. When a few of these windows are opened, the race for more effective learner-centered technologies and environments can be pursued more diligently.

I

THEORETICAL AND TECHNOLOGICAL FOUNDATIONS

1

Computer Conferencing and Collaborative Writing Tools: Starting a Dialogue About Student Dialogue

Curtis Jay Bonk
Kira S. King
Indiana University

Calls for a more "learner-centered" curriculum are heard from the pulpit of most educational reformers of the 1990s. In response, a series of studies on computer-supported collaborative learning (CSCL) tools at Indiana University have begun to demonstrate how different tools and formats impact social interaction and learning. The chapters presented in this text explore a myriad of CSCL tools available for different levels of electronic interaction that might be indicators of high-quality social interaction and student learning. Results are discussed in terms of the age levels of participants, tools utilized, and tasks selected.

This particular chapter was written for three primary purposes. First, it initiates a discussion of CSCL tools from a sociocultural perspective. Second, it categorizes these tools and associated research studies into a five-level computer-conferencing and collaborative writing taxonomy developed by Bonk, Medury, and Reynolds (1994); these collaboration levels range from electronic messaging to delayed-collaboration tools to brainstorming tools to real-time collaborative writing tools to collaborative multimedia and hypermedia. For the most part, the research projects included in this text reaffirm this collaborative writing taxonomy. Third, this chapter samples a few electronic discussion threads in both formal and informal environments to *start a dialogue about student dialogue*. This initial taste of electronic dialogue will help readers understand some of the socioculturally based research ideas and electronic coding schemes presented in this book.

In order to make decisions that productively transform learning environments, research is needed that records how schools, teachers, and students are discovering, employing, and modifying the numerous new electronic collaboration tasks and tools. However, the diversity of electronic tools and settings presents a significant roadblock to educational researchers interested in reforming education from a more learner-centered framework. Despite these struggles, electronic learning tools clearly can alter student learning environments. As the formats for electronic collaboration proliferate, computer conferencing has great potential for changing the ways students and their instructors interact with each other in the learning processes. The overall results of these efforts should inform researchers, designers, and policymakers of the importance of social dialogue resulting from the use of collaborative learning tools.

Sociocultural Theory

Vygotsky's sociocultural theory of cognitive development is rapidly influencing diverse educational arenas. Although educators are turning to Vygotskian writings to promote the social context of student learning (Gallimore & Tharp, 1990; Wells, 1994), researchers have yet to make significant inroads regarding how cognitive processes displayed on a social plane become internalized by the participants (i.e., how intermental processes impact intramental functioning; see Wertsch, 1985). In effect, ideas about student zones of proximal development (ZPDs), scaffolding, and internalization remain extremely difficult to clarify and implement (see chap. 2 of this volume by Bonk & Cunningham, for definitions).

To understand how ZPDs are addressed as well as the process of internalization, Vygotsky and his colleagues suggested over 60 years ago that the unit of analysis for educational research be the activity setting or word meaning (Vygotsky, 1978; Wertsch, 1995). Kozulin (1986) explained that perhaps educators and researchers have yet to fully understand Vygotsky's concept of activity; hence, they continue to struggle with this new focus on activities and event meanings as the fundamental unit of analysis (Meloth & Deering, 1994). However, with the advent of electronic collaboration settings for student meaning-making activities, such approaches to assess student learning and development are now vital.

Too often, tool designers neglect to ground their conferencing and composing innovations in human learning or development theory. From a Piagetian standpoint, electronic collaboration tools can foster debates and eventual disequilibrium (Piaget, 1963), the resolution of which should encourage students to decenter from their own points of view. Vygotsky's (1978, 1986) tenets about learning and development, on the other hand, emphasize the importance of social interaction with adults and more capable peers as a means to guide children to developmental levels they might not independently attain (Brown & Palincsar, 1989; Newman, Griffin, & Cole, 1989). Recent electronic collaboration studies support Vygotskian views that students internalize the scaffolding of more capable peers when collaboratively writing (Daiute & Dalton, 1988), as well as the cognitive supports or prompts provided by computer tools (Salomon, 1988; Scott, Cole, & Engel, 1992).

Technological Opportunities

Major changes in education are occurring on both technological and instructional fronts (Cognition and Technology Group at Vanderbilt, 1991; Koschmann, Myers, Feltovich, & Barrows, 1994; Pea, 1994; Scardamalia & Bereiter, 1994). During the past decade, technologies have become more interactive, distributed, and collaborative. These technological advances merge nicely with innovations in instructional strategies for collaboration, mentoring, and project-based learning. Through this marriage of technology and instruction, global networks have connected learners across time and space, resulting in a myriad of new learning communities (Harasim, 1993; Quarterman, 1993; Riel, 1993). Global learning networks such as the International Education and Resource Network (I*EARN) (Loo & McLane, 1994), the Collaborative Visualization (CoVis) Project (Pea, 1993), the World Forum (Sugar & Bonk, see chap. 6, this volume), and the Kids as Global Scientists (KGS) project (Black, Klingenstein, & Songer, 1995; Songer, in press) represent a fraction of the current technology-oriented K–12 educational reform efforts. Such global collaborative technologies support rich new apprenticeships featuring sophisticated peer dialogue and mentoring (Collins, Brown, & Newman, 1989; Koschmann, 1994; Teles, 1993). However, with all these new learning channels, educators are faced with unprecedented educational opportunities and challenges.

Without question, the formats for electronic collaboration are proliferating. Computer-mediated communication has great potential for changing the ways students and instructors interact and may prove influential in reorganizing the entire learning process. Some educators claim that the online environment is particularly appropriate for collaborative learning approaches that emphasize group interaction (Harasim, 1990). Other literature indicates that computer conferencing can facilitate text production and discussion among students in writing-intensive courses (Bonk et al., 1994) as well as when they subsequently enter workplace-writing environments (Bonk, Reynolds, & Medury, 1996). Workplaces and schools are finding that new forms of writing and communication engage workers and learners in new patterns of social interaction and promote different standards of productivity (Schrage, 1990). As the menu of technology choices on college campuses, schools, and workplaces increases, instructional decisions regarding how to communicate with learners across these settings are becoming increasingly critical.

Electronic Collaboration Roadblocks and Questions

Research in the social context of learning has provided substantial support for the assertion that traditional teacher-centered instructional approaches must be replaced with more active, learner-centered environments (Alexander & Murphy, 1994; American Psychological Association, 1993; Duffy & Jonassen, 1991; Tharp, 1993). In the case of student writing, numerous learning tools for student collaboration are elevating writing beyond silent, solitary activities and simple word processing to environments rich in discussion and interchange (Bonk et al., 1994).

Despite these trends, there are numerous logical and monetary obstacles facing the study of computer conferencing and collaborative writing. As a result, researchers have just begun to examine the social interaction differences between electronic collaboration tools such as computer network technologies and traditional writing classrooms (Bruce, Peyton, & Batson, 1993; Forman, 1992; Hartman et al., 1991). Minimal documentation presently exists, however, regarding the differences in communication patterns, teacher roles, and student writing performance across the levels of collaborative learning tools and tasks. Many pivotal questions remain unexplored, including:

- Will collaborative tasks and tools foster new expectations of teaching and learning?
- What types of writing collaborations are preferable to teachers and students?
- What kinds of electronic collaboration activities are facilitated by different tasks and tools?
- How do students assist each other during electronic collaboration?
- How are new ideas generated during electronic collaboration?
- How do different interaction structures and collaboration formats impact student writing?

The questions, unfortunately, are too often forgotten or ignored when viewing ingenious writing technologies for searching, selecting, and sharing knowledge. Of course, it may be difficult to pose profound research questions when new generations of conferencing and composing tools rapidly alter communication channels across all levels of education (Lehrer, 1993; Montague, 1990; Riel, 1993; Ruopp, Gal, Drayton, & Pfister, 1993). Our research group has attempted to overcome these barriers by documenting how different levels of collaborative educational learning tools and associated pedagogical formats can impact social interaction and resulting human learning.

Collaborative Writing Taxonomy

Whereas educators are turning to Vygotskian writing to analyze student learning in a social context, various electronic discourse coding schemes, learning ownership checklists, learning environment surveys, and other assessment tools found in the chapters of this book might offer a glimpse into the active or static nature of electronic learning environments. Of course, the use of these measurement tools coincides with historical movements in education from competitive, individual learning to recent electronic environments rich in meaning-making negotiation and collaborative text generation. The research detailed in this book, for instance, attempts to break new ground in exploring electronic environments for text conferencing and collaboration. Because every chapter discusses some form of electronic text creation, it is important to consider computer conferencing from a collaborative writing perspective.

Bonk et al. (1994) defined collaborative writing as groups of two or more people working in concert on a common text project in an environment supportive of their text and idea sharing. In offering that definition, however, they admitted that electronic collaboration tools currently offer a maze of new communication channels among participants (from one-to-one, many-to-one, and many-to-many) and a range of text support (e.g., electronic mail, delayed collaboration, brainstorming, and real-time text collaboration). Beyond the tools and communication modes, Saunders (1989) noted that the collaborative writing activity (e.g., co-writing or coediting) often results from a combination of the interaction structure (e.g., completely cooperative or helping permitted) and the task assignment (e.g., planning or editing) (for additional information, see Savery, chap. 5, this volume). As a result, beliefs about the applications and effectiveness of electronic collaboration tasks and tools vary considerably.

After surveying and testing a number of collaborative learning tools, Bonk et al. (1994) attempted to clarify this predicament by designing a taxonomy of five levels of collaborative writing tools that can be used for school learning. The next section locates studies presented in this text within the differing levels of the collaborative writing taxonomy. Although this taxonomy can accommodate different participant age levels, tools, and instructional tasks, it does not account for electronic collaboration around single machines such as in Angeli and Cunningham in chapter 4 of this volume. Although this may be a flaw in the taxonomy, it is relatively easy to fix. For the benefits of this particular discussion, therefore, consider collaborative work in stand-alone computing environments to be at Level 0. Levels 1 to 5 are described and documented in the following sections.

Level 1 Interaction: Electronic Mail and Delayed-Messaging Tools

At Level 1, electronic mail (E-mail) and delayed-messaging tools allow users to send messages or files directly from one computer to another or use a centralized server with a store-and-forward strategy. Whereas the latter may be preferred because users can log on and off without losing messages, the former may be more economical in a writing lab. This communication mode is useful for assignment reminders, scheduling, long-distance correspondence, and document feedback.

E-mail messaging can build faculty–student relationships in higher education as well as peer-peer relationships in elementary settings. Nevertheless, E-mail is not one of the most elegant or effective collaborative writing tools. In chapter 9, for instance, Kirkley, Savery, and Grabner-Hagen track the E-mail in three separate graduate classrooms to reveal varied instructional feedback on student writing as well as cultural and gender-related variations in student electronic writing participation. Despite these problems, E-mail is perhaps the most salient form of electronic collaboration in higher education today. E-mail is also beginning to infiltrate public schools. The study presented by Sugar and Bonk in chapter 6, for example, focuses on middle and high school student use of E-mail and bulletin boards over the Internet to build online telecommunities. Note that World Forum participant readings of the latest explorer, peer, or mentor electronic bulletin board postings moves that particular study beyond the E-mail issues of Level 1 to Level 2 delayed-collaboration considerations.

Level 2 Interaction: Remote Access/Delayed Collaboration

At Level 2, there are a number of remote access or delayed-conferencing and -collaboration tools that allow users, regardless of time or geographic location, to remotely access, update, and control documents, files, or messages stored on other computers or on a mainframe computer. This type of tool is effective for weekly course topic discussions as well as document reviews or exchanges. Important to note, remote access of one's work often requires security clearance.

Although there are a number of Level 2 tools for remote file transfer and access including Timbuktu (Farallon, Inc.) and MarkUp (Mainstay), the Level 2 tools investigated in this text mainly offer asynchronous computer-conferencing functions (e.g., *Common Space* from Sixth Floor Media, *VAX Notes* from Digital Equipment Corporation, and *FirstClass* from SoftArc, Inc.). As the World Wide Web (WWW) has risen in prominence, so, too, have asynchronous conferencing tools for the web such as *Conferencing on the Web* (i.e., *COW*) (San Francisco State University), *Allaire Forums* (Allaire

LLC), *Alta Vista Forum* (Digital Equipment Corporation), *Web Crossing* (Lundeen & Associates), *Lotus Domino* (Lotus Development Corporation), and *Caucus* (Screen Porch, Inc.) (see Woolley, 1997, for a review). There is ongoing debate on whether starlike conferencing structures such as *COW* or *Caucus*—with preset conference, topic, and conversation levels and temporally organized conversations—are a more effective conferencing medium than a tree structure, such as in *Allaire Forums* or *Alta Vista Forum* wherein participant comments can be inserted at any point in the electronic discussion. Note, too, that some of tools mentioned earlier (e.g., *Alta Vista Forum*) offer both asynchronous conferencing and synchronous chat capabilities that may have some interesting and useful pedagogical benefits (see Kang, chap. 13).

More than half of the chapters of this book feature at least one delayed-conferencing tool or system. The key chapter on asynchronous conferencing here by Chong (see chap. 7) is actually part of a series of studies on *VAX Notes* that was used by many college professors to create electronic classrooms. Chong documents and compares four basic models of asynchronous text conferencing. In each of these situations, instructors employed different conferencing techniques to implement a student-centered learning environment. Important to note, all these instructors attempted to explore how delayed-conferencing systems support students' self-regulated learning and electronic text collaboration. Though promising, the collaborative composing potential of these four models varies widely as new conferencing tools emerge.

As indicated in the introduction to this book, there are various other delayed–text collaboration studies profiled in this book. For instance, an indepth look at the asynchronous conferencing text generation over a 5-year period is detailed in chapter 8 by Althauser and Matuga. Chapter 11, by Zhu, in contrast, focuses on the asynchronous composing of students in just one class setting. What is unusual here is that student electronic writing and topical discussions were meant to foster a learning community in a course taught using videoconferencing technology between two classroom sites. Also relevant here is chapter 14, wherein Siegel and Kirkley recount a myriad of asynchronous text-based activities that had been used to foster adventure learning.

Level 3 Interaction: Real-Time Brainstorming and Conversation

Level 3 tools facilitate real-time dialoguing and idea generation by encouraging multiple users to simultaneously brainstorm on a topic through electronic messaging and replying. Typically, Level 3 tools have two windows: (a) a shared transcript window consisting of ongoing and scrollable group dialogue and (b) a private screen for creating and editing dialogue. Such group decision support tools tend to be popular in both business and governmental settings wherein anonymously generating alternatives and then ranking these ideas strengthens strategic direction initiatives, meeting agendas, departmental policies, and grant proposals and reports (Schrage, 1990). Level 3 tools such as *Connect* from Turner and Ann Arbor Software (1994) also are quite valuable in academic settings for the prewriting, idea generation, and postwriting phases of collaborative writing.

There are two studies in this book involving Level 3 textual interactions. Both of these studies also investigate writing at other levels of the taxonomy, however. Chapter 12 by Bonk, Hansen, Grabner-Hagen, Lazar, and Mirabelli, for instance, details how an electronic brainstorming tool was used in a computer lab to help prospective secondary teachers analyze and resolve teaching scenarios in subject-specific small groups. Such real-time text brainstorming focused students on fairly impersonal and concise content discussion. In contrast to this university network situation, chapter 13, by Kang, describes how synchronous chat tools on the WWW can be used to foster group cohesion and decision making. This latter study, moreover, illustrates how the brainstorming tools of Level 3 can be combined with asynchronous tools for Level 1 and 2 interactions. Although not originally envisioned in the design of this taxonomy, the virtual field trip activities described by Siegel and Kirkley in chapter 14 might also contain real-time electronic conversations and brainstorming.

Level 4 Interaction: Real-Time Text Collaboration

One of the higher levels of the taxonomy of electronic collaboration is Level 4, real-time text collaboration. Level 4 tools permit two or more people to enact text-related changes on a document concurrently. Changes to a shared Level 4 document are immediately visible to all participants, whereas pointing devices might be used to draw peer and colleague attention to particular parts of the shared document or to document changes during enactment. Important to note, student discussion about the appropriateness of these changes might take place in a chat box. Though such tools are useful for both text creation and revision, some have been recently discontinued due to frequent operating system changes (e.g., *Live Writer* from Research Design Associates), whereas others sound like Level 4 tools but primarily provide Level 3 collaboration opportunities (e.g., *Realtime Writer* from Realtime Learning Systems). There are no studies reported in this volume that solely relate to Level 4.

Level 5 Interaction: Real-Time Multimedia and/or Hypermedia Collaboration

According to the taxonomy from Bonk et al. (1994), at the highest level of interaction are the "cooperative hypermedia" tools of Level 5, which not only foster document-sharing capabilities of Level 4, but also include one or more other collaborative features, such as hypertext, graphics, video images, music, speech, and animation. Although, in the past, most Level 5 tools have typically required sophisticated hardware, these tools are becoming more accessible and valued to teachers across all levels of instruction. Some videoconferencing tools available today containing limited synchronous chat features (e.g., CU-SeeMe, first developed at Cornell University) would technically still be Level 3 writing technology (i.e., brainstorming tools). In contrast, other videoconferencing tools like NetMeeting from Microsoft would fit in Level 5 because they offer online sharing of applications that can foster actual document collaboration and refinement.

Chapter 11 by Cooney, for instance, features a Level 5 tool called *Aspects* (Group Logic). Here, 10th-grade English students engage in real-time text conferences over a local network to collaboratively analyze, discuss, and report on the American play *The Crucible*. Students used multiple conferencing tools here for text collaboration, chatting, and drawing. Such tools index student conceptual understanding, unique connections, and knowledge gains. Moreover, they provide external products that can be presented, compared, debated, and modified. Additionally, the externalization of one's writing can foster self-reflection and be a catalyst for later composing efforts.

Collaborative Writing Summary

All five levels of the taxonomy are important considerations for computer conferencing and collaborative writing. Each has its own strengths and weaknesses. Assessment tools to understand and enhance student text generation and evaluation skill are still in preliminary stages of development. In chapter 12 by Bonk et al., for instance, as the coding of student interaction patterns and talk structures became more specific, the analyses became less reliable. Similar problems were encountered in chapter 6 by Sugar and Bonk when attempting to code student level of questioning and perspective taking as well as forms of mentoring and learning assistance. Further dilemmas not even mentioned in this chapter include their initial attempts to use Granott and Gardner's (1994) analysis framework to examine equal–unequal collaborations and issues of dominance, which also proved unsuccessful and was abandoned.

However, without studying the social environment, certain insights into the collaborative writing process might not have taken place. The persistent coding of rich electronic transcripts, for instance, enabled Cooney to note who talked (i.e., wrote), when he or she communicated, and any patterns in student contributions. Additionally, she was able to examine the extent to which different software features (e.g., the chat box or drawing tool) were being utilized. Cooney's analyses demonstrate that these conferencing tools can result in extended and refined dialogue and enhanced written products, even among students who are normally less successful in the English classroom.

Another approach to understanding collaborative writing in electronic environments is to note the participant interaction patterns and threads of discussion. Threads provide a permanent record of the social interaction among participants; however, determining whether or where one's social interaction has impacted later independent or group writing is no easy proposition! Such questions inspire investigations of electronic discussion threads as well as the creation of better dialogue coding schemes as detailed in the following sections.

DIALOGUE IN ELECTRONIC LEARNING ENVIRONMENTS

It is difficult to envision how these technology tools impact collaboration, human interaction, and written expression without sampling some student electronic dialogue. In the following sections, we briefly present examples of dialogue in real-time and delayed modes within both formal classrooms and informal learning settings.

Formal Electronic Learning

One electronic interaction project currently being coordinated by the first author at the time of this writing involves the use of Conferencing on the Web (COW), an asynchronous conferencing tool (Bonk, Malikowski, Angeli, & East, in press). Here, preservice teachers in multiple sections of undergraduate educational psychology are creating problem-based case vignettes on the WWW related to their early field experience observations. This reflective writing activity is being employed in these classes in order to make learning more relevant, exciting, and interconnected. In addition to linking many text-related concepts and ideas to actual school activities, we hope to reduce the depersonalization and loneliness of many early field experiences because these preservice teachers will now have someone to share their insights with. Since this project is on the WWW, our students, as well as their cooperating teachers, can join COW conversations without having to be on campus. Moreover, peers, faculty, conferencing coordinators, and participants from other countries can provide students with mentoring and feedback on their cases. We are currently testing the hypothesis that heavier scaffolding and learning assistance will result in higher quality case creation and richer case dialogue.

The purpose of this study is to discover whether student electronic conferencing on the WWW about early field experiences can have an impact on their learning of educational psychology principles and theories, training to become a teacher, and sense of connectedness to the teacher education program. In linking graduate instructors, public school teachers, faculty, and students, this project is truly a university–school partnership. Equally important, this project involves students in a practical WWW activity that should help them comprehend the importance and scope of this new learning tool. In particular, we hope to sensitize these students to the use of the WWW for collaboration, dialogue, reflection, and written expression. In the near future, we will extend our work here beyond the State of Indiana to senior students in our Cultural Immersion programs in England, Australia, India, and Native American reservations in Arizona and New Mexico. Eventually, we hope to have students work with preservice teachers, faculty, and students from other countries for international electronic conversations about the teaching dilemmas they commonly witness and experience. In accordance with ideas presented in this book, it is expected that electronic conferencing tools like COW will soon extend beyond educational psychology courses to many other courses and experiences related to teacher education training.

Bonk et al. (in press) witnessed the excitement of this electronic activity when visiting labs wherein students were using COW. Here is a brief synopsis of one case, an asynchronous conferencing thread on special education under the topic heading of "Different Learning Levels":

> 1. Author: *Cindy* (Date: Feb. 20, 10:18 AM, 1997). My early field experience is in a first-grade class. There are two boys that are repeating kindergarten and sit in the first-grade class half of the day. The teacher mentioned learning disability testing, but it didn't seem like anything that is going on now. During certain lessons, specifically math and reading, I sat at a separate table with the boys working on lessons that were different from the rest of the class's. This works fine when I am there to help; I'm not positive what happens when the teacher has to teach two completely different lessons within the same class. It seems like these boys aren't really getting the attention they need and are just "sitting in" on first grade.
>
> Chapter 9 of the text talks about "between-class ability grouping." The text says that this is the most common method and also one of the most ineffective. (This is also what's going on in the first-grade class.) The members of the lower groups have an increased chance of becoming delinquent or truant and usually have a very low self-esteem and negative self-image. The best I think I can do is to keep the boys sitting with the rest of the class . . . It is kind of a sad situation; I can't say [I] will be able to deal with this as easily as I talk about it.
>
> 2. Author: *Mandy* (Date: Feb. 20, 10:34 AM, 1997). I think you would have handled this situation better than the teacher. It seems she doesn't want to take the time to make sure these boys are learning, she just lets them sit there confused or pushes them to the back of the room for help, occasionally. I think your suggestions would be helpful to the teacher because it seems like it would be more effective and less harmful to their perceptions about themselves. They would feel like normal students and not degenerates.
>
> 3. Author: *Jane* (Date: Feb. 20, 11:43 AM, 1997). I think that you have the right idea. Including these boys will help them develop socially. This is what they need to build their self-esteem. I also think that the idea of helping

these two with separate assignments while the class is writing in their journals is a great idea. This would give them the extra help they need. With this they will learn how to deal with their disability and become better students.

4. Author: *Cindy* (Date: Feb. 20, 12:29 AM, 1997). (Response Summary) I think these responsed [sic] to my case are very encouraging. They say that inclusion is definitely very important for children with special needs. Both replies also agree that it is important to keep the self-esteem of chilren [sic] high. These replies also find the idea helping the slower students while the entire class is busy a good one. This is just one way to keep these students from standing out from the rest of the children.

5. Author: *Matt* (Date: Feb. 27, 7:22 PM, 1997). I feel there should be some testing on the students, but your idea I feel would be teh [sic] best answer for the present situation, as long as they dont [sic] act up during the lecture. It would give the students the self esteem [sic] boost as well as letting the teacher deal with them in a one on one situation which it sounds like they need.

Unlike the instructor-created cases discussed and analyzed by Bonk et al. in chapter 12 of this text, these cases were generated by the students themselves. As a result, the WWW was utilized for focused conversations related to how problems and success stories encountered in the field could be better interpreted and understood. This assignment contained instructions to create cases, respond to peer cases, and summarize one's case discussion. For instance, these students were asked to suggest how their textbook author would resolve the situation and relate the dilemma to ideas and concepts from the course. In addition, when a student like Cindy lacked a direct text reference in her case, faculty or teacher mentors often suggested the need for such a connection. Electronic collaboration environments when supported with sufficient task structuring, therefore, can foster extensive content-related interactions among students. But what do we look for in this case creation and dialogue? Certainly, depth of case discussion, coherence, solution justification and rationale, peer responsiveness, and a quality summary are among the possible variables of interest here (Bonk et al., in press).

As opposed to this asynchronous academic learning environment, electronic collaboration unfolds in vastly different ways when the tools are in real-time settings and when learning is of a more informal nature. Such informal environments are explored in the next section.

Informal Electronic Learning

Outside typical K–12 and university environments, there are scores of learning forums for electronic collaboration that can be investigated. Learning in cyberspace and over newsgroups are among the new areas ripe for analyses of collaborative writing components, participant interaction, electronic training, and social dialogue. It is unlikely that participants view these electronic forums as vehicles to enhance their writing, however.

Some courses on the Internet are now offered by America Online in chat rooms. Here, people can converse with one another in real time. Such an activity setting has discussion threads, levels of participation (e.g., contributor/active or lurker/passive), tags/anonymous names, noise and off-track conversation, specific directions of who one's comment is meant for, and emoticons (i.e., symbols that represent personal feelings). In addition, instructor comments and contributions can be evaluated. When in newsgroups, in contrast, one might note who is contributing something, the institution or organization that he or she represents, the depth of this interaction, and the quality, type, and direction of this contribution. In both the cyberspace and newsgroup environments, however, documenting the interaction patterns and direction of messages may be the most difficult but beneficial analyses.

Let us give an example of learning in cyberspace. In one study at IU not reported elsewhere, O'Shea (1995) attempted to understand the learning environment of a course on screenwriting offered through America Online. This class met for 2 hours each week for 6 weeks and was conducted by a successful screenwriter located in Australia. In addition, this expert screenwriter was assisted by technical facilitators and several guest speakers. During one analysis of a 2-hour session in the course chat room, O'Shea found that only 28 of the 76 people entering the chat room remained beyond the 20 minutes deemed necessary to be considered a *participant*. The remaining 47 were labeled as *visitors*. Of the 28 session participants, 8 were labeled as *lurkers* because they failed to contribute comments during the session, 9 were labeled as *semiactive* because they made comments occasionally, and, finally, 11 were deemed *heavily active* because they were making comments during most or all of the periods. It appears that most of these cyberspace participants were less actively engaged in the learning process than they would have been in more structured, formal conferencing settings.

Though active engagement is difficult to judge, O'Shea (1995) attempted to understand it better by coding the chat room dialogue. Coding students as AAAAA (i.e., active), 00000 (i.e., inactive), or 0000L (i.e., inactive and leaving) during each 6-minute period gave O'Shea a better grasp of student participation. In this situation, off-task comments or "noise" was produced by 10 of the 47 visitors, which significantly interrupted the flow of the course. One visitor, BABE1000, for instance, asked three times if there were "Any hot boys in here?" before participants made it clear that those comments were not welcome in this particular forum. Moments later, someone nicknamed "Clueless" was true to his or her name by coming in to the chat room for a few minutes and leaving. More instructionally interesting, during just one 2-hour session, the instructor made 203 contributions to the discussion or more than 1 per minute. Also, despite the number of people in the chat room, over 60% of his comments were directed at one student at a time, mostly providing questions, answers, and positive feedback to individual prompting. Student contributions, on the other hand, were mainly directed at the group, though 40% were aimed at the instructor. Surprisingly few student–student interactions were noted.

Like others, O'Shea (1995) found synchronous social interaction on the Internet difficult to categorize. Reducing cyberspace instruction to specific social interaction categories proved daunting. Breaks in discussion threads were much more common than nonbreaks. Here is an example of some of this chat room dialogue concerning the role of Hal, the computer in the movie from *2001: A Space Odyssey* (note: the instructor's screenname is "MOVEEWRTR"):

1. Moveewrtr:	He doesn't move . . . how can have action <hint, this is a trick question>
2. KateG:	He's a character. He has a motive. Self-preservation.
3. JudyM:	Hal is a character
4. CompCom:	he can motivate others.
5. Straymouse:	action can be internal.
6. Lenswoman:	He has emotions, his actions affect everyone.
7. MaxToo:	A reflection can be a character, also.
8. WriterSuzy:	He causes things to happen
9. Shorelle:	His motive is to take control
10. Moveewrtr:	Stray and Max, Gold Stars!
11. Straymouse	:-)
12. ReelMary:	Hals actions are expressed in dialogue, then carried out with effects.
13. Moveewrtr:	Am I the only one who cried when HAL was disconnected.
14. MaxToo:	no.
15. GypsieOne:	no.
16. Moveewrtr:	Now, how does Kubrick do that?
17. WriterSuzy	I thought it was sad.
18. Real Mary:	No, my hankie's still wet.
19. Lenswoman:	(weeping uncontrollably at the thought)
20. MaxToo:	Hal expressed humanity to some extent.
21. Moveewrtr:	Lens, you always uncontrollably, have a donut.
22. GypsieOne:	Through character.
23. OnlineHost:	Cybersmit3 has entered the room.

24. Lenswoman:	thanks . . . (sniff)
25. Moveewrtr:	Suppose it was you, you have to create a character who has no external movement How should you do that?
26. WriterSuzy:	Hal reflected weaknesses and desires people have (blows nose)
27. Lenswoman:	He has that voice . . .
28. MaxToo:	Why not words on a screen . . . ?
29. Shorelle:	I would create a character that moves others.
30. GypsieOne:	With description.

With messages coming in from participants at different rates and in response to different questions or topics, the conversation appears quite confusing compared to traditional sequential classroom discussion. Despite these dialogue-tracking problems, O'Shea (1995) claimed that her coding attempts revealed the success of the course as the same students returned from week to week. In addition, she believed that finding instances of scaffolding and assisted learning in the dialogue patterns to be critical in cyberspace because one cannot see the participants. Due to the variety of participation levels, she also recommended that (a) early contributors be encouraged, (b) questions be directed to lurkers, and (c) an observation booth or "read-only areas" be established for visitors so as to limit their disruptiveness. Given the increase of synchronous web-based instruction, these guidelines are bound to increase in importance.

Contrast these findings with asynchronous newsgroup discussions on the Internet. For example, in another unpublished study from our research team, Chen (1995) explored the participant communication patterns within Usenet classical music (i.e., rec.music.classical) and the culture of Usenet (alt.culture.usenet) newsgroups. In this newsgroup data, she could determine participant country of origin as well as some information about the organizations wherein these people worked (i.e., educational institution, government, or commercial setting). As in other studies, Chen could also code the discussion context and communication patterns. She found that these Usenet conferences were dominated by those in the United States and Canada (i.e., over 80% of messages sent) with some participation from Australia, New Zealand, Europe, and Japan, perhaps because of the common use of the English language and greater technology access.

From a sociocultural perspective, Chen (1995) found that participant responses usually replied specifically to the content of the message of another, thereby creating a shared space (Schrage, 1990) or focal point for intersubjectivity. Whereas the chat room of the screenwriting example required respondents to restate such content and specifically point out with whom they were agreeing or disagreeing with, in the these asynchronous newsgroups, the system would insert the name and content of the previous message in the response, thereby enhancing the ability to track the discussion threads. According to Chen's analyses, this electronic conference was dominated by counterassertions, suggestions, personal opinions, and general information. In effect, most participants were attempting to guide the discussion. Sometimes just one message could spark significant dialogue. In one of her analyses, for example, Chen found that of the 86 messages sent on the topic of "overhauling Usenet" during a 1-week period, 31% linked to comments of a single participant. Off-task behaviors, however, were virtually nil.

Although electronic dialogue and learning on America Online and Usenet are new forms of communication, they seem limited to people with English language skills. Those functioning effectively on these systems certainly are scaffolding each other and engaging in meaning-making activities. Whereas the synchronous chat dialogue of the screenwriting example was extremely stilted, the Usenet discussion threads were more easily trackable and elaborate. From a numerical standpoint, compared to the short, 5–10 word comments in the real-time chat rooms, the more elaborate and indepth Usenet discussions ranged from 50 to in excess of 300 words. Nevertheless, both informal learning environments, the preceding synchronous and asynchronous examples, were interesting and informative research settings. Such preliminary investigations are vital because informal learning on the Internet and WWW is only bound to increase in the coming decades!

Summary of Research on Electronic Learning Environments

From these initial studies, it is evident that formal and informal electronic learning opportunities vary widely. If the goal is depth of discussion and dialogue, the previous electronic dialogue examples would give the nod to formal learning environments and asynchronous discussion. These electronic learning arenas need further exploration before such statements can be made, however. Although all these participants were heavily engaged in text generation, not much of it would be considered socially interactive or collaborative. Across both the formal and informal learning situations, analyses to date have centered on (a) the type and length of electronic dialogue, (b) the key forms of instructor assistance and peer interaction within this dialogue (e.g., modeling, contingency management, feedback, instructing, questioning, cognitive structuring, task structuring; see Tharp, 1993; Tharp & Gallimore, 1988), (c) the degree of collaborative relationship among participants, (d) forms of intersubjectivity or shared space, and (e) other salient discourse processes (e.g., roles, responsiveness, power, and authority; see Berge & Collins, 1995). As it becomes clear that collaborative learning and advanced technologies are important tools for learning, questions about the benefits of social interaction and dialogue are beginning to be answered.

Surveying all the work of this book related to social interaction and dialogue in synchronous and asynchronous computer-conferencing settings, electronic forums appear to have some definite advantages over live instruction and interaction (e.g., enhanced student involvement, writing practice, low-key publishing of ideas, and student motivation to impress peers). It is clear that collaborative learning tools can now be used to (a) change the way students and instructors interact, (b) electronically apprentice student learning, (c) enhance teamwork and collaborative learning opportunities, (d) build intersubjective or shared experiences, (e) facilitate class discussion, and (f) move writing and other literacy activities from solitary events to more active, social learning. If we begin to grapple with some of these electronic learning issues, significant progress will be made.

By examining collaborative formats used in schools and universities, our research projects to date reaffirm the Bonk et al. (1994) taxonomy of collaborative writing, while helping flesh out sociocultural factors in electronic learning. Of course, we must ask what sociocultural variables might seem important and relevant enough to assess? One area of common pursuit within the research presented in this text is to document the forms of electronic learning assistance and cognitive apprenticeship (see Collins et al., 1989; Tharp, 1993). A parallel concern is how experts or practitioners apprentice novice learners in developing new skills through the use of authentic learning experiences and timely exposure to cultural practices (Lave, 1991). A third prominent sociocultural variable often investigated relates to how meaning is negotiated and participant common knowledge or intersubjectivity acquired (Resnick, Levine, & Teasley, 1991; Rogoff, 1990). Fourth, electronic dialogue instruments might supply evidence of changes in students' ZPDs when exposed to ideas of adults or more capable peers. When these learning mechanisms are better understood and addressed, knowledge is no longer simply a transmission process with predetermined single right answers; instead, it is transformed and generated out of social experiences.

Educational Contribution and Implications

Despite many plausible linkages between computer-conferencing research and Vygotsky's (1978) sociocultural theory, Vygotsky, himself, would be amazed and confused if he were alive to witness the emergence of learning tools justified by his views. He would be amazed by the powerful new research and instructional devices, but confused by the rather trivial pursuits for which these tools are often used and the minimal theoretical justification for technology in the learning process. Of course, he would not be alone in his confusion about the theories on which most technological innovation in education is based (Koschmann et al., 1994). Vygotsky would perhaps find himself even more perplexed as to why Marxist-based psychological ideas he was wrestling with over half a century ago are finally being embraced by the West; he surely must have hoped that his theories would have been rigorously tested and then adopted, modified, or discarded long ago. At the same time, maybe enough time has elapsed between Vygotsky's death and the age of the computer so that researchers could embrace his ideas without being accused of blindly linking the latest theories with the latest technologies.

Because of this theoretical confusion, focused programs of research and development are essential for maximizing the effectiveness of collaboration-learning technologies in student learning. The results from the studies presented in this book, for example, indicate that both synchronous and asynchronous computer conferencing, when designed with peer or adult assistance opportunities, have some advantages over live discussions in terms of student engagement in learning, depth of discussion, time on task, and the promotion of higher order thinking skills. It is also hoped that when intensively exposing students to a range of electronic collaboration experiences, they will view crafting the written word as less arduous and schooling as less dry. In any event, computer conferencing and collaborative writing tools will play a key role in building local and global learning communities.

Documenting the nature of electronic collaboration formats, tools, and social interaction processes certainly responds to a broad array of educational needs. Beyond the collaborative writing taxonomy validations and electronic dialogue examples highlighted here, work in this area addresses the political clamoring for more interactive and motivating learning environments. At the same time, these findings may alter student and teacher ideas about teaching and learning and offer insight into how to use technology as a tool within a learner-centered environment.

But what is next? Given that the range of avenues for electronic writing and peer dialogue is widening, the research potential here is somewhat daunting. We hope that, by cataloguing specific social interaction patterns within distinctive levels of these tools, this set of studies and sociocultural reviews begins a dialogue on how schools and universities might effectively use computer conferencing and collaborative writing tasks and tools while providing a compass for future directions of use. If social interaction patterns and learner-centered ideas embedded in electronic learning tools and tasks are better documented and publicized by this research, both educators and educational critics will better appreciate the components of this new teaching–learning epistemology. We only hope that other researchers and educators will now join in and extend this dialogue about student dialogue.

ACKNOWLEDGMENTS

We recognize and thank Yi-Fei Chen and Laura O'Shea, whose pilot studies on informal electronic learning environments are referred to in this chapter. Many of their insights into electronic interaction coding are reflected in this chapter. Portions of this chapter were presented at a plenary session of the first international conference on Computer Support for Collaborative Learning (CSCL), 1995, Bloomington, IN. That manuscript was published in the CSCL conference proceedings and remains available on the World Wide Web (see "http://www-cscl95.indiana.edu/cscl95") at the time of this writing.

REFERENCES

Alexander, P. A., & Murphy, P. K. (1994, April). *The research base for APA's learner-centered psychological principles*. Paper presented at the American Educational Research Association annual meeting, New Orleans.

American Psychological Association. (1993). *Learner-centered psychological principles: Guidelines for school reform and restructuring*. Washington, DC: Author and the Mid-continent Regional Educational Laboratory.

Berge, Z. L., & Collins, M. P. (1995). Computer-mediated communications and the online classroom: An introduction. In Z. L. Berge & M. P. Collins (Eds.), *Computer mediated communication and the online classroom* (Vol. 1, pp. 1–10). Cresskill, NJ: Hampton Press.

Black, L., Klingenstein, K., & Songer, N. B. (1995). Observations from the Boulder Valley Internet Project. *T.H.E. Journal, 22*(10), 75–80.

Bonk, C. J., Malikowski, S., Angeli, C., & East, J. (in press). Web conferences for preservice teacher education: Electronic discourse from the field. *Journal of Educational Computing Research*.

Bonk, C. J., Medury, P. V., & Reynolds, T. H. (1994). Cooperative hypermedia: The marriage of collaborative writing and mediated environments. *Computers in the Schools*, *10*(1/2), 79–124.

Bonk, C. J., Reynolds, T. H., & Medury, P. V., (1996). Technology enhanced workplace writing: A social and cognitive transformation. In A. H. Duin & C. J. Hansen (Eds.), *Nonacademic writing: Social theory and technology* (pp. 281–303). Mahwah, NJ: Lawrence Erlbaum Associates.

Brown, A. L., & Palincsar, A. S. (1989). Guided, cooperative learning and individual knowledge acquisition. In L. Resnick (Ed.), *Cognition and instruction: Issues and agendas* (pp. 391–451). Hillsdale, NJ: Lawrence Erlbaum Associates.

Bruce, B., Peyton, J. K., & Batson, T. (Eds.). (1993). *Networked-based classrooms: Promises and realities*. New York: Cambridge University Press.

Chen, Y. (1995). *Analyses of interaction in Usenet newsgroups*. Unpublished manuscript, University of Indiana at Bloomington.

Cognition and Technology Group at Vanderbilt. (1991). Technology and the design of generative learning environments. *Educational Technology*, *31*(5), 34–40.

Collins, A., Brown, J. S., & Newman, S. E. (1989). Cognitive apprenticeship: Teaching the crafts of reading, writing, and mathematics. In L. Resnick, (Ed.), *Knowing, learning, and instruction: Essays in honor of Robert Glaser* (pp. 453–494). Hillsdale, NJ: Lawrence Erlbaum Associates.

Daiute, C., & Dalton, B. (1988). "Let's brighten it up a bit": Communication and cognition in writing. In B. A. Rafoth & D. L. Rubin (Eds.), *The social construction of written language* (pp. 249–269). Norwood, NJ: Ablex.

Duffy, T. M., & Jonassen, D. H. (1991). New implications for instructional technology. *Instructional Technology*, *31*(5), 7–12.

Forman, J. (Ed.). (1992). *New visions of collaborative writing*. Portsmouth, NH: Boynton/Cook.

Gallimore, R., & Tharp, R. (1990). Teaching mind in society: Teaching, schooling, and literate discourse. In L. C. Moll (Ed.), *Vygotsky in education: Instructional implications of sociohistorical psychology* (pp. 175–205). New York: Cambridge University Press.

Granott, N., & Gardner, H. (1994). When minds meet: Interactions, coincidence, and development in domains of ability. In R. J. Sternberg & R. K. Wagner (Eds.), *Mind in context: Interactionist perspectives on human intelligence* (pp. 171–201). New York: Cambridge University Press.

Harasim, L. (1990). Online education: An environment for collaboration and intellectual amplification. In L. Harasim (Ed.), *Online education: Perspectives on a new environment* (pp. 39–64). New York: Praeger.

Harasim, L. M. (1993). Networlds: Networlds as social space. In L. M. Harasim (Ed.), *Global networks: Computers and international communication* (pp. 15–34). Cambridge, MA: MIT Press.

Hartman, K., Neuwirth, C. M., Kiesler, S., Sproull, L., Cochran, C., Palmquist, M., & Zubrow, D. (1991). Patterns of social interaction and learning to write: Some effects of network technologies. *Written Communication, 8*(1), 79–113.

Koschmann, T. D. (1994). Toward a theory of computer support for collaborative learning. *Journal of the Learning Sciences, 3*(3), 219–225.

Koschmann, T. D., Myers, A. C., Feltovich, P. J., & Barrows, H. S. (1994). Using technology to assist in realizing effective learning and instruction: A principled approach to the use of computers in collaborative learning. *Journal of the Learning Sciences, 3*(3), 219–225.

Kozulin, A. (1986). The concept of activity in Soviet psychology: Vygotsky; his disciples and critics. *American Psychologist, 41*(3), 264–274.

Lave, J. (1991). Situating learning in communities of practice. In L. B. Resnick, J. M. Levine, & S. D. Teasley (Eds.), *Perspectives on socially shared cognition* (pp. 63–82). Washington, DC: American Psychological Association.

Lehrer, R. (1993). Authors of knowledge: Patterns of hypermedia design. In S. P. Lajoie & S. J. Derry (Eds.), *Computers as cognitive tools* (pp. 197–227). Hillsdale, NJ: Lawrence Erlbaum Associates.

Loo, M., & McLane, J. (1994, February). *Kids-to-kids: Global telecommunications in the 21st century.* Paper presented at the Association for Educational Communications and Technology, Nashville, TN.

Meloth, M., & Deering, P. (1994). Task talk and task awareness under different cooperative learning conditions. *American Educational Research Association, 31*(1), 138–165.

Montague, M. (1990). *Computers, cognition, and writing instruction.* Albany: State University of New York Press.

Newman, D., Griffin, P., & Cole, M. (1989). *The construction zone: Working for cognitive change in school.* New York: Cambridge University Press.

O'Shea, L. (1995). *Learning in cyberspace: An analyses of a screenwriting course offered through America Online.* Unpublished manuscript, University of Indiana at Bloomington.

Pea, R. D. (1993). The collaborative visualization project. *Communications of the ACM, 36*(5), 60–63.

Pea, R. D. (1994). Seeing what we build together: Distributed multimedia learning environments for transformative communications. *Journal of the Learning Sciences, 3*(3), 219–225.

Piaget, J. (1963). *Psychology of intelligence.* Paterson, NJ: Littlefield, Adams.

Quarterman, J. S. (1993). The global matrix of minds. In L. M. Harasim (Ed.), *Global networks: Computers and international communication* (pp. 35–56). Cambridge, MA: MIT Press.

Resnick, L. B., Levine, J. M., & Teasley S. D. (Eds.). (1991). *Perspectives on socially shared cognition.* Washington, DC: American Psychological Association.

Riel, M. (1993). Global education through learning circles. In L. Harasim (Ed.), *Global networks* (pp. 221–236). Cambridge, MA: MIT Press.

Rogoff, B. (1990). *Apprenticeship in thinking: Cognitive development in social context*. New York: Oxford University Press.

Ruopp, R., Gal, S., Drayton, B., & Pfister, M. (Eds.). (1993). *LabNet: Toward a community of practice*. Hillsdale, NJ: Lawrence Erlbaum Associates.

Salomon, G. (1988). AI in reverse: Computer tools that turn cognitive. *Journal of Educational Computing Research*, *4*(2), 123–139.

Saunders, W. M. (1989). Collaborative writing tasks and peer interaction. *International Journal of Educational Research*, *13*(1), 101–112.

Scardamalia, M., & Bereiter, C. (1994). Computer support for knowledge building communities. *Journal of the Learning Sciences*, *3*(3), 219–225.

Schrage, M. (1990). *Shared minds: The technologies of collaboration*. New York: Random House.

Scott, T., Cole, M., & Engel, M. (1992). Computers and education: A cultural constructivist perspective. *Review of Research in Education*, *18*, 191–251.

Songer, N. B. (in press). Can technology bring students closer to science? In K. Tobin & B. Fraser (Eds.), *The international handbook of science education*. Dordrecht, The Netherlands: Kluwer.

Teles, L. (1993). Cognitive apprenticeship on global networks. In L. M. Harasim (Ed.), *Global networks: Computers and international communication* (pp. 271–281). Cambridge, MA: MIT Press.

Tharp, R. (1993). Institutional and social context of educational reform: Practice and reform. In E. A. Forman, N. Minnick, & C. A. Stone (Eds.), *Contexts for learning: Sociocultural dynamics in children's development* (pp. 269–282). New York: Oxford University Press.

Tharp, R., & Gallimore, R. (1988). *Rousing minds to life: Teaching, learning, and schooling in a social context*. Cambridge, MA: Cambridge University Press.

Turner, M. C., & Ann Arbor Software. (1994). *Instructor's guide for use with Norton Textra Connect: A networked writing environment*. New York: Norton.

Vygotsky, L. S. (1978). *Mind in society: The development of higher psychological processes* (M. Cole, V. John-Steiner, S. Scribner, & E. Souberman, Eds.). Cambridge, MA: Harvard University Press.

Vygotsky, L. (1986). *Thought and language* (Rev. ed.). Cambridge, MA: MIT Press.

Wells, G. (1994, April). *Discourse as tool in the activity of learning and teaching*. Paper presented at the American Educational Research Association annual meeting, New Orleans.

Wertsch, J. V. (1985). *Vygotsky and the social formation of mind*. Cambridge, MA: Harvard University Press.

Wertsch, J. V. (1995). The need for action in sociocultural research. In J. V. Wertsch, P. Del Rio, & A. Alvarez (Eds.), *Sociocultural studies of mind* (pp. 56–74). New York: Cambridge University Press.

Woolley, D. R. (1997). *Conferencing on the World Wide Web* [on-line]. Available: http://freenet.msp.mn.us/~drwool/webconf.html

2

Searching for Learner-Centered, Constructivist, and Sociocultural Components of Collaborative Educational Learning Tools

Curtis Jay Bonk
Donald J. Cunningham
Indiana University

As Bednar, Cunningham, Duffy, and Perry (1995) argued, instructional strategies and tools must be based on some theory of learning and cognition. Of course, crafting well-articulated views that clearly answer the major epistemological questions of human learning has exercised psychologists and educators for centuries. What is a mind? What does it mean to know something? How is our knowledge represented and manifested? Many educators prefer an eclectic approach, selecting "principles and techniques from the many theoretical perspectives in much the same way we might select international dishes from a smorgasbord, choosing those we like best and ending up with a meal which represents no nationality exclusively and a design technology based on no single theoretical base" (Bednar et al., 1995, p. 100). It is certainly the case that research within collaborative educational learning tools has drawn upon behavioral, cognitive information processing, humanistic, and sociocultural theory, among others, for inspiration and justification. Problems arise, however, when tools developed in the service of one epistemology, say cognitive information processing, are integrated within instructional systems designed to promote learning goals inconsistent with it. When concepts, strategies, and tools are abstracted from the theoretical viewpoint that spawned them, they are too often stripped of meaning and utility. In this chapter, we embed our discussion in learner-centered, constructivist, and sociocultural perspectives on collaborative technology, with a bias toward the third. The principles of these perspectives, in fact, provide the theoretical rationale for much of the research and ideas presented in this book.

Theory certainly cannot operate within a vacuum. Views on questions such as the nature of mind are developed by considering not only philosophical questions like the form of underlying mental representation, but also the world within which learners function. Cunningham (1996) has proposed three models of mind that could guide our conceptions of learning and cognition: mind as computer (a symbol manipulation device), mind as brain (a parallel distributed processing device), and mind as rhizome (an infinity of connections with and within the social cultural milieu). Each of these metaphors points to a view of instruction in general and of collaborative learning tools in particular: (a) learning as information processing—a cognitive skills approach, (b) learning as experiential growth and pattern recognition—a cognitive constructivist approach, and (c) learning as a sociocultural dialogic activity—a social constructivist or sociocultural approach. If learning is predominantly information processing, then instruction should provide for efficient communication of information and effective strategies for remembering. If learning is predominantly experiential growth, then instruction should focus on experiences and activities that promote the individual development of the appropriate cognitive networks or mind maps. And, finally, if learning is predominantly a sociocultural dialogic, then instruction should provide opportunities for embedding learning in authentic tasks leading to participation in a community of practice.

But each of these views presumes the availability, in the world of experience, of tools and structures to support them. In a way, each of these three views can be identified and embodied in the tools and cultural practices of the late 20th century; though none is so apparent and consequential as the sociocultural. As we see later, recent developments in cultural tools and instructional practices have allowed rapid advances in sociocultural theory by providing embodiments and instantiations of this theory undreamed of only decades ago.

We truly live in interesting times (whether this is a curse or blessing, we leave it to the reader to decide)! Daily advances in fiber optics, multimedia, and telecomputing technology continue to force new sectors of society to grapple with information access, transmission, and collaboration issues. In the midst of this social and technological drama, vast resources at our fingertips are restructuring the way we humans work, live, learn, and generally interact regardless of "geography, distance, resources, or disability" (United States, Department of Labor, Secretary's Commission on Achieving Necessary Skills, 1991). Technology is becoming increasingly interactive and distributed, such that individual learners have available, at rapidly declining cost, the means to participate in incredibly complex networks of information, resources, and instruction. For instance, Internet navigation and discovery tools like the World Wide Web (WWW) have brought to many of our desktops an immense array of text, video, sound, and communication resources unthinkable even 10 years ago.

Such changes cannot fail to influence our views of the teaching–learning process and the education of our children. During the past few years we have all witnessed the exploding interest in the Internet among teachers, students, and other learning communities. But the underlying views of learning held by students and teachers of the Internet remain unclear. With the dramatic growth in both the means and impact of collaborative communication, there is a heightened need for theoretically based collaborative educational learning tool use. At the same time, educational leaders need reassurance and guidance that as the formats for electronic collaboration proliferate, computer-mediated communication will enhance student–teacher and student–student interaction and positively reorganize the learning process of K–12 schools and institutions of higher learning.

Some educators claim that online environments are particularly appropriate for collaborative learning approaches because they emphasize group interaction (Harasim, 1990). But as the menu of technology choices in schools, workplaces, and on college campuses escalates, instructional decisions regarding how to communicate with learners across these settings are becoming increasingly critical and complex. The lack of pedagogical guidance about integrating tools for collaboration and communication into one's classroom or training setting leaves instructors across educational settings with mounting dilemmas and confusion.

Predictably, the traditional teacher-centered model in which knowledge is "transmitted" from teacher to learner is rapidly being replaced by alternative models of instruction (e.g., learner-centered, constructivist, and sociocultural ideas) in which the emphasis is on guiding and supporting students as they learn to construct their understanding of the culture and communities of which they are a part (A. L. Brown et al., 1993; J. S. Brown, Collins, & Duguid, 1989; Cobb, 1994; Collins, 1990; Duffy & Cunningham, 1996; Pea, 1993b). In the process of shifting our attention to the constructive activity of the learner, we recognize the need to anchor learning in real-world or authentic contexts that make learning meaningful and purposeful.

The blending of these technological and pedagogical advancements has elevated the importance of research on electronic student dialogue, text conferencing, information sharing, and other forms of collaboration. Clearly, as specialized software is developed to support the exchange of information across workstations (e.g., text, graphics, and other digitized material) and various instructional strategies are experimented with and modified, collaborative tools will present unique opportunities for facilitating, augmenting, and redefining learning environments (Koschmann, Myers, Feltovich, & Barrows, 1994). Rapid tool development during the 1990s has naturally multiplied concerns within a number of human–computer interaction subfields for identifying, empirically examining, and adapting the design of collaborative learning tools. In fact, one such subfield, *computer-supported collaborative learning* (CSCL) (Koschmann, 1994, 1996), has merged various technological and instructional trends to offer major promise for coping with this current change.

Advances in interactive technologies for learning collaboration within CSCL are evident in new journals, conferences, technology tool announcements, instructional labs, and professional organizations. Prominent CSCL technologies for computer conferencing and collaboration are bringing students close to real-world environments and mentoring situations. As these collaborative technologies provide increasing opportunities for working with online communities of learners (Harasim, 1993), the pedagogic potential of every connected classroom multiplies. Given all these new technologies for conferencing and collaboration, faculty in higher education as well as those in public schools and the corporate world have a growing number of instructional possibilities to consider. And there is certainly no sign of a letup in collaborative tool development! The primary issue facing these educators, therefore, is what sort of framework they will have for incorporating these tools for learning collaboration into K–12, higher education, and corporate classrooms. Just what is the most effective way to understand and use these tools?

THEORETICAL PERSPECTIVES ON COLLABORATIVE LEARNING TOOLS

As indicated, the chapters in this book primarily draw on three general and overlapping theoretical perspectives on collaborative learning tools: learner-centered instruction, constructivism, and sociocultural theory. We consider each of these in turn.

A Learner-Centered View on Collaborative Technology

In 1990, the American Psychological Association (APA) and the Mid-continent Regional Educational Laboratory (McREL) joined forces to create a task force on psychology in education that recognized that research and theory on learning, development, and motivation was not having as great an impact in school reform and restructuring activities as expected. As a result, an eclectic mix of 12 learner-centered principles (LCPs) were drafted, which later evolved into 14 basic principles from the APA (American Psychological Association, 1993, 1997; see also Table 2.1). Because these learner-centered principles have extensive research backing (Alexander & Murphy, 1994), they have begun to provide a foundation for educational reform and transformation across age levels and organizations. With all the media attention on tangible and cost-effective changes in schools, these reform efforts, not surprisingly, are especially conspicuous in technology-rich learning environments wherein the role of the teacher is under intense scrutiny and transformation.

TABLE 2.1
Learner-Centered Psychological Principles Revised

Cognitive and Metacognitive Factors

1. *Nature of the learning process.* The learning of complex subject matter is most effective when it is an intentional process of constructing meaning from information and experience.
2. *Goals of the learning process.* The successful learner, over time and with support and instructional guidance, can create meaningful, coherent representations of knowledge.
3. *Construction of knowledge.* The successful learner can link new information with existing knowledge in meaningful ways.
4. *Strategic thinking.* The successful learner can create and use a repertoire of thinking and reasoning strategies to achieve complex learning goals.
5. *Thinking about thinking.* Higher order strategies for selecting and monitoring mental operations facilitate creative and critical thinking.
6. *Context of learning.* Learning is influenced by environmental factors, including culture, technology, and instructional practices.

Motivational and Affective Factors

7. *Motivational and emotional influences on learning.* What and how much is learned is influenced by the learner's motivation. Motivation to learn, in turn, is influenced by the individual's emotional states.
8. *Intrinsic motivation to learn.* The learner's creativity, higher order thinking, and natural curiosity all contribute to motivation to learn. Intrinsic motivation is stimulated by tasks of optimal novelty and difficulty, relevant to personal interests, and providing for personal choice and control.
9. *Effects of motivation on effort.* Acquisition of complex knowledge and skills requires extended learner effort and guided practice. Without the learner's motivation to learn, the willingness to exert this effort is unlikely without coercion.

Developmental and Social Factors

10. *Developmental influences on learning.* As individuals develop, there are different opportunities and constraints for learning. Learning is most effective when differential development within and across physical, intellectual, emotional, and social domains is taken into account.
11. *Social influences on learning.* Learning is influenced by social interactions, interpersonal relations, and communication with others.

Individual Differences

12. *Individual differences in learning.* Learners have different strategies, approaches, and capabilities for learning that are a function of prior experience and heredity.
13. *Learning and diversity.* Learning is most effective when differences in learners' linguistic, cultural, and social backgrounds are taken into account.
14. *Standards and assessment.* Setting appropriately high and challenging standards and assessing the learner as well as learning progress—including diagnostic, process, and outcome assessment—are integral parts of the learning process.

Note. For a full text of the principles listed as well as additional rationale and explanation, call or write to the American Psychological Association (APA) for the December 1995 report *The Learner-Centered Psychological Principles: A Framework for School Redesign and Reform* (this summary of the 14 LCPs appeared in the *Newsletter for Educational Psychologists*, "Learner-Centered Psychological Principles revised," 1996, Vol. 19, Issue 2, p. 10) or see: American Psychological Association (1997) *Learner-Centered Psychological Principles: A Framework for School Redesign and Reform* (On-line), Available at URL: http://www.apa.org/ed/lcp.html.

But what does "learner-centered technology" look like? According to Wagner and McCombs (1995), technology-enhanced instructional settings, such as distance learning, offer special opportunities for implementing learner-centered principles and demonstrating them in action. They pointed out that distance-learning technology can offer greater opportunity to experience learning activities that are internally driven and constructed, goal oriented and reflective, personally meaningful and authentic, collaborative and socially negotiated, and adaptive to individual needs and cultural backgrounds.

As indicated in Table 2.1, the framework of the LCPs begins with cognitive and metacognitive aspects of learning. In directly addressing these first six LCPs, technology is often touted as affecting the nature and goals of the learning process (i.e., LCPs #1 and #2) by placing tools in the hands of learners to build, browse, link, draw, juxtapose, represent, and summarize information (Lehrer, 1993). Such construction of knowledge and emphasis on mental operations also aligns with the third, fourth, and fifth LCPs. More strikingly, the sixth LCP, on the "context of learning," explicitly notes that learning is influenced by environmental factors such as technology, instruction, and culture. Thus, this sixth LCP has relevance to all the research presented in this text because the collaborative technologies explored in this volume have been designed, modified, and/or enhanced to create new contexts for learning. Equally important, this principle is derived from sociocultural theory and research, detailed later, which is the framework we feel is best suited for research investigations involving CSCL tools. From our point of view, therefore, LCP #6 should be the first LCP.

The three motivationally related LCPs (#'s 7–9) point to the role of novelty, optimal difficulty, curiosity, personal choice, control, effort, and emotions. Certainly these, too, have applicability in technology-mediated settings. The intrigue of answering questions posted by one's foreign peers as well as the delight of posting one's ideas and work on the WWW builds a personal sense of pride and ownership over the task (Harasim, 1990). The linkage between collaborative technologies and learner-centered instruction, therefore, is extremely strong with both the cognitive and motivational principles.

The third category of LCPs relates to developmental and social factors in learning (i.e., LCPs #10 and 11). Adapting collaborative technology to the developmental issues stated in the 10th LCP is simultaneously the most tenuous and promising of these principles, however. Technology alone is not adaptive, but the design and use of it most definitely can be. The following LCP, on the other hand, is an important corollary to the sociocultural ideas of LCP #6 highlighted previously, because it addresses the social interactional factors in learning as well as the importance of interpersonal relations and communication with others. This LCP clearly corresponds to the supposed benefits of electronic conferencing and collaboration tools. It is here, in the social relations, that the cognitive and motivational activities addressed by the first 9 LCPs spring forth. The social interactional nature of collaborative educational technologies can foster many emotions and cognitions, including: (a) the tension of debate with students from distant lands who may come within one's field of vision, (b) the query of a student seeking to fill in a gap in his or her knowledge base, (c) the warming feedback of a keyboard-generated smile, and (d) the encouragement of someone recently befriended on the electronic superhighway. In effect, a common ground of interest and understanding is becoming a more determinant factor of who one communicates with than some shared "physical" space or geographic proximity. The fortunes of the learner-centered movement may, in fact, hinge on the success of emerging collaborative technologies in promoting interaction among those with common interests as well as finding learners new proximities of interest along the way.

Finally, the last three LCPs, related to individual differences in learning such as prior knowledge (LCP #12), linguistic and cultural backgrounds (LCP #13), and challenging standards (LCP #14), each can be linked to collaborative learning technologies. The use of global communication tools can make learner differences in prior knowledge (LCP #12) more salient, while forcing learners to consider variations between the way they view the world and those individuals from distinctly different social, economic, cultural, and linguistic backgrounds (LCP #13). At the same time, when students gather information to share with classmates from other cultures, their performance becomes elevated as one does not want to "look dumb" to his or her foreign peers. In this way, perhaps more challenging learning standards are established for both parties as is hoped for in the final LCP.

These 14 LCPs have arisen, in part, to satisfy public school teachers and higher education faculty who are no longer satisfied teaching in the familiar and routine way in which they themselves were taught. Many of these educators are seeking to use collaborative technologies to build new interaction patterns and learning communities based on a philosophy that puts the learner first. But although the emergence of more learner-centered teaching practices and technology tools for constructing knowledge applies to a myriad of school settings, most teachers still lack the support and direction to use collaborative technology from such a learner-centered perspective (Blumenfeld, Marx, Soloway, & Krajcik, 1996). For instance, teachers previously trained in the benefits of collaborative learning need to know how to embed grouping strategies when using CSCL tools. Furthermore, teachers trained in teacher-centered technologies such as overheads and videotape, or tool-centered media such as computer-assisted instruction or databases and spreadsheets, are now being asked to adopt CSCL technologies that place increasing responsibility for learning squarely in the hands of the learner. Fourteen individual statements are helpful but not enough. Teachers need assistance in identifying opportunities for the use of these principles in instruction and in evaluating their effectiveness. CSCL tools should provide a number of windows for doing so.

These 14 LCPs have generated much discussion and debate among educators, and as such, have been very productive. Yet, at the same time, they seem far too broad and eclectic and are not focused upon significant issues of mind. What is the nature of meaningful knowledge representations, for example? Are thinking and reasoning strategies abstract algorithms to be transferred to the learner or are they tied to the everyday cognition of humans in action? As with the learner-centered approach, constructivism has recently achieved some prominence as a theoretical foundation for teaching and leaning. We now turn to constructivist approaches to better understand collaborative tool learning.

A Constructivist View on Collaborative Technology

Constructivism is a recent perspective or philosophy on learning with ancient roots (von Glasersfeld, 1995) that has extensive implications for the use of collaborative learning tools. In employing constructivism, some teachers believe that better learning occurs when knowledge is the result of a situated construction of reality (Brooks, 1990). Unfortunately, although constructivist revolutionaries have ventured onto the battlefield of epistemological change, most have not provided practicing educators with the wherewithal to reconstitute and embed constructivist ideas within their personal philosophies and teaching practices. Teachers might, in fact, design useful constructivistic learning environments and strategies, but may not recognize that they operate from a constructivist paradigm (Harris & Pressley, 1991). Even when constructivism is recognized as valuable, few guidelines exist for implementing and assessing it. So, when CSCL tools enter the instructional arsenal of public schools and higher education settings, constructivism may not be the theory of choice. And, undoubtedly, many scholars and researchers fuel this problem with intense debates that most practitioners simply lack the time and energy to deal with (e.g., see Ernest, 1995; von Glasersfeld, 1995).

Further muddying the debate, there is no canonical form of constructivist theory. Cobb (1994) identified two variations—cognitive constructivist and social constructivist—and there are undoubtedly more. Cognitive constructivists tend to draw insight from Piaget and focus on individual constructions of knowledge discovered in interaction with the environment (see Table 2.2). Social constructivists rely more on Vygotsky (1978) and view learning as connection with and appropriation from the sociocultural context within which we are all immersed (see Table 2.3). In Tables 2.2 and 2.3, we try to clarify some of the distinct differences in teaching practices between these

TABLE 2.2
Cognitive Constructivistic Teaching Practices and Principles

1. *Mind:* The mind is in the head; hence, the learning focus is on active cognitive reorganization.
2. *Raw Materials:* Use raw or primary data sources, manipulatives, and interactive materials.
3. *Student Autonomy:* Ask students for personal theories and understandings before any instruction. Allow student thinking to drive lessons and alter instruction based on responses. Place thinking and learning responsibility in students' hands to foster ownership.
4. *Meaningfulness and Personal Motivation:* Make learning a personally relevant and meaningful endeavor. Relate learning to practical ideas and personal experiences. Adapt content based on student responses to capitalize on personal interests and motivation.
5. *Conceptual Organization/Cognitive Framing:* Organize information around concepts, problems, questions, themes, and interrelationships, while framing activities using thinking-related terminology (e.g., classify, summarize, predict).
6. *Prior Knowledge and Misconceptions:* Adapt the cognitive demands of instructional tasks to students' cognitive schemes, while building on prior knowledge. Design lessons to address students' previous misconceptions, for instance, by posing contradictions to original hypotheses and then inviting responses.
7. *Questioning:* Promote student inquiry and conjecture with open-ended questions. Also, encourage student question-asking behavior and peer questioning.
8. *Individual Exploration and Generating Connections:* Provide time for the selection of instructional materials and the discovery of information, ideas, and relationships. Also includes encouraging students to generate knowledge connections, metaphors, personal insights, and build their own learning products.
9. *Self-Regulated Learning:* Foster opportunity for reflection on skills used to manage and control one's learning. Help students understand and become self-aware of all aspects of one's learning, from planning to learning performance evaluation. Given the focus on individual mental activity, the importance of cooperative learning or peer interaction is in the modeling of and support for new individual metacognitive skill.
10. *Assessment:* Focus of assessment is on individual cognitive development within predefined stages. Use of authentic portfolio and performance-based measures with higher order thinking skill evaluation criteria or scoring rubrics.

Note. From Bonk, Oyer, and Medury (1995), Brooks (1990), A. L. Brown et al. (1993), Duffy and Cunningham (1996), Ernest (1995), Savery and Duffy (1996), von Glasersfeld (1995), Wells and Chang-Wells (1992).

two positions as well as some of the more subtle ones, which are really more a matter of emphasis than epistemological divergence.

It is worth pointing out that collaborative learning tools can be used from both a cognitive constructivist and social constructivist perspective. CSCL tools can place students in an authentic learning situation wherein an assortment of primary data and human resources are at their fingertips. A wealth of Internet and local area network tools, in fact, are now available in many public schools and universities to offer students significant opportunities to explore personal interests and expand on prior experiences. Moreover, many technology tools enable teachers to structure learning activities that address student misconceptions, seek student elaboration of their answers, and pose questions. Perhaps, even more importantly, a few educators have come to recognize the importance of social constructivism for electronic learning

TABLE 2.3
Social Constructivistic Teaching Practices and Principles

1. *Mind:* The mind is located in the social interaction setting and emerges from acculturation into an established community of practice.
2. *Authentic Problems:* Learning environments should reflect real-world complexities. Allow students to explore specializations and solve real-world problems as they develop clearer interests and deeper knowledge and skills.
3. *Team Choice and Common Interests:* Build not just on individual student prior knowledge, but on common interests and experiences. Make group learning activities relevant, meaningful, and both process and product oriented. Give students and student teams choice in learning activities. Foster student and group autonomy, initiative, leadership, and active learning.
4. *Social Dialogue and Elaboration:* Use activities with multiple solutions, novelty, uncertainty, and personal interest to promote student–student and student–teacher dialogue, idea sharing, and articulation of views. Seek student elaboration on and justification of their responses with discussion, interactive questioning, and group presentations.
5. *Group Processing and Reflection:* Encourage team as well as individual reflection and group processing on experiences.
6. *Teacher Explanations, Support, and Demonstrations:* Demonstrate problem steps and provide hints, prompts, and cues for successful problem completion. Provide explanations, elaborations, and clarifications where requested.
7. *Multiple Viewpoints:* Foster explanations, examples, and multiple ways of understanding a problem or difficult material. Build in a broad community of audiences beyond the instructor.
8. *Collaboration and Negotiation:* Foster student collaboration and negotiation of meaning, consensus building, joint proposals, prosocial behaviors, conflict resolution, and general social interaction.
9. *Learning Communities:* Create a classroom ethos or atmosphere wherein there is joint responsibility for learning, students are experts and have learning ownership, meaning is negotiated, and participation structures are understood and ritualized. Technology and other resource explorations might be used to facilitate idea generation and knowledge building within this community of peers. Interdisciplinary problem-based learning and thematic instruction is incorporated wherever possible.
10. *Assessment:* Focus of assessment is on team as well as individual participation in socially organized practices and interactions. Educational standards are socially negotiated. Embed assessment in authentic, real-world tasks and problems with challenges and options. Focus on collaboration, group processing, teamwork, and sharing of findings. Assessment is continual, less formal, subjective, collaborative, and cumulative.

Note. From Bonk et al. (1995), A. L. Brown et al. (1993), Duffy and Cunningham (1996), Ernest (1995), Savery and Duffy (1996), Wells and Chang-Wells (1992).

because the potential for collaboration and negotiation embedded within it provides the learner with the opportunity to obtain alternative perspectives on issues and offer personal insights; in effect, to engage in meaning making and knowledge negotiation (Duffy & Cunningham, 1996).

As Scardamalia and Bereiter (1996) discovered, when CSCL tools are developed and used from a social constructivist viewpoint, new communities of learning often emerge. Whereas cognitive constructivists focus on making learning more relevant, building on student prior knowledge, posing contradictions, and addressing misconceptions (Brooks, 1990), social constructivists emphasize human dialogue, interaction, negotiation, and collaboration (Bonk, Oyer, & Medury, 1995). Across both viewpoints, constructivistic educational practices and orientations emphasize active, generative learning, with curricula wherein teachers continue to perform a critical learning function as learning consultants and guides (Cognition and Technology Group at Vanderbilt, 1991; Tharp & Gallimore, 1988). For additional discussion of constructivist uses of technology tools across different subject matter domains, see Bonk, Medury, and Reynolds (1994), Lehrer (1993), Pea (1993b), Ruopp, Gal, Drayton, and Pfister (1993), Scardamalia and Bereiter (1996), Schoenfeld (1988), Scott, Cole, and Engel (1992), and Songer (in press).

In our separate research endeavors (e.g., Bonk et al., 1994; McMahon, O'Neill, & Cunningham, 1992), we have discovered that tools fostering social interaction and learner-centered instructional practices are transforming learning from silent, solitary acts to lively, meaning-making events rich in discussion and interchange. This research has led us to believe that what is now needed is national and international leadership to move educational technology to the next phase of development focusing on social interaction and dialogue tools. As becomes clear later, we believe that sociocultural theory and social constructivist teaching practices provide the backbone for such leadership (in fact, we use the terms social constructivism and sociocultural theory interchangeably).

Sociocultural Views on Collaborative Technology

As worldwide learning forums or educational "networlds" (Harasim, 1993) arise, the resulting electronic interactions between humans should be investigated through suitable social and cultural lenses (J. Brown, 1986; Scott et al., 1992). Fortunately, paralleling the recent advances in technology for global collaboration and dialogue, many educators and human-learning researchers are finding promise in Vygotsky's (1978, 1986) sociocultural ideas about learning in a social context (Cognition and Technology Group at Vanderbilt, 1990, 1991; Duffy & Jonassen, 1991; Forman, Minick, & Stone, 1993; Moll, 1990; Palincsar, 1986). A primary tenet of Vygotskian psychology is that individual mental functioning is inherently situated in social interactional, cultural, institutional, and historical contexts. Therefore, to understand human thinking and learning, one must examine the context and setting in which that thinking and learning occurs.

Mediation. As noted in Table 2.4, which summarizes 10 key sociocultural terms and principles, individual learning and development is dependent on the institutions, settings, and cultural artifacts in one's social milieu. The tools and signs one is exposed to, therefore, influence or mediate new patterns

TABLE 2.4
Sociocultural Theory and Principles for CSCL Environments

- *Mediation:* According to sociocultural theorists, genetic or developmental analyses need to be used to understand the origins and transitions of mental functions; there are four levels of development: microgenetic, ontogenetic, phylogenetic, and sociohistorical. From this view, social and individual psychological activity is influenced or mediated by the tools and signs in one's sociocultural milieu (e.g., written language, maps, artwork, diagrams, computer screens, etc.). Because individual development is dependent on institutional settings and cultural artifacts in one's learning environment, as technology advances to alter the available cultural tools and settings, so, too, does it alter mind.
- *Zones of Proximal Development (ZPD):* This terms refers to the distance between actual or independent problem solving and performance when provided with learning assistance from adults or more capable peers. It assumes that social interaction is central to the development of new patterns of thought and strategic behaviors; hence, if computer tools can be considered a more capable peer, they might mediate new patterns of thought within one's ZPD.
- *Internalization:* Sociocultural theorists believe that development appears twice, once socially with others and later as independent problem-solving behavior; in other words, it moves from an external to an internal plane. Internalization, therefore, is the process of taking new information that was experienced or learned within a social context and developing the necessary skills or intellectual functions to independently apply the new knowledge and strategies. Private or inner speech is important to development because it can be a bridge for the internalization of self-regulatory behaviors. A key assumption here is that learning is not an exact copying process, but, instead, the learner appropriates or applies the skills or information based on his or her own skills, needs, and experiences.
- *Cognitive Apprenticeship:* Refers to a socially interactive relationship similar to the master–apprentice one in skilled trades and crafts. The concept assumes that newcomer learners should be acculturated into an established community of practice by observing and participating on the periphery. Teachers and communities, therefore, should apprentice and scaffold young learners into authentic learning activities, while gradually ceding control of the learning task to the student. Hence, novice learners move from the fringes of the culture to a more central role within it.
- *Assisted Learning:* Because learning precedes development, effective instruction can provoke developmental growth or rouse new skills to life. As a result of this malleability of intelligence to instruction, teachers are vital in creating learning environments rich in meaning making and social negotiation activities. There are a range of techniques for teachers to assist in the learning process (e.g., modeling, coaching, scaffolding and fading, questioning, directly instructing, task structuring, management and feedback, and pushing students to explore, reflect, and articulate ideas).
- *Teleapprenticeship:* As a result of advances in technology tools, there are a myriad of online learning environments that are mediated by experts, peers, mentors, teachers, and so on, to help learners and teachers build and share knowledge through access to specialized expertise and information.
- *Scaffolded Learning:* This term relates to the various forms of support or assistance provided to a learner by an expert or more capable peer that enables the learner to complete a task or solve a problem that would not have been possible without such support. Scaffolding could include hinting, elaborating, guiding, questioning, prompting, probing, simplifying, or other similar learning supports. The goal is to actively engage the learner while providing only the necessary supports for eventual independent use of such strategies.

(Continued)

TABLE 2.4
(Continued)

- *Intersubjectivity:* This concept refers to a temporary shared collective reality among individuals. Conferencing and collaborative technologies can foster such shared space or situational understanding between learning participants that can help them negotiate meaning, design new knowledge, and perceive multiple problem-solving perspectives.
- *Activity Setting as Unit of Analysis:* Sociocultural theorists argue that the proper unit of analysis for research should be the activity or word meaning. Specific circumstances of an event or activity are essential to understanding how people act in their attempt to reach their goals. In effect, because consciousness is a product of society, we should explore the individual-in-social action.
- *Distributed Intelligence in a Learning Community:* Student higher order mental functioning has its roots in social relations. The mind, therefore, is distributed in society, and extends beyond one's skin. Because knowledge is negotiated by members of a community of practice, the classroom should be organized to guide student learning toward membership in a learning community. Participation in such a classroom is no longer didactic or transmissive, but a sophisticated instructional conversation. Though technology is vital here, it is but one resource of a learning community; other resources that should also be utilized include: experts, mentors, peers, curriculum/textbooks, teachers, self-reflection, assessment, parents, and the funds of capital within one's local community.

Note. From Bonk and Kim (1998), Cobb (1994), Duffy and Cunningham (1996), Teles (1993), Wertsch (1991a, 1991b).

of thought and mental functioning (Wertsch, 1991a). One repercussion is that intelligence is no longer viewed as static, but dynamic. Mediational tools and signs could be mathematical symbols, artwork, or diagrams as well as software visualizations, electronic messages, WWW course homepages and student conferences, and other electronically displayed information. The critical point here is that as technology advances to alter cultural tools and institutional settings, the available mediational means that can impact cognitive functioning also change (Wertsch, 1991b). Given the technological changes we have experienced in recent years, there are undoubtedly a myriad of untapped human-learning possibilities from a sociocultural point of view.

Zone of Proximal Development. According to sociocultural theorists, an individual acquires new mental functions and patterns of thought from the mediational assistance of tools, signs, and human scaffolding when it is offered within his or her zone of proximal development (ZPD) (Salomon, 1988; Wertsch, 1991a, 1991b). Vygotsky defined the ZPD as the distance between a child's independent problem-solving level and that obtained under adult guidance or in collaboration with more capable peers (Wertsch, 1985). Wells (1997) cautioned us, however, that a ZPD is formed not just within an individual learner, but in the interaction between the learner, coparticipants, and available tools during involvement in a common activity. ZPDs, therefore, depend on the quality of the total interactive context as well as individual learner capabilities.

A ZPD might be evident in online communities when students teach their peers about their particular region or locale (Harasim, 1993; Riel, 1990, 1993) as well as when the teaching comes directly from a computer tool in the form of thinking-related prompts and feedback mechanisms (Daiute & Dalton, 1988; Zellermayer, Salomon, Globerson, & Givon, 1991). Such computer prompts embed strategies intended to be internalized by the learner (Bonk & Reynolds, 1992). The resulting intellectual benefits from electronic collaboration with peers, teachers, and technology tools may rest, however, on the extent of student reflection and general "mindfulness" (Salomon, 1988) during these learning collaborations and collective knowledge-building experiences (Scardamalia & Bereiter, 1996).

Internalization. Central to the premise of ZPDs, and sociocultural theory itself, is Vygotsky's suggestion that higher mental functioning is dependent on the process of internalization. From a Vygotskian perspective, electronic social interaction utilizes, extends, and creates ZPDs to foster learner skills and capacities that originally were active only in collaborative or assisted learning situations, but gradually become internalized as independent self-regulatory processes (Bereiter & Scardamalia, 1985; A. L. Brown & Palincsar, 1989). In other words, internalization has occurred when processes first performed with others on a social plane are successfully executed by a learner in an independent learning activity.

But this prompts a key question here. Can we use learning environments rich in electronic social interaction to test Vygotsky's (1978) axiom that every function in one's development must appear on an interpsychological or social plane and later intrapsychologically as independent problem-solving skills or strategies? If the answer is yes, just how do individual learners, or learning communities for that matter, come to display this internalization in subsequent independent problem-solving situations, as well as in new socially constituted ones? And how do learners, or sets of learners, within this internalization process, appropriate the new skills and information initially encountered on the social plane for their own unique needs (Rogoff, 1990).

Cognitive Apprenticeship. In asserting that learning is most effective when it approximates real-world situations or problem scenarios, sociocultural research on collaborative technology also draws on insights from cognitive apprenticeship theory (Collins, 1990; Collins, J. S. Brown, & Newman, 1989; Pea, 1993a). As highlighted in the chapter by Sugar and Bonk (chap. 6, this volume), situating students as "legitimate peripheral participants" within an authentic community, apprentices or guides their learning until they can assume a more engaged and central role in that activity (Lave & Wenger, 1991). As mentors negotiate and support novice learners through experiences suitable to their ZPDs, they, in turn, gradually cede control of the task to the student (J. S. Brown et al., 1989). When the learning participants gradually assume greater task responsibility, they begin to internalize standard cultural practices (Rogoff, 1995). Such apprenticing situations and activities do not always imply vertical "teacher-to-student" relationships, however (see Zhu, chap. 10, this volume). Teachers may, in fact, assume colearner or coparticipant role in some of these learning situations, whereas their role in others may center on performance feedback and review. Collins et al. (1989) provided a rationale for at least six teaching methods of these cognitive apprenticeships: (a) modeling, (b) coaching, (c) scaffolding and fading, (d) articulation, (e) reflection, and (f) explorations, which are briefly defined next.

Assisted Learning. Not only is the environment transformed when adopting sociocultural practices, but so, too, is the pedagogical role of the teacher. Clearly, the focus here is on assisting learning, not directing it (Tharp & Gallimore, 1988). According to Tharp (1993), adept sociocultural teaching is responsive in nature; instead of assigning tasks, relying on text readings, and fostering standard practices (e.g., teacher *i*nitiation of a question or comment followed by pupil *r*esponse and teacher *e*valuation; known as the I-R-E recitation script), sociocultural teachers value assisting or supporting the performance of their students. Tharp further argued that there are seven basic ways for teachers to "assist" in the learning process: (a) modeling, (b) feedback, (c) contingency management, (d) instructing, (e) cognitive structuring, (f) questioning, and (g) task structuring. Bonk and Kim (1998) pointed out that merging these seven forms of learning assistance with Collins et al.'s six cognitive apprenticeship techniques, mentioned above, renders the following socioculturally based teaching techniques: (a) *modeling* to illustrate performance standards and verbalize invisible processes, (b) *coaching* to observe and supervise students, thereby guiding them toward expert performance, (c) *scaffolding* and *fading* to support what learners cannot yet do and gradually removing that support as competence is displayed, (d) *questioning* to request a verbal response from learners while supporting them with mental functions they cannot produce alone, (e) encouraging student *articulation* of their reasoning and problem-solving processes, (f) pushing student *exploration* and application of their problem-solving skills, (g) fostering student *reflection* and self-awareness (e.g., through performance replays), (h) providing *cognitive task structuring* by explaining and organizing the task within students' ZPDs, (i) *managing instruction* with performance feedback and positive reinforcement, and (j) using *direct instruction* to provide clarity, needed content, or missing information. When these means of assistance are woven together, the teaching–learning situation evolves into a rich "instructional conversation" (Gallimore & Tharp, 1990, p. 196; Tharp

& Gallimore, 1988, p. 111). By using this instructional framework to imagine rich, interactive conversations among students and teachers and beyond, we are optimistic that CSCL technologies can provide effective learning assistance within learner ZPDs.

Teleapprenticeship. In merging the aforementioned strategies with global networking technologies for "teleapprenticeship" (Teles, 1993), many universities and public schools are exploring CSCL tool features that provide unprecedented student-student social interaction opportunities and momentous cross-cultural activities and events (Harasim, 1990; Levin, Kim, & Riel, 1990; Riel, 1993). Now, online apprenticeships can involve experts and peers demonstrating ideas, posing questions, offering insights, and providing relevant information when needed. Recent breakthroughs in videoconferencing tools showcase such authentic avenues for student and instructor social interaction and dialogue (Fetterman, 1996b). A series of CSCL breakthroughs, in fact, have resulted in fully accredited online PhD programs, which feature electronic file exchange, E-mail office hours, electronic libraries, virtual cafes, whiteboards, debates and opinion polls, role-taking activities, and student dialogue transcripts (Fetterman, 1996a; Harasim, Hiltz, Teles, & Turoff, 1995). Such tools and strategies collectively function to electronically apprentice and assist in student learning.

Another celebrated example of a cognitive apprenticeship is to involve students in genuine scientific data collection and reporting about the weather. Recent projects here include the Collaborative Visualization (CoVis) project (Edelson, Pea, & Gomez, 1996; Pea, 1993a), the GLOBE Program (1995), Kids as Global Scientists (Songer, in press), and the Indiana Weather Project (Bonk, Hay, & Fischler, 1996). Along these same lines, Ruopp et al. (1993) used the Internet to build communities of physics teachers who then apprenticed less skilled learners through a mix of microcomputer laboratory activities and electronic sharing of results with students and teachers at other locales. Similarly, Sugar and Bonk in chapter 6 of this text employed such apprenticeship techniques to enhance the scientific learning possibilities of students in an Arctic expedition learning adventure. In these types of projects, peer and mentor collaborations validate and enhance students' sense of participation in communities of practice.

Scaffolded Instruction. Such cognitive apprenticeships are, of course, inherently reliant on a mentor or guide who effectively uses "scaffolded instruction." In selecting scaffolded instruction, a mentor or guide provides the learner with the support or assistance necessary to complete a task that would not have been completed without the help. Examples of this support might include prompts, hints, comments, explanations, questions, counterexamples, and suggestions. A learning scaffold may be embedded in an explicit request to include additional information or a more general question or comment intended to spur new idea linkages or course connections. Of course, these learning aids are faded and removed as the learner assumes control over the activity. Through such assistance, the learner (or a team of learners) solves a problem, generates solutions, and gains insights that would ordinarily rest beyond his or her independent abilities. In terms of such scaffolded learning activities, collaborative technologies can offer opportunities for both peer and mentor electronic guidance and feedback that stimulate student discussion and internal reflection. As in both the Zhu and the Sugar and Bonk chapters of this volume, electronic experts and learning guides might instigate learning activities through timely messages, questions, and quotes. On the other hand, experts might also provide electronic demonstrations and task assistance.

Such electronic tool support and scaffolded assistance is especially important for young children because the support structure aiding the acquisition of oral communication, which has developed over many thousands of years, is not available for young readers and writers. Until recently, reading and writing were strangely removed forms of communication not necessarily driven by human interaction; they simply involved a mark-making process that *required* explicit awareness of metalinguistic aspects of language (Downing, 1979). Unfortunately, reading and writing literacies do not develop spontaneously from spoken language; they are inaccessible to consciousness without the aid of a literate partner or guide. For young children, this means that, unlike their speech system, when reading or writing, there are no outside others to support and provide feedback on their communicative ability. We argue, therefore, that electronic tools not only might enhance literacy guidance possibilities, but extensive research in this area might inform sociocultural theorists of the types and conditions of effective teacher and mentor guidance and scaffolding.

Intersubjectivity. According to the sociocultural perspective, scaffolded instruction is bound to be more effective when the players of the learning situation experience intersubjectivity. Intersubjectivity refers to a temporary shared collective understanding or common framework among learning participants. As learners find common ground (Rogoff, 1990) or shared thoughts (Levine & Moreland, 1991), they can more easily exchange their ideas, build new knowledge, and negotiate meanings. Not surprisingly, in Michael Schrage's (1990) journeys across the country to find and document collaborative communication tools, he discovered that the most promising ones were those that created a mental "shared space" (e.g., electronic whiteboards, conferencing tools, group brainstorming tools, etc.). As Schrage found, these communication tools promote new forms of social interaction and productivity. In addition to the many apprenticeship possibilities, therefore, electronic conferencing tools open up new avenues for students to take the perspective of peers and better understand their expectations and potential reactions (Bonk, Appelman, & Hay, 1996).

In moving beyond local area networks, global networks and associated curricula bring new audiences to young learners. As the work of Sugar and Bonk (chap. 6, this volume) and Siegel and Kirkley (chap. 13, this volume) points out, there are a wealth of instructional design possibilities and pedagogical strategies for fostering electronic perspective taking. Computer-conferencing and collaboration technologies, for instance, might encourage learners to consider alternative perspectives and viewpoints by providing expert feedback windows, interactive debate forums, juxtapositions of opinions, scrollable dialogue-tracking devices, private reflection notes, peer commenting windows, public text-pointing devices, and interactive prompts available on demand. These are the types of tools that need to be developed and tested to help egocentric or culturally unaware students decenter from their own narrow points of view and engage in extensive dialogue with their peers. Such tools not only bring unique opportunities for enhancing perspective taking and intersubjectivity, but, in fact, provide a glimpse into the entire "activity" of electronic collaboration.

Activity Setting as Unit of Analysis. From a sociocultural perspective, the lifeblood of new intellectual functioning is, in fact, the activity setting. The concept of an activity setting was derived from the sociocultural school of Vygotsky–Leont'ev–Luria in the Soviet Union during the 1930s (see Davydov & Radzikhovskii, 1985). Vygotsky and many of his followers emphasized the mediational role of signs in socially meaningful activity (Kozulin, 1986). As Cole (1985) further pointed out, analysis of human activity in real, not contrived, settings links individuals and social systems and provides insights into both cultural practices and individual higher order thinking. It is from activity settings that one can simultaneously begin to understand groups or individuals, products or processes, and cognitions or cultures. Similarly, Wertsch (1995) proposed using human action as the primary unit of analysis because it helps one understand the sociocultural context as well as the mental functioning of individuals operating within it.

Ideas about activity settings have penetrated psychological research in a variety of domains, including early literacy in the home (Gallimore & Goldenberg, 1993), classroom learning (Chang-Wells & Wells, 1993; Tharp & Gallimore, 1988), after-school computer play environments (Nicolopoulou & Cole, 1993), and even workplace settings such as navy vessels (Hutchins, 1993) and medical practices (Engestrom, 1993). Quotes such as, "the mind rarely works alone" (Pea, 1993b, p. 47) and the mind "can be said to extend beyond the skin" (Wertsch, 1991a, p. 90), indicate that thinking in such settings is distributed. Accordingly, by attempting to understand activity settings, the focus of evaluation has shifted from individual mental functioning to groups of minds in interaction (Hutchins, 1993).

Distributed Intelligence in a Learning Community. Whereas an activity system includes subjects, rules, communities, objects, and divisions of labor (Cole & Engestrom, 1993), it is the tools that mediate the activity and connect humans to objects and other people (Wells, 1996). And, as the research in this book demonstrates, there are a myriad of CSCL tools to create new forms of activity settings for both human–human and human–computer interaction and collaboration. The current generation of collaborative educational learning tools present unique opportunities for supporting and organizing human conversations and creating new communities of learning (Blumenfeld et al., 1996). Because human mental functioning is rooted in social relations and intellectual performance is distributed among members of a learning community, it is critical to begin to understand how electronic tools might enhance the collective intelligence of such a community. What types of electronic tools foster the negotiation of meaning and sophisticated conversations among community participants? How can they be married with other learning resources—experts, mentors, teachers, text resources, and the local community—to foster learning? When sociocultural theory is finally merged with electronic tool development and use, the answers to these questions may arise in rich, instructional conversations (Tharp & Gallimore, 1988) among learning participants wherein new meanings and insights are coconstructed and debated. Certainly that should be the benchmark for this field.

Some Sociocultural "Ifs"

Although the research on collaborative technologies is in a prime position to test and extend sociocultural theory, many questions and issues remain. For instance, if the mind is distributed in society, then the tools for collaboration should offer a unique way to illustrate this in action. But have they? Second, if cultural artifacts and institutions underpin human development, then we need to grasp unique opportunities for human development as new collaborative educational learning tools spring forth and intersect. Instead of simply purchasing the latest CSCL tools and systems, therefore, one must first grasp their utility as scaffolded learning devices. Even the social context of extremely popular instructional techniques, such as using a word processor for collaborative writing, for instance, are only beginning to be documented and better understood (Daiute & Dalton, 1988; Kumpulainen, 1996).

In terms of activity settings, collaborative tools should also offer interesting windows on the negotiation of meaning and learner interaction. If the interaction with experts and more capable peers on a social plane leads to student intellectual growth and new competencies, then we need to create and test electronic situations wherein students represent and share knowledge (Pea, 1994; Vosniadou, 1996). In order to test whether development moves from the external to the internal plane, the activities appearing within collaboration tools must be later seen in students' independent problem-solving acts. And, if speech is a bridge for movement from the external plane to new strategic behaviors, then the dialogue patterns of electronic social interaction as well as any ensuing journal writings and private reflections must be captured and inspected.

Still other sociocultural questions face collaborative learning tool advocates. For instance, if scaffolded instruction is important in moving students from novice to more expertlike behavior, then we need to create situations wherein the cognitive apprenticeship and dialogue possibilities of collaborative tools can be fostered and examined. Pedagogically intriguing electronic apprenticeship tools should allow for various types of learning assistance and social interaction. For instance, explicit displays of shared knowledge should foster greater participant intersubjectivity and perspective taking. In addition, if learning prefaces development as Vygotsky proposed, then effective forms of electronic learning assistance and scaffolding need to be better understood. Finally, this field is in dire need of learning benchmarks, signposts, and standards. How will CSCL researchers and educators really know when they have made an impact on human learning? Certainly, new collaborative problem-solving or problem-finding assessments need to be developed and tested. Perhaps some innovative assessment ideas and approaches can be found in various sections of this text. The ensuing chapters should provide some tentative answers for the questions raised earlier or at least make explicit related issues and dilemmas.

Ending the Search

The appearance on a nearly daily basis of new interactive technologies has sorely taxed the ability of educators to conceptualize and capitalize upon the processes of learning and teaching in this brave new world. Familiar definitions of school, teacher, textbook, subject matter content, and so forth seem increasingly irrelevant in a world where access to information is expanding at explosive rates and where the ability to communicate on a global basis is as simple as pointing and clicking a screen icon. In response, learner-centered, constructivist, and sociocultural models have arisen to place emphasis on guiding and supporting students as they construct their understanding of the cultures and communities of which they are a part (J. S. Brown et al., 1989; Cobb, 1994). In the process of shifting our attention to the knowledge-building and social negotiation activities of a learner in meaningful environments, we recognize the need to anchor learning in real-world or authentic contexts that give it meaning and purpose. Perhaps, even more important, we have come to recognize the significance of collaboration in learning when it provides opportunities to receive a myriad of alternative perspectives, test contrary ideas, and collect new data and insights (Duffy & Cunningham, 1996; Riel, 1993).

This search for learner-centered, constructivist, and sociocultural components of collaborative educational learning tools was in response to the dearth of theoretical grounding related to CSCL tools (Koschmann, 1994). Although our theoretical search indicates that useful components and connections are being made, more knowledge is desperately needed about the relevance, prevalence, and consequence of these innovative learning tools. For pedagogical progress to be made in electronic learning environments, educators must begin to realize that the lockstep factory model of education is out of sync with prevailing views of learning. Today, with the complementary nature of sociocultural theory and collaborative learning tools, learning is viewed as fundamentally social and derived from authentic engagement with others in a community of practice (Kahn, 1993).

Just where we are headed is uncertain given the tremors of change and parallel tension in the nature of learning and schooling in the 1990s. However, this uncertainty has been fostered, at least in part, by the emergence of CSCL tools and their associated learning activities. What is clear is that recent advancements in collaborative tools parallel new developments in psychological theory on human teaching and learning. What is also apparent is that further inroads into the use of collaborative educational learning tools will help educational researchers design more powerful learning environments during the early stages of the next millennium.

In this particular chapter, we have tried to make salient the theoretical viewpoints from which CSCL tools can be evaluated and discussed. Although the theoretical frameworks presented here—learner centered, constructivist, and sociocultural—do overlap, we find most hope for CSCL developments within the latter. And while some perspectives emphasize such critical issues as meaningful learning, developing higher order thinking strategies, and encouraging learners to link new information to old, the social context of learning too often does not play a central enough role in these approaches. In contrast, a sociocultural view on collaborative tools explicitly points to the social origin of higher mental functions, the distributed nature of learning and problem solving, and the importance of technology tools in mediating individual and cultural development. Ongoing developments in CSCL technology, therefore, make possible the embodiments of sociocultural theory not possible in Vygotsky's days. And, correspondingly, continued theoretical development will serve to strengthen the underbelly of effective tool use in both public school and higher education settings. Some of those tool developments and practices are reflected in the remaining chapters of this book. Enjoy.

REFERENCES

Alexander, P. A., & Murphy, P. K. (1994, April). *The research base for APA's learner-centered psychological principles.* Paper presented at the American Educational Research Association annual meeting, New Orleans.

American Psychological Association. (1993). *Learner-centered psychological principles: Guidelines for school reform and restructuring.* Washington, DC: Author and the Mid-continent Regional Educational Laboratory.

American Psychological Association. (1997). *Learner-centered psychological principles: A Framework for School Redesign and Reform* (Online), Available at URL: http://www.apa.org/ed/lcp.html.

Bednar, A., Cunningham, D. J., Duffy, T., & Perry, D. (1995). Theory in practice: How do we link? In G. Anglin (Ed.), *Instructional technology: Past, present, and future* (2nd ed., pp. 100–112). Englewood, CO: Libraries Unlimited.

Bereiter, C., & Scardamalia, M. (1985). Cognitive coping strategies and the problem of "inert knowledge." In J. W. Segal, S. F. Chipman, & R. Glaser (Eds.), *Thinking and learning skills* (Vol. 2, pp. 65–80). Hillsdale, NJ: Lawrence Erlbaum Associates.

Blumenfeld, P. C., Marx, R. W., Soloway, E., & Krajcik, J. (1996). Learning with peers: From small group cooperation to collaborative communities. *Educational Researcher, 25*(8), 43–46.

Bonk, C. J., Appelman, R., & Hay, K. E. (1996). Electronic conferencing tools for student apprenticeship and perspective taking. *Educational Technology, 36*(5), 8–18.

Bonk, C. J., Hay, K. E., & Fischler, R. B. (1996). Five key resources for an electronic community of elementary student weather forecasters. *Journal of Computing in Childhood Education, 7*(1/2), 93–118.

Bonk, C. J., & Kim, K. A. (1998). Extending sociocultural theory to adult learning. In M. C. Smith & T. Pourchot (Ed.), *Adult learning and development: Perspectives from educational psychology* (pp. 67–88). Mahwah, NJ: Lawrence Erlbaum Associates.

Bonk, C. J., Medury, P. V., & Reynolds, T. H. (1994). Cooperative hypermedia: The marriage of collaborative writing and mediated environments. *Computers in the Schools, 10*(1/2), 79–124.

Bonk, C. J., Oyer, E. J., & Medury, P. V. (1995, April). *Is this the S.C.A.L.E.?: Social constructivism and active learning environments.* Paper presented at the annual convention of the American Educational Research Association, San Francisco.

Bonk, C. J., & Reynolds, T. H. (1992). Early adolescent composing within a generative-evaluative computerized framework. *Computers in Human Behavior, 8*(1), 39–62.

Brooks, J. G. (1990). Teachers and students: Constructivists forging new connections. *Educational Leadership, 47*(5), 68–71.

Brown, A. L., Ash, D., Rutherford, M., Nakagawa, K., Gordon, A., & Campione, J. C. (1993). Distributed expertise in the classroom. In G. Salomon (Ed.), *Distributed cognitions: Psychological and educational considerations* (pp. 188–228). New York: Cambridge University Press.

Brown, A. L., & Palincsar, A. S. (1989). Guided, cooperative learning and individual knowledge acquisition. In L. Resnick (Ed.), *Cognition and instruction: Issues and agendas* (pp. 393–451). Hillsdale, NJ: Lawrence Erlbaum Associates.

Brown, J. (1986). From cognitive to social ergonomics and beyond. In D. Norman & N. Draper (Eds.), *User centered system design: New perspectives on human-computer interaction* (pp. 457–486). Hillsdale, NJ: Lawrence Erlbaum Associates.

Brown, J. S., Collins, A., & Duguid, P. (1989). Situated cognition and the culture of learning. *Educational Researcher, 18*(1), 32–41.

Chang-Wells, G. M., & Wells, G. (1993). Dynamics of discourse: Literacy and the construction of knowledge. In E. A. Forman, N. Minick, & C. A. Stone (Eds.), *Contexts for learning:*

Sociocultural dynamics in children's development (pp. 58–90). New York: Oxford University Press.

Cobb, P. (1994). Where is mind? Constructivist and sociocultural perspectives on mathematical development. *Educational Researcher, 23*(7), 13–20.

Cognition and Technology Group at Vanderbilt. (1990). Anchored instruction and its relationship to situated cognition. *Educational Researcher, 19*(6), 2–10.

Cognition and Technology Group at Vanderbilt. (1991). Technology and the design of generative learning environments. *Educational Technology, 31*(5), 34–40.

Cole, M. (1985). The zone of proximal development: Where culture and cognition create each other. In J. V. Wertsch (Ed.), *Culture, communication, and literacy: Vygotskian perspectives* (pp. 162–179). New York: Cambridge University Press.

Cole, M., & Engestrom, Y. (1993). A cultural approach to distributed cognition. In G. Salomon (Ed.), *Distributed cognitions: Psychological and educational considerations* (pp. 1–46). New York: Cambridge University Press.

Collins, A. (1990). Cognitive apprenticeship and instructional technology. In L. Idol & B. F. Jones (Eds.), *Educational values and cognitive instruction: Implications for reform* (pp. 119–136). Hillsdale, NJ: Lawrence Erlbaum Associates.

Collins, A., Brown, J. S., & Newman, S. E. (1989). Cognitive apprenticeship: Teaching the crafts of reading, writing, and mathematics. In L. Resnick (Ed.), *Knowing, learning, and instruction: Essays in honor of Robert Glaser* (pp. 453–494). Hillsdale, NJ: Lawrence Erlbaum Associates.

Cunningham, D. J. (1996). Time after time. In W. Spinks (Ed.), *Semiotics 95* (pp. 263–269). New York: Lang Publishing.

Daiute, C., & Dalton, B. (1988). Let's brighten it up a bit: Collaboration and cognition in writing. In B. A. Rafoth & D. L. Rubin (Eds.), *The social construction of written communication* (pp. 249–269). Norwood, NJ: Ablex.

Davydov, V. V., & Radzikhovskii, L. A. (1985). Vygotsky's theory and the activity-oriented approach in psychology. In J. V. Wertsch (Ed.), *Culture, communication, and literacy: Vygotskian perspectives* (pp. 35–65). New York: Cambridge University Press.

Downing, J. (1979). *Reading and reasoning*. London: Chambers.

Duffy, T. M., & Cunningham, D. J. (1996). Constructivism: Implications for the design and delivery of instruction. In D. H. Jonassen (Ed.), *Handbook of research on educational communications and technology* (pp. 170–198). New York: Scholastic.

Duffy, T. M., & Jonassen, D. H. (1991). New implications for instructional technology. *Instructional Technology, 31*(5), 7–12.

Edelson, D. C., Pea, R. D., & Gomez, L. (1996). Constructivism in the collaboratory. In B. G. Wilson (Ed.), *Constructivist learning environments: Case studies in instructional design* (pp. 151–164). Englewood Cliffs, NJ: Educational Technology Publications.

Engestrom, Y. (1993). Developmental studies of work as a testbench of activity theory: The case of primary care medical practice. In S. Chailklin & J. Lave (Eds.), *Understanding practice: Perspectives on activity and context* (pp. 64–103). New York: Cambridge University Press.

Ernest, P. (1995). The one and the many. In L. P. Steffe & J. Gale (Ed.), *Constructivism in education* (pp. 459–486). Hillsdale, NJ: Lawrence Erlbaum Associates.

Fetterman, D. M. (1996a). Ethnography in the virtual classroom. *Practicing Anthropologist, 18*(3), 2, 36–39.

Fetterman, D. M. (1996b). Videoconferencing on-line: Enhancing communication over the Internet. *Educational Researcher, 25*(4), 23–27.

Forman, E. A., Minick, N., & Stone, C. A. (Eds.). (1993). *Contexts for learning: Sociocultural dynamics in children's development*. New York: Oxford University Press.

Gallimore, R., & Goldenberg, C. (1993). Activity settings of early literacy: Home and school factors in children's emergent literacy. In E. A. Forman, N. Minick, & C. A. Stone (Eds.),

Contexts for learning: Sociocultural dynamics in children's development (pp. 3–16). New York: Oxford University Press.

Gallimore, R., & Tharp, R. (1990). Teaching mind in society: Teaching, schooling, and literate discourse. In L. C. Moll (Ed.), *Vygotsky in education: Instructional implications of sociohistorical psychology* (pp. 175–205). New York: Cambridge University Press.

The GLOBE Program. (1995). *The GLOBE Program*, 744 Jackson Place (Internet World Wide Web Server Address: http://www.globe.gov), Washington, DC, National Oceanic and Atmospheric Administration.

Harasim, L. (1990). Online education: An environment for collaboration and intellectual amplification. In L. Harasim (Ed.), *Online education: Perspectives on a new environment* (pp. 39–64). New York: Praeger.

Harasim, L. M. (1993). Networlds: Networks as a social space. In L. M. Harasim (Ed.), *Global networks* (pp. 15–34). Cambridge, MA: MIT Press.

Harasim, L., Hiltz, S. R., Teles, L., & Turoff, M. (1995). *Learning networks: A field guide to teaching and learning online*. Cambridge, MA: MIT Press.

Harris, K. R., & Pressley, M. (1991). The nature of cognitive strategy instruction: Interactive strategy construction. *Exceptional Children*, *57*(5), 392–404.

Hutchins, E. (1993). Learning to navigate. In S. Chailklin & J. Lave (Eds.), *Understanding practice: Perspectives on activity and context* (pp. 35–63). New York: Cambridge University Press.

Kahn, T. M. (1993). *A learning agenda: Putting people first*. Palo Alto, CA: Institute for Research on Learning.

Koschmann, T. D. (1994). Toward a theory of computer support for collaborative learning. *Journal of the Learning Sciences*, *3*(3), 219–225.

Koschmann, T. D. (Ed.). (1996). *CSCl: Theory and practice of an emerging paradigm*. Mahwah, NJ: Lawrence Erlbaum Associates.

Koschmann, T. D., Myers, A. C., Feltovich, P. J., & Barrows, H. S. (1994). Using technology to assist in realizing effective learning and instruction: A principled approach to the use of computers in collaborative learning. *Journal of the Learning Sciences*, *3*(3), 219–225.

Kozulin, A. (1986). The concept of activity in Soviet psychology: Vygotsky; his disciples and critics. *American Psychologist*, *41*(3), 264–274.

Kumpulainen, K. (1996). The nature of peer interaction in the social context created by the use of word processors. *Learning and Instruction*, *6*(3), 243–261.

Lave, J., & Wenger, E. (1991). *Situated learning: Legitimate peripheral participation*. New York: Cambridge University Press.

Learner-centered psychological principles revised. (1996). *Newsletter for Educational Psychologists*, *19*(2), 10.

Lehrer, R. (1993). Authors of knowledge: Patterns of hypermedia design. In S. P. Lajoie & S. J. Derry (Eds.), *Computers as cognitive tools* (pp. 197–227). Hillsdale, NJ: Lawrence Erlbaum Associates.

Levin, J., Kim, H., & Riel, M. (1990). Analyzing instructional interactions on electronic messaging networks. In L. Harasim (Ed.), *Online education: Perspectives on a new environment* (pp. 185–213). New York: Praeger.

Levine, J. M., & Moreland, R. L. (1991). Culture and socialization in work groups. In L. B. Resnick, J. M. Levine, & S. D. Teasley (Eds.), *Perspectives on socially shared cognition* (pp. 257–279). Washington, DC: American Psychological Association.

McMahon, H., O'Neill, W., & Cunningham, D. (1992). "Open" software design: A case study. *Educational Technology*, *32*(2), 43–55.

Moll, L. C. (Ed.). (1990). *Vygotsky and education: Instructional implications and applications of sociohistorical psychology*. New York: Cambridge University Press.

Nicolopoulou, A., & Cole, M. (1993). Generation and transmission of shared knowledge in the culture of collaborative learning: The Fifth Dimension, its play-world, and its institutional contexts. In E. A. Forman, N. Minick, & C. A. Stone (Eds.), *Contexts for learning: Sociocultural dynamics in children's development* (pp. 283–314). New York: Oxford University Press.

Palincsar, A. S. (1986). The role of dialogue in providing scaffolded instruction. *Educational Psychologist, 21*(1 & 2), 73–98.

Pea, R. D. (1993a). The collaborative visualization project. *Communications of the ACM, 36*(5), 60–63.

Pea, R. D. (1993b). Practices of distributed intelligence and designs for education. In G. Salomon (Ed.), *Distributed cognitions: Psychological and educational considerations* (pp. 47–87). New York: Cambridge University Press.

Pea, R. D. (1994). Seeing what we build together: Distributed multimedia learning environments for transformative communications. *Journal of the Learning Sciences, 3*(3), 219–225.

Riel, M. (1990). Cooperative learning across classrooms in electronic learning circles. *Instructional Science, 19*, 445–466.

Riel, M. (1993). Global education through learning circles. In L. Harasim (Ed.), *Global networks* (pp. 221–236). Cambridge, MA: MIT Press.

Rogoff, B. (1990). *Apprenticeship in thinking: Cognitive development in social context.* New York: Oxford University Press.

Rogoff, B. (1995). Observing sociocultural activity: Participatory appropriation, guided participation, and apprenticeship. In J. V. Wertsch, P. D. Rio, & A. Alvarez (Eds.), *Sociocultural studies of mind* (pp. 139–164). New York: Cambridge University Press.

Ruopp, R., Gal, S., Drayton, B., & Pfister, M. (Eds.). (1993). *LabNet: Toward a community of practice.* Hillsdale, NJ: Lawrence Erlbaum Associates.

Salomon, G. (1988). AI in reverse: Computer tools that turn cognitive. *Journal of Educational Computing Research, 4*(2), 123–139.

Savery, J. R., & Duffy, T. M. (1996). Problem-based learning: An instructional model and its constructivist framework. In B. G. Wilson (Ed.), *Constructivist learning environments: Case studies in instructional design* (pp. 135–148). Englewood Cliffs, NJ: Educational Technology Publications.

Scardamalia, M., & Bereiter, C. (1996). Adaptation and understanding: A case for new cultures of schooling. In S. Vosniadou, E. De Corte, R. Glaser, & H. Mandl (Eds.), *International perspectives on the design of technology-supported learning environments* (pp. 149–163). Mahwah, NJ: Lawrence Erlbaum Associates.

Schoenfeld, A. H. (1988). Mathematics, technology, and higher order thinking. In R. S. Nickerson & P. Z. Zodhiates (Eds.), *Technology in education: Looking toward 2020* (pp. 67–96). Hillsdale, NJ: Lawrence Erlbaum Associates.

Schrage, M. (1990). *Shared minds: The technologies of collaboration.* New York: Random House.

Scott, T., Cole, M., & Engel, M. (1992). Computers and education: A cultural constructivist perspective. *Review of Educational Research, 18*, 191–251.

Songer, N. (in press). Can technology bring students closer to science? In K. Tobin & B. Fraser (Eds.), *The international handbook of science education.* Dordrecht, The Netherlands: Kluwer.

Teles, L. (1993). Cognitive apprenticeship on global networks. In L. M. Harasim (Ed.), *Global networks: Computers and international communications* (pp. 271–281). Cambridge, MA: MIT Press.

Tharp, R. (1993). Institutional and social context of educational reform: Practice and reform. In E. A. Forman, N. Minick, & C. A. Stone (Eds.), *Contexts for learning: Sociocultural dynamics in children's development* (pp. 269–282). New York: Oxford University Press.

Tharp, R., & Gallimore, R. (1988). *Rousing minds to life: Teaching, learning, and schooling in a social context.* Cambridge, MA: Cambridge University Press.

United States, Department of Labor, Secretary's Commission on Achieving Necessary Skills. (1991). *What work requires of schools: A SCANS report for America 2000.* Washington, DC: Secretary's Commission on Achieving Necessary Skills.

von Glasersfeld, E. (1995). A constructivist approach to teaching. In L. P. Steffe & J. Gale (Eds.), *Constructivism in education* (pp. 3–15). Hillsdale, NJ: Lawrence Erlbaum Associates.

Vosniadou, S. (1996). Learning environments for representational growth and cognitive flexibility. In S. Vosniadou, E. De Corte, R. Glaser, & H. Mandl (Eds.), *International perspectives on the design of technology-supported learning environments* (pp. 13–23). Mahwah, NJ: Lawrence Erlbaum Associates.

Vygotsky, L. S. (1978). *Mind in society: The development of higher psychological processes* (M. Cole, V. John-Steiner, S. Scribner, & E. Souberman, Eds.). Cambridge, MA: Harvard University Press.

Vygotsky, L. (1986). *Thought and language* (Rev. ed.). Cambridge, MA: MIT Press.

Wagner, E. D., & McCombs, B. L. (1995). Learner-centered psychological principles in practice: Designs for distance education. *Educational Technology, 35*(2), 32–35.

Wells, G. (1996). Using the tool-kit of discourse in the activity of learning and teaching. *Mind, Culture, and Activity: An International Journal, 3*(2), 74–101.

Wells, G. (1997). *The zone of proximal development and its implications for learning and teaching.* Available at: http://www.iose.utoronto.ca/~gwells/zpd.discussion.txt

Wells, G., & Chang-Wells, G. L. (1992). *Constructing knowledge together: Classrooms as centers of inquiry and literacy.* Portsmouth, NH: Heinemann.

Wertsch, J. V. (1985). *Vygotsky and the social formation of the mind.* Cambridge, MA: Harvard University Press.

Wertsch, J. V. (1991a). A sociocultural approach to socially shared cognition. In L. B. Resnick, J. M. Levine, & S. D. Teasley (Eds.), *Perspectives on socially shared cognition* (pp. 85–100). Washington, DC: American Psychological Association.

Wertsch, J. V. (1991b). *Voices of the mind: A sociocultural approach to mediated action.* Cambridge, MA: Harvard University Press.

Wertsch, J. V. (1995). The need for action in sociocultural research. In J. V. Wertsch, P. Del Rio, & A. Alvarez (Eds.), *Sociocultural studies of mind* (pp. 56–74). New York: Cambridge University Press.

Zellermayer, M., Salomon, G., Globerson, T., & Givon, H. (1991). Enhancing writing-related metacognitions through a computerized writing partner. *American Educational Research Journal, 28*, 373–391.

3

Critical Thinking in a Distributed Environment: A Pedagogical Base for the Design of Conferencing Systems

Thomas M. Duffy
Bill Dueber
Chandra L. Hawley
Indiana University

There is a strong movement in education today away from a predominantly didactic model of instruction and toward a learner-centered model where the learning activities involve students in inquiry and problem solving, typically in a collaborative framework. The strength and breadth of this shift in the pedagogical landscape has been quite dramatic if we are to judge by the policy recommendations arising from national education organizations (American Association for the Advancement of Science, 1993; J. Brooks & M. Brooks, 1993; National Council of Teachers of Mathematics, 1991) or by an examination of the shifting focus of educational research. It is only recently, however, that similar calls for reform in postsecondary education have begun to grow as legislatures and national associations begin to question the quality of classroom experiences (Braxton, Eimers, & Bayer, 1996; Cooper, Prescott, Cook, Smith, & Mueck, 1990; Wingspread Group, 1993).

As with primary and secondary schools, there is pressure for higher education to become more learner centered. Despite this trend, university faculty have been slow to adopt these "new" learner-centered approaches to instruction. Braxton et al. (1996), in an assessment of faculty norms, found that there was little expectation among faculty to read or learn about teaching methods. In fact, their work revealed minimal indicators of a norm supportive of an egalitarian classroom in which it was acceptable for students to express views different from the instructor or direct comments to other members of the class. The lecture mode, involving direct "transmission of knowledge" with minimal student contribution, dominates not only the practice in faculty teaching but also the norms for good practice. There are exceptions, of course. Many small, liberal arts schools, for example, have a tradition of promoting critical thinking both in and out of the classroom (Fischer & Grant, 1983). However, the more common practice and expectation is that of a lecture-based environment.

In fact, a recent study by Nunn (1996) provides what we consider rather depressing data indicating the predominance of noninteractive, lecture-based instruction. Nunn examined 20 faculty teaching upper-division courses in a public university. The faculty were selected based on high student ratings and general recognition for the quality of their teaching. The courses were all in the humanities or social sciences and had an enrollment between 15 and 44 students. Furthermore, 73% of these students reported that the course was in their major. In effect, the reputation of the faculty, the level of the courses, the subject matter, and the class size were all optimal for creating a highly participatory, learner-centered environment. Yet, Nunn found that, averaged across all classes, student discussion took up only about 2% of class time. The discussion that did occur tended to be almost entirely teacher directed rather than learner centered. That is, contributions by the students tended to be in response to the teacher questions, consistent with the normative findings of Braxton et al. (1996) described earlier.

These normative and performance data do not necessarily reflect faculty opinions of what ideal or desirable learning environments should be, but rather they simply reflect the reality of classroom instruction. We assume that most faculty are interested in engaging students in meaningful dialogue in the content domain. There are too many examples of faculty spending extended periods in discussion with students outside of class time (e.g., during office hours) to believe otherwise. However, how does one carry on a meaningful discourse in a class of 40? It is only in an academic environment that we even consider that a meaningful discussion can occur with a group larger than 10 or perhaps 15.

A second "reality" of the impact of the undergraduate classroom on the opportunity for meaningful discussion is the time available for meeting: The typical class meets only 2.5 hours per week. Given the joint constraints of the class time available and the size of the class, a faculty member must weigh the alternatives of spending that brief time in discussion that is likely to be superficial because of the number of students involved or in presenting a well-designed (from the faculty point of view) lecture that he or she believes will help students understand the complex issues in the field.

In sum, we are confident that a highly interactive, learner-centered environment is a worthy goal in undergraduate education (or in any education or training environment) in terms of the quality of the learning experience (Astin, 1993; D. Johnson & R. Johnson, 1993). Interaction is valued as a vehicle for developing, through mentoring, the critical-thinking skills of students. Furthermore, we assume that most faculty agree with this premise but are unable to see it as viable with the typical class size and limited meeting time of classes. Of course, faculty can assign collaborative inquiry tasks to be completed outside of class time (or even during class time). However, it is difficult in the classroom, and impossible outside of the classroom, to monitor collaborative discussion and critical thinking. As a result, faculty can neither coach nor assess the inquiry. It is only the final product of inquiry that can be reviewed.

It is from this perspective that we focus on the design and use of network-based "conferencing" tools in this chapter. We view the large number of conferencing tools that have become available, particularly via the World Wide Web (WWW), as offering the opportunity for discussion to occur outside the classroom as well as providing an opportunity for the instructor to coach, participate in, and evaluate such discussion. Electronic conferencing systems allow the instructor to (a) observe students' contributions to the discussion, (b) include transcripts of the discussions in a portfolio for feedback or grading, (c) participate in the discussion to model critical-thinking skills, (d) interject questions and comments to coach critical thinking, and (e) provide expertise in a topic area when such input is required. In essence, the instructor can mentor and evaluate the critical-thinking skills exhibited during out-of-class discussions. It is this potential of electronic conferencing systems that we find so exciting. There is an opportunity, not just in small liberal arts colleges, but throughout the postsecondary educational system, to create learner-centered classrooms that require and "teach" critical thinking.

Clearly the development of these conferencing tools, along with the ability to supply information resources using the World Wide Web, provides a new perspective on what can be accomplished in college courses and begins to blur the distinction between residential and distance-learning environments. Whereas the World Wide Web can provide new opportunities for rich, distance-learning environments (Dolence & Norris, 1995; Harasim, 1990; Hiltz, in press), the same features can also provide new opportunities for increasing the quality of on-campus learning environments. We raise the issue of distance versus on-campus courses here only to note that the opportunities to mentor and evaluate critical thinking in a domain or particular course through the use of conferencing systems applies equally to on-campus and distributed environments.[1]

Our concern in this chapter is the design of electronic conferencing systems that support both critical thinking and the mentoring of critical thinking.

---

[1]We distinguish between distance education where students are at a distance from campus and distributed education. The fact that the learning activities and technology support can be used with students on campus as well as students at a distance is generally referred to as "distributed education" (Dolence & Norris, 1995; Oblinger & Maruyama, 1996).

We have found that computer-based conferencing systems are typically distinguished only by whether they are synchronous or asynchronous—whether the discussion is in real time or not. There is a common assumption that discussion is an undifferentiated activity—all discussion is the same and we simply need a tool that allows "it." There is little consideration given to different kinds of discussion, the goals people have for discussion, or the impact of the design of a conferencing system on achieving the goal of the discussion.

We take the position that critical thinking is a particular type of goal-oriented activity that focuses on issue analysis and problem solving. Because particular skill requirements are associated with effective critical thinking, conferencing systems must support the use of those skills. Furthermore, because students must develop critical-thinking skills, conferencing systems should support the mentoring of critical thinking. In the next section we examine the characteristics of critical thinking. From this discussion we develop a richer understanding of what is required to support critical thinking in the collaborative inquiry process. We propose an approach to the design of an asynchronous tool that highlights some features we feel are critical to supporting and promoting collaborative inquiry.

CRITICAL THINKING AND REASONING

A myriad of terms have been used to describe the focus of our interest: critical thinking, informal reasoning, informal argumentation, critical reasoning, inquiry, abduction, induction, and so on (Barrows & Myers, 1993; Ennis, 1962, 1989; P. A. Facione, Sanchez, N. C. Facione, & Gainen, 1995; Kuhn, 1991; Paul, 1993). We are not particularly interested in fine distinctions between these terms because we feel they all apply to the learning environment of our focus. In essence, we see inquiry as a key component of most learner-centered environments (Roschelle, 1992; Savery & Duffy, 1996). By inquiry, we mean that the learner encounters a puzzlement or a perturbation of their expectations—something they cannot explain and that puzzles them.[2] This inquiry process has been described as both inductive and abductive reasoning (Shank, 1987; Voss & Means, 1991). In either case, the learner must generate hypotheses, gather and evaluate evidence, consider alternatives, and come to a reasoned position on the issue. In essence, the learners must build an argument for their position. Of course, as Paul has noted so forcefully, it is not just the carrying out of these inquiry activities but it is the quality with which they are carried out that determines the quality of the critical thinking.

---

[2]Perturbation of the learner is essential. Their puzzlement is the basis for their assuming ownership of the learning activity, that is, for the environment to become a more learner-centered environment.

Critical thinking is seen as an essential skill for success in our society and has been heralded as a need not only in the Goals 2000 (H.R. Res. 1804) but in most curriculum analyses as well as statements from the corporate sector. However, Kuhn (1991) has found critical-thinking skills at a considerable deficit among a population of average adults reasoning about common societal problems. Further, the National Assessment of Educational Progress (1981), in reflecting on the performance of students in discussing readings they had just completed, noted:

> Students seem satisfied with their initial interpretations of what they have read and seem genuinely puzzled at requests to explain or defend their point of view. As a result, responses to assessment items requiring explanations of criteria, analysis of texts or defense of a judgmental point of view were disappointing. Few students could provide more than superficial responses to such tasks, and even the "better" responses showed little evidence of well developed problem-solving or critical thinking skills. (pp. 28–29)

Our goal is to support students in collaborative inquiry, which involves making sense of some problem or issue that puzzles them and building a rationale argument in coming to their position. Although there are many features of such a system that must be considered, the overall design must be informed by a clear understanding of the collaborative inquiry process we seek to support. We have identified five dimensions of critical thinking and inquiry that have informed the design of the conferencing system we are beginning to build: (a) the common beliefs and goals that define the scientific community, (b) the structuring of inquiry, (c) the elements of argumentation, (d) the quality of the reasoning, and (e) the forms of collaboration in inquiry.

Beliefs and Goals

Although inquiry always entails seeking understanding or resolution of some issue, the beliefs and goals underlying the process, and hence, how it is conducted, can vary significantly as a function of discipline. Bereiter (1992) contrasted the assumptions underlying inquiry in the political, philosophical, scientific, and judicial communities. For our part, we see scientific inquiry as most pervasive across the disciplines and the most central educational goal. Bereiter distinguished the scientific approach to inquiry by the commitment to (a) work toward a common understanding satisfactory to all, (b) frame questions and propositions in ways that enable evidence to be brought to bear, (c) expand the body of collectively valid propositions, and (d) allow any belief to be subjected to criticism.

These goals and beliefs can be contrasted to the political process where compromise is the goal as well as to the legal process where winning is the goal. The inquiry process calls for individuals to value and use alternative perspectives to test their ideas and expand their understanding. Here, coming to agreement arises not out of compromise or a vote but through gathering additional evidence to evaluate ideas as well as seeking overall parsimony and robustness.

Structure of Inquiry

What is the structure of inquiry or problem solving? What is it that individuals might not know or might forget about problem solving? There are many ways of characterizing the structure—each problem-solving model has its own representation of the process (Bransford & Stein, 1993; Hayes, 1989; Polya, 1957; Wallas, 1926). However, at a basic level we can define five components:

- *Define the problem.* First the problem solvers must identify the problem. Even though it is stated, there is a need to consider the constraints around the problem, new meanings that might arise from rephrasing the problem, and the ways in which it might be focused or expanded to provide a better understanding of the issues.
- *Develop and evaluate solution alternatives.* In seeking to develop a solution or position on the problem, they must generate possible solutions and critical issues, evidence, and counterproposals to be used in evaluating and fine tuning those possible solutions.
- *Come to some resolution.* There must be an active evaluation to the alternatives, moving toward resolving the problem using the best understanding of the moment.
- *Developing a plan of action.* The solution must be acted upon in some way. This may involve writing a paper that is an argument for the position or it might involve an implementation of a plan.
- *Reflect on the process.* Finally, it is essential that there be a reflective process to evaluate the effectiveness of the problem solving and to synthesize, evaluate, and index what was learned. This is a critical learning activity that is too often ignored. Reflection is essential not just for school environments, but for any problem-solving activity if the goal is to learn from and capitalize on the experience. In business, it is generally referred to as "debriefing" on the project or engagement.

Of course, these five components do not play out in a linear fashion. Evaluating potential solutions will almost certainly lead to new thoughts on problem constraints or parameters as well developing a plan. And, of course, developing a plan can easily lead to seeing entirely new solution options.

Rather than specific phases, these five components can be thought of as essential focus points for critical thinking in any problem-solving activity. A conferencing system that supports critical thinking and inquiry should make these components of the inquiry process visible to the learners and support the learners in organizing their thinking around each component.

Elements of Argumentation

When we suggest that each of the aforementioned components of problem solving is a focus for critical thinking, we are in essence arguing that each is a focal point for argumentation. As previously discussed, critical thinking involves building an argument for a position by considering evidence and counterarguments. In examining an argument, there are certain elements we look for as forming the foundation for critical thinking. Toulmin (see Toulmin, Rieke, & Janik, 1979), in one of the most established models of argumentation, identified the elements as claims, warrants, grounds, backing, and rebuttals. Voss and his colleagues (Voss, Fincher-Kiefer, Wiley, & Silfies, 1993; Voss & Means, 1991; Voss & Post, 1988) have used this framework in a series of studies of the informal reasoning of individuals about ill-structured problems. From a pedagogical perspective, it is unclear that a detailed system like Toulmin's would be useful. As the research discussed earlier (Kuhn, 1991; Perkins, 1992) suggests, the needs are so fundamental in this area that we would have a clear success if there was simply a consistent consideration of evidence and counterarguments for hypotheses. How often have we heard "Well, that is what I think," as *the* basis for taking a position—as if simply thinking it makes it the best solution.

In summary, a critical thinker will develop a strong argument in defining and interpreting the problem, in developing and evaluating solutions, in developing a plan based on a selected solution, and in reflecting on the learning outcomes. In each case, the essential elements of an argument that we focus on are hypotheses, counterarguments, and evidence.

Quality

Richard Paul (1993) fervently argued that we have too often focused only on the structure of thinking—judging it as "good" if the structural components are present; for example, an argument is good if the individual presents evidence. He argued that the word *critical* in critical reasoning refers to the quality of the reasoning. Hence, it is not just the structure and elements of the reasoning process that should be the focus, but also the quality of the argument and the sense it makes, for example, the quality and credibility of the evidence source and how well it supports the argument. Educators must assess the quality of the individual's analysis of the problem, the quality of the counterarguments, and the quality of the evidence and the use of that evidence. Paul proposed such indicators as clarity, precision, specificity, plausibility, accuracy, relevancy, significance, logic, depth, breadth, completeness, adequacy, and consistency be used in judging the quality of critical reasoning. In the case of problem solving, Paul suggested the following indicators of quality to judge the student's problem solving: (a) evaluating information for *relevance*, (b) constructing *plausible* inferences, (c) *accurately* identifying assumptions, (d) distinguishing *relevant* points of view, and (e) distinguishing *significant from insignificant* information.

Collaboration

Working with other people in the inquiry process is a context considerably different from individual inquiry and those differences must also be taken into account in the design of an electronic support system. In reflecting on our teaching in a learner-centered environment, our experiences in committee meetings, and in some recent pilot research on expert collaborative reasoning conducted in our laboratory,[3] it became evident to us that two distinct types of interactions occur in the collaborative problem-solving process: conversation and issue-based discussion. In effect, the structure and quality of critical reasoning discussed in the previous sections is only a part of the collaborative process.

The foundation of group work, we propose, is conversation: We talk to each other to explore issues and seek common ground. Conversation is the general discussion between team members in which there is assessment of the group knowledge base and perspectives relevant to the problem. It is primarily "me"-centered—featuring a lot of "Here is what I think" types of comments made in response to an issue presented. In conversation, there is often a seeking of common ground in terms of meanings of statements and beliefs in the broad domain of the problem. Thus, topics arise as individuals think of them, rather than through an inquiry process. In these conversations there is a lot of talking past each other, with each individual wanting to make his or her views "known." As such, conversation is exploratory rather than systematic. In addition, topics can change rapidly with little obvious link between topics and the most important topic or issue is the most recent one—statements from 5 minutes earlier are, for the most part, lost.

Educators have typically eschewed this type of conversation among students. Students are criticized for talking past each other and for not systematically analyzing the issue. Although we agree with this assessment, we want to argue that this sort of exploratory posturing is a necessary part of the collaborative problem-solving process. Reflection on virtually any committee

[3]Conducted by Barbara Maynes and Heather Sugioka.

or other collaborative problem-solving effort we have been involved in reveals that the free exploration of a range of topics, driven by personal interests and focused on "Here is what I think" statements, is an integral part of the activity regardless of the expertise of the participants.

We suggest that issues to be discussed and analyzed in detail arise out of these conversations and become the basis of more focused discussion and systematic analysis. In contrast to conversation, issue-based discussion is focused on moving to the development of the recommended solution or plan. Unlike the temporal flow of a conversation, the issue-based discussion is organized around important issues. The issue-based discussion is focused on hypotheses or issues relevant to the final product. In effect, the issue is examined in detail, with evidence, counterarguments, and alternative positions all being brought to bear. Unlike the conversation's exploratory nature, issue-based discussion is product focused. It is in an issue-based discussion that we attend to both the argumentation elements and quality of critical thinking. And also unlike conversation, comments from earlier in the issue-based discussion remain relevant and are organized around the issues.

For all the reasons already discussed, we believe that a system to support critical thinking and inquiry must support both the conversation and the issue-based discussion. Furthermore, we think that there is a need to link the two types of discussion so participants can review the context from which the issues arose and move back and forth between the issue discussion and the conversation. It is with these beliefs in mind that we are progressing toward the development of a conferencing system that supports critical thinking.

A PEDAGOGICAL MODEL FOR COLLABORATIVE CRITICAL INQUIRY

Before turning to the design of conferencing systems, we briefly examine one of the most widely discussed models for supporting collaborative inquiry in the classroom environment: problem-based learning (PBL; Barrows, 1992, 1994; Savery & Duffy, 1996). The PBL framework, as described by Barrows, provides a well-documented model for addressing many of the critical-thinking goals described in the previous section. In this sense, the design of the PBL classroom environment can serve as a benchmark for the design of a distributed-inquiry environment.

PBL is perhaps the most widely applied approach to teaching in which the focus of students' activity is collaborative inquiry and the teacher is a model and coach for critical reasoning (Barrows, 1988; Barrows & Meyers, 1993; Milter & Stinson, 1993; Savery & Duffy, 1996). In PBL, students, working with a facilitator in teams of about five, are presented a problem or issue that they must analyze and gather data on with the goal of developing a response or recommended solution. There are two types of PBL sessions: (a) collaborative problem-solving sessions, and (b) self-directed learning sessions. Both kinds of sessions require learners to gather information in order to develop, reject, or defend hypotheses as well as explain alternative solutions. Our focus here is on the collaborative problem-solving sessions.

In the collaborative problem-solving session, the group members, in a face-to-face collaborative environment, use what they know to generate and evaluate hypotheses and to determine what else they must learn to refine or evaluate their hypotheses. One member of the problem-solving team is often identified as the scribe who records on the white board the "important" points that are made in the conversation. The white board is divided into three parts: hypotheses, what we know, and learning issues (Savery & Duffy, 1996).

Using the framework for critical inquiry we have discussed previously, there is both conversation and issue-based discussion in the problem-solving session. The oral discussion is a conversation that is reasonably unstructured and moves in many directions. As in any meeting, the students discuss the problem and exchange perspectives on a range of issues and topics related to the problem. As discussion progresses, statements that the team considers important are recorded on the board as hypotheses/issues, data, or learning issues. It is these recorded statements that the team will return to and systematically analyze in putting together their proposed resolution of the problem. The use of the board provides the mechanism for moving from the temporal, conversation mode in the group discussion to an issue-based discussion where the PBL dialogue and the representation on the board are organized around hypotheses and key issues to be considered.

The teacher plays a critical role in facilitating the inquiry process. Although there are alternative structures for the inquiry process, the most typical model as described by Barrows (1992) is a hypothetical-deductive approach. Hence, in moving into the issue-based discussion, the facilitator encourages students to generate hypotheses to be evaluated—rather than beginning by generating a list of what they know. As hypotheses are generated, evidence for evaluating the hypotheses (either known evidence or that which must be gathered) is identified. Unfortunately, PBL lacks a formal process or notation system for addressing the analysis of the problem, though such analysis typically arises as part of the problem-solving process. PBL does, however, formalize the reflective process: The facilitator directs a postproblem discussion in which students evaluate both the process and the content that was learned.

The quality of critical thinking is modeled by the facilitator who asks important questions that model good reflection and critical thinking for the students. The facilitator has two goals in facilitating critical thinking. First, there is the concern with the quality of the analysis. In this context, the facilitator looks for the students to analyze the problem constraints and parameters, to provide or identify needed evidence related to hypotheses, to compare alternative hypotheses in terms of satisfying the goals, and to consider implications of proposed solutions. The questions the facilitator will model or coach if they do not develop naturally are:

- Do I know of evidence to support or refute that idea?
- What evidence should I seek?
- How does that relate to the problem/solution?
- Can we approach this problem another way?
- What do we have to do next?
- What do we know so far?
- Can I organize what we have done so far?
- What seems to be standing out in all of this?

It is also important for the learners to be able to understand whether or not they are active contributors to their group's conversation. Although each individual should be asking the sorts of analytic questions just outlined, they should also be monitoring their understanding of what others are saying and be prepared to ask questions if clarification is necessary. Hence the questions the facilitator would look for or coach are ones like:

- Do I understand the terms that were used?
- How does that fit into the discussion?
- What are the implications of that statement?

Conversation, as we noted and as we have all experienced, can go in many directions and certainly it can get off track. It is exploratory! One of the most effective strategies for developing order and focus out of the exploration is to attempt to summarize what has been discussed. Hence individuals and the group as a whole should periodically ask the questions:

- Where are we in relation to developing a solution?
- What are the key ideas and issues we have been talking about?

As noted, the PBL model can provide benchmarks for the design of conferencing systems to support students at a distance. In particular, the PBL approach supports both exploratory conversation and issue-based analysis—and provides for moving back and forth between the two. There is also a focus on coaching the learners in effective problem-solving skills and effective collaborative skills.

TECHNOLOGY TO SUPPORT COLLABORATIVE INQUIRY

Scardamalia and Bereiter's (1991) computer-supported intentional learning environment (CSILE) provides technological support for the issue-based discussion in critical inquiry. CSILE was designed as a database system in which students conduct their inquiry in science. The original CSILE design used a simple database concept in which a student could look at, for example, responses to a hypothesis that was made or see what contributions another student has made. Recent efforts have moved CSILE to a Web-based environment in which all contributions to an inquiry are visible in a branching, weblike representation (Hewitt & Scardamalia, in press; Hewitt, Scardamalia, & Webb, 1997). A key feature of both the original and the Web-based CSILE is that students are required to label their contribution to the inquiry. As an example, one set of the labels used in a CSILE-based research effort includes: *what I need to know, what I need to understand, high-level question, new learning, plan, my theory, new experiment, conclusion*, and *synthesis* (Oshima, 1994). The labels serve to mentor students in the elements of inquiry in a way analogous to the facilitator in the PBL environment. That is, the students must think about how their entry contributes to the problem-solving effort.

CSILE research efforts have focused on the computer-based entries, that is, the issue-based discussion. However, even in the Web-based applications, students are all in the same classroom. Thus, we assume there is considerable oral conversation (as defined earlier) about the problems. We hypothesize that this oral conversation is a critical component in the success of the more formal issue-based discussion that occurs in the CSILE system. Indeed, recent research from the CSILE lab (Hewitt, Webb, & Rowley, 1994), in evaluating the effectiveness of the Web-based representation, describes considerable teacher–student and student–student face-to-face interaction that appears to be central to the successful use of CSILE. Thus, the CSILE approach can extend the critical inquiry outside of the classroom in a distributed environment, but face-to-face contact in support of the conversational component of collaborative inquiry is essential to the success.

The Collaborative Visualization (CoVis) project (Edelson & O'Neill, 1994) at Northwestern University developed a Collaboratory Notebook that is similar in function to the CSILE system but is meant for use at a distance. In essence, students in different high schools use the Notebook as the vehicle for collaborative inquiry about a science problem. As with CSILE, CoVis students must label how their entry contributes to the inquiry. The labels used in the Notebook include *Information, Commentary, Question, Conjecture, Evidence for, Evidence against, Plan*, and *Step in the plan* (Edelson & O'Neill, 1994). As with CSILE, this labeling process captures some of the coaching function of the facilitator in the PBL environment.

The Collaboratory Notebook is a relatively new product so there is not yet extensive data on its effectiveness. However, based on our earlier analysis, we would predict that students will find the Notebook difficult to use if there is no additional support for the conversation from which issue-based discussion arises. Fishman (personal communication, May 9, 1997), a project manager for the CoVis project, confirmed our perspective in noting that, "When we designed the Collaboratory Notebook, we always believed that there would be other forms of communication surrounding its use, e.g. synchronous tools like Cruiser."

Although CoVis and CSILE are important products to the use of computer-based collaboration, they have distinct limitations if used in the context of distance learning. The lack of a tool to support conversation, for example, could cripple a problem-solving effort. There are, of course, dozens of Internet-based conferencing systems. However, CoVis and CSILE are the only two that seem to make any attempt to address the pedagogical goals of supporting student inquiry. It is the limitations of these systems that has led us to the development of a new system.

SUPPORTING COLLABORATIVE INQUIRY AT A DISTANCE

At this point, we turn our attention to the design of a networked conferencing system (including both tools and processes) that supports collaborative critical inquiry in any distributed environment: at a distance or as a supplement to face-to-face meetings. Consistent with the PBL framework and in accordance with most on-the-job problem-solving teams, we are working under the assumption that the system will be used by small groups (3 weeks or more with little or no face-to-face communication). We are currently involved in the design and implementation of a portion of such a system that we refer to as ACT (Asynchronous Collaboration Tool), a WWW-hosted, asynchronous, text-based conferencing system. We are currently beta testing the two types of conferencing systems in ACT, but it should be recognized that all of the features outlined in this chapter have not yet been implemented. In particular, we have not yet built the links between the conferences; this is a work in progress.

Design Goals

The ACT project is an attempt to use the theoretical underpinnings of critical inquiry already addressed in this chapter to drive the design of artifacts and processes that can be used to support small-group collaboration. Through this effort, we hope to better understand both the general nature of small-group inquiry and the practical considerations of conducting such inquiry in an asynchronous environment. Let us emphasize that although our design goals are focused on smoothly supporting those activities necessary to the process of critical inquiry, we are not attempting to make inquiry itself "effortless." We firmly believe that critical thinking is an effortful, often difficult process and we seek to both encourage it through the inclusion of specific tools related to inquiry and support it by focusing students on the process and structure of the inquiry.

Our design strategy can be distilled into four main goals, as follows.

Focus the User on Problem Solving. The process of critical inquiry must drive the basic design of the system. Students must be purposefully engaged in analyzing the problem, generating possible solutions, gathering evidence, and systematically evaluating the options. The various phases of the problem-solving process must be visible to the learner, and the analytic process in those phases must be in focus. Related discussions and off-task discussions must be separated from the primary problem-solving activity. By providing distinct areas for on-topic conversations and issue-based discussions, we attempt to make the problem-solving process itself a little *less* transparent to the user. The goal is to remain cognizant of the task at hand and indeed, guidance to the user should focus on the inquiry strategy at least as much as on the mechanics of using the application. The design goal is to lead the user toward a more focused dialogue in the group's work areas.

Promote Attention to, and Reflection on, the Argument and the Goals. Helping students attend to the quality of an argument (their own or that of another) is critical to the learning process. Indeed, as the work of Paul (1993), Kuhn (1991), and others has demonstrated, children and adults remain largely unaware and inattentive to the quality of an argument—responses tend to be gut-level reactions based on belief systems, not on hard evidence and logic. Using Schon's (1987) framework, our design goal is to promote both reflection-in-action and reflection-on-action. We want individuals to be reflective of the argument and their contribution to the argument in the action of making a contribution. If they are analyzing a problem they must be thoughtful of the way in which their contribution fits into an effective argument. But we also want the individuals to reflect on the ongoing discussion quite irrespective of their impending contribution. That is, as we discussed in the case of problem-based learning, there is an important activity of taking stock of where the group is in the process. Whether it is a conversation about the problem or an analysis of the issues, we want to encourage reflecting on the overall activity, asking and providing their answer to questions like "where are we now," "where should we be going next," "how well are we doing in our analysis/discussion." We want to permit the students to easily see what has happened and we want to facilitate their instantiating answers to questions like these as part of their participation in the inquiry.

Provide Appropriate Structures for Each Communication Need. Collaborative inquiry is a complex activity involving a variety of types of interactions. Social conversation, for example, is, by its nature, unstructured and without explicit focus. Scientific discussion, on the other hand, is topically organized and requires the ability to engage in very well structured exchanges built around a common core of data and hypotheses. In between lies communication that addresses a problem holistically: brainstorming, problem definition, question generation, and so forth. By examining the needs of each type of communication, we hope to build an electronic space appropriate for each type of interaction that can support the necessary organization without becoming a burden to the users as well as support movement of information between the spaces.

Support Coaching by a Facilitator. One of our central goals in this design effort is to help individuals develop effective critical-thinking and -inquiry skills. We have no doubt that a facilitator plays an essential role in this activity. In essence, it simply is not possible to build all of the PBL facilitator responsibilities into a conferencing system. Thus, a design goal is to aid the facilitator or teacher in monitoring the problem-solving activity in a way that will enhance his or her ability to offer constructive guidance on problem solving and critical thinking to the group as a whole and to individual participants.

Key Design Features

We have identified two communication styles (conversation and issue-based discussion), several communication needs (social, administrative, brainstorming, in-depth hypothesis examination, etc.), and a desire to organize and archive ongoing inquiries for various purposes. At this point, we turn our attention to the creation of communication spaces that can support the activities associated with critical inquiry. There are seven key design features of ACT supporting the goals outlined earlier.

Two Conference Structures. Based on our characterization of conversation and issue-based discussion, we provide two conference structures that can be used to provide the spaces necessary to support critical inquiry. By supporting both, we hope ACT can more readily cover the breadth of communication needs associated with small-group problem solving. Conversation is supported in a linear conference structure (see Fig. 3.1). Messages are organized temporally (with the newest messages at the bottom of the

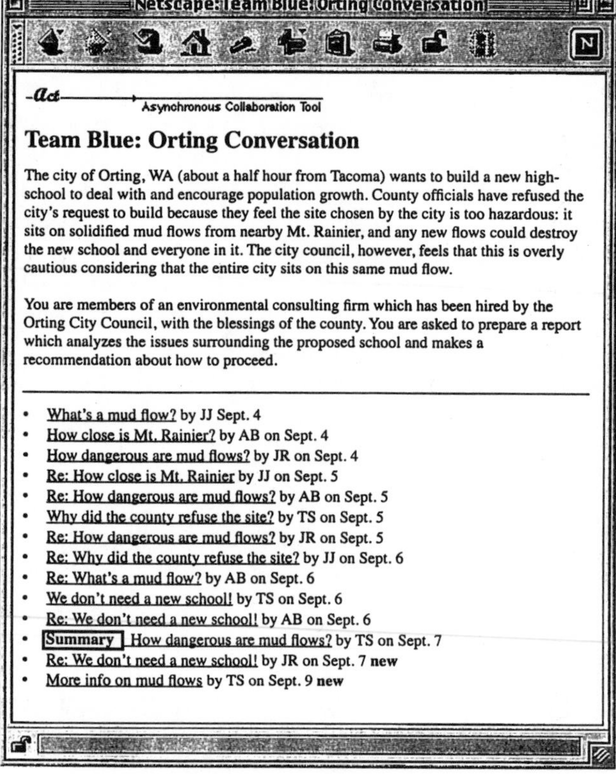

FIG. 3.1. A conversational space. Messages are arranged temporally to keep the focus on recent activities and the rapid advancement of ideas. (Note: Label is color coded to support ease of scanning.)

document), reflecting the natural flow of a face-to-face conversation and mirroring the organization of bulletin board systems such as COW[4] or The Well.[5] By eliminating a deliberate structure, the linear conference promotes the quick exchange of ideas. Reexamination of a particular line of thought, however, is difficult. Linear conferences are suited to social and administrative chatter, brainstorming, holistic problem definition, and any other application that requires a safe, fast-paced environment.

Issue-based discussion is supported through a hierarchical conference structure (see Fig. 3.2). Messages are organized by topic in an outline structure, with new messages indented under the post that inspired the reply. The need to pick a location in the hierarchy makes inserting a message a

[4]COW can be seen at http://thecity.sfsu.edu/COW2/

[5]The Well can be found at http://www.well.com/

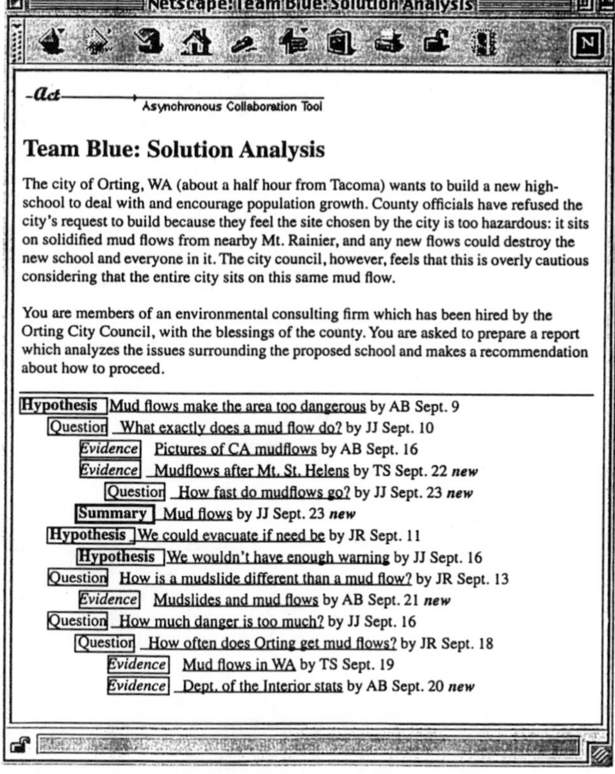

FIG. 3.2. A solution analysis space. In the analytical discussion spaces, messages are organized by topic. Each message is also categorized along several dimensions to encourage *in situ* reflective thinking and allow for later searching and sorting. (Note: Labels are color coded to support ease of scanning for message types.)

more reflective, effortful process, but should help students become more critically aware of their own contribution. The structure also makes it easy to review issues examining the discussion of an issue in a coherent manner and identifying which issues may need more attention. The hierarchical structure does make it more difficult to quickly locate new messages. Although we do have a label for all unread messages, the user must still scroll the discussion for the "new" labels. The hierarchical structure also reduces the use of more exploratory messages that don't have a well-defined place in the current hierarchy. But of course that is the intent of the design—the exploratory discussion belongs in the conversation conference.

Let us emphasize that these two conferencing structures are distinct. Many conferencing systems have a single conference in which the user can reorganize messages to reflect the hierarchical relations or the temporal relations. We do not advocate that strategy because we see the design of the conference as an integral component of the type of activity. A temporal organization is simply not appropriate for an issue analysis process nor is an hierarchical arrangement appropriate to an exploratory conversation. Structurally misrepresenting the goals of the exchanges, in our view, can only lead to less effective if not frustrating and muddled exchanges.

Issue Board. A problem-solving activity begins with a conversation and the analytical activity grows out of that conversation. This is not a linear process, of course, but rather there is movement back and forth between exploratory conversation and structured analysis. It is critical to support this interchange between conversation and analysis. Although we have not yet built this component of the ACT system, our current view is to provide a transitory *issue board*—much like a white board—onto which users can move messages from the conversation and from which they can export messages to the issue-based discussion.

An alternative to the issue board design is to simply permit users to move messages from the conversation directly to the issue-based conference. From an interface perspective that is certainly an easier task to accomplish. However, from the perspective of supporting effective inquiry, it seems to us that the immediate transfer will lead to a confusing issue-based structure. Our strategy is to support users in identifying what in the current context are important hypotheses, issues, and evidence before these contributions get "lost" in the conversation. We think there is a need to let things evolve so that everyone can pause and reflect not only on the continued relevance of the message, but also on where it fits into the issue-based conference. This will be especially important in the early stages of problem solving, when the exploratory conversation is essential to developing a framework for an issue analysis. It is likely to become less important as the problem-solving activity progresses.

Defined Communication Spaces. The goal of focusing the users' attention on the goals of the conferencing leads to a potentially complex conferencing space for the user. Clearly, this environment will require considerable user testing and revision. However, as we have argued throughout this chapter, we feel it essential to focus the learners' attention on the problem-solving goal and to coach and promote high-quality arguments.

When a user first logs in, she is presented with a list of links to the discussion spaces she is allowed to participate in. For most students, these will consist of those spaces that pertain to the entire class and associated small-group or satellite conferences. Because the conferences are password protected, the student will typically only include the spaces that are specific to her group. An instructor may of course choose to allow students to keep track of the progress of other small groups, probably by offering the rest of the class read-only access to these conferences.

Included with each discussion space listed in the conversation and analysis areas is information showing how many total messages have been posted, how many have not yet been read, and what type of conference (linear or hierarchical) it is. This meta-information allows the user to quickly locate discussions relevant to her particular goal in contributing, showing her which conferences she can participate in and where new messages are located. Our current design of the interface for this discussion space is shown in Fig. 3.3. The interface consists of general class conversation, problem-focused conversation, and issue-based discussions on the key problem-solving tasks.

Of course, the conference headings are all definable and thus this structure can be modified or even eliminated. However, within the administrative system, the prompted selection for conference headings are as shown in Fig. 3.3. Furthermore, the default setting in the administration of ACT gives control for creation of new conferences to the system administrator (who

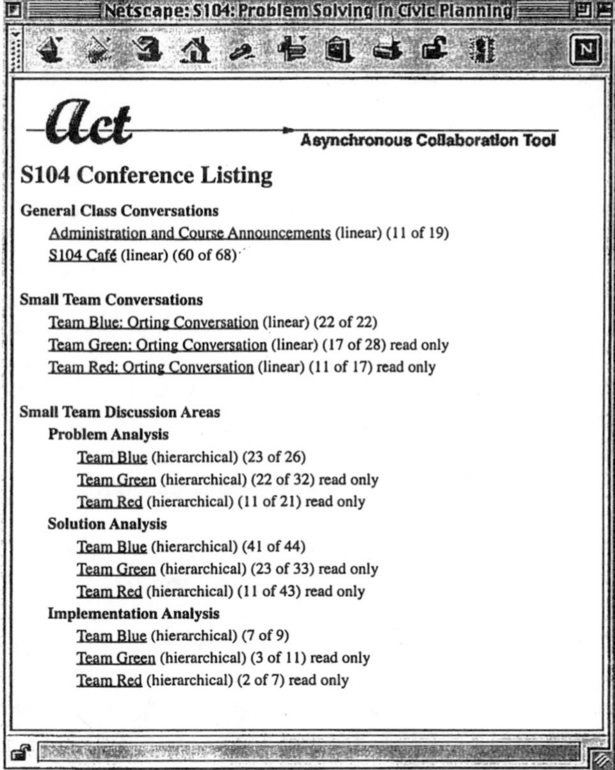

FIG. 3.3. A sample course conference listing. The list of discussion spaces has links to the individual conferences, as well as information about how they are organized and how many messages (total and unread) are in each conference.

may be the instructor or who may be a group member). In essence, although the system permits flexibility in designing the conferencing space, the default settings are designed to promote planful design of conferences that focus on the structure and process of problem solving.

General class conversations (see Fig. 3.3) are set up as linear conversations available to all students. These conversations serve two purposes. First, they provide a social area in which students interact with each other and the instructor, resulting in general-interest and class discussion. Second, and more important, they provide spaces for students and instructors to address administrative issues such as syllabus changes and clarification, announcements of upcoming events, technical questions about the software being used, attempts to borrow a textbook, and so on. This general class space helps prevent these kinds of issues from being included in the more structured work areas that focus on the specific problem or issue being addressed.

Small-group conversations are also linear conferences, but are restricted to the members of a specific work group. Here, we take advantage of the simplicity and low overhead of the conversational organization to support brainstorming, hypothesis generation, looking at the problem holistically, and generating potential solutions. Clearly, students must feel safe to offer unsupported opinions and ideas in getting their issues on the table at any time. Consistent with the purpose of this problem-solving-oriented conversation area, and reflecting the familiar sequential nature of face-to-face conversation, a single conversational space is available for each group.

The analytical discussion areas in ACT are implemented as hierarchical conferences because they are designed to support intensive, indepth discussion of specific topics. The administrative default settings are for three separate analysis spaces: problem analysis, solution analysis, and implementation analysis. All have the same structure, but each is dedicated to a different problem-solving activity and we anticipate that each will be most heavily used at different stages in the inquiry process. The user help system provides guidance to the users as to the goal for each analysis, outlined as follows:

- *Problem Analysis.* This is an area reserved for discussion about the nature of the problem statement itself, so group members can come to consensus about what the problem is "really" asking. The goal of the problem analysis area is a succinct encapsulation of the problem being solved and the conditions and constraints that will inform decisions about picking and implementing a solution. Activity in this space will likely be intense at the beginning of the project and slowly taper off (without disappearing completely).
- *Solution Analysis.* Solution analysis will be a primary focus and dominate the middle portion of the inquiry process. It is in this space that hypotheses are presented and criticized, evidence is gathered and interpreted, and

solutions are proposed and slowly dissected by the group members. In most cases, the majority of analysis will take place in this space.

- *Implementation Analysis.* This area is dedicated to the creation of an implementation of the agreed-upon solution strategy. Its use is most obvious in distance education (when students cannot get together face-to-face to discuss implementation issues) and when the problem presented is in the hard or social sciences (as opposed to, e.g., literary criticism). Implementation analysis will obviously be empty at the very beginning of the problem-solving process, but will become more active as a solution is agreed upon and implementation details begin to surface.

Required Labeling of the Elements of an Argument. We use labels, much like those in CoVis and CSILE, to focus students' attention on their contribution to the problem solving (reflection-in-action) and to support their reflection on the ongoing discussion. The labels are used differently in the two conference structures, reflecting the different goals of conversation and analysis.

The issue-based analysis areas are the places where the argument concerning the problem, solutions options, and implementation are a central focus. Hence, the goal here is to promote attention to the elements of the argument as one vehicle for judging the quality of the argument, for determining what is missing, and for determining how the user's post fits into the argument. We have already discussed how the issue-based analysis areas are organized with these reflective activities in mind. The very structure of the conferences invites a student to ask the question, "Where does this information fit best within this discussion?", thereby immediately initiating reflection-in-action.

We focus additional attention on these issues of argument structure and "my" contribution, by requiring users to categorize their post in terms of the contribution it makes. Rather than letting the student generate his or her own label, the label is selected from a menu. The list can be edited by the system administrator, thus reflecting particular needs of a problem-solving activity or the particular framework of the instructor/facilitator. The default labels, shown in Table 3.1, reflect both the elements of effective argumentation as discussed earlier in this chapter and the requirements for

TABLE 3.1
Examples of Potential Message Categories and Labels

Type of Message	*Content Source*	*Perceived Importance*
Hypothesis	Summary	Data
Important Point	Personal Opinion	Interesting Tangent
Evidence	Anecdote	Useful Thought
Learning Issue	Expert Opinion	Important Point
	Published Word	Critical Issue

effective collaboration, for example, asking a question about someone's post. The narrow scope of many of the labels encourages the message to be succinct and focused, thereby preventing clutter and keeping the organization of the conference clean and easy to scan for relevant information.

The labels remain a highly visible part of the posts. A color coding and verbal label for each classification supports easy scanning of the structure of the argument developing, thus aiding the users to review the nature of the discussion regarding key issues, focusing in, for example, on the evidence provided or the counterproposals offered.

The conversational conferences are exploratory and involve brainstorming. Labeling each post in terms of its contribution would be cumbersome and counterproductive to the goals of the conference. Hence, we do not require labels in conversational conferences. Indeed, with one exception, we do not even make the labels available. That exception is the label *summary*. In our work with PBL, we found that pausing to summarize progress in a conversation is very important in refocusing a group's efforts on key issues and in helping them to take stock of the progress and important points in the conversation. Thus, we encourage that a participant periodically assume responsibility for posting a summary of the conversational key points up to that point in time. In general, we find that the summary process is extremely useful for focusing attention on issues and paths and, because it remains very visible in the list of conference posts, it is easy to locate for review at any point in the conversation.

Selective Viewing of Argument Structure. All posts are stored in a database making selective access to particular classes of posts possible. In contrast to systems that rearrange posts into hierarchical or temporal-based sequences or that allow the user to specify the depth of the hierarchy displayed, in the next version of ACT we will permit users to present selected argument elements. Thus, for example, a user could ask to see only the *hypotheses* and *evidence* posts. The goal is to focus attention on and support users in their analysis of the argument structure. We also see this as a tool for the facilitator or instructor to monitor the developing arguments in ways that will facilitate coaching the teams.

Visual Streamlining. One of the problems with conferencing systems is the small window into the conference: It is difficult to get a large perspective on the discussion. This problem is compounded by a clutter of messages that are primarily simply responses or acknowledgments to previous posts.[6] We

[6]The clutter is especially evident in synchronous conferences, where there is an administrative message acknowledging each person's entry and exit from the conference as well as their greeting to other participants. One significant problem in synchronous conferences is that the amount of this clutter sometimes exceeds the messages of substance.

have tried to provide an environment in which the user can easily see the structure of the argument by using three tools. First, the default presentation of the messages in a conference is one in which only the header information is presented, that is, the classification of the message, the author, subject, and date. Thus, the entry view is structural rather than a myopic view of the first message or two.

Two sorts of clutter are prevalent in asynchronous conferences: a tendency to simply acknowledge having read a message and the need to register agreement or disagreement (vote) on a proposal or statement in a message. In both cases, the screen is littered with a string of posts that are empty except to say "Thanks for your thoughts" or "I agree" and it is difficult to see the larger organization of the discussion. Of course, both types of responses are necessary. There is no greater frustration than making a post that you have thoughtfully constructed and wondering a week later if anyone has read what you had to say. We address the acknowledgment "I read this" need by providing a history of who read the post. The list of users (identified on login) who read the post is available by selecting history off of the menu bar. The history tool is not only a benefit to the conference participants but it also provides data for the instructor to assess level of participation by students.

We will address the voting issue by providing a "vote" response to a message along with a component of the message header that displays the vote tally. Thus, rather than a vote resulting in a message below the one being responded to, the tally is simply displayed in the message header.

Post Before Viewing. One pedagogical strategy for promoting more effective collaboration in problem solving is to begin by having each participant take a position on an issue. In essence, before an idea or a person dominates, each person should get a say. This could be done in the conversation mode where each person takes a position to start the discussion. It could also be in the issue-based discussion where each person registers a response to the problem before considering alternatives. The problem could be academic—come to some agreement on the key issues in the chapter and how they should be presented—or it could be initial statements of key parameters of a nonacademic, authentic problem.

Of course, the difficulty in achieving this pedagogical goal is that students will view other statements before posting their own and hence in many cases they will modify their thinking to be more in tune with what has already been stated. To aid instructors in better achieving this pedagogical goal, we have provided an option of "post before viewing" that can be set for any conference. If this option is chosen, when users *first* enter a conference, they are required to post before they can see any of the messages or message headers that might already have been posted. This only happens on the first entry into the conference.

Current Status

ACT is not a finished product. The discussion of design features identified what is completed and what is not. Important to note, the conversational and issue-based conferencing systems are complete (as a version 1.0) along with the requirement to label contributions. In essence, the system features displayed in the figures in this chapter are complete. However, the issue board, or some other mechanism for moving between conversation and issue-based discussion is not complete. Because we firmly believe the design of the system must be consistent with the goals (conversation or issue analysis) of the discussion, we do not think either conferencing design alone is sufficient to support inquiry. And without the strategy for movement of ideas between conferences, the use of both types of conferences in an inquiry is cumbersome. So, our developmental priority is the design of the linkage between discussions.

We have used the issue analysis and the conversation discussion formats in several classes and we have used them in experimental contexts to understand the collaborative inquiry process and the difficulties in using one or the other discussion format as a vehicle for inquiry. The systems have been stable and effective. The interface clarity has been well received. However, as we anticipated, the use of just one system—regardless of which one—to sustain collaborative inquiry at a distance, presents difficulties and frustrations when there is a mismatch between the particular goal (analysis or conversation) and the design of the conference.

CONCLUSION

Asynchronous discussion environments like ACT afford us enormous pedagogical opportunities—opportunities that could not be realized in the classroom. In a traditional classroom, if there is even an opportunity for discussion, students must be bold and quick on their feet if they are to contribute. The asynchronous environment, however, affords students the time for thoughtful analysis, reflection, and composition as their discussion of an issue evolves. Furthermore, the discussions are products that the faculty member can review and grade and on which he or she can give feedback.

The key difficulty here is that too many designers of conferencing systems have had a simplistic view of discussion as simply talking. There has been little recognition of the different rhetorical structures and of the requirements for supporting those rhetorical structures in a text rather than oral mode. We have experimented informally with both conversation and issue-based discussion forums in our classes and have found that even experienced computer users have difficulties with each. The assignment in one case was solving an ill-structured problem—designing a course for a distributed-learning environment. When students worked in the conversation environment, it was hard to stay focused. Certain individuals dominated and, when an inferior idea was presented, there was an enormous amount of space taken up talking about why it was "bad." Not surprisingly, the good ideas got lost. Furthermore, people were constantly talking past each other—posturing with their ideas, or simply trying to get an idea out that struck their fancy at the moment. Furthermore, there was a tendency to only look at "unread" messages—there was little motivation or time to venture back and sort through "old" conversations. And although there was prodding of the participants to stay focused and reminders of the ultimate goal, there was little, if any, sense of progress.

The issue-based forum provided a different set of difficulties. Although there was a need for discussion, the hierarchical structure and labeling of the contribution was too constraining. No one knew how their contribution fit, especially when the discussion was just getting going or when there was simply an idea to share. Eventually conversation took place as a string of responses to one another—moving progressively inward in the hierarchy until someone decided to put their contribution down as a "new issue." In effect, the issue-based structure was not usable in these earlier stages of problem solving.

There is no doubt that the system we are proposing and building is complex both in design and in use. Other conferencing systems provide for the ability to reorganize the conference posts so that they may be viewed grouped by author, by topic, or by time. We argue that this reorganizing strategy is inadequate. The structures are suited to different rhetorical goals and hence each will lead to or support different types of conversations. As noted earlier, it is awkward, at a minimum, to conduct a discussion when the conference structure is not consistent with the rhetorical goals.

There are a host of instructor tools that we have not discussed—tools essential to managing the class and assessing students. In the ACT environment, we have built or are building three support tools. First, there is a toggle to be able to see the messages in a discussion either all closed or all open. The former option permits one to see the structure and the participants in the discussion, whereas the latter permits efficient reading and evaluation of the contributions. Second, we provide an option where the instructor can see the contributions organized by author thereby enabling him or her to assess individual contributions. Finally, we will provide a history on each post, showing who has read it and thereby providing the instructor with yet another index of participation.

Finally, let us reemphasize that our goal in creating ACT is to promote critical thinking and, as we noted earlier, critical thinking is work. We have no doubt that if students are forced to focus on issues and consider how their contributions relate to these issues, they will find it to be substantial work. However, we are convinced that asynchronous conferencing environments offer the potential for realizing the intellectual goals of postsecondary education, to move beyond transmitting information and testing for facts and procedures. Asynchronous conferencing affords the opportunity for students to engage in critical thinking in the domains, to become participants in the intellectual discussions of the professions they are studying. It also affords the faculty the opportunity to demand increasing intellectual rigor and to coach and assess students based on the quality of their thinking. It is with these goals foremost in our minds that we engage in the pedagogically-based design of an asynchronous conferencing system.

ACKNOWLEDGMENTS

This report and the research and development described were supported through a grant from the Proffitt Foundation, School of Education, Indiana University, a grant from the CIC Consortium, and a contract with the School of Continuing Studies, Indiana University.

REFERENCES

American Association for the Advancement of Science. (1993). *Benchmarks for science literacy: Project 2061*. Washington, DC: Author.

Astin, A. (1993). *What matters in college*. San Francisco: Jossey-Bass.

Barrows, H. S. (1988). *The tutorial process*. Springfield: Southern Illinois University School of Medicine.

Barrows, H. S. (1994). *Practice-based learning: Problem-based learning applied to medical education*. Springfield: Southern Illinois University Medical School.

Barrows, H. S., & Myers, A. C. (1993). *Problem-based learning in secondary schools*. Unpublished monograph, Problem-Based Learning Institute, Lanphier High School and Southern Illinois University Medical School, Springfield.

Bereiter, C. (1992). Implications of Postmodernism for science, or, science as progressive discourse. *Educational Psychology, 29*, 3–12.

Bransford, J. D., & Stein, B. S. (1993). *The ideal problem solver: A guide for inproving thinking, learning, and creativity*. New York: Freeman.

Braxton, J. M., Eimers, M. T., Bayer, A. E. (1996). The implications of teaching norms for the improvement of undergraduate education. *Journal of Higher Education, 67*, 603–625.

Brooks, J., & Brooks, M. (1993). *In search of understanding: The case for constructivist classrooms*. Alexandria, VA: Association for Supervision and Curriculum Development.

Cooper, J., Prescott, S., Cook, L., Smith, L., & Mueck, R. (1990). *Cooperative learning and college instruction*. Long Beach, CA: Trustees of the California State University.

Dolence, M. G., & Norris, D. M. (1995). *Transforming higher education: A vision for learning in the 21st century*. Ann Arbor, MI: Society for College and University Planning.

Edelson, D. C., & O'Neill, D. K. (1994, April). *The CoVis collaboratory notebook: Computer support for scientific inquiry.* Paper presented at the annual meeting of the American Educational Research Association, New Orleans.

Ennis, R. H. (1962). A concept of critical thinking. *Harvard Educational Review 32*(1), 81–111.

Ennis, R. H. (1989). Critical thinking and subject specificity: Clarification and needed research. *Educational Researcher, 18*(3), 4–10.

Facione, P. A., Sanchez, C. A., Facione, N. C., & Gainer, J. (1995). The disposition toward critical thinking. *Journal of General Education 44*(1), 1–25.

Fischer, C. J., & Grant, G. E. (1983). Intellectual levels in the classroom. In C. L. Ellner & C. P. Barnes (Eds.), *Studies of college teaching* (pp. 47–60). Lexington, MA: Heath.

Harasim, L. (1990). *On-line education: Perspectives on a new environment.* New York: Praeger.

Hayes, J. R. (1989). *The complete problem solver.* Hillsdale, NJ: Lawrence Erlbaum Associates.

Hewitt, J., & Scardamalia, M. (in press). Design principles for the support of distributed processes. *Educational Psychology Review.*

Hewitt, J., Scardamalia, M., & Webb, J. (1997, April). Situative design issues for interactive learning environments: The problem of group coherence. In M. Scardamalia & C. Bereiter (Chairs), *Sociocognitive design issues for interactive learning environments across diverse knowledge building communities.* Symposium conducted at the annual meeting of the American Educational Research Association, Chicago.

Hewitt, J., Webb, J., & Rowley, P. (1994, April). *Student use of branching in a computer-supported discussion environment.* Poster session presented at the annual meeting of the American Educational Research Association, New Orleans.

Hiltz, S. R. (in press). Impact of college-level courses via asynchronous learning learning networks: Some preliminary results. *Journal of Asynchronous Learning Networks.*

H.R. Res. 1804 (Goals 2000: Educate America Act), 103d Cong., 2nd Sess. (1994).

Johnson, D., & Johnson, R. (1993). What we know about cooperative learning at the college level. *Cooperative Learning, 13*(3), 17–23.

Kuhn, D. (1991). *The skills of argument.* New York: Cambridge University Press.

Milter, R. G., & Stinson, J. E. (1993). Educating leaders for the new competitive environment. In G. Gijselaers, S. Tempelaar, & S. Keizer (Eds.), *Educational innovation in economics and business administration: The case of problem-based learning* (pp. 30–40). London: Kluwer.

National Assessment of Educational Progress. (1981). *Reading, thinking, and writing.* Princeton, NJ: Educational Testing Service.

National Council of Teachers of Mathematics. (1991). *Professional standards for teaching mathematics.* Reston, VA: Author.

Nunn, C. E. (1996). Discussion in the college classroom: Triangulating observation and survey results. *Journal of Higher Education, 67*, 23–26.

Oblinger, D. G., & Maruyama, M. K. (1996). *Distributed learning* (CAUSE Professional Paper Series, No. 14). Boulder, CO: CAUSE.

Oshima, J. (1994, April). *Coordination of solo- and joint-plane of student activity in CSILE: Analysis from the perspective of activity theory by Leontiev and Engestrom.* Paper presented at the annual meeting of the American Educational Research Association, New Orleans.

Paul, R. (1993). *Critical thinking: What every person needs to survive in a rapidly changing world.* Santa Rosa, CA: Foundation for Critical Thinking.

Perkins, D. (1992). Person-plus: A distributed view of thinking and learning. In G. Salomon (Ed.), *Distributed cognition: Psychological and educational considerations* (pp. 88–110). New York: Cambridge University Press.

Polya, G. (1957). *How to solve it: a new aspect of mathematical method.* Princeton, NJ: Princeton University Press.

Roschelle, J. (1992, April). *Reflections on Dewey and technology for situated learning.* Paper presented at annual meeting of the American Educational Research Association, San Francisco.

Savery, J., & Duffy, T. (1996). Problem based learning: An instructional model and its constructivist framework. In B. Wilson (Ed.), *Constructivist learning environments: Case studies in instructional design* (pp. 135–148). Englewood Cliffs, NJ: Educational Technology Publications.

Scardamalia, M., & Bereiter, C. (1991). Higher levels of agency for children in knowledge building: A challenge for the design of new knowledge media. *The Journal of the Learning Sciences, 1*, 37–68.

Schon, D. A. (1987). *Educating the reflective practitioner: Toward a new design for teaching and learning in the professions*. San Francisco: Jossey-Bass.

Shank, G. D. (1987). Abductive strategies in educational research. *The American Journal of Semiotics, 5*, 275–290.

Toulmin, S., Rieke, R., & Janik, A. (1979). *An introduction to reasoning*. New York: Macmillan.

Voss, J. F., Fincher-Kiefer, R., Wiley, J., & Silfies, L. (1993). On the process of arguments. *Argumentation, 7*, 165–181.

Voss, J. F., & Means, M. L. (1991). Learning to reason via instruction in argumentation. *Learning and Instruction, 1*(4), 337–350.

Voss, J. F., & Post, T. (1988). On the solving of ill-structured problems. In M. Chi, R. Glaser, & M. Farr (Eds.), *The nature of expertise* (pp. 261–285). Hillsdale, NJ: Lawrence Erlbaum Associates.

Wallas, G. (1926). *The art of thought*. New York: Harcourt Brace.

Wingspread Group on Higher Education. (1993). *An American imperative*. Racine, WI: The Johnson Foundation.

II

STAND-ALONE SYSTEM COLLABORATION

4

Bubble Dialogue: Tools for Supporting Literacy and Mind

Charoula Angeli
Donald J. Cunningham
Indiana University

Literacy (i.e., reading and writing) has been one of the most prominent and controversial issues in education for several decades (Noll, 1995). The debate has often centered on two different approaches of teaching reading and writing, namely the phonics approach and the whole language approach. Chall (1967, 1989), an advocate of the phonics approach, warned us that whole language does not provide enough structure for children who come from homes that are not reading-supportive and recommended that this structure be systematically provided. On the other hand, Goodman (1986), an advocate of whole language, asserted that the phonics approach makes language learning difficult because it breaks language into arbitrary and abstract little pieces. Language, as a consequence, too often becomes unrelated to the needs and experiences of learners. Although the debate continues, and no matter which side of the debate one belongs to, the fact that there are currently 14 million children in the United States who have failed to reach satisfactory levels of literacy cries for our immediate attention, fresh conceptions of literacy, and innovative ways to support its development.

One promising approach has been to focus on the importance of dialogue in literacy. Oakshott (1962) drew attention to the critical relationship between language, thought, and dialogue. He hypothesized that humans have evolved a dialogic competence that is both private and public. This dialogue can take place in collaboration with other people in a social environment, or it can take place within ourselves in the form of an internal dialogue, often called reflective thought. Vygotsky (1962) has proposed that learning is a social process, and that children first learn "social speech," talk directed at others, in their attempt to communicate with their significant others. He argued that children's social speech is later turned inward, and experienced as thought.

Following a similar line of reasoning, Tharp and Gallimore (1988) asserted that literacy events should be experienced by learners as collaborative social activities with goals embedded in natural settings, and not as isolated and decontextualized events. Likewise, Bruffee (1984), who viewed dialogue as a vital element in composing thoughts, claimed that collaborative writing groups provide the social context and the structure for such dialogue to take place. In arguing that all knowledge is constructed and that social interactions are critical in knowledge construction, he laid the theoretical groundwork for using dialogues and conversations among socially interacting people jointly negotiating text. Hall (1987) also agreed that learners develop acceptable literacy skills when they are involved in meaningful and collaborative activities.

As Downing (1979) asserted, however, literacy involves a mark-making and interpretive process that requires explicit awareness of the meta-linguistic aspects of language. Awareness of those aspects of language required for literacy does not develop spontaneously from spoken language; they are inaccessible to one's consciousness without the aid of a teacher, mentor, or collaborative community. Hence, what is required for literacy is a language awareness support structure, which incorporates the more conscious, deliberate, meta-linguistic processes that help make meaning in reading and writing. The support structure has to be such that it is grounded in the social and physical worlds in which children find themselves, so that the ensuing discussion and knowledge construction is meaningful and driven by their concerns. Of equal importance, the shift from spontaneous conversation to conscious dialogue has to be made. It is here, in one's reflection on dialogue, that language is turned in upon itself and becomes a tool for thought (D. J. Cunningham, Angeli, Morton, & M. L. Cunningham, 1997).

Learning how to read and write can most effectively take place in learning environments where learners engage in a process of socially constituted and constructed meaning, and where a language awareness support structure is provided. We believe that computer-mediated systems can effectively support innovative environments for language development where such reflective dialogue can take place.

Bubble Dialogue, a computer software tool developed by the Language Development and Hypermedia Research Group (D. J. Cunningham, McMahon, & O'Neill, 1992), was intended to provide such a language awareness support structure for the acquisition of literacy. The purpose of this chapter is to examine the instructional framework within which we used Bubble Dialogue, discuss the different modes of interaction or communication that took place during the literacy process, and present our current thinking on how Bubble Dialogue can be used as an assessment tool for literacy. Finally, we conclude with recommendations for the design of collaborative learning environments as these emerge from our research with Bubble Dialogue.

BUBBLE DIALOGUE

As we mentioned earlier, Bubble Dialogue provides a language awareness support structure for the development of literacy. More specifically, Bubble Dialogue is a HyperCard application that combines elements of role play, comic strip creation, and reflexive dialogue analysis (The Language Development and Hypermedia Research Group, 1992). A master stack, called BubbleMaker (see Fig. 4.1) has been written to create customized Bubble Dialogue stacks for later use.

The scene in which the discussion is to take place is established by the participants. A graphic is then chosen, and the setting is described by writing a prologue. In each customized stack created by BubbleMaker, four icons, representing a speech bubble (public/social speech) and a think bubble (inner speech), are presented alongside each of at least two characters on the screen. The comic genre is so well established in many cultures that even very young children, when presented with empty bubbles, feel compelled to speak for the characters playing out their roles.

Bubble Dialogue can operate in two distinct modes: the creation mode and the review mode. In the creation mode (see Fig. 4.2), one can only move forward to the next empty think or speech bubble. When in this generative

FIG. 4.1. The BubbleMaker workspace.

FIG. 4.2. The tool in creation mode.

mode, the course of action is transferred to the other character once a speech, and optionally, one think bubble have been used. This turn-taking protocol ensures that a user cannot have an extended conversation with him or herself.

In contrast, in review mode (see Fig. 4.3), the user can move forward or backward to add notes, edit existing bubbles, or even extend the dialogue. Most important, the review mode provides the user with an opportunity to reflect on the dialogue that took place, as well as the quality of his or her writing. One of the features that is activated while the application is in review

FIG. 4.3. The tool in review mode.

TABLE 4.1
Short Section of a Bubble Dialogue Script

Mary thinks:	Shall I tell him the word?
Mary says:	**I know a good word that might fit.**
Peter thinks:	I don't want help from her. I didn't want to work with her anyway.
Note:	*Peter has a strong dislike for Mary, so he doesn't want her to give him the word.*
Peter says:	**Wait a minute, I've almost got it. It's on the tip of my tongue.**
Mary thinks:	I bet he doesn't know it.
Mary says:	**OK, then what is it?**
Note:	*Mary gets cocky.*
Peter thinks:	Oh no! What am I going to tell her? I'm really in the soup now!
Peter says:	**I'm not telling. You just want to know so that you can say you knew it from the start.**

mode is the notes field. This feature is powerful in a variety of ways. For example, when users review their dialogues they can use the notes field to add comments about "what's happening," or comments on the motives and feelings of the characters. Teachers and researchers may also use this feature to annotate the dialogues in any manner they see fit, such as commentary, reminders, and questions for the users to consider as they review their work.

In addition, Bubble Dialogue has the capability to automatically save all dialogues in a script format. Table 4.1 provides as an example the script of Mary and Peter's dialogue (see Figs. 4.1, 4.2, and 4.3).

All these features of Bubble Dialogue make up the language awareness support structure that is needed for learners to transition from conversation to written dialectic discourse. Think and speech bubbles enable the learner to function in both the interpersonal and intrapersonal levels (Vygotsky, 1962), as well as learn to take turns in a dialogue. The review mode allows learners to reflect and revise their dialogues appropriately.

RESEARCH PROCEDURES

We tested Bubble Dialogue with 50 school children at an elementary school in a midwestern city of about 60,000. Thirty of those students were in second grade, 5 were in third grade, and 15 were students from a multiage classroom for fourth-, fifth-, and sixth-grade levels. Fifteen of the 50 students were reported as students with special needs, and 5 were identified as gifted. Thirty-eight of the students were White, 10 were African American, 1 was Hispanic American, and 1 was Native American. The school drew from the predominantly low-income areas of the city.

Our primary role as the researchers for this study was to use Bubble Dialogue with the children, in a collaborative manner, to write stories. For each dialogue, we created a script that children could take home for later review. These scripts were the main source used for data analysis. Other sources that were also used for analysis were the researchers' field notes and semistructured student interviews. Data were analyzed qualitatively into categories and themes (Lincoln & Guba, 1985; Merriam, 1988).

THEORETICAL FRAMEWORK

The theoretical framework we adopted for this research project was based on learner-centered principles for learning and instruction. The 14 learner-centered psychological principles (LCPs) "provide an essential framework to be incorporated in new designs for curriculum and instruction, and assessment systems for evaluating educational goal attainments" (American Psychological Association, 1995, p. 2). The psychological principles deal with learning in the context of real-world learning situations, and focus on learners' cognitive skills and learning strategies. The principles are divided into four categories: (a) cognitive and metacognitive, (b) motivational and affective, (c) developmental and social, and (d) individual differences (see chap. 2 by Bonk and D. J. Cunningham, this volume, for more information).

In brief, we used the LCPs as a guiding framework because we believe that learners are active, goal directed, and capable of attaining high levels of agency in their learning process. As the LCPs state, learning occurs more effectively when it is an intentional process of constructing meaning from experience and information. This view emphasizes that learners need the support and instructional guidance of a mentor, coach, or collaborative community to learn how to create meaningful representations of knowledge and engage in projects that will help them pursue their goals. In addition, learners need assistance in constructing and integrating new knowledge with existing knowledge, in part, by using a variety of cognitive strategies. Salient in the 14 LCPs is the development of the learner's thinking processes and strategies. Successful learners are the ones who are engaged in problem solving and reflection, have developed reasoning skills, and know how to apply prior knowledge to new situations. But the LCPs also caution that how much learners learn largely depends on how motivated they are. Curiosity, perceived relevance of the task to the learner's goals, and personal choice and control, for instance, are all factors that contribute to a learner's motivation. Learning is also influenced by the learner's developmental level, as well as by how he or she interacts in social environments when collaborating with others.

The instructional process we used was modeled after these LCPs. This process is introduced and discussed in the next section.

INSTRUCTIONAL MODEL

Based on the design characteristics of Bubble Dialogue and the theoretical framework of the LCPs, we developed the instructional model shown in Fig. 4.4 as follows. In accordance with the LCPs, using this model, learning and instruction were viewed from cognitive, metacognitive, developmental, and social perspectives. Instruction, therefore, took on many different dimensional forms but always within the framework of dialectic discourse.

The instructional process, shown in Fig. 4.4, consisted of seven different phases.

Phase 1

First of all, we established rapport with the students. Our goal during this first stage was to get to know the students better and inform them of the purpose of the computer activity. Even though we wanted to make the instructional process purposive and intentional, we also wanted the students to find the task relevant to their interests. As Short and Burke (1991) stated, "whenever students are involved in experiences where they have choices, there is a greater likelihood that they will be able to make choices that allow them to connect with what they already know" (p. 36). Therefore, we asked students to draw from their life experiences and select the topic they wanted to write a story about. Older students (in third-, fourth-, fifth-, and sixth-grade levels) easily referred to their family life or hobbies to select the topic they were interested in talking about, but when the younger second-graders were given the option to choose, they claimed that they did not know what they wanted to talk about.

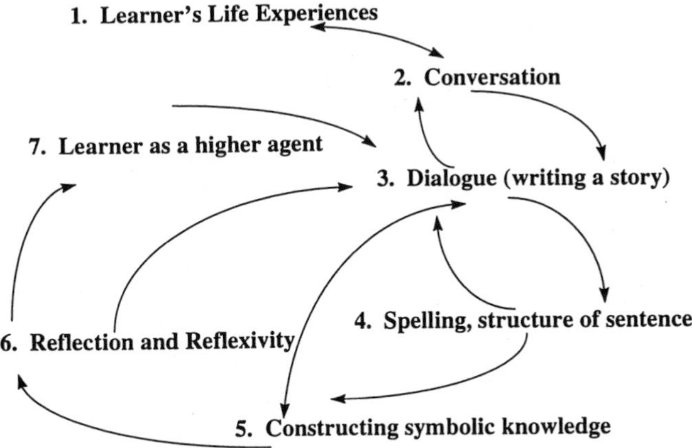

FIG. 4.4. The collaborative learner-centered instructional model.

Therefore, this introductory phase lasted longer with second-graders, as we helped them select a topic that was of interest to them.

Phase 2

After we established a topic, we engaged the students in purposive conversation to learn more about the topic they selected. Although this phase did not last long, we used it as a bridge to shift from casual conversation to conscious dialogue. Initially, all children found it difficult to get familiar with the structure of dialectic discourse that Bubble Dialogue provided. We had to constantly remind them that they had to use the computer to talk to us by typing their responses in a speech or a think bubble.

Phase 3

Once we made the transition from conversation to dialogue, we modeled the speech and think bubbles for the students, and asked them if they knew the difference between the two. Because many students initially felt hesitant and unsure about the use of think bubbles, they avoided them. We continued modeling their uses for the students, and we noticed that after four or five speech bubbles, the students tried at least one think bubble.

Phase 4

Once the students felt comfortable with these Bubble Dialogue tools, we asked some of them to read aloud what they were typing in the bubbles. Our reason for this request was to increase their metacognitive awareness about the mechanics of their language use, because many of them were misspelling words and writing sentences that were not grammatically correct. Once they began reading aloud what they wrote, they became aware of the fact that what they wrote did not "sound" too well. Accordingly, they began asking questions about how to spell certain words, if they used punctuation correctly, and if their sentences were well formed.

Postman (1995) stated that "there are many ways to teach the young the connections between language and world-making" (p. 84), and he argued that teachers make a major mistake by focusing students' language use on how to spell words correctly and use punctuation rules properly. Therefore, literacy becomes a game of trivia. As a result, during the fourth phase, our role as the "teacher" became extremely difficult and challenging. As Sternberg and Horvath (1995) noted, a good teacher is one that is insightful and that holds a bag of different tools to use appropriately. Because not all students were at the same level of language development, the biggest challenge for us was to diagnose when the time was right to make a student aware about the technical aspects of language. Some (10%) students were aware from the beginning about their language use by just watching the way we wrote. More (60%) gradually became aware of their writing as we were constantly asking them questions to think about their writing. The remaining students (30%) failed to discriminate between our writing and their writing.

D. J. Cunningham (1992) stated that knowledge does not consist of a number of objects that learners acquire; instead knowledge is better thought of as knowing or as a process. In tandem with this notion, we viewed literacy as a process of how learners come to mature thought and reason about abstract concepts (Bruner, 1966) and worldviews (Postman, 1995). At the same time, we recognized the importance of learning how to write correctly. Our strategy for dealing effectively with a number of different zones of proximal development (ZPDs; Vygotsky, 1962), therefore, was to first assess the readiness of students for new learning, and then, through a process of appropriation (Rogoff, 1990), introduce them to grammatical and punctuation rules by using language to talk about language. Therefore, not all children entered the fourth phase at the same pace. For those students (10%) who were aware about their language use from the beginning, the instructional process shown in Fig. 4.4 was systematically used in a linear fashion. In contrast, students who gradually became aware of their writing (60%), were guided from Phase 3 to 5 and returned to 4 at a later time. There were two reasons for this tactic: (a) We wanted the students to question by themselves the quality of their writing, and ask for help when they felt they needed it, and (b) we did not want students to think that the only goal of the activity was to learn punctuation and grammatical rules. The rest of them (30%) were also guided from Phase 3 to 5 and returned to 4 when the researchers felt that it was appropriate to introduce language mechanics.

Phase 5

During the fifth phase, our goal was to help children develop their cognitive skills by asking them questions about the topic they selected. Initially, our questions were simple and required them to recall certain facts. Gradually, we shifted to questions seeking their personal experiences to reason and make inferences about the topic. For example, if the topic was friends, we asked questions such as: "Why do you like Tim as a friend?", "What qualities should a friend have?", "Are friends important?", "What do you do to be a good friend to somebody?". Our goal was to activate their belief system about friendship through a process of inductive and deductive questioning. When the question was one that they had not encountered before, we helped them to build a context within which the question could be answered meaningfully.

This last process is known as abduction (D. J. Cunningham, 1992; Shank, 1987). Our instructional strategy for fostering abduction was to present students with a perspective different than their own; most of the time this was our own perspective. Therefore, students came to know how their knowledge templates and belief system were situated in relation to somebody else's belief system, while enhancing theirs as needed.

Phase 6

The sixth phase of reflection and reflexivity was also of particular interest.[1] We used reflection and reflexivity as an instructional strategy to help students develop metacognitive and higher order skills. We defined reflection and reflexivity as a "reflection of our reflections, thinking about our thinking process, knowing how we know" (D. J. Cunningham, 1992, p.187). Our goal was to encourage students to think about the dialectic discourse reported in speech bubbles, analyze the arguments presented, synthesize all that was said so far, edit and revise appropriately, and decide how to respond next.

Our findings indicate that students found it either difficult or irrelevant to use think bubbles as they made limited use of them. Nonetheless, when they did employ them, the students used them to evaluate their current state of knowledge and say "I don't know, why is she asking me that question?", or express a concern they had about what the other person had said. When we asked students why they were not using think bubbles as much as intended, they responded that they did not have to think about what to say, they already knew. However, in our observations, students stopped and thought on numerous occasions about their answer without using a think bubble. Therefore, it seems that students either felt that it was too much work to type in their thoughts, or they did not see the connection between speech and think bubbles and how they could use both to shape their internal and external dialogue. We believe that a certain amount of practice with Bubble Dialogue is needed for a student to make the connection between think and speech bubbles. We also expected that the notes field feature of Bubble Dialogue would provide an appropriate opportunity for reflexivity to take place but our students also made limited use of this feature. Here, again, we propose that with increased use of Bubble Dialogue, reflexive use of the notes field and other features will increase.

Phase 7

In all six stages of the instructional process used here, the "teacher" provided scaffolding while the student was constructing a set of negotiated beliefs. But even in this prevailing teaching model it is the teacher who asked ques-

---

[1]Although we have distinguished between reflection and reflexivity in other writings (e.g., D. J. Cunningham, 1992), here we use the terms interchangeably.

tions, directed inquiry, and provided direction. As a result, the learners were dependent on the teacher's assessment of what constitutes knowledge, because the teacher was the one who was in control of movements within the ZPD. To help them grow out of this dependency, we tried another activity using Bubble Dialogue, which encouraged learners to assume higher levels of agency in the learning process by asking us questions. This movement out of dependency is really a question of ZPD control. Therefore, in attempting to shift control of the ZPD from the teacher's control to mutual control, we were hoping to balance the learning process. Previous research (e.g., Brown & Palinscar, 1989; Palinscar, 1986; Scardamalia & Bereiter, 1985) has shown that such a shift in power and control can be achieved only in learning environments that support the dialectic process, wherein learners, with the appropriate scaffolding, take over the asking of questions, and, thereby, direct their own inquiry. Bubble Dialogue proved to be an effective vehicle for supporting the development of such student self-agency. Student opportunities for self-agency are evident in our analyses of dialectic discourse.

For each dialogue we facilitated with this instructional process, we created a script we could later print out and review. To give the reader a better sense of the format of these scripts and how we facilitated a dialogue, we provide an example in the next section.

THE DIALECTIC DISCOURSE AS A PROCESS OF FACILITATION

In the following dialogue, one of the researchers is engaged in a problem-solving activity with three students. Two of these students were in sixth grade, and one was in fourth grade.

Researcher says: What have you been doing in math this week?
Students say: Adding and subtracting fractions.
Researcher thinks: *It's been a long time since I had that.*
Researcher says: Do you find adding and subtracting fractions hard?
Ann says: Sometimes, but not always.
Researcher says: Why do you want to talk about math?
Ann says: Because math is one of my favorite subjects.
Note (by Ann): *I got an award in math.*
Researcher says: What kinds of problems do you have to solve? Are they word problems?
Katie says: Sometimes they are word problems.
Researcher says: Can you come up with a word problem we can all solve together?
Note (by Researcher): *Usually word problems are more difficult because you need to set them up first.*
Students think: *Umm, there are 283 dimes and 398 pennies. How many were there all together?*

Students say: There are 283 dimes and 398 pennies. How many were there all together?
Researcher says: Why is this a fraction problem?
Students think: *Umm, we don't know.*
Students say: We don't know.
Researcher thinks: *Hmm. They don't seem to be understanding.*
Researcher says: OK, let me help more. Can we add the two numbers together?
Ann thinks: *No! Because you can't add a story problem.*
Ann says: No! Because you can't add a story problem.
Researcher says: Roger what do you think?
Roger thinks: *Well, you have to subtract a story problem.*
Roger says: Well, you have to subtract a story problem.
Researcher says: What do you mean by subtracting a story problem?
Roger says: Well, you said that you don't add a story problem, so you subtract it.
Note (by Roger): *I learned that you don't always have to subtract.*
Ann thinks: *I wonder what she [the researcher] will do next?*
Researcher says: OK, let's think about this. The question is "how many were there all together?" Right? Now, this question is vague to me. Do you mean how many coins, or pennies or dimes?
Students say: Oh, yes. We mean how many coins.
Researcher says: All right, in that case I think you know the answer. What do you need to do to get the total number of coins?
Katie says: I think you should add. The answer is 681.
Researcher says: Do we all agree? Now let's solve a more difficult problem. Suppose we want to find how many dimes were there all together. How do we do that? Work as a group to find the answer.
Katie thinks: *OK, this is very hard.*

[Roger is attempting to solve the problem by writing on a piece of paper, but with no success. One of the group members had this reaction.]

Ann thinks: *I don't know what Roger is doing. It seems strange.*
Researcher says: Roger, do you want to explain to us what you are doing?
Roger says: I don't know.
Researcher says: OK, well we need to use fractions to solve this one, don't we? We know we have 283 dimes and 398 pennies. We want to find how many dimes we have. Can we add the two numbers together like before?
Students think: *No, because before we wanted to find the total number of coins not dimes.*
Ann says: We need to find how many dimes there are in 398 pennies first.
Researcher says: You got it. Can you show us how to do that?
Ann says: Divide 398 by 10, and add the number to 283. So, there are 322 dimes and 8 pennies left.

The main goal of the preceding dialogue was to test the students' ability to set up their problem space and develop their understanding about fractions within an activity. That was the reason we asked them to come up with a word problem that we could all solve together. During the early stages of our dialogue with the students, we realized that even though they were able to come up with a word problem, they did not understand fractions very well. Moreover, these students also held a number of misconceptions about word problems. As the script indicates, we chose to provide support for the students from a simple to complex sequence, by asking them to first solve an easier version of the problem and then gradually move to one that was more complex. As a result of this approach, their learning was never decontextualized; instead, the problem-solving activity was always embedded in a context. The only difference was that the students started from a familiar problem before moving to one that was more challenging and one step beyond their current level of competence. Finally, the students came to construct their answer after a series of questions from the researcher. The researcher's questions prompted them to compare what they already knew with what they wanted to find out, and draw appropriate analogies from a problem they already solved to an unknown one.

It was interesting to see how students who were engaged in reflective thought gradually eliminated their misconceptions either by using think bubbles or the notes field. In effect, Bubble Dialogue efficiently and effectively supported those interactions by providing a cognitive structure that enabled the students to engage in both reflective thinking and experiential learning by reacting to our questions and taking action.

In previous research (D. J. Cunningham & Angeli, 1995; D. J. Cunningham et al., 1997), we approached teachers with whom we established a working relationship, and invited them to work with us in evaluating the dialogue scripts. Even though we already reported on the result of this collaboration (see D. J. Cunningham et al., 1997), we would like to briefly discuss it again in the next section.

SCRIPT ANALYSIS

Teachers and researchers together, in a collaborative effort, found that Bubble Dialogue as a tool for literacy development has great potential as it promotes (a) the articulation and development of young learners' thought processes, (b) natural language teaching, and (c) sentence structure awareness.

Articulation of Young Learners' Thought Processes

The teachers we worked with were impressed by the amount of information the students typed in the computer, as well as the extent of conceptual development. The teachers claimed that one of the main problems they were facing in their traditional lessons was to teach their students to write more in their journals. They also mentioned that, most of the time, students' thinking was not well reflected in their writing. But with Bubble Dialogue, this was no longer a problem. The dialectic process allowed the students to exchange ideas and collaborate to solve a problem or write a story. Therefore, writing became a meaningful activity, a vehicle to shape their thinking.

Natural Language Teaching

One of the first things that we noticed once we started working with the children, was the fact that they wanted to work with us all the time. They never said they wanted to quit and we had to somehow end the dialogue to move on to other things. We believe that the reason for their motivation and eagerness was the fact that the Bubble Dialogue sessions were holistic and focused on the discussion of a topic that was interesting to them. Specifically, during our interviews with the students, we were informed that Bubble Dialogue was a tool that enabled them to speak and write as if they were at home with their parents or with friends, and that they would love to have permanently in their classroom.

Sentence Structure Awareness

Rogoff (1990) has explored the concept of cultural learning in terms of the metaphor of apprenticeship. Following Vygotsky, she sees learning as occurring through the participation of a "novice" in a jointly undertaken cultural activity in which the expert assists the novice's performance.

Accordingly, our main goal was to facilitate the literacy process by creating opportunities for the children to learn language without making them conscious that they were learning language (Speidel, 1984). Through questioning, we assisted the children to express themselves to the maximum of their abilities, and through feedback, we helped them write grammatically correct sentences. The teachers also stated that students wrote more complete and well-formed sentences with Bubble Dialogue. When we informed the students that they wrote better sentences with Bubble Dialogue, they said that the speech and think bubbles allowed them to organize their ideas effectively and efficiently, thereby making them aware of how they formed their sentences.

So far, we discussed the dialectic discourse as both (a) a process of facilitation or coaching, and (b) a product or outcome (script analysis). In addition, we analyzed the dialectic discourse as a process of engagement or communication. The result of this analysis is presented next.

ZONES OF ENGAGEMENT

Figure 4.5 identifies three different zones of engagement. These are (a) "Direct Interactions," (b) "Identification," and (c) "Knowledge Construction and Beliefs."

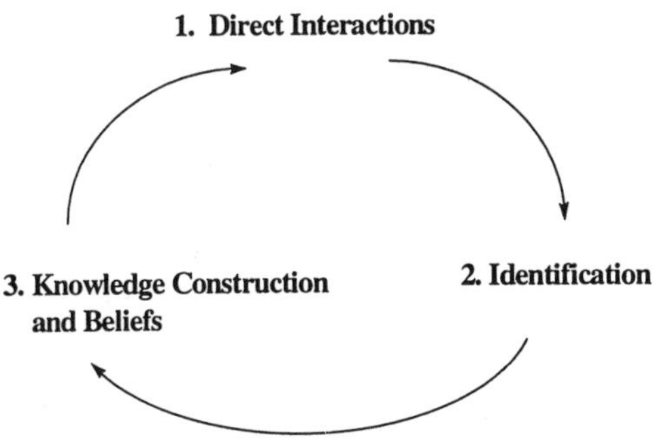

FIG. 4.5. Zones of engagement.

The Zone of "Direct Interactions"

The zone of "Direct Interactions" regulates the etiquette of dialogue. This was primarily controlled by the turn-taking protocol built in Bubble Dialogue. The turn-taking protocol ensures that all voices of the community are heard. It also ensures that interacting parties are committed to responsible participation in a genuine knowledge-building community (Scardamalia & Bereiter, 1991). Therefore, writing at this stage is seen as a balanced exchange of ideas among participants who respect each other. In our case, this exchange of ideas was facilitated by asking questions.

The Zone of "Identification"

Once learners are engaged in social discourse (the use of speech bubbles), they venture through a process of identification, which mainly involves determining the key roles and audiences for one's writing (i.e., who am I and to whom I am talking). In our case, there were a number of different roles and audiences that were identified. Students, for instance, talked to other students from the same class, friends from their neighborhood, and their teachers. Students in teacher roles, on the other hand, talked mainly to students and other teachers. The zone of "Identification" has important implications for the entire writing cycle. First, it sets the stage for the kinds of language constructs that are the most appropriate to use, enabling writing to become purposive wherein writers use the appropriate means to express their ideas (i.e., debate ideas, set agendas, establish relationships, defend one's position). Second, through the zone of "Identification" students become aware of different writing styles and strategies.

The Zone of "Knowledge Construction and Beliefs"

Once the form of language constructs is set, the process of discourse is shifted to the construction of knowledge and beliefs. The dialogic interactions that take place at this point are of two types. One type is the external dialogue that ensues as participants negotiate meaning and construct new understandings in an attempt to develop a common mind and a common voice (Wertsch, 1991), thereby establishing a community of learners. At the same time, as learners strive to negotiate and construct meaning, they interact with their belief system through internal dialogue or debate with one's self-reflective thought (Ward, 1994). This is what Vygotsky called interpsychological processing and intrapsychological processing. Interpsychological processing occurs when the child interacts with others to construct or negotiate meaning; intrapsychological activity results from internalized knowledge, jointly constructed with others, in a meaningful way.

We now turn to the subject of assessment and how Bubble Dialogue can be used to assess literacy.

BUBBLE DIALOGUE AND ASSESSMENT

Instruction and assessment become increasingly blurred with Bubble Dialogue. We view assessment as a dynamic and continuous process that takes place concurrently with instruction. Brown et al. (1993) have noted the many similarities between assessment and instruction in a learner-centered framework where typically both involve guided collaboration, strategy modeling by a mentor, discussion of strategies, provision of hints, multiple attempts, and so forth. Brown and her colleagues have used the term *dynamic assessment* to describe those methods of assessment where children are presented with problems just ahead of their existing competence, and then provided with help as needed for them to reach independent mastery. According to Brown et al., four main principles are involved in the design of dynamic assessments: (a) understanding the procedures, rather than just speed and accuracy, (b) expert guidance for diagnosing and scaffolding as well as promoting independent competence, (c) microgenetic analysis to permit estimates of learning as it actually occurs over time, and (d) the assessment is forward anticipating or "proleptic," directed toward levels of competence not yet achieved individually, but possible within supportive learning environments. Based on these principles, the assessment framework of literacy that we developed with Bubble Dialogue is shown in Fig. 4.6.

Assessment must serve the needs of schools, teachers, parents, and students themselves to have accurate information concerning students' level of development and learning. For example, Bubble Dialogue may be a proven technique for engaging students in a dialogue, but can it also provide an accurate and useful picture of the literacy development and progress of individual students?

The naturalistic model of assessment shown in Fig. 4.6 advocates that students' learning should be observed in a variety of activities. For example,

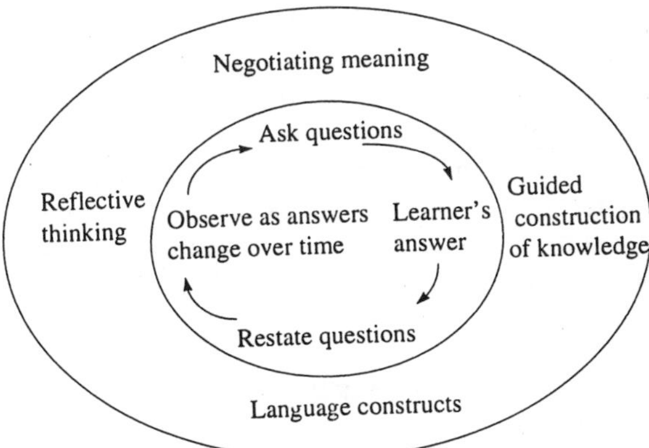

FIG. 4.6. Assessment model.

students might be observed in (a) social activities negotiating meaning, (b) learning from experts through scaffolding and modeling in apprenticeships, (c) settings for direct instruction of language constructs when needed, and (d) instructional activities that foster reflective thinking. The observation process is based on a system of questions that the teacher develops to assess each stage of the writing process discussed earlier. Whereas for student learning we began with simple, personalized questions to scaffold the child's movement to competence beyond their current level, for the later assessment of this activity we begin with relatively challenging questions and provide assistance in a prespecified format until we reach the child's level of independent functioning. In other words, our assessment questions are designed to assess student need in constructing a dialogue, rather than to assist the process. We also focus our assessment practices on the individual student, although the task continues to be a collaboration between the assessor and the student. A particular focus of our assessment work has been on reflexivity, on the development of student awareness, and the understanding of the dialogic process. Many of our questions and probes have been designed to foster students' externalization of the processes they are embodying: Why did you use a think bubble? Why did this character say that? Why do you think that is important?

But our questions also move beyond the process of constructing Bubble Dialogues to the dialogic process itself: Is it OK for a friend to ask a question like that? How could that character persuade the teacher? What is that character thinking? Questions such as these are designed to enhance the students' awareness of dialogic discourse with the intention that this awareness will allow the students to take control of that process.

Preliminary results of our work on assessment show that the teachers with whom we have worked have been amazed at the literacy accomplishments shown by some of the children using Bubble Dialogue; students who had previously shown only modest skill on traditional tasks like reading aloud or writing stories in class. We believe that Bubble Dialogue taps literacy development that is obscured or discouraged by traditional measures and will provide a much needed addition to literacy assessment techniques. As a result, we conclude our chapter by discussing design issues that instructional designers should consider for developing collaborative learning environments that can impact children's literacy development.

DESIGN OF COMPUTER COLLABORATIVE LEARNING ENVIRONMENTS

Our research with Bubble Dialogue has taught us that instructional efficacy does not reside in either external (the medium as the stimulus) or internal events (within the learner solely), but rather in complex interactions between the learner and the instructional environment. Bubble Dialogue is a collaborative computer tool that effectively handles the complexities of the learning and instructional processes, by providing a cognitive structure for learning and, at the same time, managing an interplay between the learner, the teacher, and the medium itself. There are a number of design features that still require further examination.

Organization of Knowledge

In environments where there is more than one person participating, such as collaborative learning environments, the medium must provide support for the organization and structure of the interactions. In Bubble Dialogue, this was accomplished by creating the characters to participate in the process and by allocating a unique space for each one of the characters to "speak" or "think." Consequently, knowledge was organized in a systematic way that was easy to retrieve and modify.

Provision for Cognitive and Metacognitive Structures

As Norman (1993) stated, cognitive and metacognitive structures are the artifacts that make us smart. In Bubble Dialogue this was implemented with the language awareness support structure that was built in the system. Because some learners have limited memory capabilities and often a short attention span, the purpose of our cognitive artifact was to help learners strengthen their mental powers by engaging them in a process with which they are already familiar—dialogue. The language awareness structure in Bubble Dialogue, such as the think and speech bubbles, provides a model and a scaffold for learners to use while they are engaged in the process of literacy development. Similarly, the features of the notes field and the review mode provide the learner with tools for reflective thought.

Adaptive Environments

We know that learners differ in terms of their knowledge bases, their learning preferences, and the cognitive and metacognitive skills they possess. Bubble Dialogue has provided us with useful insights into how much control should be given to learners, by changing the amount of support provided. We identified four different types of control: (a) no support—the learner is independent and able to engage in self-directed learning effectively; (b) partial support with an emphasis on cognitive strategies—the learner receives help to develop his or her cognitive skills such as planning, elaborating, and organizing knowledge; (c) partial support with an emphasis on metacognitive strategies—the learner learns how to examine and question his or her learning process; and (d) full support—the learner is told what problems to solve, in what sequence, and what strategies to use. As a result of operating within an adaptive environment, the teacher assumes a variety of roles. The role of the teacher may change from being in total control of the instructional process, to that of a facilitator or guide.

Access to Information

Of course, computer collaborative environments (and all other computer environments) should provide easy access to information. For example, learners may need to access work that was done some time ago to either review it online or get a printout for later use. The learning tool should be able to allow access to the information stored (this may need to be authorized), as well as provide the user with the capability of printing out his or her own work.

CONCLUSION

The purpose of this chapter was to discuss how tools like Bubble Dialogue can be used for the development of literacy. We started out by presenting the learner-centered instructional model that we used to model the language awareness support structure built in Bubble Dialogue and scaffold students' learning. Next, we presented and discussed an example of dialectic discourse. Then we discussed the results of the Bubble Dialogue script analysis, followed by a discussion of how learners communicate while engaged in the writing process. After that, we presented ideas regarding how Bubble Dialogue can be used as an assessment tool for literacy. Finally, we offered guidelines for the design of collaborative computer-learning environments.

Our experience with Bubble Dialogue illustrates that literacy is not a game of trivia. Instead, it is a process of exchanging ideas, jointly constructing and negotiating meaning, and becoming aware of the dialogic process. This research, therefore, provides us with a number of insights of how to design collaborative learning environments to foster literacy development. Specifically, such learning environments should be designed to (a) allow learners to collaborate in social activities, (b) foster learner-centered instruction, (c) provide for adaptive instruction to meet individual needs, (d) empower the learner with cognitive structures to facilitate his or her learning, (e) promote natural language teaching, (f) encourage learners to guide and assess their own learning, and (g) nurture reflexivity. We believe that the collaborative learner-centered instructional model discussed in this study has great potential for impacting the debate on literacy issues, as it overcomes the weaknesses of the two predominant approaches currently used for teaching literacy, and offers the means to reduce the tremendous amount of childhood illiteracy.

REFERENCES

American Psychological Association. (1995). *Learner-centered psychological principles: A framework for school redesign and reform*. Washington, DC: Author.

Brown, A. L., Ash, D., Rutherfold, M., Nakagawa, K., Gordon, A., & Campione, J. C. (1993). Distributed expertise in the classroom. In G. Salomon (Ed.), *Distributed cognitions: Psychological and educational considerations* (pp. 188–228). New York: Cambridge University Press.

Brown, A. L., & Palinscar, A. S. (1989). Guided, cooperative learning, and individual knowledge acquisition. In L. B. Resnick (Ed.), *Knowing, learning, and instruction. Essays in honor of Robert Glaser* (pp. 393–451). Hillsdale, NJ: Lawrence Erlbaum Associates.

Bruffee, K. A. (1984). Collaborative learning and the conversation of mankind. *College English, 53*, 452–466.

Bruner, J. S. (1966). *Toward a theory of instruction*. Cambridge, MA: Harvard University Press.

Chall, J. (1967). *Learning to read: The great debate*. New York: McGraw-Hill.

Chall, J. (1989). Learning to read: The great debate 20 years later. A response to debunking the great phonics myth. *Phi Delta Kappan, 70*, 521–538.

Cunningham, D. J. (1992). Beyond educational psychology: Steps toward an educational semiotic. *Educational Psychology Review, 4*, 165–194.

Cunningham, D. J., & Angeli, C. (1995, October). *Language awareness support structures: Tools for literacy*. Paper presented at Hypermedia, 95, Bloomington, IN.

Cunningham, D. J., Angeli, C., Morton, M. L., & Cunningham, M. L. (1997). Language awareness support structures: Tools for literacy. In M. Collins & Z. Berge (Eds.), *Wired together: The online classroom in K–12* (Vol. 4). Washington, DC: Hampton Press.

Cunningham, D. J., McMahon, H., & O'Neill, W. (1992). Bubble Dialogue: A new tool for instruction and assessment. *Educational Technology Research and Development, 40*(2), 59–67.

Downing, M. (1979). *Reading and reasoning*. London: Chambers.

Goodman, K. (1986). *What's whole in whole language*. Portsmouth, NH: Heinemann.

Hall, N. (1987). *The emergence of literacy*. London: Hodder and Stoughton.

The Language Development and Hypermedia Research Group. (1992). Bubble Dialogue: A new tool for instruction and assessment. *Educational Technology Research & Development, 40*(2), 59–67.

Lincoln, Y., & Guba, E. G. (1985). *Naturalistic inquiry*. Newbury Park, CA: Sage.

Merriam, S. B. (1988). *Case study research in education: A qualitative approach*. San Francisco: Jossey-Bass.

Noll, J. W. (1995). *Taking sides: Clashing views on controversial educational issues* (6th ed.). Hartford, CT: Guilford Press.

Norman, D. A. (1993). *Things that make us smart: Defending human attributes in the age of the machine*. New York: Addison-Wesley.

Oakshott, M. (1962). The voice of poetry and the conversations of mankind. In *Rationalism in politics* (pp. 196–247). New York: Basic Books.

Palinscar, A. S. (1986). The role of dialogue in providing scaffolded instruction. *Educational Psychologist, 21*, 73–98.

Postman, N. (1995). *The end of education: Redefining the value of school*. New York: Vintage Books.

Rogoff, B. (1990). *Apprenticeship in learning*. New York: Oxford University Press.

Scardamalia, M., & Bereiter, C. (1985). Development of dialectic processes in composition. In D. R. Olson, N. Torrance, & A. Hildyard (Eds.), *Literacy, language and learning. The nature and consequences of reading and writing* (pp. 307–329). New York: Cambridge University Press.

Scardamalia, M., & Bereiter, C. (1991). Higher levels of agency for children in knowledge building: A challenge for the design of new knowledge media. *The Journal of the Learning Sciences, 1*(1), 37–68.

Shank, G. (1987). Abductive strategies in educational research. *American Journal of Semiotics, 5*, 275–290.

Short, K. G., & Burke, C. (1991). *Creating curriculum: Teachers and students as a community of learners*. Portsmouth, NH: Heinemann.

Speidel, G. E. (1984). *Conversation and language learning in the classroom*. Paper presented at the Third International Congress for the Study of Child Language, Austin, TX.

Sternberg, R. J., & Horvath, J. A. (1995). A prototype view of expert teaching. *Educational Researcher, 24*(6), 9–17.

Tharp, R. G., & Gallimore, R. (1988). *Rousing minds to life: Teaching, learning, and schooling in social context*. New York: Cambridge University Press.

Vygotsky, L. (1962). *Thought and language*. Cambridge, MA: MIT Press.

Ward, I. (1994). *Literacy, ideology, and dialogue: Towards a dialogic pedagogy*. Albany, NY: State University of New York Press.

Wertsch, J. V. (1991). *Voices of the mind: A sociocultural approach to mediated action*. Cambridge, MA: Harvard University Press.

5

Fostering Ownership for Learning With Computer-Supported Collaborative Writing in an Undergraduate Business Communication Course

John R. Savery
DePaul University

For 17 years, Anna Weston and Judy McCloud used a lecture/lab approach to teach the skills and knowledge for effective business communications to class after class of undergraduates. However, both were dissatisfied with the results of their teaching; and as McCloud said, "There has to be a better way, a more valuable way for students to learn to write than by listening to lectures on how to write." Concurrently, within the School of Business, there was increased concern with the inability of undergraduate students to demonstrate effective problem-solving skills. Thus, Weston and McCloud were supported in their efforts to redesign their business communications course to foster problem-solving skills through the use of an integrated instructional simulation, collaborative learning, problem-based learning instructional strategies, and a learner-centered approach. Students taking business communications in this alternative format were required to demonstrate their ability to (a) recognize different business-writing situations and apply the heuristics followed by good writers, (b) work effectively in a collaborative team environment, and (c) use computers applications (word processing, spreadsheet, graphics and communication) to generate business communications.

This chapter reports on a semester-long study that examined the experiences of these two instructors and 20 sophomore business students enrolled in the redesigned course. The more narrow focus is on the sociocultural aspects of this learner-centered instructional environment and the incorporation of computer technology to support the learning environment. Therefore, the experiences of the students participating in this study are examined in terms of (a) the patterns of collaboration in the writing process, (b) the intersubjectivity between students, (c) the instructional scaffolding and coaching provided by the teachers, and (d) the integration of technology into the learning environment. Before proceeding, however, it should be noted that these aspects of the environment were studied within the context of a larger study (Savery, 1996) that focused on the demonstration of student ownership for learning. Therefore, to set a context for this discussion, an explanation of the model of ownership for learning is provided followed by a detailed examination of the topics listed earlier.

MODEL OF OWNERSHIP FOR LEARNING

Most educators consider it important that students take ownership for their own learning. Langer and Applebee (1986) identified ownership as one of the five essential components of effective instruction. Honebein, Duffy, and Fishman (1993) claimed that ownership for learning is essential to the development of metacognitive and critical-thinking skills. Scardamalia and Bereiter (1991) argued that with ownership for learning (obtained through appropriate interactions in the zone of proximal development), students will have primary responsibility for noticing what is important, recognizing what must be learned to accomplish a given task, setting and evaluating criteria for understanding, and applying effective performance in the transfer environment. The concept of ownership has roots in self-regulation (Zimmerman & Schunk, 1989) in that it views learners as metacognitively, motivationally, and behaviorally proactive participants in their own learning process. The common elements are reflected in the model of ownership for learning (Fig. 5.1) developed for this study.

The terms in bold (e.g., cognitive and metacognitive factors) name the cluster of factors that are examined in each quadrant. The indicators or descriptors (i.e., self-monitoring) refer to observable student behaviors related to the cluster of factors. The learner-centered psychological principles described by McCombs (1993) provided the naming conventions used in the model and several of the behavioral indicators inserted in each quadrant. The *cognitive and metacognitive factors* affecting ownership are represented in the upper left quadrant, while the sociocultural factors are represented in the lower left quadrant labeled *personal and social factors*. The *affective factors* related to ownership are represented in the upper right quadrant whereas *individual differences* are represented in the lower right quadrant.

The personal and social factors are particularly important in the context of this chapter as they address the interpersonal aspects of learning. Vygotsky (1978) and others writing from a sociocultural perspective (Gallimore & Tharp, 1990; Rogoff, 1990, 1994; Tharp & Gallimore, 1988; Tudge, 1990;

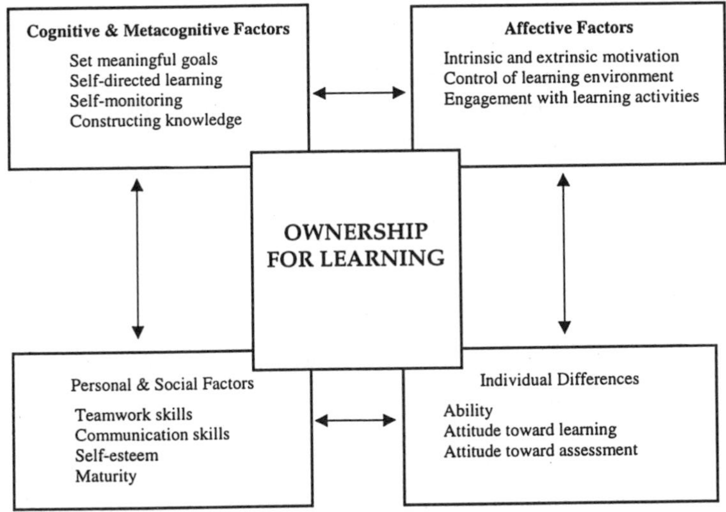

FIG. 5.1. Ownership for learning.

Wertsch, 1991) argue that the social milieu within which learning occurs has a significant influence on what is learned. (See chap. 2 of this volume for a more complete examination of sociocultural theory.) Based on the premise that knowledge is socially negotiated, the development of a learning community where ideas are discussed and understanding enriched (Cognition and Technology Group at Vanderbilt, 1991; Fosnot, 1989; Pea, 1993) becomes a critical component in the design of an effective learning environment (A. L. Brown & Palinscar, 1989; Lave & Wenger, 1991; Rogoff, 1990; Tudge, 1990). The design of learning communities may be fostered by the application of specific instructional principles (J. G. Brooks & M. G. Brooks, 1993; Duffy & Cunningham, 1996; Savery & Duffy, 1995). In this alternative format for the business communications course there was evidence that the teachers (a) anchored all learning activities to a larger task or problem, (b) designed an authentic task such that the task and the learning environment reflected the complexity of the environment students should be able to function in after instruction, (c) gave the learner ownership of the process used to develop a solution and supported the learner in developing ownership for the overall problem or task, (d) supported and challenged the learner's thinking while encouraging the testing of ideas against alternative views and contexts, and (e) provided learners with an opportunity for and support for reflection on both the content learned and the learning process.

Because the model of ownership for learning was intended as a theoretical framework for the research study, it was necessary to translate the model into a form that could be used to collect and collate evidence gathered in the study. The checklist (see Table 5.1) is intended as a tool for instructors to use to assess the level of ownership being demonstrated by their students. By observing and recording student behaviors on this form, teachers could begin to develop a pattern for each student indicating which cluster of factors might be helping or hindering the student to develop ownership for his or her own learning. Examples of contrasting behavioral indicators related to high versus low levels of ownership are provided in the Appendix.

TABLE 5.1
Ownership Checklist

Quadrant #1	*Cognitive & Metacognitive Factors*	
Indicators	*Examples of Student Behaviors*	*Observed Behaviors/Evidence*
Sets meaningful goals	Articulates reasons for taking course. Reflects on what has been learned and describes what they hope, want, or need to learn.	
Self-monitoring	Identifies gaps in understanding and role of self within group. Adapts to changes in environment.	
Self-directed	Actively seeks information to solve problems. Utilizes available learning resources. Considers alternative solutions.	
Constructs knowledge	Utilizes prior knowledge to understand new experiences. Applies course experiences to build new knowledge.	
Quadrant #2	*Affective Factors*	
Indicators	*Examples of Student Behaviors*	*Observed Behaviors/Evidence*
Balance between intrinsic-extrinsic motivation	Examples of flow experiences vs. teacher/other dependent behaviors. States reasons for taking course, doing tasks.	
Control of learning environment	Class time spent working on-task vs. off-task. Attendance and reports on tasks performed outside of class. Uses learning resources/tools.	
Engages with learning tasks	Indicates interest in content domain/problems, perceived relevance of course goals/content, expectations of success in domain and satisfaction with outcomes (rewards).	

(Continued)

TABLE 5.1
(Continued)

Quadrant #3	*Social/Personal Factors*	
Indicators	*Examples of Student Behaviors*	*Observed Behaviors/Evidence*
Collaborative teamwork, helps & tutors peers	Shares in all aspects of writing tasks. Teaches rather than just tells/shows. Willingly shares expertise. Supports the efforts of teammates.	
Leadership	Sets agendas, schedules meetings, assigns tasks, and holds teammates accountable. Leads by example, knowledge/skill, or personality.	
Effective communication	Listens to teammates/teachers. Works to ensure clear communications, avoids misunderstandings, offers tactful and constructive criticisms.	
Self-esteem	Demonstrates honest self-esteem vs. low self-esteem or a false sense of importance.	
Maturity	Accountable to self, team, and teacher. Accepts responsibility for results of individual and team tasks vs. blames others.	
Quadrant #4	*Individual Differences*	
Indicators	*Examples of Student Behaviors*	*Observed Behaviors/Evidence*
Ability	Success levels in other academic courses. Estimate performance relative to ability.	
Attitude toward learning	Accepts challenges, shows self-struggle to make content meaningful. Focuses on learning.	
Attitude toward assessment	Applies feedback on performance and other forms of assessment to learn/improve.	

This study subscribed to the multiple-case study design guidelines provided by Yin (1992) and used the following research methods: (a) participant observation of each team for 26 class sessions, (b) documentation including: forms completed by students, teacher-developed writing scenarios, quizzes, and course-grading sheets for individuals and teams, (c) rating surveys completed by individual students after each writing project (a.k.a. a department within the simulation), (d) interviews with each student at midcourse and during the final week of class, (e) two structured interviews with each teacher, and (f) in-class videotaping of each team during four consecutive classes (a complete project cycle). Taken as a complete set, the data collection strategies provided multiple perspectives on the learning experiences of individual students, student teams, and the course instructors.

Finally, it is important to note that the business communications course taught writing skills. There is a considerable body of literature supporting the notion that the act of writing, particularly collaborative writing (Collins, J. S. Brown, & Newman, 1989; Daiute, 1986; Scardamalia & Bereiter, 1987), influences the development of cognitive and metacognitive skills (Bidwell-Bowles, P. Johnson, & Brehe, 1987; Bonk & Reynolds, 1992; Caccamise, 1987; Hayes & Flower, 1983). Thus, the combination of content domain and the instructional approaches provides a rich classroom environment within which to examine these important learning issues.

In the sections that follow, we examine the learning environment, the patterns of collaboration in the writing process, the intersubjectivity between students, the instructional scaffolding and coaching provided by the teachers, and the integration of technology into the writing process within this learning environment.

WHAT WAS THE LEARNING ENVIRONMENT LIKE?

On Day 1 of the course, Weston and McCloud welcomed the students and stated very clearly that there would be no lectures, that each student was expected to be mature, responsible, and self-directed in their learning, and that much of their grade depended on collaborative teamwork. They encouraged any students who felt they lacked the maturity to be responsible learners, or felt uncomfortable with the collaborative team approach to transfer to a lecture-based section of the course as soon as possible. They took turns explaining how the course would be run like a business and how business criteria for effective correspondence would be used consistently. Thus, students were "hired" into Starr Corporation and given a detailed Employee Handbook (which effectively functioned as the course syllabus) containing a history of the corporation, the organizational structure, clearly stated expectations for all employees (course objectives), as well as the policies and procedures to be followed by all employees. Starr Corporation was an instructional simulation developed by the teachers to provide a business context for the writing assignments and an organizational framework for the course.

The new employees were offered training on the word processor, spreadsheet, graphics, and communication programs to be used in their new jobs. Students with acceptable skill levels could sign a waiver and skip the training sessions. External instructors provided the skills-based training during Days 2, 3, and 4 of the course. On Day 5, the teachers assigned students to their teams for the rest of the semester and gave each team a nongraded training unit to complete. On Day 6, they reviewed the training unit with the teams, rewarded accomplishments, and set expectations for high standards on the next assignments. On Day 7, the student teams began their rotation through the various departments within Starr Corporation and received their first set of writing assignments expressed as problem situations.

During the semester, student teams rotated through four 2-week-long departments (Human Resources, Marketing, Accounting, and Purchasing) and one 4-week-long department (Operations) according to a master schedule created by the teachers. Both teachers were familiar with all the writing assignments, but coached and graded separately to ensure consistency between teams and classes. Thus, Weston was the teacher/coach, resource person, and evaluator for all student teams working in the Purchasing and Human Resources departments, whereas McCloud fulfilled the same responsibilities for teams in the Marketing and Accounting departments. The primary teacher resource for each team was determined by the departmental rotation, not the room assignment. Teachers moved constantly between the adjoining computer labs to help the teams that had rotated into their departmental responsibility area. In contrast, when a team rotated into the Operations Department, the teacher in their assigned home lab became their mentor during the 4 weeks allocated for the assignment. This teacher was also the person to whom they presented their written and oral reports.

The 20 sophomores volunteering for this study were representative of the 200 students enrolled in the course. Fourteen students were male and 6 students were female. Nineteen students were White and 1 was African American. All 20 students passed the course and each of the four teams remained intact for the complete semester. One volunteer team[1] from each of the four classes was chosen for this study based on their willingness to participate, their group composition, and the computer lab in which they were physically present for the semester: two teams from Weston's home lab, and two teams from McCloud's. Three of the four teams had the same gender composition, two female students and three male students. The fourth team had five male students.

The semester during which the study took place was the fourth time Weston and McCloud had team taught their alternative format of business communications course and they were well prepared with multiple sets of problem situations for each department. New problem situations drawn from articles in business journals/newspapers were added each semester and problem situations from previous semesters were modified to increase or decrease the level of difficulty based on past student performance. The following assignment for the Human Resources department illustrates the writing situations presented to the student teams:

---

[1]No teams in the 8:00 AM class volunteered, so one team in the class was asked directly for their participation.

> You are employees of the Human Resources Department of Starr Services, a subsidiary of Starr Corporation. You will work in this department for two weeks. During this two-week period, you are to write memos and letters, submit a payroll report to Accounting, and summarize a *Wall Street Journal* (*WSJ*) article.
>
> *Writing Assignments:* Here is a summary of a report you received this morning.
>
> [Deleted were details of research reports on the hazards of smoking cigarettes]
>
> After reading these statistics about smoking, you decide to write a memo to Starr Corporation President Miles Kanne suggesting a no-smoking policy for Starr's buildings. *Write this memo.*
>
> Mr. Kanne agrees with your suggestion and wants Starr to be smoke free. *Write a memo to your employees* announcing the new policy and explaining the reasons for it. Use any of the previous information that would make a more effective memo. Remember that some of your employees will be unhappy with this decision, so use your persuasive writing techniques to emphasize the reasons for this policy.
>
> As Human Resources Manager, you have interviewed William Sears and Alicia Stewart, two applicants for the same position. It's a difficult decision because you were impressed by both candidates. You decide to offer the job to Alicia because her work experience more nearly matches the requirements of the job. *Write a letter to Alicia offering her the job.* Be sure to identify the position, the salary, and the starting date.
>
> In addition, you want to send a tactful letter to the other applicant, William. While William didn't have quite the right experience for this job, you were impressed with his energy and motivation. There are no other openings at the company right now, but you may want to hire him for another position in the future. *Write a letter explaining to William that he didn't get the job.*

The team in this Human Resources Department wrote a memo to a superior within the organization, a general memo to all employees, a good news letter to one job applicant, and a bad news letter to the other applicant. Regardless of the department the student teams worked in, they would encounter variations on the four basic types of letter-writing situations: good news, bad news, persuasive, and routine. The teachers deliberately gave students an opportunity to become expert with these four most frequently used types of business correspondence in significantly different contexts.

In theory, each student would learn each of the four letter types by authoring or coauthoring at least one of each type, and by reviewing or critiquing the work of teammates. By the end of the course, each student should have written or edited at least four examples of each type of business correspondence. In practice, the extrinsically motivated students often chose to repeat a letter type in hopes of improving their grade or expending less effort. The intrinsically motivated, self-directed learners chose a different writing situation each time to expand their understanding of all the letter types. How students selected their writing assignments was often an indicator of their cognitive/metacognitive awareness and their source of motivation.

The assessment/grading criteria were clearly described in the employee handbook and verbally reinforced by the teachers. As Weston said, "The important thing is that each of you shares in each of the documents your team produces. You will share the grade, so you should share the product. I don't want you to wait until after the grade to say I should have put that in." Students were expected to write at a level that would be acceptable for authentic business communications. Thus, a letter was graded superior, acceptable, or not acceptable. Team members shared the grade for group work and were expected to participate fully to ensure that the best quality of writing was produced.

The 60% of the individual grade based on group work was balanced by 40% for individual scores, earned through peer evaluations (15%), attendance (10%), exams (10%), and *Wall Street Journal* (*WSJ*) article summaries (5%). Students completed three peer evaluation forms over the semester. The teachers tabulated the scores and informed students with very high scores or very low scores of their peer approval rating. The final exam was a timed writing situation similar to the three spot quizzes, but weighted more heavily. The *WSJ* article summary task required students to read an article supplied with each department folder, write a concise summary, and send it via electronic mail (E-mail) to the teacher. Graded assignments and tests were returned to the students in a timely fashion, that is, during the next class session.

All classes were held in two interconnected computer labs each equipped with 25 networked desktop computers that had been reserved for this course for the entire semester. Students were encouraged to treat the computer lab as an office and to act as they would in a work environment. Teams typically found an area in the lab that became their self-designated work area. As in most work environments, there was time for socializing. Students talked about other courses, relationships with boyfriends or girlfriends, holiday plans, sports events, recent adventures, and a multitude of other topics. The learning environment was relaxed, and, except during individualized testing (spot quizzes), there was a constant hum of multiple conversations (both on- and off-task) that was pleasant and never disruptive. Students were very effective at tuning out extraneous noise, concentrating on their writing assignments, and using their time in the computer lab efficiently. In particular, students pressed for time with full course loads and part-time jobs expressed their appreciation at being able to complete their writing assignments during class time. Many teams stayed on-task during class to complete assignments and also encouraged the less well organized members of their team to do the same. This produced more on-task behaviors, use of available resources (e.g., teachers, textbooks, resource books), discussion between team members, and helping behaviors.

The use of this computer lab as the scene for most class activities encouraged student social interaction and negotiation of meaning. It was here in the computer lab that students faced each other and debated the problem situations, possible solutions, sought information and references from textbooks and other sources, and eventually produced a written solution. Preliminary drafts and the results of brainstorming activities could be printed out for further team discussion, which enabled this electronic text space to function as a permanent record of team productivity and choices. Even stand-alone electronic writing tools, therefore, can play a significant role in supporting and elevating the level of classroom discourse and learning. Although many educators are becoming excited about the possibilities of overcoming geographic and time constraints through various electronic conferencing and collaborative devices, this study points out that exciting electronic collaboration can take place among small teams of students who are not physically distant nor time independent.

Although it was not directly apparent to the students, this learning environment was well planned and highly structured, particularly in the design and implementation of projects (Blumenfeld et al., 1991) that were both challenging and motivating. It reflected the teachers' stated intention of helping students to become more independent, responsible, and self-directed or, as Weston described it, "doing their own reading, own thinking, and not always asking the teacher for answers." Recall that the intended learning outcomes addressed (a) effecient business writing, (b) effective collaborative teamwork, and (c) productive use of computer applications. These three goals were realized in the organization of the course content and the design of the learning environment.

PATTERNS OF COLLABORATION IN THE WRITING PROCESS

The teachers used collaborative learning groups as one strategy for achieving a community of learners (Cohen, 1994; D. W. Johnson & R. T. Johnson, 1975, 1990; Kagan, 1992; Pea, 1993). Students provided biographical information and a self-report on current strengths in selected areas by completing an employee profile form on Day 1. Using these data and their experience, Weston and McCloud assigned students to teams based on gender (two female students per team or none), amount of part-time work by members on the same team, associations (separate sorority sisters and/or fraternity brothers), computer expertise (one expert as team resource), and at least one team member who was willing to take a leadership role. Their stated intent was to create teams with the best chance of being successful.

The decision to use five-person teams was entirely pragmatic. Each course section had 25 students and that divided evenly into five teams of five persons each. The Starr Corporation (simulation) was organized into five departments (analogous to instructional modules) and, because each department contained four writing assignments, teams with five members could cover for absent members and the extra person could collaborate on the more challenging assignment. Of the 40 teams in the four classes, only three teams experienced problems requiring direct teacher intervention, and in all cases the problems were caused by external events (two illness, two withdrawal, and one suspension).

The level of collaboration on each team was indicated by the manner in which they handled their writing assignments. Saunders (1989) described a range of interaction structures (e.g., completely cooperative, cooperative, helping obligatory, and helping permitted) that, combined with the tasks assigned (e.g., planning, composing, reviewing, and correcting), produced four primary categories of collaborative writing activities: *cowriting*, *copublishing*, *coresponding*, and *coediting*. In Saunders' hierarchy, cowriting is the most collaborative and coediting the least collaborative. The four teams studied in this learning environment demonstrated the following patterns.

Cowriting involved a completely cooperative interaction structure during all stages of the writing process, but was the least frequently demonstrated pattern of writing in this environment. Cowriting interactions were more apparent at the beginning of the course, possibly because students were unsure how to proceed and preferred to move together into the unknown. The question of document ownership was not a significant issue during the first writing assignments. To illustrate, the 9:30 AM team members worked together to plan the writing assignments in their first department. Mike wrote a draft memo and presented it to his teammates during the next class. Linda, a better typist, sat at the keyboard while the other three team members clustered around her and made suggestions for changes to Mike's draft concerning the format, that is, spaces between headings, verb tense, grammar, and specific word choices. This first memo took 45 minutes to rewrite collaboratively and when the final copy was printed, the team gave a genuine cheer and applauded their efforts. However, this was the only assignment completed in this fashion. Subsequent assignments used a copublishing or coediting strategy.

Also during the first writing assignment, four team members of the 11:15 AM team sat together to help a teammate write a good news letter. One student typed the brainstorms offered by the group members, but when the group reached an impasse, individuals returned to their separate tasks leaving completion of a final draft to the original author. During Week 10 of the semester, Susan and Janet on the 1:00 PM team worked together to plan and edit a memo, but they did not actually cowrite the document. Susan typed a first draft of their negotiated content, while Janet created a graphic to be included in the memo. Janet edited and commented on Susan's draft and they made revisions together. As a counterexample, Bob on the 8:00 AM team always found a partner for his writing assignments. However, Bob's contributions were minimal and in all cases his partner did the majority of the thinking, researching, and writing. Bob was definitely not a cowriter, and the level of interaction was decidedly not collaborative.

Copublishing stipulates that team members work together to develop a collective document, share ownership and responsibility for the collective document, and yet retain personal ownership of their individual contribution. This pattern was demonstrated by all four teams, but *only* during rotation in the Operations Department. Team members negotiated individual assignments related to the larger document, gathered their research materials, wrote their individual section, and then combined their individual sections within the group document. I believe one reason for the success of the Operations project as a learning activity was the high degree of goal and resource interdependence (D. W. Johnson & R. T. Johnson, 1990) that forced teammates to work together to complete the larger task.

Coresponding was a pattern in which students did not share ownership for the texts they planned and composed individually, but were expected to help each other with the review process. This was the dominant form of collaborative writing for assignments in any department other than Operations. Coresponding was particularly evident during the second half of the semester as student teams began to repeat familiar types of business correspondence (i.e., the second good news letter). On surveys completed after each department, 96% of the students stated that they divided the assignments so that individuals could write a first draft, then have the group (or teachers) help with the revisions.

Coediting was a pattern of collaboration with the sole purpose of correcting mechanical errors rather than errors in content or meaning. All teams included a proofreading step in their writing activities, although in practice, the best grammarian on the team took the lead in performing this task. Team members weak in grammar and mechanics benefited from comments and corrections made to their work, but provided minimal corrective feedback on the work of their teammates.

INTERSUBJECTIVITY BETWEEN STUDENTS

In analyzing the experiences of these teams, it became apparent that more successful teams were aware of and concerned with each other's lives outside of the classroom setting. The more familiar the team members were with each other as individuals with cares and concerns, and likes and dislikes, the better able they were to relate to the individual as a team member. It also became apparent that teams functioned more effectively when there was a clear group leader. It must be pointed out, however, that these 20 sophomore students were assigned to collaborative teams with little or no training in team dynamics, or how to operate effectively as a group. The relationships that developed between individuals on each team represent a broad range of intersubjectivity that defined the overall functioning/personality of the team. Space restrictions make it difficult to adequately describe the experiences of all 20 students with the proper degree of rich detail. As an alternative, selected comments by students on the same team during their end of the semester interviews are juxtaposed to demonstrate these differences in their experiences.

The 9:30 AM team developed a mutual support group wherein the team members accepted that they had to work together and made a pact to cooperate and act responsibly. This decision was based on discussions between team members and the realization that the points earned through the peer evaluations affected each individual's grades so cooperation benefited everyone. Leadership was shared by all members of the team with the two female students, Linda and Mary, providing most of the logistical organization and often holding the three male students accountable for task completion. There was a good balance of abilities, an equal sharing of work responsibilities, a positive work ethic, and no serious personality conflicts. Attendance in class was high (95%) and they gave each other the highest possible scores on the peer evaluation forms.

Team camaraderie was developed through constant social chatter while working intently on their writing tasks. Members of this team often crowded together (were physically close regardless of gender) when working at the computer and changed writing partners frequently. There were frequent examples of team members helping each other out with troublesome writing tasks, inquiring about the health of a team member, or offering to do something extra for the group. These behaviors were evident in other groups, particularly the 11:15 AM team, but within this 9:30 AM team, the frequency of demonstrations of concern, consideration, and helpfulness was consistently high. This high level of intersubjectivity helped them achieve course goals and personal goals. All five team members received an A– for the course, although Bert demonstrated a low level of ownership for learning because of his dependency on the teacher and his teammates to do his thinking for him.

The 8:00 AM team mirrored the 9:30 AM team with the same gender combination and rotation schedule through Starr Corporation departments. However, their experience was completely opposite. Personality differences, uneven ability levels, a negative attitude toward the content, a cynical attitude toward education, and a poor work ethic contributed to the group's lack of success. The team was minimally cooperative with each member having as few interactions with other team members as possible. Bill attempted to lead and organize but was constantly thwarted by the negative attitude of Nash, the laziness of Bob, and the apathy of the two female team members.

This team had the lowest attendance in class of the four teams studied at 92.5% and they consistently rated each other poorly on the peer evaluation forms. They were the least talkative team and maintained their physical distance from each other. There was no discussion of the problem scenarios prior to writing, and no evidence of team members holding each other accountable for completion of tasks. Where the 9:30 AM team had individuals motivated to succeed, the 8:00 AM team had individuals motivated to just get by with the least amount of effort required. Bob's comment that follows is a poignant example of this undergraduate apathy. Bill received a B+ and the others a B or B– grade. Bill demonstrated a moderate level of ownership, but the rest of the team demonstrated a low level of ownership for learning. During their exit interviews, Bill and Bob commented as follows:

> Bill said:
> [I like this format because] there's not really anybody standing over you all the time. Sure they give you a deadline, but you've gotta when you're in your own group you decide what you're doing, how you're gonna go about and do it, and I just feel you learn it a little better because you're controlling it. Maybe it's just me but, we come in here and we're expected to write something every day, which is good. I'd rather get in and do things than sit back and have someone tell me how to do it. I'd rather try it for myself.

> Bob said:
> Like, she [my teacher] just let us be, like free. She lets us do what we want. Like, I mean she took attendance, but that's about it. She talked with us maybe five minutes a day. She didn't like, lecture the whole class or anything. I don't know [if I'd recommend this course] . . . it would depend like on what kind of student they were. If they were an A student I would say take it by yourself [lecture]. But if you're a B or C student, I'd say take it [this way]. I think it's really hard to get an A, but it's really easy to get like a B or high C.

The entire 1:00 PM team worked collaboratively on the first two projects but soon developed a pattern wherein four team members worked together, but the fifth team member was excluded. Roger and Susan tended to lead the other team members. Steve who had difficulties working in a team setting became an outcast within the group. This team had a 95% attendance rate and received the highest overall academic grades of the four teams studied: four A's and a B+. However, there was a wide range in the peer evaluations as team members struck out at each other through this medium. Roger and Steve both contributed to the success of their team's Operations report but had very different perceptions of that experience. As illustrated in the following, Roger was emotionally involved with the project, excited, and motivated. In contrast, Steve maintained an intellectual and emotional distance from the learning tasks and his teammates.

> Roger said:
> Operations was totally like that [engrossing] . . . It was almost like you forgot you were doing it for a class, you just wanted to get this project done and we had all these ideas floating around in your head and we kept revising it, and going over it making sure everything was perfect and . . . it was kinda neat. That doesn't happen to me very often in these classes. Usually I'm trying to get the work done, learn what I can, and get good grades.

> Steve said:
> I wasn't really that proud of [the Operations project] . . . I did my part, but in the group setting, I did not feel that it was more of mine . . . Like for me, group projects are just a lot harder. Not that I'm a loner, but one of the things I do is work by myself . . . personally, I take more pride in that Accounting test where I studied for it and I did this, this, and this and I got an A on it. Not that you don't want to work with the team but, for me at least it's self-satisfaction.

The five male students on the 11:15 AM team were excited to be part of the study and were highly verbal about their experiences in the course. They developed a social club approach wherein team members formed friendships, had a good time in class, but often did less than expected on the course assignments. Their experience was unique because of the extremes within the group. Sam was a strong and capable leader, whereas Mitch stubbornly refused to adapt to a learner-centered approach. Carl demonstrated his lack of maturity by blaming his poor grades on a perceived gender bias by the two female instructors. Although others on the team listened to his complaints, none actively supported that position. Grades ranged among an A–, three B's, and a C. Poignant examples of the differences between Sam and Mitch in the areas of self-regulation, motivation, collaboration, attitude toward learning, and ownership for learning were provided during their exit interviews.

> Sam said:
> I think the course is very relevant, because [from] what everybody says, corporations and people who come visit the university, they say that group and teamwork is *the* key to success now and [particularly] working in teams where you just get thrown together. I think it's a good alternative to other classes where you just sit and get lectured. This is more hands-on, more doing, more experiencing rather than reading how its supposed to be which I think is good. I think with this class it's more of a self-struggle to learn because we're not getting lectured to. We have to read the book ourselves, we have to read the examples ourselves, we have to synthesize the letters ourselves . . . We have to

read and we have to prepare and we have to know what we're doing. It's more of a struggle . . . I mean, if you want to learn anything you've got to do it yourself. You can't expect to go to class, get notes and just read those notes. You have to do it yourself, so I think it's very focused on me, and my learning how to do these things.

Mitch said:
I don't think this course is particularly relevant . . . some of the writing assignments are a little far-fetched in my opinion . . . I think more than any other class, this class is pretty much self-taught. I mean, there really isn't that much instruction per se, which irritates me to some extent, and I think I wrote this on the evaluation of the class. There's a certain aspect of college right, that you come and you pay a lot of money for a professor to teach you something and you get a class like this where you're really not taught anything. I mean, you buy an expensive book and [you know] they pass out assignments and it's pretty much all self-taught in my opinion. To that extent it irritates me a little bit because you know, the teachers really don't do that much instruction which I'd like to see a little bit more because you know, sure they can make bad comments and . . . some of their comments I don't really agree with and they never get to say why they grade the way they do and. . . . So, I mean they don't really teach what they're correcting, so I don't understand how they expect us to really understand some of the things that we're doing wrong when they've never taught it correctly to begin with.

Sam and Mitch had strikingly different experiences of the course. Sam accepted responsibility for his own learning, made an effort to improve his understanding of the domain, and developed a high level of intersubjectivity with each of his teammates. Sam recognized and praised the positive contributions of each team member and helped maintain an emotional stability within the group. For example, as Marty was grousing about the poor grade on the Operations project, Sam reached over, put his arm around his shoulders, and said in a loud voice, "Marty don't leave us now! We need ya!" Marty was mollified and his usual good humor resurfaced. In contrast, Mitch did not form friendships with his teammates, often missed the first day in a new department, and made minimal efforts to learn new skills. He expected to be told what he needed to know and resented the lack of direct instruction by the teachers. He continually discounted feedback and assessment by the teachers, preferring to rely on his own "superior" experience.

In general, there were very high levels of intersubjectivity between students. The learning environment afforded the students an opportunity to debate and discuss their interpretations of the problem scenarios and the appropriate writing solutions. This negotiation generated a great deal of verbal discussion, pointing at screen displays, marking of drafts, and references to textbooks and other authorities as the final product was negotiated. It was evident throughout the semester that the high degree of goal interdependence and resource interdependence (D. W. Johnson & R. T. Johnson,

1990), though related to the shared grade for team assignments, appears also to have been the preferred way to complete tasks.

INSTRUCTIONAL SCAFFOLDING AND COACHING

Both instructors were aware of the need to support students as they developed self-directed learning skills, so for the first writing project they provided extensive coaching and mentoring and occasionally direct instruction. Teams were encouraged to use a four-stage writing process—plan, write, revise, and edit—explicitly taught in the nongraded training unit. In the first department, both teachers stressed that the goal for the team their first day was to discuss the writing situations as a group and plan how they would structure their letters or memos. For the remainder of the session, they met with individual teams to discuss their writing assignments.

When the teachers met with the team, students asked questions that revealed their thinking about the problem. Within the context of the specific problem, the teachers provided both cognitive structuring and global questioning strategies. These included the heuristics of effective writers, such as: What is your primary purpose? What is your secondary purpose? Who is your audience/reader? What do they need to do with this information? Is the direct or indirect approach appropriate in this situation? The teachers effectively utilized all six means of assistance identified by Gallimore and Tharp (1990) as appropriate with their students. The six means of assistance were (a) modeling—offering behavior for imitation, (b) contingency management—rewarding desired behaviors while controlling undesirable behaviors, (c) feeding back—responding to performance in relation to a given set of criteria, (d) instructing—direct teaching/telling and assigning of tasks, (e) questioning—stimulating thinking and provoking creations by the student, and (f) cognitive structuring—helping the learner organize raw experience by providing a structure for thinking/acting. As Bonk and Cunningham (chap. 2 of this volume) point out, a seventh means of assistance, cognitive task structuring, has been added to the other six, to address relevant task-related scaffolding.

The teachers responded with factual answers (instructing) where appropriate (e.g., use a full colon in a formal letter or put two spaces below the address), questioning (who, why, when, etc.), and feeding back (grades and comments on every project and test). They also modeled the thinking of an expert writer and verbalized the heuristics they used, or would use, in the context of the problem to which the students were responding. They provided cognitive structuring at the start of each writing assignment through their initial discussions with the teams, and during the reviews of draft letters. Through probing questions, and occasionally direct instruction, they helped students resolve difficulties and/or referred them to specific sections in the textbook for additional information. Contingency management (class control) was seldom required because the design of the learning environment placed responsibility for self-directed learning on each student and self-policing of negative behaviors (absenteeism, failure to complete assigned tasks) on each team.

In subsequent class sessions the teachers reviewed and commented on initial drafts prepared by individuals, but encouraged students to use their teammates as their first source of information and assistance. As the semester progressed, and most sharply after the midterm break, the teachers reduced their level of support for the teams and insisted that team members became more self-directed, independent, and responsible. This was done openly and the teams where told what to expect. Students that asked for teacher support without using the available resources, and particularly their teammates, returned to their teams with their questions unanswered. Student reaction to this nonlecture approach was mixed. Students with a high degree of teacher dependency were resentful and tried many different tactics to get the teacher to answer their questions or confirm that they had it right. Students on teams where there was minimal collaboration relied more heavily on the teacher for guidance and support. Students that were more self-directed in their learning and comfortable with the course format and content adapted to the reduction in teacher support with little or no difficulty.

Both teachers frankly admitted that moving between groups and responding to context specific questions could be very challenging. However, they both found this format more rewarding than responding to the same questions asked repeatedly by students in a large class working on the same assignment. The 5 to 10 minutes per class that a teacher spent with an individual team was highly focused and contextualized. Consequently, students were provided with the assistance that they needed as they moved from novice to more expert writers.

INTEGRATION OF TECHNOLOGY IN THE WRITING PROCESS

McCloud commented that because students would use computers regularly in their jobs, they should learn to use them effectively in class. Thus, students were expected to use the computers in the labs as office productivity tools to originate their correspondence and conduct research (library, Internet). The intensive workshops on software applications ensured that all students had the necessary entry-level skills with each application, and the problem situations were designed so that students needed to use the word processor, spreadsheet, and graphic programs to complete the writing assignments. For example, in the Accounting Department the team prepared a payroll report (spreadsheet) for the entire class; in the Marketing Department the team prepared a newsletter incorporating multiple columns and graphics; and in the Operations department the team produced a fully indexed report (50+ pages) and developed a presentation incorporating overheads created with the graphics program.

Unfortunately, some students practiced superficial rather than deep learning and learned only the specific parts of the software application needed to accomplish the given task. If the task were to write a memo, they would copy an existing memo, reuse the format, and insert new content. Although this was efficient under certain conditions, if the conditions changed, they were easily confused because their understanding was incomplete. Team members with more developed skills usually shared their knowledge with their teammates through peer tutoring. In cases where the team lacked expertise, one or more members would volunteer to learn the necessary procedures to complete the assignment. On occasion, this meant asking a friend from another team for assistance. The teachers encouraged this information seeking, as it was similar to what employees do on the job. And because the teachers were not computer experts, they utilized the technical support staff assigned to the labs to assist students having mechanical or network problems, thereby further modeling the use of external resources. Of the 20 students in the study group, only 2 made no effort to learn the applications and passively let their teammates perform tasks for them. The majority of students learned new skills and significantly improved their level of expertise with the application programs.

During the initial stages of composing their letters and memos, students often invited a teammate to view the draft on screen. Changes and revisions were then incorporated directly into the draft. Later in the process, the finished draft was printed out with letterhead and shared with teammates for further editing and feedback. The computing environment also provided tools that students used to improve their performance including application specific "help" systems, and, in the word processor, the spell-checker, thesaurus, and grammar-checker programs. Student use of these tools was very uneven. One or two members of a team would use the tools regularly, whereas other team members would totally ignore them. During the Operations project, all teams used the spell-checker program because various authors were contributing to the combined document. Also, in the Operations project, there was extensive use of the presentation software (e.g., PowerPoint and Freelance Graphics) by student teams to enhance as well as organize their presentations.

As noted earlier, students wrote summaries of *Wall Street Journal* articles and E-mailed their summaries to the teacher. Students also E-mailed their teammates to inform them of their whereabouts if they were ill or away from class. The online resources, library, and Web browsers were used by most students for class assignments and also for entertainment during free time. When viewed as a complete environment, it is evident that computer technology was an important and well-integrated aspect of this course, and that students used the technology to increase their effectiveness in both individual and collaborative writing tasks.

SUMMARY OF OWNERSHIP FOR LEARNING

Student comments collected during interviews, self-reports from surveys, academic achievements, and observations of classroom behaviors were consolidated to create an ownership profile for each participating student based on the four quadrants of the model and the indicators in each quadrant. Of these 20 students, 6 demonstrated a high of ownership for learning, 7 a moderate level, and 7 a low level of ownership for learning, indicating a fairly normal distribution of this characteristic. In contrast, final grades in the course (11 A's, 8 B's, and 1 C) were skewed to the high end of a normal distribution.

Students identified as having high ownership demonstrated frequent, positive behaviors in each quadrant, whereas students with low ownership consistently demonstrated more negative behaviors in each quadrant. Students demonstrating high ownership were consistently more self-directed and teacher-independent than students demonstrating low ownership, who were more likely to rely on the teacher as an authority. Students who demonstrated high ownership for learning struggled with the problems and issues in the domain of business communications. For instance, high-ownership students attempted to integrate their experiences in the course with their prior knowledge in order to perceive meaningful relationships and become competent in the domain. These students were predominantly motivated by an intrinsic desire to master the content for their own purposes as preparation for a future career in business. They were completely cognizant of the relationship between good grades and acceptance into the School of Business, but viewed grades as a necessary evil rather than as the proof of their knowledge or the reason for taking the course.

The seven students who demonstrated low ownership trivialized the problems and issues in the domain. They commented that they selected this course format because it was rumored to be easier and less work. Their goal was to pass the course so they would be accepted into the School of Business: Learning valuable skills in the course was secondary.

The seven students classified as having moderate ownership were usually aware that they needed to be more responsible and self-directed in their learning, yet they continued to want large amounts of direct instruction and teacher support. Thus, their behaviors indicated both high and low levels of ownership at various times during the semester. They struggled to make the transition from a teacher-centered to a learner-centered instructional environment and would possibly benefit greatly from instructional interventions that could support them as they learned to be more self-directed and responsible. Although the current criteria were effective at sorting the behaviors demonstrated by these students into the four quadrants of the model of ownership for learning, additional refinement is required to determine the relative importance of each quadrant on the development of ownership.

SUMMARY OF COMPUTER-SUPPORTED COLLABORATIVE WRITING

Over a series of curriculum redesign efforts, these teachers had designed a problem-based learning situation rich in electronic as well as live collaborative writing.[2] The learning environment resulting from their efforts provided an exciting opportunity to examine and evaluate learning issues, such as problem ownership, self-regulatory behaviors, collaborative learning, building intersubjectivity, and the incorporation of technology in support of learning. This course set out (overtly) to develop a set of skills and knowledge related to the writing of properly formatted, concise, clear, and effective business communication. The course also set out (less overtly) to increase the level of self-directed learning, self-regulation, and teacher independence of these undergraduate students. Through the design of this learner-centered instructional environment, the teachers were able to help improve the writing skills of all 20 study participants while simultaneously enhancing the self-regulated learning skills of at least 13 students as demonstrated by their level of ownership for learning.

It is significant, but not surprising, that the majority of these undergraduate students adapted well to this learner-centered environment. Many students commented that they appreciated being treated as responsible adults, where they were encouraged to discuss their writing situations, collaborate with a peer, share their knowledge, and negotiate a meaningful response to the problem situations. They further commented that the course had significantly less busywork than most courses, provided extensive focused mentoring by an experienced expert in the field, and provided an environment that rewarded the efficient use of class time.

Although this study focused more on issues of ownership for learning and self-regulatory behaviors, student collaborative writing and problem solving

---

[2]This course was revisited a year after the study was completed. Teams in the Operations Department project were now required to create a Web page to organize information about their company and link to the Starr Corporation intranet.

was structured around electronic tools and teamwork. These electronic venues provide insight into how collaboration and ownership are fostered in face-to-face team settings within the parameters of various technology supports and resources materials. The four learning teams were studied by directly observing their social interaction patterns as well as through video- and audiotape replays of such, rather than using electronic dialogue transcripts as have other studies in this volume. As such, it breaks new ground on the discourse of electronic collaboration, while posing new questions about how to foster learner-centered instruction within a technology-rich environment.

It is apparent that even simple word-processing tools can offer powerful frameworks for electronic collaboration. There is a need for additional qualitative and quantitative probing in these environments, thereby adding to the residue of what we now understand about how students acquire and maintain their sense of learning ownership. Although this researcher was fortunate to find this undergraduate course ripe for qualitative and quantitative analyses, there are undoubtedly thousands of situations in K–12 and higher education classrooms that would display similar success stories if they were examined in more detail.

APPENDIX

Contrasting the Behavioral Indicators in Each Quadrant

High-Ownership Characteristics	*Low-Ownership Characteristics*
Cognitive/Metacognitive Factors	
Students set personally meaningful goals.	Students took course because it was required and did assignments to please teacher.
Practiced self-regulation, self-monitoring, self-directed learning, and reflection. Applied higher order thinking skills to solve problems.	Practiced limited cognitive and metacognitive behaviors and engaged in minimal reflection. Matched new situations to previous examples rather than applying higher order thinking skills and problem-solving skills.
Actively constructed knowledge and integrated prior knowledge.	Treated content domain as separate from prior experience.
Affective Factors	
Intrinsic motivation (aware of grades, but not obsessed).	Extrinsic motivation (focus on grades and passing course).
Took control of learning environment—used class time and available resources effectively, completed assignments with time for revision/reflection.	Limited control of learning environment—ineffective time/resource management, hurried to complete assignments at last minute.

(Continued)

APPENDIX
(Continued)

High-Ownership Characteristics	*Low-Ownership Characteristics*
Enjoyed appropriately challenging and realistic problem situations.	Often nonreflectively chose to repeat prior, superficial behaviors. Complained of situations being unrealistic.
Social and Personal Factors	
Worked on tasks both independently and collaboratively.	Worked independently. Provided minimal feedback to peers.
Voluntarily shared expertise with teammates (often effective as peer tutors). Asked teammates for help as needed.	Shared expertise with teammates (when asked). Often told rather than taught. Asked teacher for help, rather than peers.
Demonstrated mature, responsible, considerate behavior toward teammates and instructors.	Demonstrated immature, irresponsible, inconsiderate behavior and often blamed others for problems (whined/complained frequently).
Self-confident, but not arrogant (no low self-esteem problems).	Evidence of low self-esteem expressed as arrogance, anger, or superiority attitude.
Individual Differences	
Demonstrated a positive attitude toward learning, i.e., recognized need and value of content domain. Directed efforts to acquire content knowledge/skill.	Demonstrated a negative attitude toward learning, i.e., discounted relevance of domain and failed to master content domain.
Demonstrated a positive attitude toward assessment, i.e., used assessment as feedback to improve performance.	Demonstrated a negative attitude toward assessment, i.e., failed to utilize feedback to improve performance.

REFERENCES

Bidwell-Bowles, L., Johnson, P., & Brehe, S. (1987). Composing and computers: Case studies of experienced writers. In A. Matsuhashi (Ed.), *Writing in real time: Modeling production processes* (pp. 81–107). Norwood, NJ: Ablex.

Blumenfeld, P. C., Soloway, E., Marx, R. W., Krajcik, J. S., Guzdial, M., & Palinscar, A. (1991). Motivating project-based learning: Sustaining the doing, supporting the learning. *Educational Psychologist, 26*(3/4), 369–398.

Bonk, C. J., & Reynolds, T. H. (1992). Early adolescent composing in a generative-evaluative computerized prompting framework. *Journal of Computers in Human Behavior, 8*(1), 39–62.

Brooks, J. G., & Brooks, M. G. (1993). *In search of understanding: The case for constructivist classrooms.* Alexandria, VA: Association for Supervision and Curriculum Development.

Brown, A. L., & Palinscar, A. S. (1989). Guided cooperative learning and individual knowledge acquisition. In L. Resnick (Ed.), *Knowing, learning, and instruction: Essays in honor of Robert Glaser* (pp. 393–451). Hillsdale, NJ: Lawrence Erlbaum Associates.

Caccamise, D. J. (1987). Idea generation in writing. In A. Matsuhashi (Ed.), *Writing in real time: Modeling production processes* (pp. 224–253). Norwood, NJ: Ablex.

Cognition and Technology Group at Vanderbilt. (1992). Technology and the design of generative learning environments. *Educational Technology, 31*(5), 34–40.

Cohen, E. (1994). Restructuring the classroom: Conditions for productive small groups. *Review of Educational Research*, *64*, 1–35.

Collins, A., Brown, J. S., & Newman, S. E. (1989). Cognitive apprenticeship: Teaching the crafts of reading, writing and mathematics. In L. B. Resnick (Ed.), *Knowing, learning and instruction: Essays in honor of Robert Glaser* (pp. 453–494). Hillsdale, NJ: Lawrence Erlbaum Associates.

Daiute, C. (1986). Do 1 and 1 make 2? Patterns of influence by collaborative authors. *Written Communication 3*(2), 382–408.

Duffy, T. M., & Cunningham, D. J. (1996). Constructivism: Implications for the design and delivery of instruction. In D. Jonassen (Ed.), *Handbook of instructional technology*. New York: Macmillan.

Fosnot, C. T. (1989). *Enquiring teachers enquiring learners. A constructivist approach to teaching*. New York: Teachers College Press.

Gallimore, R., & Tharp, R. (1990). Teaching mind in society: Teaching, schooling and literate discourse. In L. C. Moll (Ed.), *Vygotsky and education* (pp. 175–205). New York: Cambridge University Press.

Hayes, J. R., & Flower, L. S. (1983). Uncovering cognitive processes in writing: An introduction to protocol analysis. In P. Mosenthal & L. Tamor (Eds.), *Research on writing: Principles and methods* (pp. 207–220). New York: Longman.

Honebein, P., Duffy, T. M., & Fishman, B. (1993). Constructivism and the design of learning environments: Context and authentic activities for learning. In T. M. Duffy, J. Lowyck, & D. Jonassen (Eds.), *Designing environments for constructivist learning*. Heidelberg: Springer-Verlag.

Johnson, D. W., & Johnson, R. T. (1975). *Learning together and more: Cooperation, competition and individualization*. Englewood Cliffs, NJ: Prentice-Hall.

Johnson, D. W., & Johnson, R. T. (1990). Cooperative learning and achievement. In S. Sharan (Ed.), *Cooperative learning: Theory and practice*. New York: Praeger.

Kagan, S. (1992). *Cooperative learning*. San Juan Capistrano, CA: Kagan Cooperative Learning.

Langer, J. A., & Applebee, A. N. (1986). Reading and writing instruction: Toward a theory of teaching and learning. In E. Rothkopf (Ed.), *Review of research in education* (Vol. 13, pp. 171–194). Washington, DC: AERA.

Lave, J., & Wenger, E. (1991). *Situated learning: Legitimate peripheral participation*. Cambridge, MA: Cambridge University Press.

McCombs, B. L. (1993). *Learner-centered psychological principles: Guidelines for school redesign and reform*. Washington, DC: American Psychological Association and the Mid-continent Regional Education Laboratory. (ERIC Document Reproduction Service No. ED 371 994)

Pea, R. (1993). Practices of distributed intelligence and designs of education. In G. Salomon (Ed.), *Distributed cognition* (pp. 47–87). New York: Cambridge University Press.

Rogoff, B. (1990). *Apprenticeship in thinking: Cognitive development in social context*. New York: Oxford University Press.

Rogoff, B. (1994). Developing understanding of the idea of communities of learners. *Mind, Culture and Activity, 1*, 209–229.

Saunders, W. M. (1989). Collaborative writing tasks and peer interaction. *International Journal of Educational Research, 13*(1), 101–112.

Savery, J. R. (1996). *Fostering student ownership for learning in a learner centered instructional environment*. Unpublished doctoral dissertation, Indiana University, Bloomington.

Savery, J. R., & Duffy, T. M. (1995). Problem-based learning: An instructional model and its constructivist framework. *Educational Technology, 35*(5), 31–38.

Scardamalia, M., & Bereiter, C. (1987). Knowledge telling and knowledge transforming in written composition. In S. Rosenberg (Ed.), *Advances in applied psycholinguistics: Vol. 2. Reading, writing and language learning*. New York: Cambridge University Press.

Scardamalia, M., & Bereiter, C. (1991). Higher levels of agency for children in knowledge building: A challenge for the design of new knowledge media. *The Journal of the Learning Sciences, 1*, 37–68.

Tharp, R., & Gallimore, R. (1988). *Rousing minds to life: Teaching, learning and schooling in a social context*. New York: Cambridge University Press.

Tudge, J. (1990). Vygotsky, the zone of proximal development and peer collaboration: Implications for classroom practice. In L. C. Moll (Ed), *Vygotsky and education* (pp. 155–172). New York: Cambridge University Press.

Vygotsky, L. S. (1978). *Mind in society: The development of higher psychological processes*. Cambridge, MA: Harvard University Press.

Wertsch, J. (1991). *Voices of the mind: A sociocultural approach to mediated action*. Cambridge, MA: Harvard University Press.

Yin, R. (1992). *Case study research: Design and methods*. London: Sage.

Zimmerman, B. J., & Schunk, D. H. (1989). *Self-regulated learning and academic achievement: Theory, research and practice*. New York: Springer-Verlag.

ASYNCHRONOUS ELECTRONIC CONFERENCING

6

Student Role Play in the World Forum: Analyses of an Arctic Adventure Learning Apprenticeship

William A. Sugar
Southern Connecticut State University

Curtis Jay Bonk
Indiana University

As society rides the crest of the information age wave, futuristic predictions become pedestrian. Numerous societal conventions and rules are being transformed in the wake of the ability to transmit data in dichotomous bits of information. Although the information superhighway is only beginning to materialize, it is important to consider the potential educational ramifications of embracing this massive, multiaccess information turnpike. In what ways will schools connect to, collect, and share this information? How might students be apprenticed in their initial attempts to drive the highway and form new learning collaborations? What new learning and collaboration patterns will occur? What level of dialogue will occur between students of differing grade levels, nationalities, and domain interests within global information networks?

In response to these questions, researchers must begin to analyze and describe student interactions and learning activities when using celebrated, new learning tools for networking and collaboration. For instance, as the computer-conferencing networks spawn innovative educational activities and partnerships for apprenticing young learners (e.g., real-world environmental debates and scientific explorations), questions regarding the social and cognitive benefits of new interaction patterns should be raised in regard to the forms of dialogue, the types of learning and teaching assistance, the forms and benefits of mentorship, and the impact of globally shared meaning.

One area ripe for investigation is the impact of new computer-conferencing and global networking tools on student perspective taking and audience awareness (Bonk, 1990). Just how do these tools foster an appreciation for other perspectives, global events, systemic change, and multicultural issues and customs (Riel, 1993)? Given the power of conferencing and networking technology to expose students to new issues and ideas, it is surprising to find minimal research in this area. One of the key aspects of this particular study on adventure learning with Arctic explorers, therefore, was to address the effects of role play on student electronic perspective taking and social dialogue. Before describing this Arctic learning adventure, key theoretical perspectives on global collaboration are presented.

Online Global Collaboration

Among the new partnerships of information age learning are tools for networking and global collaboration. As advances in telecommunications build the necessary foundation for collaboration (Ishii, 1993), ubiquitous online educational communities will shift instructional design concerns from the prevailing human–computer interaction issues to more personalized human–human agendas (Lauzon & Moore, 1989). Already, it is increasingly common to hear about students sending messages to distant peers or distinguished experts on a topic, while their teachers simultaneously collaborate with their colleagues and peers on the same network. Riel (1993) argued that these online communities will provide *global educations* for students in the 21st century that will empower them to examine and appreciate the complexity of real-world events and information through the eyes of experts and practitioners as well as their foreign peers.

Collaborative work in online communities is already becoming an effective way of using the many information age offspring (Harasim, 1990; Ruopp, Gal, Drayton, & Pfister, 1993). Bannon (1986), for instance, noted that computer-mediated communication networks are emerging to foster new communities among geographically distant people bound primarily by shared interests or backgrounds. Riel (1992) contended that these networks present excitingly fresh possibilities for cooperative learning and student interactions because they engage students in both generative and evaluative aspects of negotiating and sharing meanings.

Theoretical Framing With a Sociocultural Lens

Mindful engagement when electronically collaborating (see Salomon, 1993; Salomon, Perkins, & Globerson, 1991) should enhance student sense of audience or perspective taking. From a Vygotskian or sociocultural viewpoint (Bonk & Cunningham, chap. 2, this volume; Vygotsky, 1986), more capable peers or adult guides on a computer network might lead students into cognitive processes of writing and communication that they might not independently consider (Bonk, Medury, & Reynolds, 1994). Likewise, neo-Piagetian studies indicate that debating with peers over a network might guide and challenge learners to new levels of growth and understanding

(Clements & Nastasi, 1988). From this viewpoint, when students in an electronic community are confronted by alternative views and opinions, cognitive dissonance or disequilibrium is triggered, thereby prodding individuals to seek additional information to resolve that conflict (Piaget, 1963) and, as numerous computer-networking experiences indicate (see Golub, 1994; Riel, 1993), they do not want to look dumb to their foreign peers. Clearly, then, both Vygotskian and Piagetian developmental theories are helpful is explaining why collaborative technologies might succeed in helping children learn.

Another developmentalist, Robert Selman (1980), suggested that educators need to devise new ways for students to progress beyond their egocentric views of the world (i.e., to grow interpersonally). His developmental construct, perspective taking or social cognition, relates to the ability to see the world from another person's perspective or "infer another's capabilities, attributes, expectations, feelings and potential reactions" (Selman, 1971). Such skills are critical to successful human functioning and involvement in everyday social interaction (Bjorklund, 1995). Based on Piaget's (1963) cognitive developmental theory, Selman (1980) has outlined a social cognitive developmental model of five distinct stages (Stages 0–4) that delineates children's increasing abilities to take alternative viewpoints into account.

Because social cognition is directly linked to school performance (Muuss, 1988) and is at the core of human intelligence (Mead, 1934), it seems ironic that few scholars are studying the impact of global collaborative technologies on student perspective taking. Muuss suggested that systematic role-taking opportunities might enable students to decenter from their own points of view, while fostering collaboration and enhanced interpersonal understanding. Clearly, situating Muuss' idea of systematic role-play experiences in global education curricula (e.g., the sharing of views on a computer screen while taking on specific roles) could elevate students' social cognitive skills.

Merging Theory and Technology Into Cognitive Apprenticeships

Although global learning communities might heighten social cognitive skill and directly scaffold countless struggling learners, there is no guarantee that peer collaboration and interaction will trigger critical reflection on one's ideas or enhance interpersonal understanding. Fortunately, scaffolding and feedback are no longer restricted to one's peers and classroom teacher, but, in the late 1990s, guidance often comes from other teachers, peers, consultants, and experts who apprentice learning in these socioculturally based forums. As a result, educators are finding fresh avenues for developing mentor–apprentice relationships and embedding novice student learning in a more legitimate social context (Collins, Brown, & Newman, 1989).

Lehrer, Erickson, and Connell (1994) recently asserted that a learning apprenticeship might translate sociocultural principles into "good" instructional practices. In a related article, Lehrer (1993) contended such sound instructional practices might guide student knowledge quests by making expert thinking visible, promoting student–student dialogue, providing tools for information selection and organization, and encouraging integration, presentation, and multiple representation of that knowledge. Wells and Chang-Wells (1992) further argued that adults should guide student participation in challenging and internally controllable educational activities that empower them to assume a greater portion of the responsibility or intellectual burden of these educational tasks. Apparently, there is growing belief that expert assistance of neophyte learner performance effectively apprentices them into a community of practice (Lave & Wegner, 1991). As a result, sociocultural researchers are searching for situations wherein inexperienced students actively construct new knowledge in authentic settings under some expert guidance.

One rich vein of sociocultural research during the early moments of the upcoming century will undoubtedly be in determining whether online educational networks provide us with the technologies to build communities of practice which teleapprentice (Teles, 1993) less skilled learners through social interaction and dialogue. Already, an expert can arrive on a network to provide data or demonstrations and later participate with learners in a joint learning activity. Novice learners on this network, in contrast, might seek additional information, ask questions, or offer tentative conclusions. Teachers might mediate between these expert and novice roles by setting the initial goals, stating necessary assumptions, modeling expected thought processes, and guiding the overall learning process through various supports and suggestions. Though additional roadmaps are needed, the cognitive apprenticeship situation reviewed here may be one plausible means to enter these exciting but uncharted student learning territories and virgin global networks. The expert apprenticeship and mentoring of students reported next took place using telecommunications from both explorer tents in the Arctic ice and tundra as well as from the relatively more safe confines of faculty university offices in the United States.

METHOD

The World Forum Background Information[1]

During the early 1990s, the *World School for Adventure Learning* was a program created and regulated by Indiana University, the University of St.

[1]The authors were not members of the World School for Adventure Learning nor the World Forum, but performed the analyses reported here. Note, also, that some of the events we describe here were later reused and replayed as World Forum simulations. More complete descriptions of such activities and electronic exercises are available from the Interactive Communications and Simulations (ICS) program at the University of Michigan (for more information, see URL: *http://ics.soe.umich.edu/* or write to *info@ics.soe.umich.edu*).

Thomas, Hamline University, and the University of Michigan (for more historical information and related projects, see Siegel & Kirkley, chap. 14, this volume). The events this consortium designed were intended to help intermediate, middle, and high schools foster innovative teaching and learning opportunities by utilizing telecommunications for real-life events. In World School programs, the adventure aspect of learning occurred when students tracked animal migrations, debated issues with peers and teachers, interacted with real explorers, and performed community and environmental service. The goal here was for students to be the learning adventurers, not passive watchers; hence, the real-life expedition discussed in this chapter was meant to stimulate and guide such activities.

The *World Forum*, developed primarily by the University of Michigan, was a key component of the World School for Adventure Learning. The World Forum, which remains in operation at the time of this writing, is an online asynchronous telecommunications project designed to give middle and high school students the opportunity to interact with peers globally about critical environmental and social issues, while broadening their understanding of the world through travel experiences. The World Forum supports student participation in both actual and simulated adventures to exotic parts of the world.

The project evaluated here was a highly structured curriculum in environmental, global, and multicultural education, incorporating an actual 4-month expedition across the Arctic Ocean mounted by the International Arctic Project (IAP). The IAP, which used dog sleds and canoes during the spring of 1994 to traverse the Canadian Arctic, was comprised of a group of six explorers and 33 sled dogs spearheaded by explorer Will Steger. These explorers sent World Forum student groups daily expedition reports from March to May 1994 (curricular ideas related to an expedition by this team during the following year are reported in Siegel & Kirkley, chap. 14, this volume). Explorer reports were composed daily on a portable computer and then transmitted to a polar orbiting satellite, which relayed them to the World School for Adventure Learning network through a ground station in Washington, DC. As a result, within hours of an experience, text accounts of explorer activities and observations were posted to a worldwide listserv available to millions of children from across the planet. By using telecommunications to link explorer and scientist text-based reports to student participants throughout the world, the project hoped to motivate students with authentic and current scientific data.

This particular study involved students in six middle schools and six high schools participating in the World Forum. The students ranged in age from 13 to 18 years old. The majority of these schools were in the United States, with some participating schools representing such countries as Japan and Canada. Though students were expected to connect online with the World

Forum daily, student Internet messages and responses were dependent on their daily classroom schedules. Hence, as opposed to real-time systems, student reading and responding to explorer, mentor, and peer postings varied in this delayed-messaging format.

Role playing was incorporated to engage World Forum students in more authentic problem solving and encourage multiple perspective taking during this particular expedition. To situate the role-playing activity, the classes from these 12 schools constituted a World Congress of distinguished individuals (see Table 6.1 for a list of characters). The delegations of notable individuals were balanced for ethnicity, nationality, gender, organization, and philosophical background. Within each delegation, two or three students would assume the identity of the person they were assigned; for example, one student group might portray Jacques Cousteau (an oceanographer) whereas another student group might assume the role of Margaret Thatcher (a politician). In their respective two- or three-person groups, students would conduct background research on their particular character in order to effectively participate in the World Forum activities. In assuming the persona of these noteworthy individuals, World Forum students responded to a multitude of environmental, social, and political issues related to the Arctic while being guided by the expedition team as well as by five World Forum mentors.

TABLE 6.1
List of Characters Role-Played by World Forum Participants

Green Delegation
- Professor Stephen Jay Gould
- Monsieur Jacques Cousteau
- Señor Roberto Clemente
- Señora Eva Peron
- Professor Sissela Bok
- Mr. E. F. Schumacher

Red Delegation
- Sir Edmund Hillary
- Mahatma Mohandas Gandhi
- Ms. Anna Freud
- Pres. Relix Houphouet-Boigny
- Ms. Marjory Douglas
- Governor Dixy Lee Ray

Blue Delegation
- Dr. Andrei Sakharov
- Ms. Rachel Carson
- Dalai Lama
- Prime Min. Margaret Thatcher
- Professor Edward Said
- Professor Shoshanna Zuboff

Purple Delegation
- President Lech Walesa
- Ms. Petra Kelly
- Pope John Paul II
- Prime Min. Kazimiera Prunskiene
- Mr. Ernest Hemingway
- Mr. Stephen Biko

Yellow Delegation
- Professor Barbara Jordan
- Mr. Farley Mowat
- Professor Linus Pauling
- Ms. Aung San Suu Kyi
- Madame Simone de Beauvoir
- Mr. Akio Morita

Brown Delegation
- Mr. Richard Leakey
- Ms. Dian Fossey
- Sheikh Hassan Turabi
- Professor Milton Friedman
- Ms. Toni Morrison
- Prime Minister Lee Kuan Yew

Note. Each delegation was represented by one middle school and one high school.

World Forum Activities and Variables of Interest

The main participants in the World Forum were the organizers, mentors, students, and explorers. The World Forum organizers created four key instructional activities: *Flash Points*, *Arctic Alerts*, *Questions for Explorers*, and *Explorer and Scientist Reports*. Given these participants and activities, there were four key variables of interest here: (a) the average number of postings per activity, (b) the forms of mentor assistance exhibited in these postings, (c) the level of student questioning to explorers, and (d) student perspective taking in their Flash Point and Arctic Alert responses.

In the Flash Point activity, student groups were asked to respond to controversial sayings or statements in a similar voice and expression as their character might answer. For example, students voiced their opinions on statements such as, "*The pen is mightier than the sword*," "*Knowledge is power*," "*Nature and man can never be friends*," and "*Education is the instruction of the intellect in the laws of nature*." Additionally, students rated their agreement with each statement on a 1 (i.e., Strongly Agree) to 5 (Strongly Disagree) scale. Typically after agreeing or disagreeing with a Flash Point, students would state their reasons for their particular opinion. Here are two sample Flash Points and responses:

1. Flash Point: "The world will always be governed by self-interest, we should not try to stop this."

> Sample Response: "I am Dian Fossey, I disagree. Because when I was in Africa, and I was trying to save the mountain gorillas [sic] the government didn't care about the gorillas, and all they wanted was the money from cutting off the gorilla's hands and selling them. I tried to change that because I thought they had a chance and I could help them survive. Just because the government wanted one thing [sic] I tried to stop it because to me it was totally wrong. If you want something bad enough, fight for it." (Dian Fossey)

2. Flash Point: "Most people are on the world, not in it." John Muir.

> Sample Response: "I strongly agree with John Muir that . . . In my work as a humanitarian I have witnessed many people let the world pass them by. We are only on this world for a short time, and we need to leave our mark while we are still here. We also need to take into account that those who are less fortunate than us make a difference, before it's too late for them also. Therefore, I believe that everyone gets something from the world but there are only a few who choose to put something back into it." (Señor Roberto Clemente)

Arctic Alerts, the second instructional activity, consisted of news reports that described critical environmental and social issues in the Arctic region. One Arctic Alert explored the possibility of oil exploration on native Eskimos' land. As indicated in the responses that follow, World Forum participants responded positively or negatively to these issues based, once again, on their respective roles:

> I sympathize for all horrendous deeds done to natives of the lands but to advance technology of mankind, I feel the oil must continue to be pumped. The oil offers much profit for the natives and the producers of the oil as well. To achieve an ultimate goal there must be sacrifices, and I feel we are experiencing the worst before the beneficial aspects of technology. (Mr. Akio Morita)

> I John Paul II, say that we were all put on this Earth as equals, animals and man, and that it is unfair to disrupt the lifestyles of our fellow man or animal. In short I am saying that I disagree with them drilling unless we are prepared to put the environment back into its original condition. (Pope John Paul II)

These student groups also were encouraged to pose questions to the Arctic expedition team, which we labeled as Questions for Explorers. Expedition leader Will Steger (1996) noted that the most common expedition questions they received concerned how their dogs survived in the cold. Other questions World Forum students asked explorers included high-level concerns regarding Russia's dumping toxic waste into the Arctic, how much authority Eskimos had in determining land use, and the effects of oil on the water supply. They also requested basic facts such as the ratio of men to women in the expedition, the distance traveled, the people encountered during the expedition, and the food eaten.

A final instructional component of this project, Explorer and Scientist Reports, was not as rigorously evaluated in terms of the interaction patterns and mentoring, in part, because it was the least structured of the World Forum components. It is important to note, nevertheless, that these reports helped participating schools and students follow the IAP as the explorer team studied indigenous people and animals, traveled to new sites, and reflected on environmental issues (Siegel & Kirkley, chap. 14, this volume). In explorer report #16, for instance, IAP team members reported on weather conditions (e.g., –25°C and windy at 7 AM), latitude and longitude of the expedition, a camp encounter with 10 wolves, traveling conditions (e.g., 10-meter snow drifts), caribou sightings, proximity to the tree line, equipment problems, and the present condition of the dogs. With the later reports and comments about improving weather, beautiful scenery, meals, wolverine encounters, native plants, distance traveled, an explanation for the color of the Northern Lights, local housing, identifiable as well as unknown animal tracks, and local employment opportunities, student learning was definitely highly contextualized.

Although student and school participation ultimately varied, as indicated earlier, students were instructed to log in to the World Forum each day and record their reactions and opinions to the aforementioned activities. As part of the World Forum curricula, student discussions of key Arctic environmental, social, and political issues were assisted by prompting, probing, encouragement, and guidance from the five World Forum mentors.

Exploring student interactions via the World Forum might lend insight into the process of effective asynchronous collaboration and ultimately enhance the designs of asynchronous learning communities. Questions about how this teleapprenticeship guided students' learning effectively transforms common technological concerns (e.g., networking and information access) into sociocultural questions about mentor assistance and scaffolding embedded in electronic mail (E-mail) dialogue. Therefore, the data analysis frameworks selected for this study were meant to offer insight into how electronic social interaction impacts student learning. The four key analyses, mentioned earlier, (a) the postings per activity, (b) the forms of mentor assistance, (c) the level of student questioning, and (d) the degree of student perspective taking, are discussed in the following section.

Data Analysis Approaches and Guidelines

Although the data collected during this 8-week unit was already anonymous (i.e., students had assumed fictitious identities), all school indicators were removed during the four analyses. As indicated earlier, the explorer notes to students were not included in these evaluations. The four primary analysis techniques selected here were based on the particular content of the Flash Point, Arctic Alert, and Student Questions for Explorer activities. Next, we briefly describe each analysis technique and how we applied these techniques to World Forum interactions.

World Forum Postings. The first analyses of the middle and high school data entailed a direct counting of the number of student postings concerning the Flash Points, Arctic Alerts, and Questions for Explorers. After taking out posting headers, we conducted a computer count of the total number of words composed by middle school and high school students during the three activities. The number of postings was divided into the total word counts to calculate words per posting. Counts of the number of mentor–student postings also were noted (see Table 6.2 for results).

Tharp and Gallimore's Seven Means of Assistance. Tharp and Gallimore (1988) offered insights into effective means of facilitating students' understanding, with their argument that schools should provide *assistance* for the entire school community. Though Tharp and Gallimore originally identified six means of assisting performance including: *modeling*, *contingency management*, *feeding back*, *instructing*, *questioning*, and *cognitive structuring*, Tharp

TABLE 6.2
Student and Mentor Postings by Activity in the World Forum Dialogue

	Mentor Postings	*Student Postings*	*Total Postings*	*Total Student Words*	*Average Student Words/Post*
Flash Points—middle school	13	99	112	4,808	48.6
Flash Points—high school	42	88	130	7,805	88.7
Arctic Alerts—middle school	6	51	57	4,369	85.7
Arctic Alerts—high school	1	41	42	3,898	95.1
Questions for Explorers—middle school	1	29	30	625	21.6
Questions for Explorers—high school	16	14	30	1,030	73.6
Total Middle School	20	179	199	9,802	54.8
Total High School	59	143	202	12,733	89.0
Total	79	322	401	22,535	70.0

(1993) later added a seventh, *task structuring*. These seven techniques of assisting students are an initial step in understanding mentor and student participation from Collins et al.'s (1989) *cognitive apprenticeship* framework (see also Bonk & Cunningham, chap. 2). For the purposes of this study, mentor assistance was assessed using guidelines from Tharp (1993) and Gallimore and Tharp (1990), which were adapted and modified as follows:

1. Modeling: Instructor offers sample behavior for imitation, thereby giving the learner information or images that serves as a performance standard or valuable information about the skills required.

> *Example:* "Hey Pope . . . I just sent the following message to Jacques Cousteau. Notice how I also asked for his opinions about oil dumping in the Arctic region. He will probably send me a reply to my message." (Note: This is a hypothetical example because no mentor modeling actually occurred during the World Forum activities we investigated.)

2. Contingency Management: When the instructor applies principles of reinforcement (e.g., praise, privileges, tokens, and rewards) and punishment (e.g., reprimands) to the learning situation in order to increase or decrease certain behaviors presented or deemed warranted.

> *Example:* "Mr. Mowat—you are an expert on this region and these people . . . please share more of your reasons for supporting native cultures instead of technology."

3. Feedback: Process of providing feedback on performance, thereby guiding him or her to improve or continue performance on the next attempt. In comparing the learner to a standard of performance, there is increased opportunity for self-correction.

Examples: "I like this question because it focuses the group on the lives of the native people and the changes they are going through." "Hm . . . this working group is filled with insightful comments . . ." "Gosh, many interesting points have been raised here . . ."

4. Instructing: Using traditional teaching techniques such as providing correction, clarity, decision making, or other information. Most helpful when the learner can perform some segment of the task but cannot yet analyze the entire task or make judgments about which elements to choose.

Example: "Akebono: Greenpeace may have been correct (that the Russians were dumping waste) but I still question the 'correctness' of their pursuit. The longer we discuss this point, the less I agree with Greenpeace. *This does not mean I condone what the Russians may be doing.* My concern is with Greenpeace's methods. Granted, Greenpeace tried to get Russian permission. But failing to get permission does not allow them to violate Russian territory. The international community should band together and confront the Russians about dumping. This approach has a far better chance to reaching a long-term solution than a grandstand (and dangerous) maneuver by a lone group . . . all communities have rules, including the international community. Greenpeace violated those rules hoping their actions would help."

5. Questioning: Requests for a verbal response that also assists the learner by providing a mental operation (e.g., "Another reason might be?") that the learner would have difficulty producing on his or her own. Such requests provide metacognitive information about the development of the learner's understanding.

Example: "What say the rest of you? Is this like the Native Americans? How so? What should be different this time? What should be the same? I'm sure a big debate is about to happen . . ." "What are your suggestions for these people? How can they continue to grow and progress? Imagine this group is their consultant . . . what would your recommendation be?"

6. Cognitive Structuring: Explanations or elaborations that provide new belief structures that organize and justify new learning and perceptions, perhaps even leading to the creation of new schemata.

Example: "Hindsight *is* the best teacher, Akebono. The last News from the North tells us that the Greenpeace Organization was correct in their pursuit. Can you relate this incident to the 'Knowledge is Power' quote? If you look at both sides, just who had the power, and who had the knowledge? What sort of power would Greenpeace have possessed if Russia had been exposed a year earlier? Certainly, the power to embarrass Russia—but what of the power to possibly save the seals, or other wildlife? What power did Russia have by keeping its actions secret from the rest of this planet?"

7. Task Structuring: Chunking, sequencing, detailing, reviewing, or any other means to structure the task and its components so as to fit it into the learner's zone of proximal development.

> *Example:* "[Mentor's Note: You'll notice that the Mentors (and now some of you) have been writing our Role's name before our text—when you start moving into your Working Groups, you *won't* have to do this. VisConfer has been set up so that it'll automatically sign your Working Group role (e.g., Edmund Hillary) to the comment.]"

Questions of interest here included whether the assistance varied across age the groups and tasks. For instance, what types of learning assistance do students need? And does the form and quantity of mentor assistance vary with younger students and older students or from the beginning to ending sessions? To initiate answers, percentages of mentor postings involving each assistance mode were calculated for each level of schooling (i.e., middle and high school).

In surveying the forms of assistance provided by the project mentors in the World Forum (across Flash Points, Arctic Alerts, and Questions for Explorers), interrater reliability between the two raters was below 50%. After refining the scoring guidelines, these statements were entirely rescored by a third rater as well as one of the original raters. Interrater reliability improved to 74.2%. These two raters then reviewed and negotiated disagreements until 100% agreement was obtained. Note that the complexity of many postings necessitated multiple codings within some of the messages, hence, the lower interrater reliability experienced here.

Bloom's Taxonomy of Educational Objectives. Paralleling the forms of assistance analysis was a concern with the level of questioning in electronic social interaction and discourse. Although decades old, Bloom's (1956) taxonomy of educational objectives—from low-level knowledge, comprehension, and application goals to higher level cognitive skills of analysis, synthesis, and evaluation—was useful for cognitive analysis of this electronic discourse. Though these question types have been used for four decades to illustrate the lack of high-level classroom questioning, we were interested in whether electronic interaction in a community of discourse would raise student level of questioning.

In accordance with sociocultural theories and ideas of cognitive apprenticeship, we speculated that while students were immersed in the key World Forum activities (e.g., Flash Points and Arctic Alerts), they would gain some geographical and environmental expertise and express this new awareness with higher level questioning of explorers. Along these same lines, we wondered whether students would internalize and exhibit the types of questions asked by their World Forum mentors. Here is a sampling of what we found in student questioning of explorers across the six levels of Bloom's taxonomy:

1. Knowledge-level questions: "When you get cut does your blood freeze? Does it stick to you? Is it true human blood bounces on ice?"—Madame Simone de Beauvoir.
2. Comprehension-level questions: "Since my profession deals with nature, I am really curious and excited about the trip the explorers are taking. Will they depend on their survival skills for food, or have they brought their own food? Are they taking precautions to leave the natural habitat as they came upon it? I do sincerely hope that they are being as careful as they can be."—Monsieur Jacques Cousteau.
3. Application questions: None of the 60 coded Student Questions to Explorers among World Forum participants were at this level.
4. Analysis-level questions: "Could there be a chance that the nuclear dumping will cause mutations in the sea animals, and the humans who drink the water? If there is, what kind of mutations would occur?"—Sir Edmund Hillary.
5. Synthesis-level questions: "What kind of developments should be made for Eskimos in order for them to have alternate sources of food so that whales, etc., do not become extinct?"—Professor Linus Pauling.
6. Evaluation-level questions: "Dear Mr. Steger, Do you feel that your expedition of the Arctic will benefit mankind in any way?"—Sincerely, Mahatma Gandhi.

Two raters were used to rank the level of questioning in the student Questions for Explorers. Though initial interrater reliability was deemed sufficient at 83.6%, a third rater was utilized for statements of disagreement until 100% agreement was obtained.

Selman's Perspective/Role-Taking Scheme. As indicated, online collaborations have the potential to raise student perspective taking and interpersonal understanding. Robert Selman's (1980) developmental theory of social cognitive skills, mentioned earlier, offered one tool for exploring this possibility.

According to Selman's (1980) social cognitive scheme, children at ages 3 to 6 years initially are at the *Stage 0: Undifferentiated and Egocentric Role Taking*. During this stage, children cannot make any clear distinction between their own and other points of view. In the next stage, *Stage 1: Differentiated and Subjective Role Taking*, children ages 5 to 9 years realize that others do have different perspectives than their own, but they cannot accurately determine the other person's perspective. The *Stage 2: Self-Reflective/Second-Person and Reciprocal Role Taking* stage is where the 7- to 12-year-old child realizes that the other person does have his or her own perspectives and knows that this other person thinks about this child's thinking. The *Stage 3: Third-Person and Mutual Role Taking* stage is where the adolescent (ages 10 to 15 years) not only interprets the other person's perspective, but can take on a third-person role. This role enables children to see their own perspective and the other person's perspective from a neutral viewpoint. During the last stage, *Stage 4: In-Depth and Societal Role Taking*, adolescents and adults are provided the means to not only take the neutral third-party perspective, but also to assume a societal or multidimensional perspective where some mutuality and deeper communication with others is seen. Selman also indicated that individuals at this stage can compare and contrast different levels of perspectives.

These levels have been investigated by Selman's camp by having students view or hear open-ended dilemmas from which interview and probing techniques are used to determine the subjects' perspective- or role-taking level (e.g., Selman & Byrne, 1974). Selman's work indicates that by age 10, 60% of children are at Stage 2 and another 20% at Stage 3 (Selman & Byrne, 1974). More important, Selman's (1980) age-based norms indicate that the 13- to 18-year-old World Forum youth in the present study should be progressing from Stage 2, Self-Reflective/Second-Person and Reciprocal Role Taking to Stages 3: Third-Person and Mutual Role Taking and 4: In-Depth and Societal Role Taking. Although the Mutual Role-Taking level (Level 3) is a preadolescent phenomenon and the In-Depth Societal level (Level 4) most often occurs during adolescence and early adulthood, many of the oldest students in this study may still be operating at the second or third level.

Instead of measuring students' entry or exit social cognitive levels, we adopted Selman's role-taking categories when coding student postings within both the Flash Points and the Arctic Alerts. Of course, most students in World Forum activities engaged in role playing from the perspective of another person; hence, participants were already operating above the initial egocentric level of Selman's scheme. The primary question asked here was whether students' perspective taking would be elevated during their role-playing activities. Perhaps more important, which World Forum activity, Arctic Alerts or Flash Points, would encourage higher levels of perspective taking? Second, we asked whether older students would exhibit higher levels of perspective taking in their responses than middle school students.

It must be pointed out that no claims are made here that we were measuring students' social cognitive skill or development during World Forum activities; instead, this research component simply attempted to link student dialogue within World Forum tasks to ideas of social cognition. As indicated, Selman's (1980) scheme for measuring social cognitive skills was developed to analyze protracted interview sessions, not specific comments or answers. Given World Forum activities and goals, however, an indication of participant social cognitive processing level was deemed useful and implicitly available. Detailed next are sample student Flash Point and Arctic Alert postings coded according to Levels 1 to 4 of Selman's model:

1. Level 1: Differentiated and Subjective Role Taking.

"I, Sir Edmund Hillary disagree with this quote because I thought a lot during school and I ended up with a very good education. I did not want to just say no and quit. I kept going and worked very hard."

"I, Felix Houphouet-Boigny, am against getting involved in the world's problems."

2. Level 2: Self-Reflective/Second-Person and Reciprocal Role Taking.

"I disagree strongly with Pope John Paul II. I Sir Edmund Hillary, think that the pope is wrong in my religion [sic]. But he is talking in his own religion, so it is his right to believe it."

"I strongly agree [#1] with Ms. Freud, because if desire was not the essence of man, the world would not have been blessed with my great writing or the writings of many other writers. Ms. Freud, your opinions are very well expressed for a woman and I recognize that you achieved a lot when women were unable to do so. Thus desire must have played a great role." Mr. Ernest Hemingway.

3. Level 3: Third-Person and Mutual Role Taking.

"Ms. Aung San Suu Kyi would not agree with the statement that people deserve what they get. That is not necessarily true unless they have worked hard and long to achieve their gaols. [sic] If it is something that is not good, then they don't necessarily deserve it unless it is their fault. Sometimes government is the fault of others."

"Everyone is and should be involved in all the worlds problems, but whether or not someone would choose to fight about them is there own business. You do not have to get to involved with them if you choose, but I choose to." Governor Dixie Lee Ray.

4. Level 4: In-Depth and Societal Role Taking.

"I strongly agree with Thomas Hobbs. In my country of Poland change came very slowly because we did not know enough and knowledge was kept from us. As we have moved from [sic] into the technical age more and more information was available to us. As our standard of living declined we all knew there must be a way to build better lives for the people of Poland. But I would change the quote. I would say 'knowledge, together with courage, is power.'

For if you know a lot, it makes no difference unless you have the courage to pursue change." President Lech Walesa.

"I, Gandhi, strongly agree that we are involved in the world's problems because we are the people of the world that make up the world. Everything we do affects the world. We cause the wars and violence. We are involved in the economics problems. As you can see, we are the world."

Using two raters, interrater reliability for these task transcripts was 78%, slightly lower than the reliability reported for the interview data of Selman (1980). Therefore, a third rater, once again, was utilized to review and rescore disagreements until 100% agreement was obtained by all three raters.

Results

In our first analysis, we looked at the data quantitatively. First of all, when examining the total number of postings recorded in World Forum by grade level, we found that the middle school students recorded more messages in each of the three World Forum activities (i.e., Flash Points, Arctic Alert responses, and Questions for Explorers) (see Table 6.2). However, as noted in Table 6.2, high school students, however, composed more elaborate messages in their Flash Point responses and in their electronic questioning of explorers than did middle school students. High school students, in fact, wrote 62.4% more text per posting than middle school students across their electronic commenting, averaging 89 words compared to 54.8 words per posting. Analyses by activity revealed that whereas World Forum Flash Points promoted 60% of the student participation, the Arctic Alerts nurtured more elaborate responses than the other two activities, averaging about 90 words per posting.

Table 6.2 also indicates that Arctic Alert mentor postings and resulting learning assistance was minimal, though favoring the middle school student youth. However, mentor responses to high school student Flash Point and Questions for Explorer postings was considerably higher than to middle school students. Although high school student mentoring was nearly triple the assistance provided middle school youth, most electronic activity was created by students and not the mentors. Surprisingly, however, the student posting activity decreased during the 8 weeks and direct student–student interaction throughout the project was minimal.

The coding scheme, based on Tharp and Gallimore's seven forms of learning assistance, disclosed that questioning was the most frequently used technique with novices, followed closely by feedback and cognitive structuring. Mentors spent over 75% of their time engaged in these three activities (see Table 6.3). In contrast, instruction accounted for slightly over one in seven of the mentor assistance techniques provided, whereas contingency management

TABLE 6.3
Forms of Mentor Teaching Assistance in World Forum Flash Point and Arctic Alert Dialogue

	Form of Assistance						
Activity	*Feedback*	*Questioning*	*Cognitive Structuring*	*Instruction*	*Contingency Management*	*Task Structuring*	*Total*
Flash—middle school	4	9	6	5	1	3	28
Flash—high school	18	31	12	12	2	5	80
Arctic—middle school	6	4	4	0	1	1	16
Arctic—high school	1	1	1	0	1	0	4
Questions—middle school	0	0	0	0	0	0	0
Questions—high school	12	12	6	6	0	0	36
Total Middle School	10	13	10	5	2	4	44
Total High School	31	44	19	18	3	5	120
Total	41	57	29	23	5	9	164
	25%	34%	18%	14%	3.0%	6%	

Note. Within the 79 mentor postings, we noted the above 164 distinct instances of learning assistance. However, modeling, the seventh form of assistance, was nonexistent in mentor electronic postings.

(i.e., behavioral rewards and punishment) and task structuring were rarely employed. Modeling was totally absent.

Our third analysis indicated that a majority of both middle school and high school student questioning activities to the Arctic explorers (see Fig. 6.1) were at lower levels of Bloom's (1956) taxonomy (i.e., knowledge and comprehension levels). However, with only 60 questions asked of explorers during this project, few conclusions can be made here.

By examining students' perspective-taking abilities, we found that both World Forum activities (i.e., Flash Points and Arctic Alerts) promoted fairly high levels of perspective taking (Figs. 6.2 and 6.3). Though 41% of middle

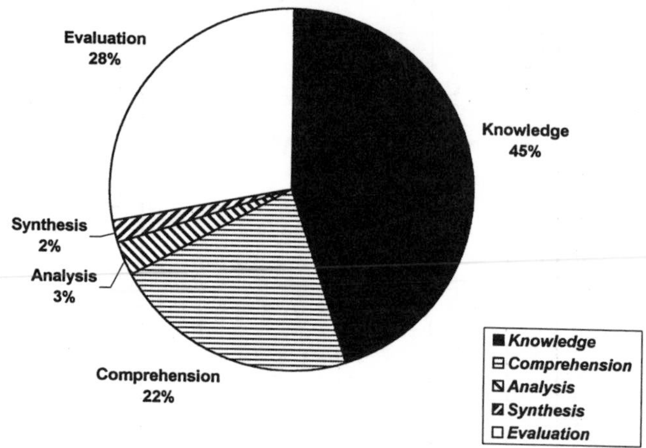

FIG. 6.1. Student questions to Arctic explorers according to level of Bloom's taxonomy.

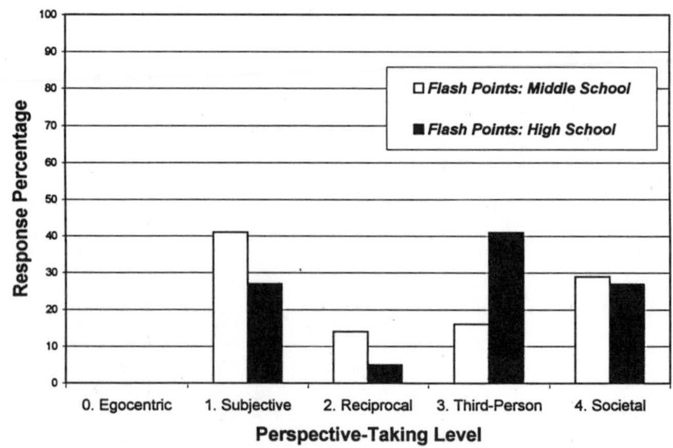

FIG. 6.2. Comparison of middle school and high school student degree of perspective taking reflected in World Forum Flash Point postings.

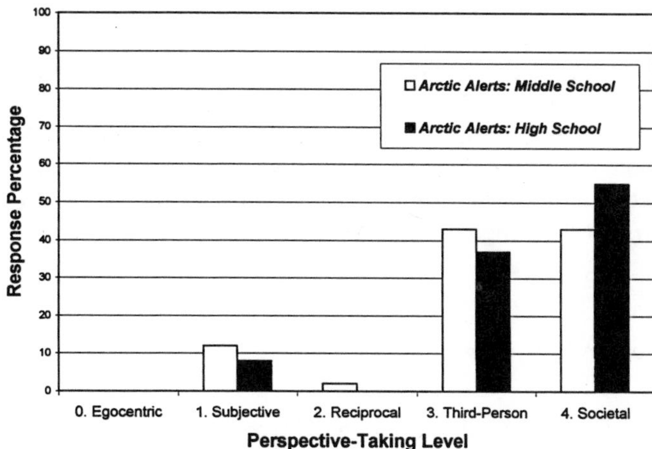

FIG. 6.3. Comparison of middle school and high school student degree of perspective taking reflected in World Forum Arctic Alert postings.

school students' responses to Flash Points were scored a "1" (*subjective* perspective taking), 14% of the time they participated at Level 2, 16% at Level 3 (*third-person* perspective taking), and almost 29% of their responses were a "4" (*societal* perspective taking). High school students fared even better with Flash Points; 41% of their responses were a "3" (*third-person* perspective taking) and 27% of their responses were a "4" (*societal* perspective taking). When responding to the Arctic Alerts, moreover, both middle and high school students engaged in even higher perspective-taking levels. Though few Arctic Alert student postings were noted at Levels 1 and 2 (14% for middle school students and 8% for high school students), there were significantly fewer Arctic Alerts coded (i.e., 94) than Flash Points (235). Though this seems higher than the developmental data reported by Selman (1980) and Selman and Byrne (1974), conclusive developmental statements are not warranted here due to the wide age range of the students in this study and limitations of the data mentioned earlier.

Figures 6.2 and 6.3 indicate that the Arctic Alerts promoted more Level 3 and 4 perspective taking among both groups of students than its Flash Point counterpart. Because the anonymity of the data made it impossible to match responses to specific individuals and comments, conservative non-parametric statistics were employed to compare perspective-taking levels in the different activities and grade levels. Mann–Whitney U comparisons of the social cognitive level of discussion displayed in the Flash Points and Arctic Alerts indicated that the latter resulted in significantly higher levels of perspective taking (Arctic Alerts $X = 3.25$, $SD = .93$, $n = 94$; Flash Points $X = 2.52$, $SD = 1.22$, $n = 235$; $U = 7{,}404.5$, $p < .0001$). Descriptively speaking, it appeared that the high school students were interacting at a predictably higher level of perspective taking than were middle school youth. However, Mann–Whitney U comparisons found that the differences between high school student and younger student responses to the Arctic Alerts, although favoring the older group, were, nonetheless, insignificant. Grade-level comparisons on the more abstract Flash Points, on the other hand, revealed significant differences favoring the older students (middle school $X = 2.31$, $SD = 1.27$, $n = 108$; high school, $X = 2.69$, $SD = 1.14$, $n = 127$, $U = 5{,}836.5$, $p < .05$).

Conclusion and Implications

The World Forum, developed by the University of Michigan, simulated an online discussion between middle and high school students about critical environmental issues (for other forms of learning adventures, global as well as local, see Siegel & Kirkley, chap. 14, this volume). The intention of this instructional activity was to encourage students to assume the identities of famous characters and communicate with their peers, explorers, and mentors about these environmental issues. To analyze participant interaction patterns on the World Forum, four different analysis methods were utilized: (a) quantitative summaries of the response frequencies, as well as more subjective cognitive and social interactional analyses derived from the work of (b) Tharp and Gallimore (1988), (c) Bloom (1956), and (d) Selman (1971). The goal of these analyses was to inform others about the levels and types of cognitive and social cognitive processing activity that students might engage in when role taking within online learning communities, not to evaluate specific World Forum programs or curricula.

Although there are at least seven forms of assistance available to mentors (see Bonk, Malikowski, Angeli, & East, in press; Tharp, 1993), one of them, modeling, was totally absent. Perhaps mentors could have used modeling to promote more interactions among students. For instance, in the beginning of the World Forum, prototypical interactions patterns could have been demonstrated to middle and high school students. This technique might help instruct students on how to interact with other World Forum participants. Task structuring also could have been used to facilitate additional interaction. For instance, in the beginning of the World Forum, mentors could have more extensively reminded World Forum participants that they should be responding to their counterparts, while also passing out sample question-asking or reflection sheets to guide early peer interactions. Overall, World Forum mentors appeared to concentrate their learning assistance on asking questions, instructing, providing positive feedback, and supplying cognitive structure to the task, but they failed to provide a framework for how students should properly interact with one another. Other possible forms of learning assistance not analyzed here include scaffolding, coaching, articulating, dialoguing, and fostering student exploration and application of skills (see Bonk & Cunningham, chap. 2, this volume).

Though our social cognitive analyses were crude, the results indicate that during World Forum role-play activities, participants assumed higher levels of perspective taking than typical preadolescent and adolescent youth. This occurred despite the minimal peer collaboration and responsiveness noted in the dialogue. As a result, instead of students jointly learning new information, helping each other grasp the task better, or engaging in extended debate, most commenting was in response to the environmental, social, or political issues in question. Nevertheless, when students assumed the roles of illustrious individuals and responded to these environmental predicaments, they began to discern alternative points of view and perspectives important to understanding the complexity of the problem.

Regarding particular tasks, World Forum participants demonstrated fairly high perspective-taking abilities while engaging both in Flash Points and Arctic Alerts. The highly current Arctic news stories were more contextually rich than the terse Flash Points and were responded to at a significantly higher levels of perspective taking. In effect, even though there were fewer Arctic Alert interactions, they promoted more elaborate discussion and interpersonal understanding. In terms of age, perspective-taking differences among the middle and high school youth were more noticeable in responses to the briefer Flash Points. Perhaps, this indicates that despite the role-playing activities, the younger children were unable to comprehend the gist of abstract Flash Point quotes and comments.

The analyses also corresponded with expectations of developmental differences from middle to high school. For instance, the perspective-taking analyses indicated that older students responded to Flash Points and Arctic Alerts more often at Selman's upper levels of social cognitive ability or judgment than the early adolescent students in this study. As predicted, as children mature, role-taking activities become easier (Muuss, 1988).

Though students demonstrated these higher level social cognitive abilities, especially high school students, this skill failed to transfer when asking questions of Arctic explorers. Instead two thirds of their questions remained primarily at the knowledge and comprehension levels. Nevertheless, most of their remaining question asking was at the highest level of Bloom's taxonomy, evaluation. This indicates that the events and activities embedded in the World Forum did, in part, encourage students to reflect beyond the basic factual types of questions.

Among the other developmental trends, high school students, on average, wrote more lengthy responses than middle school youth. The fact that the Flash Points and Questions for Explorers were better utilized by older students corresponds with their ability to cognitively reason at high levels than younger students (Piaget, 1963). Notice, moreover, that the younger middle schools students engaged in deeper correspondence on the more concrete Arctic Alerts. In terms of the level of questioning, too few questions were asked to infer any developmental differences. Of course, as indicated earlier, no direct modeling of how to ask questions was evident in this forum.

These four analyses indicate that timely mentoring of students in computer-mediated communications environments should scaffold students to new social cognitive heights and possibilities. Although extremely tentative, our codings of electronic data begin to detail why innovative social interaction formats may need to consider student developmental level. Despite the limited mentor modeling and reduced use of the medium over time, this particular invention functioned to raise perspective taking and vary the levels of questions students were concerned with. If the World Forum becomes promoted as a way to encourage students to consider critical environmental and social issues from another person's perspective, it may become a means to marry recent advances in sociocultural theory and collaborative technologies. For instance, as more apprenticing opportunities emerge from computer-mediated communication environments, additional understandings are needed regarding how unique cognitive strategies and processes displayed electronically between participants become internalized as independent problem-solving processes. Additionally, extensive research is needed to examine how to best design similar instructional approaches.

Future Directions

Future research ideas spin off from each limitation of this study. First of all, we did not manipulate the interactions among participants, but simply analyzed student role-playing dialogue and mentor assistance within an existing program. In a follow-up effort, researchers might want to suggest tasks or collaboration patterns that participants will use. Variations in the role taking or questioning of explorers, for instance, may enhance our initial findings found here. At the same time, additional training of mentors or explorers may scaffold their ability to model even higher levels of thinking, questioning, and perspective taking than witnessed here. Peer training also may prove fruitful, because few direct student–student interactions were noted within these 12 participating schools. Of course, other researchers might want to perform similar analyses on the pieces of data we were missing, namely, the explorer responses to students as well as explorer notes to the student participants discussing their daily expedition activities.

Recap

Despite these limitations, some of the tasks and approaches used here help clarify the impact of electronic social interaction on student learning. In using sociocultural and cognitive learning theory, new procedures were developed for assessing the impact of World Forum interaction structures on student dialogue and meaning making. Certainly these coding schemes for analyzing the questions asked, help provided, and perspectives taken can be further refined or altered for other collaboration formats and structures. Indeed, there are many additional variables, coding schemes, technologies, networld activities, and instructional design models to consider. Graphical communication among World Forum participants (e.g., still images or movies of the IAP), for instance, would likely have required vastly different assessment devices.

Many learning apprenticeship and research possibilities certainly abound here. For instance, other teleapprenticeships might experiment with debates and role plays using additional concrete and contextually rich situations like the Arctic Alerts to prompt more elaborate discourse and higher levels of interpersonal understanding. As our review of student dialogue in the World Forum transcripts indicates, role play appears to develop a broader and deeper understanding of worldly environmental, social, cultural, and political issues. Forcing student opinions about controversial statements within extremely diverse roles forces student disagreement and resulting perspective taking. Additionally, whereas student character research and interactive dialogue engrosses them in important historical and geographical data, real-world expedition findings apprentice them in authentic scientific data analysis and discoveries. Across these learning opportunities, it is clear that sociocultural learning theory can assist in theoretically grounding the use of global networking technologies.

Though network and online educational technologies are changing faster than research studies can be designed, in this study, we used four assessment techniques that were specific to the unique social interaction and mentorship activities of the World Forum program. It is a start. Future activities might explore additional World Forum data and refine these initial social interaction coding schemes for other aspects of collaborative learning and electronic dialogue. Clearly, we are just beginning to contemplate and examine how social interaction and discourse influence electronic group activities and resulting cognitive change. In a recent *National Geographic* article, Will Steger (1996), the IAP expedition leader, confirmed that we need more World Forums and World Schools for Adventure Learning, not fewer, when he declared, "As a teacher as well as an explorer, I'm glad we had the chance to share these moments with so many young people, who may now understand a little better the importance of adventure in every life" (p. 89). Certainly this quote and our initial findings indicate that electronic messages sculpted from the frozen tundra to our north can instantly ignite cognitive battles among millions of children in dozens of countries around the world. As the World Forum leaders rerun these activities as simulations, such hot cognition springing from messages beamed long ago through the chilly Arctic air becomes a cheap, renewable networld energy resource simply awaiting another imaginative use. What will be yours?

ACKNOWLEDGMENTS

This manuscript will be reprinted in *Interactive Learning Environments* with permission of Lawrence Erlbaum Associates. Portions of this chapter were also presented at the 1995 annual convention of the Association for Educational Communication and Technology (AECT) in Anaheim, CA, and the 1994 Midwestern Educational Research Association annual meeting in Chicago, IL. The authors would like to thank Douglas Scott and Fred Goodman from the University of Michigan and Marty Siegel from Indiana University for their help in obtaining access to this World Forum and World School program data and in explicating the specific International Arctic Project (IAP) events. We also are grateful to Gladysin Huerta-Stark for her data analysis assistance as well as Robert Fischler for his timely editorial services. Authorship order here was strictly arbitrary because the two authors contributed equally to this manuscript.

REFERENCES

Bannon, L. (1986). Computer-mediated communication. In D. Norman & N. Draper, (Eds.), *User centered system design: New perspectives on human-computer interaction* (pp. 399–410). Hillsdale, NJ: Lawrence Erlbaum Associates.

Bjorklund, D. F. (1995). *Children's thinking: Developmental function and individual differences.* Pacific Grove, CA: Brooks/Cole.

Bloom, B. (1956). *Taxonomy of educational objectives; the classification of educational goals, by a committee of college and university examiners.* New York: Longmans, Green.

Bonk, C. J. (1990). A synthesis of social cognition and writing research. *Written Communication, 7*(1), 136–163.

Bonk, C. J., Malikowski, S., Angeli, C., & East, J. (in press). Case-based conferencing for preservice teacher education: Electronic discourse from the field. *Journal of Educational Computing Research.*

Bonk, C. J., Medury, P. V., & Reynolds, T. H. (1994). Cooperative hypermedia: The marriage of collaborative writing and mediated environments. *Computers in the Schools, 10*(1/2), 79–124.

Clements, D. H., & Nastasi, B. K. (1988). Social and cognitive interactions in educational computer environments. *American Educational Research Journal, 25*(1), 87–106.

Collins, A., Brown, J. S., & Newman, S. E. (1989). Cognitive apprenticeship: Teaching the crafts of reading, writing, and mathematics. In L. Resnick (Ed.), *Knowing, learning, and instruction: Essays in honor of Robert Glaser* (pp. 453–494). Hillsdale, NJ: Lawrence Erlbaum Associates.

Gallimore, R., & Tharp, R. (1990). Teaching mind in society: Teaching, schooling, and literate discourse. In L. C. Moll (Ed.), *Vygotsky in education: Instructional implications of sociohistorical psychology* (pp. 175–205). New York: Cambridge University Press.

Golub, J. N. (1994). *Activities for the interactive classroom.* Urbana, IL: National Council of Teachers of English.

Harasim, L. (1990). Online education: An environment for collaboration and intellectual amplification. In L. Harasim (Ed.), *Online education: Perspectives on a new environment* (pp. 39–64). New York: Praeger.

Ishii, H. (1993). Cross-cultural communication and CSCW. In L. Harasim (Ed.), *Global networks* (pp. 144–151). Cambridge, MA: MIT Press.

Lauzon, A., & Moore, G. (1989). A fourth generation distance education system: Integrating computer-assisted learning and computer conferencing. *The American Journal of Distance Education, 3*(1), 38–49.

Lave, J., & Wegner, E. (1991). *Situated learning: Legitimate peripheral participation.* New York: Cambridge University Press.

Lehrer, R. (1993). Authors of knowledge: Patterns of hypermedia design. In S. Lajoie & S. Derry (Eds.), *Computers as cognitive tools* (pp. 197–227). Hillsdale, NJ: Lawrence Erlbaum Associates.

Lehrer, R., Erickson, J., & Connell, T. (1994). Learning by designing hypermedia documents. *Computers in the Schools, 10*(1/2), 227–254.

Mead, G. H. (1934). *Mind, self, and society.* Chicago: The University of Chicago Press.

Muuss, R. E. (1988). *Theories of adolescence* (5th ed.). New York: Random House.

Piaget, J. (1963). *Psychology of intelligence.* Paterson, NJ: Littlefield, Adams.

Riel, M. (1992). A functional analysis of educational telecomputing: A case study of learning circles. *Interactive Learning Environments, 2*(1), 15–29.

Riel, M. (1993). Global education through learning circles. In L. Harasim (Ed.), *Global networks* (pp. 221–236). Cambridge, MA: MIT Press.

Ruopp, R., Gal, S., Drayton, B., & Pfister, M. (Eds.). (1993). *LabNet: Toward a community of practice.* Hillsdale, NJ: Lawrence Erlbaum Associates.

Salomon, G. (1993). On the nature of pedagogic computer tools. In S. Lajoie & S. Derry (Eds.), *Computers as cognitive tools* (pp. 179–196). Hillsdale, NJ: Lawrence Erlbaum Associates.

Salomon, G., Perkins, D. N., & Globerson, T. (1991). Partners in cognition: Extending human intelligence with intelligent technologies. *Educational Researcher, 20*(3), 2–9.

Selman, R. (1971). Taking another's perspective: Role-taking development in early childhood. *Child Development, 42,* 1721–1734.

Selman, R. (1980). *The growth of interpersonal understanding: Developmental and clinical analysis.* New York: Academic Press.

Selman, R., & Byrne, D. (1974). A structural-developmental analysis of levels of role taking in middle childhood. *Child Development, 45,* 803–806.

Steger, W. (1996). Dispatches from the Arctic Ocean. *National Geographic, 189*(1), 78–89.

Teles, L. (1993). Cognitive apprenticeship on global networks. In L. Harasim (Ed.), *Global networks* (pp. 271–281). Cambridge, MA: MIT Press.

Tharp, R. (1993). Institutional and social context of educational reform: Practice and reform. In E. A. Forman, N. Minnick, & C. A. Stone (Eds.), *Contexts for learning: Sociocultural dynamics in children's development* (pp. 269–282). New York: Oxford University Press.

Tharp, R., & Gallimore, R. (1988). *Rousing minds to life: Teaching, learning, and schooling in social context.* New York: Cambridge University Press.

Vygotsky, L. (1986). *Thought and language* (Rev. ed.). Cambridge, MA: MIT Press.

Wells, G., & Chang-Wells, G. L. (1992). *Constructing knowledge together: Classrooms as centered of inquiry and literacy.* Portsmouth, NH: Heinemann.

7

Models of Asynchronous Computer Conferencing for Collaborative Learning in Large College Classes

Siat-Moy Chong
Indiana University

Higher education is currently undergoing its most significant changes in decades. Student populations are shifting from high school graduates to adults who have been in the workplace for many years. More and more of these students demand alternatives to the full-time, on-campus study arrangements of the past. Those students who come fresh out of high school show increasing signs of unpreparedness and lack of motivation for higher learning (Erickson & Strommer, 1991). Decreases in public funding and efforts to contain the steadily rising costs of tuition are forcing universities to rethink the ways in which they deliver instruction. National studies of higher education have been critical of the result, claiming that many degree programs have failed to develop students' critical thinking and social values (Boyer, 1987; Knox, Lindsay, & Kolb, 1993). Despite these problems universities continue to award degrees in record numbers and compete fiercely for new students. Classroom sizes remain high—especially during the first college years when individualized attention and support are most important—and many students seem more disengaged than ever.

In an effort to adjust to the demands of these new realities, faculty and instructional developers are exploring different instructional strategies and new educational technologies that might effectively transform the traditional college classroom. For about a decade now, the collaborative learning movement has made its way into postsecondary education. Encouraged by new, socially contextualized concepts of learning in and out of school (Resnick, 1989; Rogoff, 1990) and compelled by the ineffectiveness of the stand-and-deliver model of instruction, teachers have begun to look for new classroom procedures that put more emphasis on the students' role in their own education. In addition, new computer technologies are laying the groundwork for a communication infrastructure that will allow instructors and students to distribute initiatives for the learning process in more democratic and reflective ways (Harasim, Hiltz, Teles, & Turoff, 1996; Harrison & Stephen, 1996).

Even before the arrival of the Internet, asynchronous computer conferencing offered itself as a medium that combined a potential for collaboration, increased participation and reflection, peer tutoring, close monitoring of student learning, and time-and-space–independent extension of classroom learning. Now integrated into the Internet, it may become the key to an interactive alternative to the live classroom. The current study was conducted before the Internet had begun what probably will amount to a new era of distance education and possibly education in general. In the early 1990s, instructors had just started to explore the value of asynchronous computer conferencing. Their struggle to come up with specific instructional formats for this new medium may prove useful now that people seem to have accepted the technology itself. This study is a descriptive record of how several instructors from different disciplines adopted asynchronous computer conferencing to supplement instruction of their large on-campus courses. It includes descriptions and analyses of the various collaborative learning models on which these instructors based their use of the technology.

PURPOSE OF THE PROJECT

The purpose of this research project was to explore the educational potential of computer conferencing technology in college teaching. More specifically, the goal was to investigate how computer conferencing might facilitate collaborative learning and enhance social interaction in instructional contexts where high enrollment minimizes opportunities for students to get to know each other and engage in meaningful discussions.

The courses described in this research were conducted between 1990 and 1993 at Indiana University, Bloomington. The computer-conferencing system available at that time was VAX Notes from Digital Equipment Corporation, referred to on campus as the "Electronic Classroom" (EC). The EC system was accessible from all computer clusters using networked PCs and Macintoshes across the campus as well as via modems from workstations in offices and homes. The EC was a computerized bulletin board that allowed its users to post messages for other participants to read and reply to. Each of the classes described here was given a separate conference (in some cases more than one) under its course and section number enabling the instructor to structure and monitor exchanges via the bulletin board. Additional material could also be added as the need arose.

These electronic conferences were structured using key topics and replies. Topics were usually (but not necessarily) posted by the instructor, whereas students responded to these topics on a secondary "reply" level. The system was strictly hierarchical and linear. Topics and replies were entered only in ascending sequence. The software did not provide flexibility for online resequencing or for attaching one reply directly to another. Because entries within a conference could become numerous and lengthy, keywords were sometimes used to search through them. Important to note, in some of the electronic classes, it was possible to extract individual notes or an entire conference for printing purposes, as well as to up- and download conference files for composing or editing off-line on personal computers.

METHODOLOGICAL APPROACH

A multisample case study approach was used in this research. The intent in following a number of courses utilizing the EC throughout an entire semester or academic year, was to describe how instructors utilized an asynchronous computer-conferencing system in large-section college classes. This study also sought to observe how students would accept and participate in collaborative learning activities via computer conferencing.

The respondents in this study included the professors who taught the courses, the student volunteers enrolled in the courses, the associate instructors (if any), and the instructional developers when present. Demographic characteristics varied widely among respondents. Table 7.1 describes the

TABLE 7.1
Data Collection Procedures

Interviews	*Observations*	*Questionnaires*	*Documents*
Participants: • Faculty • Students • Associate instructors • Instructional developers	Participants: • Faculty and students	Participants: • Students	E-mail messages: • Faculty—students • Faculty—developers
Method: • Face-to-face and E-mail • Nondirected, open-ended • Focused • Taped	Method: • Class sessions • Electronic class conferences • Training sessions		EC Class Notes Meeting Summaries: • Researcher-faculty • Instructional development team Researcher Records: • Log of interviews • Personal reflections

interview participants and methods, key observations and subjects, questionnaires utilized, and documents analyzed in this study.

The pedagogical dynamics of the electronic conferences were analyzed according to such criteria as the following:

- How did students use the relatively undefined parameters of the EC?
- What effect did the EC have on classroom climate?
- How was the EC integrated into the course?
- How much interaction was generated by the EC?
- How did EC use develop over the course of a semester?
- Which aspects of the medium's potential were left unutilized in a given application?
- How did face-to-face and electronic collaboration complement each other?

RESULTS

Within the context of this project, instructors worked with variations of three basic models of computer conferencing to engage in highly interactive and challenging activities (see Fig. 7.1): (a) ongoing electronic discussions

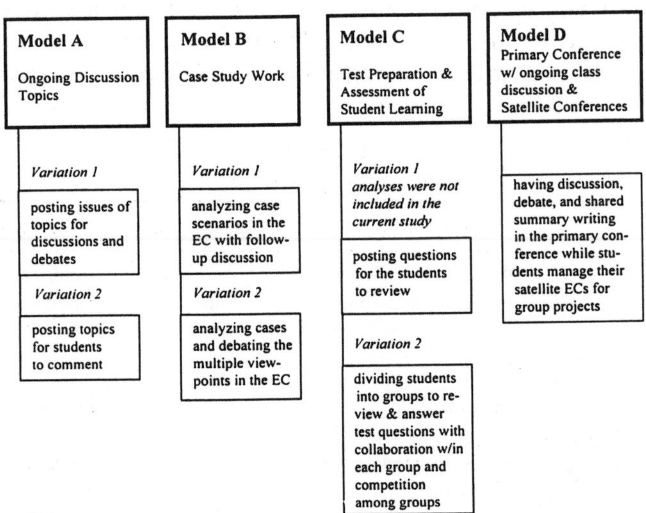

FIG. 7.1. Sample models of asynchronous conferencing in large college classes. *Note.* Model D has not been discussed in this chapter. Refer to author's unpublished dissertation for details and description (Chong, 1998).

throughout the semester on instructor-selected topics (Model A), (b) case study analyses (Model B), and (c) collaborative test preparation and assessment of student learning (Model C).

Each of these functions required different levels of involvement from students and instructor alike (see Chong, 1996, for more details).

MODEL A: ONGOING DISCUSSION TOPICS

Because opportunities for student participation in large classes are extremely limited, the first model utilized the delayed electronic conferencing medium as a forum for open-ended discussions. Lectures typically cover vast amounts of course content, which form the main basis for student assessment. This seems to restrict instructors in many cases to the transmission of factual knowledge that is easily testable on multiple-choice exams. The deeper issues of a subject matter or discipline, which rarely have a right or wrong answer, often remain untouched. Some instructors, therefore, have used the EC to create additional opportunities for discussion, oftentimes dealing with topics that could not be fully addressed during regular class time.

Model A was used by two instructors, one from computer science and one from sociology, who both used computer conferencing to incorporate debates on complex issues into their courses. Although both instructors used the conferencing for ongoing discussion, as described later, each adopted a different approach within this model.

In Model A, generic categories or topics were available for students to enter their comments, for example, the Coffee House. The basic functions of Model A provided an extension of the classroom for indepth discussion for arguments, perspectives, and insights. The discussion was carried out weekly or by topic.

As indicated, the instructors used two variations of electronic discussion. The major difference between the two was the nature of the topics posted in the EC. In Variation 1, the EC topics were selected for discussion and dialogue. In Variation 2, the instructor simply provided categories of notes, such as an Opinion Page, under which students could enter their comments. Each topic category had a different function. For instance, some were directed at fellow students—for example, the Coffee House, the Opinion Page, the Self-Introductions—whereas others were more applicable to the instructor, for example, Questions Before/After an Exam, the Class Suggestion Box, Can You Explain. The remainder were for both instructor and students to read and respond to (the Opinion Page, Collaborative Learning, the Class Project, EC Technical Assistance). These distinctions in audience were not predefined; rather, the discussion emerged gradually, as did the patterns in which students entered their comments.

Variation 1: Posting Issues for Debate

The first course examined was a beginning-level computer science class for nonmajor students. Of the total 317 students 90% were undergraduates, whereas the remaining 10% were graduate and continuing education students. Basically, the course consisted of weekly 1-hour lectures and small-group lab sections. The professor taught the lecture, while teaching assistants led the lab sessions. Students received a participation grade based on the frequency with which they got involved in class discussions or in EC debates.

The discussion topics for the EC with the number of replies to each are listed in the Table 7.2. The EC provided a secondary forum, besides the live classroom, for addressing the ethical issues that surround the increasing computerization of society. Although the instructor's use of open discussion usually led to lively participation from students, only a fraction of this huge class was able to voice its opinions during class time. The EC, therefore, was an appropriate instrument to draw those who did not have a chance to speak in class into the discussion. During later interviews, the teacher also stressed another advantage of the EC: It fostered the development of a community not typically witnessed in large college classrooms. In effect, providing everyone the opportunity to publish his or her opinion on a topic of common interest was a step toward overcoming silence and anonymity.

Findings for Model A, Variation 1

Focusing only on the EC medium's potential for fostering debate, initial analysis suggested that students in this class did not measure up to common criteria for collaborative learning through computer conferencing. Apparently, students did not utilize the EC to the extent expected by the instructor. However, one has to keep in mind that the instructor had used a variety of

TABLE 7.2
EC Debate Topics for Computer Science Class

Topics	*Number of Replies*
1. Technology & the Media in the Persian Gulf War	71
2. Ethics and Morals: Is There a Difference?	62
3. Ethical Constructs for Telecommunications	69
4. Software Piracy and Ethics	28
5. Abusing Computer Privileges	50
6. Intellectual Property	50
7. Computer Myths	100
8. Lifestyle Information vs. Factual Information	40
9. Can you get out of the computer?	30
10. Long Privacy Article	24

means to encourage student interaction. Writing comments in the EC was only one way of fulfilling the participation requirements of the course, typically accounting for merely 5% of the total course grade. Apparently, this was not a strong enough incentive for many undergraduate students who are not worried about competing for top grades.

Moreover, there were some traditional student expectations that interfered with a more effective use of the medium. Most young students still preferred to receive their feedback directly from the instructor rather than from their peers. The instructor went to great lengths to provide such feedback in her other assignments, far more than might normally be expected in such a large class. Thus, the EC was only one of a variety of methods in which students were reassured that they counted as individual members of a larger community. Had these circumstances been different, the EC could have played a more active role in developing a sense of community and interaction. For example, an instructor who had less time to devote to personalized feedback and direct student involvement in a large lecture might organize the EC more specifically to compensate for the loss of classroom interaction. Elements of such an organization of the EC are outlined later.

Variation 2: Posting Topics for Students to Comment On

The second instructor using Model A taught a junior-level class on the sociology of work. Typically this course enrolled about a hundred students, but there were only 56 undergraduate students enrolled during this particular semester. The course had a lecture format complemented by occasional small-group work, class discussion, short inclass writing ("minute papers"), guest lecturers, and some films. Course requirements included: four exams, a class project, and mandatory test preparation in groups using the EC (see Model C). Several generic topics were created by the instructor to help students learn to express their opinions on multiple levels. The number of topics grew over time as students could create new ones of their own (see Table 7.3).

The instructor was eager to create new structures in his class that mirrored the collaborative work approaches found in the "real" world. A presentation at a conference on collaborative learning in higher education had introduced him to a model of collaborative test preparation that seemed to fit his needs. It also provided a first look at the potential of computer conferencing for collaborative learning. When he and a team of instructional designers discussed a combination of the two approaches, electronic teamwork and self-testing, he agreed to pilot the new format in his class and soon became immersed in all aspects of this experiment.

Although the instructor monitored the conference several times a day, he did not enter into the discussion unless it was absolutely necessary. In fact, he exercised considerable restraint in his comments. Even on seeing such

TABLE 7.3
Generic EC Topics and Student Meeting Places for Sociology Class

Topics	*Number of Replies*
1. Students' Self-Introductions	
2. EC Technical Assist Shop	
3. Questions Before & After an Exam	
4. Informal "Coffee House"	150
- Sports (baseball & basketball)	20
- Special events (recreation)	21
- Jokes	5
- Apartment sublets	8
- Sightseeing for a classmate's parents	10
- Medical horror stories (started in class)	8
- Specific questions to anyone in class	8
- General announcements	5
- Movies (mostly relating to class topics)	9
- Class suggestions/discussions about class	16
- The university's change of tuition policy	9
5. Can you explain what . . . means?	
6. The Opinion Page	
7. About Current Readings Assigned	
8. Class Suggestion Box	
9. About Collaborative Learning	
10. About My Class Project	

entries as "Can you explain what . . . means?" he usually waited for a student to give an answer before "scaffolding" or intervening in student learning (Tharp & Gallimore, 1988). If his expertise was directly requested, however, he always responded promptly. This style of close but restrained monitoring was important in order for students to recognize that although this medium was theirs to use, their comments were heard and taken seriously by the instructor. Whenever possible, the instructor incorporated students' written, electronic, and oral suggestions into the course to give them a sense of ownership and to encourage participation. In my interviews with him, he stressed how helpful the medium was in providing new insights into his students' thinking, claiming that he now saw his students as more serious in their goals and efforts than in previous years.

Findings for Model A, Variation 2

During transcript analysis, three topics were prominent: the Coffee House, the Opinion Page, and About Collaborative Learning. The Coffee House was a topic in the EC where the students would "meet" and "socialize" with each other (see also Harasim, 1990a). Here, students could simply stop by and drop a note, whereas others might arrive and join the conversation.

Because even a comment of the most informal nature in the Coffee House earned the students points, it was difficult to determine the degree to which this informal forum fulfilled a real academic or true social need among the students. Because the class turned out to be much smaller, and hence, more collaborative and interactive than originally expected, the Coffee House outlet became less important. Of the 150 comments entered by 38 students in the Coffee House, 61 could be considered announcements, whereas 73 were classified as replies to these announcements. Further analysis revealed numerous subtopics, such as sports (baseball and basketball), jokes, medical horror stories, movies, and apartment sublets.

As a first activity in the electronic classroom, each student was asked to write one full screen of self-introduction. In this informative exercise, students revealed a significant amount of meaningful information about themselves, probably due to the instructor's request and a model provided by a graduate teaching assistant. In contrast, when students in other ECs on campus had been asked for self-introductions, the exercise was never very productive, presumably because the expectation was not modeled carefully.

Notes in the Coffee House fluctuated between a serious and a more chatty tone. About 11 or 12 weeks into the semester, there was a general turn toward more serious comments. Considerable discussion focused on two topics, a proposal by the university for a flat-fee tuition and stories of medical malpractice based on personal experience or news reports. By the end of the semester, many people seemed to tire of the casual, conversational replies, for example, baseball, weekend fun, and jokes.

In stark contrast to the Coffee House were students' comments on the Opinion Page topic. The Opinion page was initiated by one student's debate on labor–management relations—and resulted in 39 more notes over the course of the semester. This topic proved to be extremely fruitful for the discussion, in which every entry built on a previous note. Eventually other topics branched off, although none was as successful as the first one.

The Opinion Page was probably the best example of how the medium can enrich course content. First, it functioned as an extension of the class discussion. For those who could not get into the live class discussion, or were hesitant to do so, this was the perfect forum to contribute to this class. Second, it encouraged a synthesis of course materials with students' experiences in the outside world. Relating theory to practice requires time for reflection. The written medium of the EC provided the opportunity for students to thoughtfully relate what they themselves had experienced on a job, picked up in the papers or from TV, and heard and read about in class. Still, surprisingly, students' attitudes toward the EC were rather negative. Among eight main instructional elements in class, the EC was ranked lowest by the students. The mandated weekly participation in the EC was viewed by many students as relatively unproductive. Furthermore, the awarding of participation points for leaving a note in the Coffee House was considered particularly inappropriate, because this suggested that students were rewarded for doing busywork.

The students' negative evaluation of the weekly use of EC can be explained by several factors. First of all, this medium was new to both the instructor and the students. Like most innovations, electronic conferencing required an initial acclimation period, especially for finding out what the most productive activities were under various topic options. Student interviews and evaluations indicated that because the course had above-average requirements, everything that did not seem absolutely essential to the final grade was jettisoned or given low priority. Moreover, a large number of students had insufficient access to computers. Having to wait in line in a public computer cluster or make extra trips to campus to do the weekly commenting transformed the innovative idea of students electronically dialoguing about the sociology of work into a chore. One of the medium's greatest assets, its potential to facilitate reflection by allowing the user to engage in a discussion at his or her leisure, was diminished by the students' limited access to computers.

Evaluation of Model A (Ongoing Discussion Topics)

Advantages. Ongoing discussion stimulated by the instructor through the periodic insertion of new topics opens up a variety of opportunities to use the Electronic Classroom. For instance, students can become more actively involved with the course materials. A topic or series of topics that deals with the weekly readings, for instance, might be a useful mechanism for encouraging students to keep up with the assignments while, at the same time, providing an immediate opportunity to test the meaningfulness of the new knowledge.

Clearly, this model can help students reflect on their own learning behavior. Student reflection may be accomplished by inserting a topic that asks students to discuss their experiences with this new electronic medium. In addition to active involvement in metacognitive reflection, delayed computer conferencing is a strategy to help foster student ownership of and responsibility for learning. Students can take more ownership in a course when they are given the opportunity to create their own discussion topics, moderate the discussion of their peers, or suggest changes in the way the course is taught. Furthermore, such enhancing of student ownership is likely to result in student involvement and learning in the traditional classroom setting. Hence, a learning community may be sparked. Students may enjoy a class, even a large class, considerably more if they have the opportunity to use part of its electronic meeting facilities to establish a "subculture" or shared space (Schrage, 1990) of their own; that is, to tell their kind of stories, voice their hopes and their frustrations, and so forth. Such an outlet also has the potential to help a predominantly TV-oriented culture express itself verbally. Students in large classes can now enhance their social lives by identifying, through their computer contacts, fellow students with corresponding interests. Similarly, students may seek and find assistance from other classmates by posting public announcements in the EC.

A diverse EC forum such as the one presented in Variation 2, allows students to provide the instructor with a multitude of feedback that ranges from humorous remarks in the Coffee House to substantive criticism in the Opinion Page as well as proposals for improving classroom teaching in the Suggestion Box. Traditional assessment procedures, in contrast, do not allow students this degree of course analysis and teaching feedback.

Disadvantages. When the function of the technology and the requisites of its use are not carefully integrated into the overall course activities, tasks in the EC will quickly take on the character of busywork. If this occurs, the innovative potential of the medium will be rejected by the students while the instructor may lose credibility because students feel that their time has been wasted. Students also face possibilities of rejection or lack of feedback in the EC when, for instance, they insert isolated statements that fail to create the interaction and discussion they intended.

On the other hand, in large classes with high student response rates, individual topics can receive considerable input within a short amount of time. The sheer quantity of input can lead to information overload, discouraging students who log in once or twice a week from following the arguments of their peers. Close monitoring can prevent such situations if the conference moderator recognizes topic saturation and regroups new or emerging arguments into separate topics.

MODEL B: WORK ON CASE STUDIES

The instructor may use the electronic conference as a bulletin board to publish the products of individuals and groups in preparation for further discussion face to face. The logistics of sharing written information becomes a complicated (and costly) problem in large classes. At the same time, electronic classrooms offer the opportunity for comparing opinions and interpretations that are typically quantitatively and logistically unmanageable. One way to exploit this opportunity is in conjunction with the case study approach to teaching. In this approach, students analyze relevant case scenarios on their own and then use the multiple viewpoints generated by the whole class as stimuli for further electronic and "live" discussion.

In Model B, the EC served as an extension of the classroom. The students met in this virtual place to share case scenarios for indepth discussion and interpretation. There are two variations provided here: Students analyze relevant case scenarios in the EC on their own and debate their viewpoints electronically, or use the multiple viewpoints generated in the EC as stimuli for further inclass discussion.

Variation 1

The first variation of Model B was observed in a sophomore/junior-level education course with an enrollment of 125 students traditionally taught in a straight lecture format. Course requirements that semester included two exams, a portfolio, and a class project.

The instructor's motivation for experimenting with a new teaching approach originated largely from her desire to modify the students' attitudes toward people with special needs. The instructor assumed that having students work on cases might be an appropriate way to deepen their awareness and develop their critical judgment relative to the complex issues facing society in its treatment of special populations.

The need to develop the students' analytical skills and their ability to construct logical arguments were additional motivations for trying a case study approach. Authentic cases taken from real life provided the complexity necessary to encourage critical thinking and logical argumentation. They simultaneously were seen as a means of challenging students to be more active and to become self-directed learners who would rely on themselves and each other for answers, rather than on the instructor. In addition, electronic cases can function as an apprenticing tool for student knowledge construction (Reisbeck, 1996).

Using a jigsaw type of approach, the instructor divided the class into groups of four students. Each student in a group worked on a different case provided by articles from popular news magazines, although all four cases had some common underlying issue. Students were required to analyze their cases by following a case-analysis template. These individual analyses were posted in the EC. To gain a more sophisticated understanding of their case, students would then read the analyses of their peers. This procedure was to prepare them for the subsequent face-to-face meeting with their group, in which they compared the similarities and differences of their cases. The final goal was to find the common issue underlying all four cases and to analyze the concerns raised by this issue for different levels of society.

Findings for Model B, Variation 1

The students were highly enthusiastic about the group work. From the 78 feedback sheets collected after two group sessions, only eight students (in 6 of the 34 groups) questioned the benefits of their group meetings. The others had positive comments about their group experience, claiming that they had benefited tremendously from the different viewpoints contributed by other group members as well as from the magazine articles that provided current information on social issues they had not previously considered. The authentic "feel" of current news articles from newspapers or journals contributed significantly to the positive comments about the group work. When asked in group interviews whether they preferred case descriptions that had been edited to reduce complexity and length, students overwhelmingly endorsed the original news articles.

On the downside, there were problems from a variety of sources, including logistics, teaching approach, course expectations, students' collaborative skills, the novelty of the technology, and deficiencies in the planning and administration of this instructional experiment.

Training 120 students to use EC was a formidable task: Preparation of handouts and articles was time consuming; many groups had difficulty finding a mutually acceptable time for their meetings. Overall the students' frustrations resulting from the various logistical problems affected their readiness to embark on this experiment. Worse still, electronic case analysis became an add-on course feature, thereby indicating to students a fairly low level of importance. In fact, as problems became more abundant, the instructor relegated the activity to the status of an out-of-class project for extra credit.

As far as the group work was concerned, it turned out that the majority of students did not exhibit the skills to meaningfully challenge someone else's viewpoint during a discussion, or to put themselves into someone else's position. Regrettably, these had been the main goals that the case study approach, together with the use of the electronic conferencing technology, had been intended to promote. However, what could have been done differently?

Clearly, students needed more guidance throughout the exercise. Electronic communication alone was incapable of providing this guidance to students who were simply not prepared to use it independently. Without the direct involvement and encouragement of the instructor, any activity was bound to fail.

If the instructor can afford the time and effort for such a classroom innovation, a few elements are essential to make it work. First of all, appropriate behavior needs to be modeled in class. For instance, the instructor might model or explain behavior, such as actively listening, supporting the ideas of others, encouraging shy group members to take their turn, questioning fast and easy solutions, and verbalizing conflicts that tend to threaten successful teamwork. Second, detailed feedback pertaining to the students' work in the electronic medium needs to be given in class. Students are accustomed to receiving individualized feedback, at least in the form of a grade, when they hand in a written assignment. Third, clear grading guidelines need to be established affirming the importance of the EC exercise, while describing exactly how the students' work will be evaluated. Otherwise, resulting EC activity will be difficult to grade, due to students' differing kinds of input. Finally, the assignments need to be structured in ways that guarantee thoughtfulness and diversity among student products published in the EC. In individual case analyses, special incentives could be given for creative viewpoints, whereas student groups could compete in designing original plans and in contributing suggestions for solutions.

Variation 2

The course utilizing Variation 2 of Model B was a 500-level course in library science enrolling a total of 58 students from two sections, including undergraduates (seniors) and graduates. Each section met twice a week, and used the EC at other times. The course requirements included two exams, four assignments, and a class participation grade. Besides the case study discussion, the EC also served as a place for information dissemination and class discussion.

The case study discussion was the final assignment posted by the instructor in the EC. Each issue was posted as a separate topic (see Table 7.4). In response, students would select a topic and then post their position or argument. Afterwards, they were required to post a reply to a response received about the issue.

Sample electronic dialogue generated by assignment #4 and the case, "Letter of Reference" follow (note that there were 41 replies for this case):

> Case 3: The Letter of Reference
>
> Eloise has been a reference librarian at [the] Local College Library for six months. It is clear that she is not the right person in the right job—she comes to work late about once a week, and her assistance to patrons is sometimes less than her colleagues can accept. Suzannah, the reference supervisor, knows that Eloise wants to move out of town and is looking for other jobs. Eloise has asked Suzannah to write a letter of reference.

TABLE 7.4
Course Using Case Study for Discussion in the Electronic Classroom

Topics for Case Studies	*Number of Replies*
1. Assign 4 : Encyclopedia	4
2. Assign 4 : Write Off!	16
3. Assign 4 : Letter of Reference	41
4. Assign 4 : Online Catalog	18
5. Assign 4 : Electronic Ref.	17
6. Assign 4 : VAX Obscenities	28

The instructor posted questions related to whether Suzannah should write the letter, and if so, whether it should be a glowing recommendation or an honest assessment of Eloise's strengths and weaknesses. Here is one student's electronic response:

> Suzannah should agree to write the letter, but should tell Eloise that it will be an honest assessment of her capabilities and will include comments about her late arrivals and her poor assistance with patrons. She should then ask Eloise if she still wants her to be a reference, leaving the decision to Eloise. (3 of 41)

Evaluation of Model B (Using Case Studies)

Advantages. The use of the EC for case studies or for similar project formats involving proceduralized argumentation templates and out-of-class group work is, at this point, the least explored model. It is also the most involved. Nevertheless, as the preceding dialogue indicates, students become more actively involved in the practical and ethical dimensions of a field when using more authentic case material. Cases, especially when presented in the form of an authentic news report, function as an important counterbalance to the limitations of textbook knowledge. Pedagogically valuable cases have no clear right or wrong answers and thus challenge students to develop their reflective judgment beyond the rules of textbook prescriptions.

Students' cognitive skills are also exercised when using this approach. As indicated earlier, large segments of the undergraduate population need considerable work in developing the ability to analyze arguments logically. Students need guided practice in identifying issues, finding supporting evidence, analyzing underlying assumptions, and drawing conclusions for their own positions and about the actions required.

Disadvantages. Some disadvantages resulted from both the logistical and pedagogical complexity of this approach. For instance, if Model A requires the instructor to make EC activity worth at least 15% of the course work, Model B requires 30%. The effort required of the instructor in preparing the activities and of students in handling the system makes the approach inappropriate for simply an occasional exercise. In addition, key critical-thinking and teamwork skills need to be modeled repeatedly in class or students' work in groups and in the EC will be unsatisfactory. Outside of class some students tend to avoid doing their share of the work resulting in complaints from team members whose grade depends on the efforts of the whole team.

When large classes have a set of common cases for everybody to answer, "information overload" results and individualized feedback becomes a problem. The instructor cannot provide individualized comments to each one of 100 or more case analyses as many as six times during the semester. Consequently, alternative feedback modes need to be developed to help students improve their skills. Such alternative modes may include exemplar forms of feedback in the EC, peer feedback, individualized feedback to different portions of the class each time, and oral discussion and feedback in the regular classroom. Irrespective of the format, students need to understand the criteria for a good case analysis and for the grading of individuals and groups.

MODEL C: COLLABORATIVE TEST PREPARATION

This series of studies of delayed electronic collaboration has revealed that the more central the function of a given technology is within a course, the higher its chances of being accepted by students and faculty alike, and the more it may contribute to student learning. Examination of student performance is an element that is taken very seriously in every course. Model C focused on the medium's potential to assist with this assessment task. Instead of leaving it up to the individual student to prepare for an exam through the time-honored method of cramming, Model C stretches the exam preparation process out over a longer period and, at the same time, makes it a collaborative effort. The asynchronous electronic conference seemed an ideal medium for removing this endeavor from the noncommittal format found in most private study groups, to a more systematic course activity outside of class. Once again, two variations of this approach were attempted with differing degrees of success. Only the second version is detailed here.

This more complex model was embedded in one of the courses described earlier (see Model A, Variation 2). As indicated earlier, the instructor wanted to experiment with a different approach to testing that could assess students' critical-thinking abilities without long essay exams. This approach to collaborative test preparation was adapted to the EC. The class was divided into small study groups (usually four students per group) and clusters consisting of three or four groups. Each student in a cluster was given the same cluster ID number, allowing group members to log on to the system under the same name. The idea was for the students in one cluster to be able to post answers to share among themselves while shielding them from the other clusters. To reduce "free-riding" and motivate each member of a cluster to perform, the instructor encouraged "cooperative competition" with extra credit for above-average performance by individuals and individual clusters (Slavin, 1990).

About 1 week before the test, the instructor inserted 20 test questions into the EC (mostly multiple choice), creating a separate topic for each one. Each student in a cluster was assigned to answer and discuss 10 of the 20 questions. Because each question was addressed by about five different cluster members, this effectively allowed students who entered their answers later to discuss the answers of their peers. Important to note, students could see only the answers given by their own cluster members, because every cluster was hiding its input from the others by using its special cluster ID. The instructor left it up to the study groups to meet face to face shortly before the test and make final decisions about the best answers to each question.

During the test, students answered the previewed questions individually from memory. The instructor usually selected 10 of the questions and requested brief (one- or two-line) justifications for the multiple-choice answer. The instructor also included additional questions that had not been previewed, again to avoid a situation in which some students relied too heavily on the efforts of their peers. To assign the credit for the students' individual preparation and that of their cluster, the instructor randomly selected a small number of EC notes from each student and cluster for grading. Individual students received credit according to the sophistication of their answers, whereas the clusters were evaluated based on the quality of the team's discussion of a given question.

Sample of Test Preview in the Electronic Classroom

The EC is a rich source of course evaluation information. For example, there were 27 replies for Question 9 on Test 2 under Topic 53. This particular question was based on an article by Burawoy:

> Instructor Question:
>
> QU9: According to Marx's theory, the fundamental conflict of interest between workers and capitalists leads to constant hostility between workers and management in any capitalist enterprise. True or false?
>
> Two Different Student Responses:
>
> CL4 Brad (#1): *False!*—(page 86)—The workers and management that Burawoy studied are a definite exception to this rule. The management's interests were served because they were making a nice profit due to the 140% piece rate (this was controlled for the most part by the workers). While the workers' interests were served by keeping the piece rate at 140% without having the management increase the piece rate. The workers were, in effect, enforcing the restriction of output (something which Marx said they were not organized enough to do).
>
> CL3 Kevin (#5): *True!* I have just studied this in my Soc. 210 class. The Marxian view holds that conflict between workers and management creates alienation of the proletariat (working class). The capitalists try to extract surplus value from the workers who resist as a matter of principle.

Findings for Model C

Table 7.5 shows the counts of self-test responses on preview material by day for each of the three tests. Note that in all three cases, the number of responses did not reach 85% of its total before the day prior to the test. In the case

TABLE 7.5
Student Daily Self-Test Answer Input

Test 2 (Answer Input)		*Test 3 (Answer Input)*		*Final Exam (Answer Input)*	
Feb. 14	16	March 20	8	April 17	0
Feb. 15	1	March 21	5	April 18	0
Feb. 16	26	March 22	21	April 19	0
Feb. 17	14	March 23	32	April 20	0
Feb. 18	166	March 24	121	April 21	0
Feb. 19	220	March 25	169	April 22	3
Feb. 20	82	March 26	210	April 23	1
Total =	525	March 27	101	April 24	7
		Total =	667	April 25	9
				April 26	30
				April 27	40
				April 28	79
				April 29	202
				April 30	225
				May 1	101
				Total =	716

of the final exam, it was not until the very day of the exam that 85% of maximum was reached. This was in spite of the fact that half of the preview questions for the final exam were given out 2 weeks in advance. Only a week had been given for each of the other two test previews. Apparently, none of the students took advantage of the first 5 days of extra time allowed for the final preview.

Limited access to computers as well as a lack of interest in the other students' responses may, in many cases, provide an explanation for the large numbers of responses being entered just prior to an exam. Also, students may have been unwilling to spend more time on this one class. It was obvious to an observer in the classroom that the necessary preparatory reading was often not done until shortly before a test. A correlation coefficient for the relationship between the overall quality of EC response during the semester (as judged by the professor in the course) and overall performance in the class, revealed a significant positive relationship between overall quality of performance in the EC and the performance in the class for the semester (Pearson $r = .694$).

Whereas study group discussion and exchanges in the EC were most successful, the face-to-face discussions held in class were much less effective. The latter typically were centered around four to six people who were willing to participate in the large-class setting (most likely the ones who had done the readings). Their thoughtful comments, however, limited the participation of the remaining students in the class discussions. The EC, by contrast, not only allowed all the students to participate in a large-group discussion, but forced all students in the class to participate in study group meetings. Additionally, requiring EC responses forced all members of the study group to think about the test prior to the meeting and to do some advance preparation.

The use of the EC and study group work was complementary in this instructional model. Unfortunately, some of the positive aspects of the interaction in the EC and in the study group meetings might have detracted from the class meetings themselves. Low attendance figures suggest that students did not always find it necessary to come to class because they had a reliable method for getting the class notes from someone else. At least one member in every group interviewed expressed this as an added "convenience" of the EC. In this respect, added flexibility for the individual probably contributed to decreased responsibility to the class and to the instructor.

Evaluation of Model C (Test Preparation)

Advantages. The EC has great potential as a tool for collaborative test preparation and is a serious alternative to traditional practices of testing based on memorization. Model C confounds the truism that large classes of undergraduate students can be assessed only on factual knowledge acquisition. Because what is to be tested usually defines what students are willing to study, the result has been memorization and lower-order concept learning. Providing students with a mechanism to debate real problems that cover the most relevant areas of a test communicates the content difficulty more accurately.

When the preparation for a test is an integral part of the course agenda, deeper understanding and longer retention result. Instead of "cramming" for a test the night before, students are forced to go over the material a week or more ahead of time. When students choose to add study group meetings to the discussion in the EC, they come prepared and reduce the number of unmotivated group members. In accordance with Vygotsky's sociocultural theory (see Tharp & Gallimore, 1988; Wertsch, 1985), collaborative test preparation helps students view each other as sources of information and expertise, thereby fostering self-confidence. Learning to solve problems in a group of peers, instead of relying on the instructor, makes students less dependent on authority figures. It also teaches them the value of looking at problems from multiple perspectives.

Instructors, at the same time, gain important insights into the learning patterns of their students. Student rationales for solving a problem are documented step by step in the electronic medium. Consequently, tools like the EC provide a means of analyzing students' typical misconceptions and systematically addressing them in subsequent class sessions.

Disadvantages. Of course, the collaborative test preparation approach in Model C is not without problems. Although it is not so demanding of the instructor as Model B (case study work), it does require considerably more preparation and structuring than Model A (ongoing topic for discussion). The basic requirement for Model C is that a class has a minimum of three to four tests or significant quizzes per semester. A midterm and a final exam alone will hardly allow students to familiarize themselves sufficiently with the various procedures to discover their usefulness. Along these same lines, the instructor needs to generate a pool of appropriate test questions that are challenging enough to generate engaging discussions on the most appropriate answers.

The setup of the EC can become extremely elaborate. If clusters of students compete against each other, separate spaces must be created for each cluster, requiring either the provision of special cluster IDs or of separate ECs for individual clusters. Furthermore, student groups can only compete with each other if high and low performers are evenly distributed. If group members are self-selected and too homogeneous, fair competition is unlikely. Some groups will consistently score poorly and, thus, reduce their motivation for improvement. Perhaps the most severe drawback of Model C is that students may perceive the test preparation in the electronic medium as a shortcut through the course. Instead of coming to class regularly or doing the readings on a weekly basis, they may try to crunch their active learning for the course into the electronic discussions. Perhaps Model C should be combined with Model A, thereby forcing students to keep up with the course materials by requiring regular discussions of class readings in the EC.

OVERALL RESULTS

Students across all classes using the EC were surveyed as to their reactions to the new technology in instruction. Because these surveys were conducted at different times over 4 years, the questions and resulting data are not altogether consistent, but some questions were similar across the questionnaires. In the following discussion, data from seven courses and a total of 468 students are combined to provide some overall impressions of student backgrounds and opinions.

Given the relatively low degree of prior experience, most students became familiar with electronic mail (E-mail) rather quickly. When the instructor actively encouraged its use, many students logged on to the system more than twice a week (40% in class A, 60% in class B, 90% in class C). These students overwhelmingly came to like the medium (70%, 83%, 98%, respectively). One tendency was apparent: The more they used E-mail, the more they liked it. It is not surprising that, compared to E-mail, the overall approval rating for the EC was significantly lower. Four out of five classes had EC approval ratings of 40% to 66%. In the fifth class, which used it marginally, only 18% of the students liked the medium and 53% disliked it. But even within the two classes that used the EC most, not all students were enthusiastic about it. When asked whether they would take another course using the EC, only 29% of the students in each of these two classes answered positively, 51% and 62% were uncertain, and 20% and 9% responded negatively.

In three of seven classes, what the students clearly appreciated most about the EC was the opportunity and ease of receiving supplemental information from their instructor. Students in three other classes focused more on how the EC improved their ability to express themselves or to learn from each other. Some student comments included:

- ". . . the project/assignment completion-discussions were illuminating."
- "It was great. This was the only course I have taken so far that used notes as part of the class activities."
- "The VAX Notes provided a forum for student opinion that I do not think would have been expressed otherwise."

Between 31% and 77% of the students in five classes surveyed complained about problems with access to networked computers, in part because most students did not own a computer. In the case of one undergraduate course, only 1 out of 96 students owned a modem. Few computers were available in dorms. Logging on to the system for most students meant, at the very least, having to make an extra trip to one of the computer clusters on campus. Often, it also meant waiting for a computer to become available in the cluster: "Last night I tried to put it into the computer from 9 PM all the way until 4 AM. I was trying to use the computer facilities in the Fine Arts building and the VAX system was down the entire time."

What students liked least about the EC was the time and inconvenience involved in doing their assignments away from home, especially if these assignments seemed to be of low priority in the course. The second aspect that students disliked about the EC was having to deal with a software application whose functions were not very intuitive and rather clumsy compared to the more familiar microcomputer applications. Students were reluctant to learn the commands for a software tool they could not use on a PC, one that seemed to have no utility beyond the boundaries of that particular course.

In contrast, the faculty seemed extremely willing to experiment with the student-centered aspects of the technology. For instance, despite all the problems the instructor using Model C encountered, he learned from and enjoyed reading the student reasoning in the EC discussion related to the previewed test questions. For him the experiment with the new technology paid off because he got to see new sides of his students' personalities that he did not have access to previously. They became more personable to him, and their thinking became more transparent.

CONCLUSIONS: THE BENEFITS, CONSIDERATIONS, AND GUIDELINES

Although the EC was not used to its full potential in any of the courses described, these case studies show that thoughtful use of the medium can improve student involvement in the learning process, even in very large classes. Computer conferencing can help reduce the feeling of anonymity that many students have in high-enrollment courses. It can even contribute to a sense of community if students recognize that their conference notes are read by their instructor and classmates, and that, accordingly, they can have an impact on elements of the course content and format.

In courses incorporating the EC, a larger number and greater variety of students have the opportunity to participate in class discussions. Those not comfortable speaking in front of a large audience or who simply express themselves better in writing have an opportunity to share their thoughts with the class in a less pressured situation. Students can carefully compose their ideas before submitting them to the scrutiny of their peers. They have time to reflect on what was said in class and incorporate relevant personal experiences into their responses. The development of professional judgment skills based on people's value and belief systems can be dealt with much more extensively in this medium than would usually be possible in a large class. Instructors can widen their own horizons regarding their students' patterns of interest and understanding. They gain a new means of studying the teaching–learning process, because their students' written discussions provide a convenient database of information that allows them to customize their teaching.

All this can work only if some important pedagogical mechanisms are put in place. The instructor needs to indicate support for the technology by structuring the course so that activities incorporating the medium are weighted equally with other, more traditional classroom activities. In some of the cases discussed here, too little emphasis was placed on the medium. Many students will not bother to learn the mechanics of a new technology, much less explore its potential for more meaningful learning, simply for the sake of some extra credit or for a participation grade that comprises only 5% of the final course grade. The second important element is careful modeling of what is expected from students in this new medium. In some cases, this modeling has to be performed by the instructor. At other times, modeling is more effective when done by peers operating close to students' zones of proximal development (Vygotsky, 1978, 1986). The instructor can facilitate this by delegating responsibility for moderating certain parts of the electronic conference to small groups of students.

Another consideration concerns the role of the instructor in the EC. Students often pay more attention to what their instructors do or fail to do than to what they say. For students to take ownership in the new technology, thereby making it a medium for student collaboration, it is important that instructors restrain themselves from excessive intervention once the basic structure is in place. The instructor's main work for the EC, careful planning of a sequence of activities and procedures, should probably happen before the semester begins. Once the semester has started, much of the initiating and monitoring work is better performed by designated groups of students. However, the instructor needs to be aware of what is happening at all times and respond promptly if his or her expertise or authority is required. Sometimes, it can be more beneficial to student collaboration if the instructor takes on a coaching role and provides feedback to individual students' contributions by private E-mail.

DELAYED COLLABORATION RECAP AND REFLECTION

All three models can be recommended for use in regular and large classes as well as distance-education courses. However, there are vast differences in what each requires from students and instructor, and in what they might accomplish.

Model A (ongoing discussion topics) is the most generic and can be adapted to almost any class without much risk of negatively influencing other class activities (see Table 7.6). Probably the best mix for most courses would be a combination of generic topics (a) for socializing (Coffee House)

TABLE 7.6
Analysis of Model A: Ongoing Discussion Topics

Advantages	*(Possible) Disadvantages*
1. Assists students to become more actively involved with course materials.	1. Becomes busywork.
2. Helps students to reflect upon their own learning behavior.	2. Fails to create interaction and meaningful discussion.
3. Provides the students the opportunity to take ownership in the course.	3. Causes "information overload."
4. Enhances students' social life through contact in the virtual place.	4. Provides the opportunity for inadvertent or intentional verbal abuses of peers.
5. Provides a place for students to establish their "subculture."	
6. Provides the instructor with a window into their students' "souls."	
7. Provides a place for students to critique the course or to propose improvements in classroom teaching.	

and (b) for open discussion of anything relating to the course (Opinion Page, Suggestion Box), and weekly or biweekly topical issues (Class Readings, Class Topic of the Week). Enlisting student help in moderating, especially in the latter category of topics, can be extremely beneficial.

Model C (collaborative test preparation) can become much too involved for novices in computer conferencing (see Table 7.7). Planning the logistics for groups or clusters of students in electronically protected EC spaces, developing test questions capable of generating discussion, and creating a workable system for selectively reading and evaluating student input are tasks requiring some experience with the management of collaborative learning approaches and with the technology itself. This model is much more feasible when groups of students take turns debating weekly review questions in an open conference. Moreover, this approach considerably reduces the workload for both students and instructors.

Model B (case study work) is very different from the other two in that it completely subordinates the technology to face-to-face collaboration (see Table 7.8). It is possible to avoid many of these problems, however, by transferring the group collaboration into the electronic conferencing medium. As in the variations of Model C, student groups can debate cases in the EC. The argumentation template provides a structure for the conference topics. Student groups either compete with each other for the most insightful case interpretations, or take turns debating different cases across the semester.

Designing EC activities for Models B and C is more likely to succeed once the instructor has had experience with Model A. Nevertheless, all three approaches are viable options for creating active and collaborative learning conditions. Computer conferencing will not solve the problem of overcrowded classrooms, but it may help prepare instructors and students for better times in which collaborative learning and attention to individual students becomes standard practice in our college classrooms. The cases detailed here are merely an indication of the potential of delayed electronic collaboration in large-en-

TABLE 7.7
Analysis of Model C: Collaborative Test Preparation

Advantages	*(Possible) Disadvantages*
1. Provides students with a mechanism to debate real problems for test preparation.	1. Requires more preparation and structuring.
2. Helps students to prepare for the test ahead of time.	2. Needs a minimum of three to four tests.
3. Helps students to look upon each other as sources of information and expertise.	3. Needs to generate a pool of appropriate test questions.
4. Instructors gain important insight into the learning patterns of their students.	4. Needs to have more planning due to the complexity of the Electronic Classroom.
	5. Requires good formation of groups with high and lower performers in one cluster.
	6. Increases grading task.
	7. May cause low attendance.

TABLE 7.8
Analysis of Model B: Work on Case Studies

Advantages	*(Possible) Disadvantages*
1. Assists students to get more actively involved in the practical and ethical dimensions of a field of study.	1. Too time consuming relative to its benefits (Variation 1).
2. Helps students to develop their cognitive skills.	2. Needs significant amount of time for training the students to perform the task (Variation 1).
3. Improves the students' group skills and social skills.	3. Without clear provisions, group work may cause frustration (Variation 1).
4. Provides a chance for indepth discussion.	4. Not possible to provide individualized feedback.
5. Helps students to see different aspects of an issue.	5. Grading problem if there are no well-defined grading criteria (Variation 2).
	6. "Information overload" may occur if there are only limited numbers of cases.

rollment college classrooms. They also outline the potential and the pitfalls involved in moving instruction increasingly into an electronic distance-education format that relies on learner collaboration where students never actually meet face to face.

ACKNOWLEDGMENTS

Portions of this chapter were presented at the annual convention of the Association of Educational Communication and Technology (AECT) in Washington, DC, 1992, and the Midwestern Educational Research Association's annual meeting in Chicago, IL, 1994. The majority of this research was done while the author was working in the Department of Development and Special Projects (DDSP) at Indiana University. The author would like to thank Edmund Hansen, now at Emporia State University, for his assistance in accessing the findings of an earlier evaluation project on delayed computer conferencing, summarized as ERIC document ED 334 938 in 1991. I am indebted to Dr. Hansen for his support and thoughtful ideas throughout this 4-year project. The author also is grateful to Curt Bonk and Kira King for their timely editorial help and encouragement.

REFERENCES

Boyer, E. L. (1987). *College: The undergraduate experience in America.* New York: Harper & Row.

Chong, S. M. (1998). *Case studies of computer conferencing to enhance collaborative learning in college classrooms.* Unpublished doctoral dissertation, Indiana University, Bloomington.

Erickson, B. L., & Strommer, D. W. (1991). *Teaching college freshmen.* San Francisco: Jossey-Bass.

Harasim, L. M. (1990). Online education: An environment for collaboration and intellectual amplications. In L. Harasim (Ed.), *Online education: Perspectives on a new environment* (pp. 39–64). New York: Praeger.

Harasim, L., Hiltz, S. R., Teles, L., & Turoff, M. (1996). *Learning networks: A field guide to teaching and learning online.* Cambridge, MA: MIT Press.

Harrison, T. M., & Stephen, T. (Eds.). (1996). *Computer networking and scholarly communication in the twenty-first-century university.* Albany: State University of New York Press.

Knox, W. E., Lindsay, P., & Kolb, M. N. (1993). *Does college make a difference? Long-term changes in activities and attitudes.* Westport, CT: Greenwood.

Resnick, L. B. (Ed.). (1989). *Knowing, learning, and instruction: Essays in honor of Robert Glaser.* Hillsdale, NJ: Lawrence Erlbaum Associates.

Riesbeck, C. K. (1996). Case-based teaching and constructivism: Carpenters and tools. In B. G. Wilson (Ed.), *Constructivist learning environments: Case studies in instructional design* (pp. 49–61). Englewood Cliffs, NJ: Educational Technology Publications.

Rogoff, B. (1990). *Apprenticeship in thinking: Cognitive development in social context.* New York: Oxford University Press.

Schrage, M. (1990). *Shared minds: The technologies of collaboration.* New York: Random House.

Slavin, R. E. (1990). *Cooperative learning: Theory, research, and practice.* New York: Longman.

Tharp, R., & Gallimore, R. (1988). *Rousing minds to life: Teaching, learning, and schooling in a social context.* New York: Cambridge University Press.

Vygotsky, L. S. (1978). *Mind and society.* Cambridge, MA: Harvard University Press.

Vygotsky, L. S. (1986). *Thought and language* (Rev. ed.). Cambridge, MA: MIT Press.

Wertsch, J. V. (1985). *Vygotsky and the social formation of mind.* Cambridge, MA: Harvard University Press.

8

On the Pedagogy of Electronic Instruction

Robert Althauser
Julia M. Matuga
Indiana University

At many state and some private universities, faculty teach large classes of 80 to 350 students. Depending on how selective admissions are, student ability and prior educational experience can vary a great deal. As a way of grappling with large classes and these inequalities of preparation and ability, some faculty explore the use of electronic conferencing. But technology by itself does not teach students anything or solve recurring structural course problems. Especially technology used on the margins of serious course instruction! For example, creating a computer conference but not requiring students to participate characterizes roughly 50% of the conferences established each semester at Indiana University.

In any first-time experience, as with conferencing, we educators can make sound as well as unsound decisions about how to utilize new technology. Sometimes, what we do seems to work at first. Not understanding why this happened, we proceed to make changes that do not work as well the second time around. At that point, or when things do not work out at first, we may conclude that the technology detracts from our usual success in the classroom. But something vital is missing in all of these scenarios: pedagogy.

This chapter seeks to develop some ideas about key pedagogic elements of successful electronic conferencing. In the conferences described later, students posted answers to previewed exam questions or to discussion questions while working as members of small cooperative learning groups. In the first section that follows, we offer a narrative of the classroom experiences of the first author, extending over courses intermittently taught during the past 5 years. The focus of this discussion is on several sections of an undergraduate course in the sociology of work. We identify three key structural features of these conferences: the effective group size, the structure of assignments, and the grading procedures.

The remainder of this chapter reviews socioculturally based research in an attempt to pedagogically inform the effective use of electronic conferencing. This research provides a theoretical foundation for the manner in which these electronic conferences were initially organized. After becoming more familiar with this research, the first author realized that his decisions about group size, assignments, and grading criteria were unknowingly consistent with many sociocultural ideas. To illuminate this linkage, specific concepts suggested by this research are retrospectively applied to textual excerpts from electronic conferences and from the second author's observational notes on the first author's classroom instruction. Among these concepts, scaffolding (see chap. 2 by Bonk & Cunningham for a description) is perhaps the most interesting and promising, particularly because the concept has not been commonly applied to large-classroom instruction or to electronic conferencing. We apply some rudimentary codes to those excerpts, thereby tagging aspects of scaffolding and deepening our understanding of this vital pedagogical concept.

ON THE ROAD TO THE USE OF CONFERENCING

In the fall of 1990, the Bloomington campus of Indiana University hosted a conference on Collaborative Learning (CL). This conference exposed the first author to the advocacy of active learning and to criticism of traditional "passive" learning methods—the heavy reliance on the lecture in particular. Specific ways of doing CL were presented. During this conference, an anthropology colleague described how her students worked in groups outside of class, on 50 multiple-choice exam questions prior to an exam in class. Her often detailed questions required concept application or comprehension skills. On exam day students marked their answers to these questions and then, without prior warning, had to briefly justify their answers to a few of the questions. The instructor explained that this step was an antidote to "free-riding" by group members who used group work only as an occasion for memorizing answers.

As it happened, the conference keynoter was Linda Harasim, an early pioneer of electronic conferencing (see Harasim, 1990). She stressed that conferencing would be successful if it was required of students and if faculty devoted the time required to design the conference and its materials. Although she did not make conferencing look easy, she did make it look well worth the effort.

TABLE 8.1
Courses Taught by First Author

Course	*Date*	*Class Size(s)*	*Software*	*Tasks*
Sociology of Work	Spring 1991	60	VAX Notes	Previewed exam questions; individual entries, cluster of three groups shared a conference.
Sociology of Work	Fall 1991	25	VAX Notes	"Intensive Writing Course": previewed exam questions; short writing assignments.
Sociology of Work	Spring 92–Spring 93	40–120	5-by-8 cards	Groups used cards to convey group answers to previewed exam questions.
Sociology of Work	Fall 1995	40, 9	FirstClass	Individuals submitted, discussed others' answers to discussion questions.
Introduction to Sociology	Fall 1996	80	web page forms	Individuals submitted answers to review questions, groups answered previewed exam questions.

As described in the sections that follow, the use by the first author of collaborative groups and simultaneously, electronic conferencing, grew out of the these initial experiences. For the first few courses, this author concentrated on the use of conferences as a venue for out-of-class group work on previewed exam questions (see Table 8.1). Base collaborative learning groups were formed and sometimes talked together at designated moments during class, but they were not utilized in class as much as in more recent classes. Descriptions of the first of these courses appear elsewhere (Althauser, 1992; see also Chong, chap. 7 of this volume). In the most recent course that used electronic conferencing, minilectures were sandwiched between video excerpts and groups working together in nearly every class, discussing and answering questions posed on worksheets. In this undergraduate class, electronic conferencing entailed extensive group work on discussion questions. The work was spread throughout the semester, starting as early as the end of the first week, unlike the more intermittent conference work on previewed exam questions in previous semesters.

ELECTRONIC CONFERENCING ABOUT PREVIEWED EXAM QUESTIONS

In all of the classes described here, semester-long learning groups of four to five were formed and assigned seats together. During the first class (spring of 1991), students would occasionally be asked to talk over an assigned question and select a spokesperson for whole-class discussion of their findings. With 4 weeks of time afforded for out-of-class training before the first exam, the students were prepared to use the assigned VAX Notes software when the first set of previewed exam questions was handed out.

Group members worked on 20 questions, a subset of a longer (40–50 question) inclass exam scheduled for 1 week later. Each student prepared answers to 10 of these 20 questions. Before posting these answers, students in collaborative groups of four were assigned to a cluster with two other groups. Each cluster shared a common site within the electronic conference not visible to the other clusters. Thus, each of the 12 students sharing this site would post their thoughts about the best answers to each of 10 questions and work toward achieving a single best answer for their group. *Each cluster had their own, separate and private, electronic conference.* Five such clusters were needed for a class of 60 students, with each cluster developing justified answers to the same set of 20 exam questions.

Specific student assignments of 10 questions each were staggered so that all 20 questions received equal numbers of answers. A sample of two answers per student were evaluated by the instructor. The degree of overall participation by the groups in each cluster (i.e., posting answers and commenting on each other's answers) was also assessed as part of the group's grade on this assignment.

ELECTRONIC CONFERENCING FOR DISCUSSION QUESTIONS

In a more recent sociology of work course (fall 1995), the class utilized electronic conferencing, but using FirstClass software instead of VAX Notes. Training began in the second class meeting using a laptop and a network connection to pull in and project the conference to the class. With the confidence building first steps of having students submit a screen of biographic information by the end of the first week of class, and the benefit of having students increasingly acclimated to computing relative to the 1991 experience, this class was able to commence electronic conferencing work by the beginning of the second week.

Because of the centrality of exams in traditionally taught classes and their continued use in the courses described here, there was an urgency about preparing students for exams that made discussions of previewed exam questions engaging for students. In the most recent work course, however, there were other goals in mind. Although reasoning and justification of answers still mattered and were used as grading criteria, the questions used were designated to draw the class into the discourse of the readings and class materials, and thereby provide a better foundation for their skills in applying concepts.

To embrace such discourse, a student should be able to relate what he or she has read or heard to the pros and cons of an argument. Thus, students were asked questions like this:

> What is a "pro" and "con" argument to this statement: "general skills and knowledge have value throughout one's career, while the value of more specialized skills and knowledge is limited to the first job or two after training is completed"? In stating your arguments, work with specific examples from any source—readings, class materials, news clippings, shared experiences, etc. What specific general or specialized skill does your answer refer to? What kinds of jobs or careers?

More ambitious questions were those that required deeper reflection and critical thinking. For example:

> In chapters 2–3 of Garson's (1988) *Electronic Sweatshop*, the author gives us accounts of individuals pressured to change the way they did their jobs. Garson certainly thinks that her workers are being "deskilled." Yet she describes various forms of resistance to this pressure in some instances, which may partially undercut her "deskilling" viewpoint. To shed some light on this ambiguity in her argument, analyze the types of skills which workers actually use, according to Garson's accounts. Where you see connections, apply the discussion of skills and knowledge from Monday's class in your analysis.

There are three key features of FirstClass that permit instructors to appropriately structure student work. First of all, by making the entire conference "private" to members of the class only, the instructor (as moderator) is able to assign any number of students into smaller subgroups of students working in separate subconferences. Using the old VAX Notes system, this could be accomplished only by having separate computer accounts for the clusters, with a password shared among cluster members. In FirstClass, all access to private conferences requires unique user names and passwords. This ensures responsible and accountable behavior among participants. Second, unlike either VAX Notes or Web forms, FirstClass permits instructors (qua moderators) to directly insert comments into previously posted student writing. Third, everyone in a conference can view the user names of those who have viewed any given submission, as well as the date and time of this access. As a consequence, students know that the instructor and others have at least viewed their work. This panoptican (from the Greek meaning "all visible") consequence helps establish the widespread participation of classmates.

KEY STRUCTURAL FEATURES OF CONFERENCES

The organization of students' conferencing has three key structural features: (a) the effective sizes of the groups working electronically on these questions, (b) the way students are assigned specific questions out of the total set of previewed questions to be answered, and (c) the manner in which student work is graded. Let's look at each of these in turn.

Effective Group Size

One of the virtues of small-group interaction in face-to-face collaborative groups is that each member is likely to contribute ideas and receive critical responses to their ideas. That virtue is less fully realized in any whole-class discussion, with the instructor and single students speaking in turn. Many instructors unfortunately assign the entire class to one class-sized conference. From the outset, however, the first author sought to replicate the effectiveness of smaller group sizes in conferencing, so that individual students would be writing and responding to other students they were also becoming acquainted with during inclass group discussions. To do this, some attention was paid to creating separate spaces within the overall conference for subsets of students to work in. These would achieve a simulacrum of small-group discussion. But how should the actual discussion groups be constituted and sized?

Our school experiences make many of us familiar with the strengths of thought-provoking social interaction and debate as well as the weaknesses of ill-prepared and half-hearted discussion. Familiar as well are the variations in the quality of discussion as this reflects the degree to which we are acquainted with other participants. From this, we could predict that the experience of inclass, small-group discussions would create a supportive atmosphere for out-of-class conferencing. To the degree that students have been induced or instructed to collect their thoughts before the discussion begins, we would expect that this initial exchange of perhaps conflicting ideas and understandings would be more productive as well.

However, faculty have less chance to structure, and, thus, affect the quality of the discussion that occurs outside of class, except through class modeling. When outside the boundaries of the traditional class, group members may not come to discussion fully prepared. Students, especially those in groups who have become friends, may prematurely and uncritically converge on answers. After hearing or reading one answer, the next participant might simply support it and move on. In an asynchronous conference, where students can easily review previously expressed ideas before commencing to add their own, such convergence is no less likely. If preparation for discussion consists of dividing questions among members, so that each question has only one thoughtful answer prepared beforehand, there is minimal opportunity for cognitive confrontation. Even if differences emerge, students may be less likely to criticize the views of a fellow group member than the views of a student in a different group.

Taking these notions into account, the first author opted to engender both the support expected from working with fellow group members and the confrontation that was more likely from having two to three groups working in the same area of an electronic conference. Hence, three quad groups were combined into a cluster and completed their work on previewed exam questions in a separate conference. In hindsight, this was a crude attempt to stage and sequence the kind of discussion desired. Not surprisingly, long runs of identical answers turned up, though with varied justifications of answers. But on the whole, the modest size of the clusters—about 10–12 students each—achieved a better balance of support and critical response than was observed in the later course where the entire class of 25 shared a single conference. There, similar student answers were even more common, the incidence of refreshing dissent less.

As noted earlier, the software used for the more recent conference was FirstClass. FirstClass software permits faculty moderators to easily insert permissions into subconferences, thereby creating whatever size group the instructor wishes for a given discussion. In the initial conference, a morning ($N = 30$) and a smaller afternoon class ($N = 11$) were assigned to separate conferences. After moving through the first cycle of class readings and a practice conference, the groups were reformed into smaller and more appropriate sizes by dividing the larger class into two separate subconferences (from 12 to 15 students). Consequently, there were a total of three separate subconferences, each comprising one third of the total enrollment (roughly 40 students) in both classes.

Structure of Assignments

When group members structure their own work, they do not necessarily recognize how a group grade objectively creates a degree of interdependence on each other, individually or collectively. The first author has long observed graduate student groups utilizing a "detailed division of labor" for group assignments. The risk here is that each student executes his or her responsibilities to the group in such a way that their work is not independently discussed or reviewed by other group members. With previewed exams, for example, one student might prepare the answers to Questions 1–3, the next 4–6, and so on. By assigning staggered sets of questions to the group members, we avoided some of these hazards; otherwise, groups could suffer when their group grade reflected the deficiencies in certain individual's answers. In a later course, groups worked on previewed exam questions using 5-by-8 cards, each containing one answer/question and supposedly signed off on by all group members. In this course, there was clear evidence of this kind of division of labor, and, consequently, of the possibility that weak group members could turn in poor answers to the group's detriment.

In the more recent FirstClass conference, specifications of assignments evolved somewhat as we proceeded through conferences on four topics in the span of 11 weeks. At the outset, the students were instructed to answer one question from the first set by midweek and one question from the second set by the end of the week. As the class completed work on the second of the four topics, overly friendly and uncritical commentaries among group members became apparent. These may have reflected the influence of group work, now a somewhat more common classroom activity than in earlier classes. Hence, knowing each other better seemed to reduce disagreement and debate.

So by the third and fourth topics, there was a lot more structure added to the announced assignments. The total number of questions worked on collectively was reduced, so as to focus each student's effort and discussion on fewer questions. This additional structure ensured that:

1. No one in a given collaborative group worked on the same question, thus, potentially creating miniexperts within the group on given questions.
2. Students answered only one question but were expected to comment on answers posted to two questions in their conference other than the question they first answered. This meant that each student was commenting on the work of at least one or two students not in their own collaborative learning group and sometimes not even in their section of the course.
3. After many submissions had been completed, a subset of students were assigned the additional task of "wrapping up" the discussion on a given question. The members of this subset rotated among the students, so that each student served as a "wrapper" for one discussion (for similar tasks, see Zhu, chap. 10 of this volume). To facilitate this summary and reflection task, these students were "permitted" to view the answers in a second conference in which they had not participated.

What this structure tried to accomplish can be best explained by the following anecdote. A former student was asked in a more recent course if his group had worked hard on the previewed exam questions (discussed face to face, not electronically in this case). He affirmed that his group had worked several hours in the library developing their answers (submitted without justification on a single page—a bare-bones version of justified and reasoned answers that had previously been electronically posted). When this group had finished and was leaving the library, they ran into another group. To his dismay, the two groups had arrived at different answers on several questions, which led to a joint meeting of both groups for further discussion and argument.

This example outlines a sequence of events that should be the objective of electronic conferences. Ideally, the sequence begins with each student having written out a defensible answer to each question, then posting this answer electronically, only to find contrary views in the group's first electronic meeting. As discussion electronically continues, group consensus is reached on all questions. But to offset any lingering uncritical assent, the groups would then be exposed to the possibly contrasting views of another group. One way we have done this is to assign the role of wrapper to a student who would be given access to the answers of another group before composing and posting a summary statement about what has been argued and concluded. In FirstClass conferences, a moderator or instructor can arrange for this progressive expansion of the groups' discussions at well-timed moments, as part of an instructionally more effective sequence of submissions and replies. The first author once used networked computers in a single classroom to synchronously accomplish this progressive widening of discussion following the posting of initial answers to various questions.

Grading Criteria

From the outset, students in this first course were informed that their group grade for this work would be based on (a) the percentage of their group that participated in the conference, (b) the percentage score on the two graded questions (out of 20), and (c) the sheer quantity of comments on other posted answers.

As with the task of answering previewed exam questions, the grading of the discussion questions used criteria that stressed justifications based on course materials and reasoning, rather than a "right" answer. In practice, even with these criteria, there was a need to develop a simple method of scoring answers that took a manageable amount of time while providing both congratulatory and corrective feedback. Most answers received a number that indicated that the answer met certain expectations. The first author also utilized a special feature of FirstClass that permitted the insertion of comments into student answers. Because other students could read both the student answer and the instructor's comments, concrete feedback was available to an entire class about what made an answer strong or weak.

A RETROSPECTIVE LOOK USING SOCIOCULTURAL THOUGHT

Pragmatic issues of electronic conferencing such as group size, task structure, and assessment, though important, are framed by various theoretical perspectives on teaching and learning. In discussing our pedagogy of electronic conferencing, it is necessary to investigate the theoretical underpinnings of our position, namely, sociocultural theory. How do sociocultural principles help us address the problems of large class sizes, the variability of student capabilities and prior experiences, and the initial failure of some attempts to utilize electronic conferencing? Teaching a large "mass" of students of varying abilities using a relatively "new" technology would hardly seem an ideal arena for applying sociocultural principles, especially in light of the high priority on classroom control by traditional instructors. Our response is that we *can* create a setting for large classes in which many sociocultural concepts are implemented, by using collaborative group activities in class and group-based electronic conferences out of class.

The underlying sociocultural principle pertinent to this discussion is that learning and teaching are grounded in social interactions via cultural tools. According to sociocultural theory, each individual functions within a zone of proximal development (ZPD). The ZPD is the range or difference between what an individual may accomplish in an activity or task alone and what he or she may accomplish in the company of others. Effective teaching, according to sociocultural theory, should fall within the area of each student's ZPD and foster effective collaboration and mentoring of students (Gredler, 1992; Hedegaard, 1990; Moll & Greenberg, 1990).

Electronic conferencing (whether for previewing exam questions or discussing general questions) can be viewed as a means of moving students toward the more skillful and capable side of their own ZPD. Whether conferencing actually accomplishes this is another matter. Asynchronous discussion can suffer from a lack of intersubjectivity or of shared knowledge among students, even though in principle, the activity of group members working electronically to answer questions is a collaborative activity among participants. Groups of students working face to face (FTF) in class and in informal out-of-class meetings, which we know (and sometimes explicitly expect) some groups arrange for themselves, should enhance the conditions for intersubjectivity during conferencing work. In all of the instances reported previously, *the underlying foundation of electronic conferencing was the ongoing operation of collaborative groups in the classroom context*, thus creating a collaborative classroom climate that extended to electronic conferencing.

AN UNDERLYING MODEL OF SCAFFOLDING

The collaborative context of learning and individual development is a major component of the sociocultural perspective (Lunt, 1993). Models for the implementation of the various socioculturally based teaching techniques become apparent upon further examination of this collaborative context. Forman and McPhail (1993), for instance, offered this description of two students collaborating in a series of problem-solving activities: "They listened to each other's explanations and reflected on their logical consistency and precision. They watched each other's experiments and used their observations to modify their own task conceptions. Thus they provided a zone of proximal development for each other that facilitated the growth of higher mental functions (e.g. voluntary attention, logical reasoning)" (p. 224).

As in the one-to-one setting of these two colearners (or of a learner with trainer, coach, teacher) or in the comparable, one-to-a-few setting of small-group work, *it is the individual learner that is interactively engaged by peer, teacher, trainer, or tester*. The participant in the teacher's role might undertake direct and immediate modeling by verbalizing thought processes and illustrating performance standards. Encouraging learners to articulate their thought processes while pushing them to independently explore and apply their skills is a sociocultural feature of instruction within these small-group settings.

We mentioned earlier that managing the "effective group size" of students participating in a conference was an essential component of conferencing pedagogy. Fortunately, one of the reasons why small collaborative groups embody the principles of the sociocultural perspective is that their activity replicates the one-to-one or one-to-a-few model implicit in many of the socioculturally based teaching techniques (Bruffee, 1992; Rogoff, 1990). Structuring assignments and grading to build interdependence among group members during collaborative activities (both in class and out of class) is imperative for task success (Slavin, 1991) and when employing sociocultural theory (Tharp & Gallimore, 1988). Scaffolding is another key component of electronic conferencing that is based in sociocultural theory (Gredler, 1992).

ELEMENTS OF SCAFFOLDING IN INSTRUCTION

Wood, Bruner, and Ross (1976)[1] introduced the concept of scaffolding to describe the process through which an instructor may support students in learning tasks that may be *beyond* their current capabilities by creating and controlling task elements that make learning manageable *within* their current capabilities. There are three key structural features of scaffolding that instructors have to consider: the kind of scaffolding used, how much assistance or scaffolding needs to be provided, and when the structure is removed or the support withdrawn (Diaz, Neal, & Amaya-Williams, 1990; Rogoff, 1990; Tharp & Gallimore, 1988). Scaffolded interactions also may be affected by nonverbal cues, linguistic devices, interpersonal relationships, connotative meanings, and nuances of semiotic mediation, all of which are intertwined within the interaction in an extremely complex and multifaceted manner (Stone, 1993). Although many of these qualitative aspects of scaffolding may be beyond the scope of this chapter (as well as the current capabilities of electronic conferencing), there is one aspect we noticed occurring frequently in our coded examples, the negotiation of intersubjectivity.

Intersubjectivity is a shared understanding among participants about what is being said, communicated, and discussed. Prior to scaffolded instruction,

[1]This has been challenged by van der Veer and Valsiner (1991), who claimed that the term scaffolding was actually introduced by Vygotsky 30 years prior to the publication of Wood et al. (1976).

the teacher (or more capable peer) must be able to share the perspective of the learner's view of the problem at hand (Rogoff, 1990). Without the foundation of intersubjectivity or common knowledge, scaffolded learning is impossible.

Scaffolding begins with the deliberate provision of initial support by the instructor or more capable peers, provoking the active engagement in the task by students. As the learning episode unfolds, an instructor manages the amount of support or assistance provided, contingent upon the learner's level of cognitive functioning and involvement in the task at hand. As the learner exhibits mastery of the task or develops their cognitive functioning, the instructor gradually withdraws elements of support or guidance. Although one would hope that a gradual withdrawal of support is accomplished, it is not inconsistent with the concept of scaffolding that a teacher sometimes has to reverse direction and reinstate support or guidance during the learning episode (Tharp & Gallimore, 1988).

Scaffolding can be accomplished within a series of microscopic teaching and learning events as well as in a more macroscopic context where different types of mutually supportive and reinforcing learning activities are carried out. Working on previewed exam questions, answering discussion questions, solving problems, and other course activities can be structured as a series of interdependent, scaffolded activities. Whether at the macro- or microlevel, the long-range goal is to help the learner move from initially solving a problem with the help of "others" (instructor, peers, etc.) to independently possessing and applying the required skills and knowledge. Yet, the concept of scaffolding makes sense only through its association with the concept of the ZPD.

To scaffold student learning, a teacher may utilize a variety of teaching techniques that could be appropriately sequenced and made responsive to feedback from students. Providing hints, elaborating, requesting feedback, and prompting are some of the teaching techniques that may be used in scaffolded learning (see Bonk & Kim, 1998, for further discussion on this topic). Yet, how is an instructor to provide "graduated hints" in a classroom of 40–400 students with various ability levels (i.e., different ZPDs)? It seems obvious that one instructor lacks the capacity to deliver personally customized scaffolding to students in classrooms of this size. As alluded to earlier, it is this general impracticality of individualized instruction within larger classrooms that warrants the search for appropriate and effective pedagogic approaches to out-of-class instruction. However, instruction out of class cannot for long remain isolated from the expectations and experiences of inclass instruction. Although it may prove easier to apply the concepts of scaffolding to the structuring of electronic discussion (manipulating effective group size, specificity and structure of assignments, and grading criteria), it is equally important to develop methods for use in the large class that address, if not entirely resolve, the difficulties of extending the concept of scaffolding to larger groups.

PRELIMINARY CODING FOR SCAFFOLDED INSTRUCTIONAL INTERACTIONS

We have developed some codes for key instructional moments of scaffolded learning, after reviewing an exceptionally clear videotaped example of scaffolding amid the interactions between schoolteachers and elementary school children,[2] as well as the student-to-student interactions during several of the electronic conferences discussed earlier and the second author's observations of the first author's interactions with students in the large classroom. These codes are divided into the categories of entry-level, transfer-focused, facilitative, and management interactions.

Type 1: Entry-Level Interactions

Entry-level interactions are based on the assumption that a foundation for the assigned task, a problem to be solved or some instructional goal, has been established and communicated to the students. The simplest element of a task or problem, in the examples illustrated here, would be a question. When students are "initially presented" **[IP]** with a question, depending on the level of difficulty, the first occasion of face-to-face or asynchronous interaction begins. Initially, many students may not understand enough of the course material to make independent progress, prompting a "repeated presentation" **[RP]** of the question, problem, or relevant materials. These instructional situations may call for several repeated presentations until intersubjectivity concerning the problem or question is established among the participants. See Table 8.2.

Type 2: Transfer-Focused Interactions

Assuming that the instructor has determined (perhaps via dynamic assessment techniques) that a majority of the students have grasped the material, a second type of interaction applies familiar understandings or concepts in a more challenging, but practical and applicable, context. We call these "test

[2]A videotape of scaffolded interactions between schoolteachers and elementary school children was obtained from Dr. William Lynch, Emeritus Professor of Educational Psychology, Indiana University, Bloomington.

TABLE 8.2
Entry-Level Interactions

IP	Initial Presentation The first moments of instructional scaffolding when a teacher (or a peer displaying teaching behaviors) initially presents [IP] an appropriate example or poses a new question for students to respond to.
RP	Repeated Presentations Enlarging the circle of students who have achieved an initial understanding of their earlier classroom work, classroom activities, or conference discussion by supplying repeated presentations [RP] of questions or examples, at the same or slightly lower level of difficulty.

and transfer" steps in scaffolding learning. The interactions here could entail "initial presentations of examples or questions," which are at a slightly higher level of difficulty or abstraction. The source of the greater difficulty could be the fact that the materials are unfamiliar **[IPup-M]**, in contrast to the use of familiar examples or easier questions at the initial presentation. It may also be true that the skills (rather than the material) needed to apply the concepts are more demanding, perhaps because students are asked to apply more abstract definitions of the concepts **[IPup-C]**. A different form of interaction with emphasis on transference of skills and initial knowledge is one in which the instructor "solicits metacognitive statements" **[SMC]** from learners to force reflection on learning processes. See Table 8.3.

Type 3: Facilitative Interactions

The aim of the third type of interaction is to facilitate student responses, if needed. These may be in the form of helping the learner by "direct assistance" **[DA]** (e.g., supplying rudimentary answers) or simply by encouraging or "validating" **[VAL]** student answers. These facilitative interactions serve to guide or support student responses when students appear to be unsure of their understanding of new concepts. See Table 8.4.

TABLE 8.3
Transfer-Focused Interactions

IPup-M	(Material) Initial presentation of example/question at a higher level of difficulty USING unfamiliar material.
IPup-C	(Conceptual) Initial presentation of example/question at a higher level of difficulty USING related but more difficult (abstract) concepts.
SMC	Solicit Metacognitive Statements Solicit metacognitive statements from students (i.e., statements that illustrate their understanding of principles, criteria for applying concepts, etc.).

TABLE 8.4
Facilitative Interactions

DA	Direct Assistance Direct assistance to the students by providing answers to lower level questions.
VAL	Validating Student Responses Encouraging feedback that validates student responses, aids in self-confidence, and facilitates student thinking.

Type 4: Management Interactions

Finally, when students take missteps (insisting that a clearly incorrect answer is correct or misunderstanding the meaning of a text, event, or question), it is necessary for the instructor to confront these incorrect responses [**R**esponse to **S**tudent **M**issteps-]. This type of confrontation may take many forms. In some instances, the instructor may respond by restating the original question or by providing a more effective question [**RSM-Q**], a counterexample [**RSM-CX**], or a counterargument [**RSM-A**]. See Table 8.5.

Although these preliminary codes for scaffolded instructional interactions were derived from a videotaped episode between an elementary teacher and her students, we feel that they adequately illuminate key instructional moments during electronic conferences and large-classroom interactions. In the following section, we apply these codes to two electronic conferences (featuring student–student and instructor–student responses) as well as to an observation of teacher–student(s) interactions in a large undergraduate introduction to sociology class.

INSTRUCTIONAL SCAFFOLDING ILLUSTRATED

Case 1: Electronic Conference (Student–Student)

This first application of codes for scaffolded instructional interactions draws on an electronic conference in the first sociology of work course (mentioned

TABLE 8.5
Management Interactions

RSM-Q	Responding With a Question Responding to student inaccurate conclusions by restating original question or redirecting with a new, more effective one to redirect student thinking.
RSM-CX	Responding With a Counterexample Responding to student inaccurate conclusions by providing a counterexample to redirect student thinking.
RSM-A	Responding With a Counterargument Responding to student inaccurate conclusions by providing a counterargument (playing devil's advocate) to redirect student thinking.

previously). The discussion question concerns the students' understanding of a challenging passage from a reading in Robert Jackall's (1988) *Moral Mazes*. Although this book is widely used in business ethics classes, it is far from an ethics primer. Based on interviews and observations, the author develops a sound structural understanding of the politicized interactions among various layers of management, including CEOs and their loyalist supporters. The students are asked to read the question or statement as well as the passage from Jackall's book to determine whether or not the posed statement is true. The following example illustrates this form of scaffolded instruction between two students in electronic conferencing:

> [75.0 Discussion Question] Is this statement True or False?:
>
> At Covenant Corp, the power of the Chief Executive is reinforced by an ideology of centralization.
>
> Passage from the book:
>
> At the same time, all of these struggles take place within the peculiar tempo and framework each CEO establishes for an organization. Under an ideology of thorough decentralization—the gift of authority with responsibility—the CEO at Covenant actually centralizes his power enormously because fear of derailing personal ambitions prevents managers below him from acting without his approval. A top official at Alchemy comments, "What we have now, despite rhetoric to the contrary, is a very centralized system. It's [the CEO] who sets the style, tone, tempo of all the companies. . . ." (Jackall, 1988, p. 36)

The challenge this passage poses to students is to understand the meaning and context of centralization and decentralization. Decentralization in this context refers to an ideology that decisions and power are actually delegated. But the practical reality is that the echelons receiving this responsibility end up deferring even more to the inclinations and signals of the higher-ups, or CEOs. In short, the statement posed above is false.

We begin our case study with Mike's response to this true–false question: [Mike] TRUE. pg. 36—"What we have now, despite rhetoric to the contrary is a very centralized system."

Although Mike's citation from the book is accurate, there is no reasoning given that justifies his conclusion that the statement is true. Another student, Adam, is the first to respond in the electronic conference to Mike's incorrect conclusion (refer to previous tables for interaction code meanings):

> [Adam] Okay Mike, you are correct **[VAL]** if you take exactly what you have typed on your reply; but if you look at the sentence just before the one quoted **[RSM-CX]**, you will see that "Under an ideology of Decentralization . . ." It is true that the CEO centralizes his power, but he does so with the ideology

> of decentralization, which is how the question is worded [RP]. Therefore the answer is false.

Adam's reply to Mike offers a wonderful illustration of validating someone's initial attempts to solve the problem ("Okay Mike, you are correct . . .) and responding to a misstep by providing a counterexample, in this case, a different but nearby passage. Because Mike has taken his quotation out of context, Adam responds by contrasting that passage with another that reestablishes the original context and restates the wording of the original question. This display of Adam's reasoning effectively supports his conclusion that the answer is false.

The following statements between Charlie and Scott, also concerning the same question described previously, were posted in the same electronic conference.

> [Charlie] False. The CEO actually centralizes his power "under an ideology of thorough decentralization." Power and authority are given to the individual companies but only to follow what the CEO tells them to. So the idea is of having autonomous divisions, but in reality [they] are centralized under the CEO's control.
>
> [Scott] Charlie, I understand what you are saying **[VAL]**, but I interpreted what was written differently. I believe the answer to be True. The CEO is cloaking centralization in the appearance of decentralization **[IPup-C]**. He gives the impression that things are decentralized, but because everyone is so fearful of screwing up they do not utilize the power that they supposedly have—hence the centralization **[RSM-A]**. The CEO is offering the fruits of decentralization, but everyone is too fearful to accept, so the CEO has not given anything (decentralization) away **[RP]**.

In his response, Scott seems to be very familiar with the material and restates his beliefs that the answer is true by repeating examples interpreted from the original passage and using an appropriate metaphor. Despite offering a counterargument midway through this excerpt, Scott does not offer the reasoning needed to justify his conclusion. Charlie is not persuaded:

> [Charlie] Scott, I understand what you are saying also **[VAL]**, but I still think that the answer is false. The IDEA is of a decentralized corporation, but through the fear he has installed [he] is able to maintain a centralized command—so he is actually reinforced by the ideology of decentralization **[RSM-A]**.

Both Charlie and Scott reply to opposing viewpoints courteously, announcing that each student "understands" what the other is claiming (negotiating for intersubjectivity), and presenting their reasons for contesting each other's answers. However, the point at issue between them is the reasoning involved in linking the material with their different conclusions. What each does, in turn, is respond to what they perceive is the other's misstep by providing counter-arguments. Charlie ties the wording of the question about ideology to the idea of a decentralized corporation; his argument is sound. Although Scott's earlier response uses a metaphor (forbidden fruit) effectively, his answer merely recites materials without developing a reasoned connection between these materials and his conclusion that his statement is true.

Case 2: Electronic Conference (Instructor–Student)

The following interactions are taken from the most recent use of electronic conferencing:

> [Question 2] This question recalls the distinction in class Monday between general and specific skills. What is a "pro" and "con" argument to this debate statement: ". . . general skills and knowledge have value throughout one's career, while the value of more specialized skills and knowledge is limited to the first job or two after training is completed?" In stating your argument, work with one or more specific examples, from any source—readings, class materials, news clippings, shared experiences. What specific general or specialized skills and knowledge does your answer refer to? What kinds of jobs and careers?

The wording of this questions clearly suggests a structure for the answer to take. By forming the question in this manner, the instructor is providing students with a form of direct assistance **[DA]**. In the passages that follow, the instructor inserted comments into the electronic conference after the period for discussion was over:

> [Student #1]Now, I will switch to my pro and con argument about the question concerning the importance of general skills vs. specialized skills in the workplace. I will use illustrations from my job at Delco Electronics in Kokomo this past summer. In coming out of college it is understandable to think that one has a better chance for success with a more specialized background than a general knowledge. After all, one can not be a good engineer or good accountant or good in finance just having a general background. You need a specialized background so you know what is going on and why and how to deal with it a majority of the time. A majority of the time problems cannot be solved with a general background.

> Insert → [Instructor]But don't forget this is about general SKILLS and by implication, high or low levels of same; "specialized background" sounds pretty . . . [vague] to me in this context.

> [Student #1]Also, in order to move up you must be exceptional at your initial assignments. And to say that all you need is a general background as you

move up is a bit weird, since you will interact with more problems and areas of concern. If you do not understand what is going on in depth, you are in serious trouble. A specialized background is the way to go.

Another view, [that] general skills will benefit you more in your future career makes a lot of sense also, and one I have found to be true at Delco. True, to get hired on at a major company, one needs a field of specialization. But in all reality [here Student #1 shifts his support back to the prospecific skill side of the question], you will be taught what you need to know at Delco. You will learn to do things Delco's way. And once you get things done Delco's way consistently, you will have the opportunity to move up. [Student #1 then balances this notion with one of general understanding.] But in order to be a true success in the upper-levels, you must have a general knowledge of the company all over. You will go through a variety of different positions, possibly including: human resources, supervision, quality control, and so on. You need to have a general understanding of the whole company and what is going on to be a success. True, there will be areas that need the attention of specialists, but these people will now be working for you and it is . . . [their] job to get things done while you manage several other activities of all different kinds going on. I definitely believe that general skills and knowledge have more value throughout one's career, while the value of more specific or specialized skills and knowledge is limited to the first job or two after training and graduation.

Insert → [Instructor]Engaging argument you offer **[VAL]**. Making use of an example extensively was also great **[VAL]**. However, you don't really have a sense of general SKILLS. What are those skills in your example **[RSM-Q]**? Knowledge of the company, its various departments, is certainly important **[VAL]**, but you need a better sense of the skill side, which may cause you to have a second look at your position re specific skills **[SMC]**.

[Student #2]In response to your [Student #1] comments on question 2, I would like to add that in terms of your career, most people switch jobs about 9 times in their working life (according to the Wall Street Journal), which is to say that specialized skills might not help you in every working environment **[RSM-CX & RSM-A]**. But your definition of general skills appeared to me to be more along the lines of knowledge, not skill **[RSM-A]**. In class we discussed that skill dealt with proficiency, ability, dexterity, experience, and technique regarding the use of your body **[RP]**. So an example of a specialized skill would be something perhaps that required a license like a doctor specializing in brain surgery **[DA]**, but a general skill would be a doctor with skills in all parts of the anatomy **[RSM-CX]**. A mechanic has general skills about motors/engines, but he might have specialized in foreign cars **[RP]**. General knowledge is a familiarity or awareness of that [what] you have gained from studying or past experience **[RP]**.

The comments by the instructor and a peer direct the first student to reevaluate and expand upon the response and examples given, thereby guiding the student's thought processes. The response and comments posted by the second student presents new materials and reiterates an earlier inclass discussion defining skills, thus extending or applying their argument to these new materials.

Case 3: Classroom Interactions (Instructor–Student)

Ideally, scaffolded instruction would be employed in both the classroom and electronic learning environments, even if electronic conferencing is an activity appended to a traditional, lecture-based class. The experiences we desire students to have in the electronic conference would then be prefigured in earlier classroom interactions between instructor, student, and peers. As someone trained in sociocultural theory and experienced in coding scaffolded instruction, the second author observed two class meetings of the first author's introductory sociology course in the fall of 1996. The topic for this class session described later was "culture" (e.g., the elements of culture, and the ways in which culture influences human behavior). Her notes from this class identified a number of interactions between the first author and members of his class, some of which illustrate the type of scaffolded instructional interactions covered by the codes in Table 8.6. These interactions occurred between periods of minilectures and the viewing of video excerpts that generally characterize this class. This excerpt, from the second author's field notes, does not represent verbatim speech between the instructor and his students but it does describe particular interactions that could be coded as examples of scaffolded instruction. This selection does not include a description of the variety of media (overheads, Power Point outlines, videotape excerpts) used by the instructor, but, instead, highlights how these instructional aids were used in conjunction with scaffolded instruction.

As introduced, the purpose of this class was to help students develop the ability to recognize the elements and influence of culture. The stated overall goal was that students be able to analyze a culture—its essential elements and how it influences people. As an initial step in this development, students were asked to list examples on their daily "worksheets" of their present

TABLE 8.6
Summary of Scaffolding Codes

Entry-Level Interactions:		Facilitative Interactions:	
IP	Initial Presentation	DA	Direct Assistance
RP	Repeated Presentations	VAL	Validating Student Responses
Transfer-Focused Interactions:		Management Interactions:	
IPup-M	(Material)	RSM-Q	Respond With a Question
IPup-C	(Conceptual)	RSM-CX	Respond With a Counterexample
SMC	Solicit Metacognitive Statements	RSM-A	Respond With a Counterargument

concept of culture. These were briefly sampled in a whole-class discussion, and some examples were used to illustrate the first set of concepts then introduced in a minilecture on identifying a culture's "key ideas about what is good, true, and beautiful."

The second instructional tactic was to employ the use of analogy. When it became obvious that students were struggling with the concepts of what is good, true, or beautiful in a culture (i.e., no responses to questions posed by instructor), the instructor explained that culture is very much like an onion with many layers. If we peel away the skin and outer layers, we would find these concepts at its very core **[IPup-C]**.

The second step in cultural analysis was to identify three features of social life—rituals, material artifacts, and symbols—that embody these key ideas. The instructor proceeded to ask students (often by name or asking for their name when it was not known) for their own examples of each of these concepts, which were written on the overhead projector **[VAL]**. This request for familiar illustrations of the concepts, prior to the formal definition or technical illustration of those concepts, allowed the students to establish a foundation of initially presented **[IP]** student-generated examples that would support the subsequent steps of cultural analysis. The instructor gave positive feedback (praise) **[VAL]** for good examples and connected them to ideas or concepts **[IPup-C]** while expanding on those responses that were found to be particularly insightful **[RP]**. The final step in this phase was for the students to interact with each other by asking them to check their neighbor's apparel for various identifying items of culture, namely, symbols and material artifacts **[IPup-M]**.

The next phase of this learning episode was for students to practice applying these increasingly familiar concepts of cultural analysis to a selected video excerpt from the film *Avalon* **[RP]**. Prior to viewing the video, the instructor outlined what to focus on in the segment and provided an overview of the context in which the segment is situated. He also explained that some of the parts may be difficult to understand and that closed captioning would be displayed at the top of the screen. It is important to note that this video excerpt was chosen because it presented fresh examples of ritual, symbol, artifact, and conversation among characters regarding the key truths and values of a multigenerational immigrant family. The two sets of concepts, the key ideas (good, true, and beautiful) and aspects of culture (rituals, artifacts, and symbols), from the first phase of the episode were displayed just above the video image as the class viewed the movie excerpt **[IPup-M]**. After the clip was viewed, students worked in groups to identify examples of these concepts. After this brief period of consultation in groups, the instructor wrote reported examples of concepts on an overhead **[VAL]**.

The third phase of this learning episode focused on the different ways in which culture influences us. For example, how does such a culture influence or shape the individual's actions and feelings? This set of concepts regarding cultural influence was more abstract, and, therefore, more challenging for the students to learn and apply **[IPup-C]**. After providing students with the definitions (simple to complex) of the ways in which culture influences its members **[DA]**, the students were asked for examples, which were again presented on the overheads **[VAL]**. When students encountered problems identifying or providing an example, the instructor would mention scenes from a different video excerpt shown in a previous class **[IPup-M]**. In doing this, the instructor deflected an overly facile answer as well as guesses or premature answers and was able to respond to remaining confusion among some students by providing counterexamples **[RSM-CX]**, which led students to think more carefully about their answers **[SMC]**.

The last phase of this learning episode asked students to apply what they learned about how culture influences us to the initial video excerpt from *Avalon.* At this moment, the pedagogical question was whether students could now transfer and apply the concepts about cultural influence to a different example. By reintroducing the familiar video excerpt, he modestly reduced the complexity of the experience. However, it is important to note that in a way this previewed excerpt was unfamiliar **[IPup-M]** in that it had not been viewed with an eye toward applying these new concepts. Again, students viewed the familiar video excerpt on a screen that also contained the text of what they would be looking for (ways in which culture influences us). Because this set of concepts was more abstract and difficult than the elements of culture, he suggested that the group develop justifications for answers by referring to "checklists" of key definitional elements. These checklists were also provided for students on the overhead. The suggested use of checklists represents a solicitation of metacognitive statements as students worked with the definitions of these concepts **[SMC]**.

By this time in the learning episode, there was an increase in the amount and level of discussion among students, with more interaction and confrontation between and among groups. During the whole-class discussion following this exercise, the instructor started to respond to student missteps by inviting the students to provide counterexamples **[RSM-CX]** and to consider alternative matches of concepts with illustrative statements, effectively modeling the development of counterarguments **[RSM-A]**.

This example taken from a learning episode in a rather large course illustrates scaffolded instruction in action. At the beginning of the episode, much of the structure was provided by the instructor although the examples were grounded in the students' own experiences. Presenting the unfamiliar material found in the first viewing of the *Avalon* segment in conjunction with the more familiar key elements of culture provided a scaffold for students to later apply the more difficult and abstract concepts concerning culture's influence. In the final phase, the instructor gradually removed some of his support and guidance by asking the students to be responsible for evaluating their assumptions and conclusions. As the class progressed through these various phases, it seemed as if the students were more comfortable and took more risks (e.g., more hands were raised, there was an increase in jokes, etc.) during the discussions. This was perhaps due to the fact that student attempts to provide examples or answer questions were validated in some manner (i.e., answers were written on the overhead, attempts were made by the instructor to use their name, etc.). From all appearances, as the episode progressed and instructional scaffolding was partially withdrawn, it seemed that many students were able to independently identify aspects of culture and ways in which culture influences people.

MACROLEVEL SCAFFOLDING: BRINGING THE CLASSROOM AND CONFERENCE TOGETHER

As the concept of scaffolding has grown on us while writing this chapter, our focus has gradually shifted from a more microlevel to a mixture of micro- and macroperspectives. This parallels our own evolutionary course from the initial use of groups and conferencing to a broader grasp of instruction as socioculturally understood. The underutilization of electronic conferences mentioned at the outset of this chapter is only one illustration of typical faculty "gradualism" in implementing change in our instruction, whether or not the use of new technology is involved. Early on, we too viewed electronic conferencing as a supplement to regular and customary course instruction. Students' expectations change gradually as well. Although perhaps inevitable and practical, gradualism obscures a fuller understanding of why combinations of new and old instructional activities work well together.

From the beginning, Linda Harisim taught us to at least *require* work in computer conferences. Forming groups for inclass work and similarly grouping students working in conferences created possibilities not initially well exploited for each activity to support the other. But sociocultural theory has led us to see what that mutual support actually looks like—that modeling collaborative work in face-to-face group work should engender the same in electronic conferencing, and that practice applying concepts in class sets up opportunities to articulate reasons for applying concepts to new examples in a conference discussion (and vice versa in each case). Using one set of codes, we have identified moments of scaffolded instruction in both inclass activities and in conferencing work out of class. This coding exercise has subtly broadened our initial focus, in our teaching practice and in this chapter, from one of simply identifying microlevel scaffolding in the daily work of ourselves and our students to recognizing in these combinations of activities a macrolevel of scaffolded course instruction.

The general applicability of the codes reflects the larger point that we have come to understand in writing this chapter. Scaffolded instruction at the macrolevel of an entire course requires the coordination of microlevel scaffolding that is apparent in the electronic conferences with the scaffolded instruction during teacher–student classroom interactions.

It is in the classroom that students can most directly comprehend the difference between traditional instruction (active lecturer, passive student) and scaffolded instruction (coconstructors of the learning episode). The field notes of the second author reveal a transition between initial hesitancy and mild responsiveness to quite noticeable engagement of students later in the class period. Scaffolding, in general, requires a sea change of expectations about faculty–student (and student–student) interactions. Students learn through a multitude of activities, tasks, problem solving, and discussion, even in the midst of intermittent minilectures. The instructional objective of scaffolding is that students come to think, reflect, make sense of, and thereby understand and apply new materials by actively participating in learning activities. At the same time, the instructor is equally active, seeking to clarify, question, and provide support and then slowly withdraw such guidance, while encouraging the independent functioning of students as they acquire a new discourse and accept a different style of dialogue with their instructors and peers.

FUTURE DIRECTIONS OF FACULTY DEVELOPMENT AND INSTRUCTIONAL PRACTICE

Notwithstanding any greater clarity about the workings of effective electronic conferencing, collaborative group work, and classroom interactions, the first author has yet to teach a course in which all of the scaffolded instructional elements described in this chapter are simultaneously operative and coordinated. His most recent classroom teaching has been large introductory sociology sections, with enrollments ranging from 40 to 135 students. Electronic conferencing has not yet been utilized at this introductory level. To be sure, inclass collaborative groups are extremely active here. However, collaborative group work out of class has focused on previewed exam questions, where students post their answers or via an Indiana University Web-based Quiz-site system that accepts short text answers to posted questions. These submitted texts are compiled into one file by Quiz-site but remain inaccessible to other students. At the current stage of development of the introductory course, as the observational notes recalled earlier suggest, the most demanding activity is the implementation of scaffolded instruction in large classes.

Our vision of the future direction of instruction is that we begin to bring all venues of scaffolding together in each of the two courses discussed previously—the introductory and the work course—so that otherwise separate enterprises of electronic conferencing as well as FTF interactions within collaborative learning groups and student–faculty instructional interactions become mutually supportive and reinforcing. The next steps are clear. The discussion questions that students in large introductory courses are now answering over the Web must be selectively shared and commented upon, by posting general or several specific and focused comments alongside examples of student entries on the World Wide Web or via electronic mail. After pilot testing of asynchronous conferencing software that utilizes the Web, which is now in progress, we anticipate a synergistic combination of electronic conferencing and other Web-based instructional and assessment activities in the introductory class.

In the smaller but upper division, undergraduate work courses, we continue to use asynchronous conferencing in combination with Web-based activities and highly active collaborative groups. In the current semester (fall 1997), students in the work course are again doing conferencing work, as we pilot test Alta Vista Forums, a Web-based software designed to facilitate group work. To structure the successive stages of individual contributions, initial group consensus, confrontation with the different views of another group, and a final forming of a "best answer" as a group, groups complete answers to questions posed in three phases. They first bring their individual answers to a common group workspace. Then that workspace is temporarily expanded by adding members of a second group. Commentary on the work of the other group is exchanged. Finally, each group works alone again to compose their best answer to each question.

We stressed the importance of the scaffolded instruction in the regular classroom as the lynchpin of effective, scaffolded instructional experiences in electronic conferences and student FTF collaborative group work. We have found that critically applying sociocultural concepts like scaffolding is an exciting occasion for self-reflection [SMC!]. Prior to developing the codes described in this chapter, we were aware that exciting instructional moments were sprinkled throughout the texts of our electronic conferences. It is true that codes are inherently arbitrary and can be applied to a wide array of instructional interactions. But applying the codes has helped us become more aware of what is happening in the classroom, in the electronic conferences, and presumably inside the collaborative learning groups. Perhaps, most important, we are closer to understanding how all venues of instructional interaction will be more effective when consistent with the ideas, goals, and values of the sociocultural perspective.

ACKNOWLEDGMENTS

The authors would like to acknowledge Dr. William Lynch, Emeritus Professor of Educational Psychology, Indiana University, Bloomington, for the use of videotaped scaffolded interactions between school teachers and elementary school children.

REFERENCES

Althauser, R. P. (1992). Collaborative learning via study groups and the electronic classroom. In S. J. Hamilton & E. Hansen (Eds.), *Sourcebook for collaborative learning in the arts and sciences at Indiana University* (pp. 142–146). Bloomington: Indiana University.

Bonk, C. A., & Kim, K. A. (1998). Extending sociocultural theory to adult learning. In M. C. Smith & T. Pourchet (Eds.), *Adult learning and development: Perspectives from educational psychology* (pp. 67–88). Mahwah, NJ: Lawrence Erlbaum Associates.

Bruffee, K. A. (1992). Collaborative learning and the "conversation of mankind." In A. Goodsell, M. Maher, V. Tinto, with B. L. Smith & J. MacGregor (Eds.), *Collaborative learning: A sourcebook for higher education* (pp. 23–33). University Park, PA: National Center on Postsecondary Teaching, Learning, and Assessment.

Diaz, R. M., Neal, C. J., & Amaya-Williams, M. (1990). The social origins of self-regulations. In L. C. Moll (Ed.), *Vygotsky and education: Instructional implications and applications of sociohistorical psychology* (pp. 127–154). New York: Cambridge University Press.

Forman, E. A., & McPhail, J. (1993). Vygotskian perspectives on children's collaborative problem-solving activities. In E. A. Forman, N. Minick, & C. A. Stone (Eds.), *Contexts for understanding: Sociocultural dynamics in children's development* (pp. 213–229). New York: Oxford University Press.

Garson, B. (1988). *Electronic sweatshop.* New York: Penguin.

Gredler, M. E. (1992). *Learning and instruction: Theory into practice.* New York: Macmillan.

Harasim, L. A. (1990). *Online education: Perspectives on a new environment.* New York: Praeger.

Hedegaard, M. (1990). The zone of proximal development as basis for instruction. In L. C. Moll (Ed.), *Vygotsky and education: Instructional implications and applications of sociohistorical psychology* (pp. 349–371). New York: Cambridge University Press.

Jackall, R. (1988). *Moral mazes: The world of corporate managers.* New York: Oxford University Press.

Lunt, I. (1993). The practice of assessment. In H. Daniels (Ed.), *Charting the agenda: Educational activity after Vygotsky* (pp. 145–170). New York: Routledge.

Moll, L. C., & Greenberg, J. B. (1990). Creating zones of possibilities: Combining social contexts for instruction. In L. C. Moll (Ed.), *Vygotsky and education: Instructional implications and applications of sociohistorical psychology* (pp. 319–348). New York: Cambridge University Press.

Rogoff, B. (1990). *Apprenticeship in thinking: Cognitive development in social context.* New York: Oxford University Press.

Slavin, R. E. (1991). Synthesis of research on cooperative learning. *Educational Leadership, 48*(5), 71–82.

Stone, C. A. (1993). What is missing in the metaphor of scaffolding? In E. A. Forman, N. Minick, & C. A. Stone (Eds.), *Contexts for learning: Sociocultural dynamics in children's development* (pp. 169–183). New York: Oxford University Press.

Tharp, R. G., & Gallimore, R. (1988). *Rousing minds to life: Teaching, learning, and schooling in social context.* New York: Cambridge University Press.

van der Veer, R., & Valsiner, J. (1991). *Understanding Vygotsky: A quest for synthesis.* Cambridge, MA: Blackwell.

Wood, D., Bruner, J. S., & Ross, G. (1976). The role of tutoring in problem-solving. *Journal of Child Psychology and Psychiatry, 17*, 89–100.

9

▼▼▼▼▼▼▼▼

Electronic Teaching: Extending Classroom Dialogue and Assistance Through E-mail Communication

Sonny E. Kirkley
Indiana University

John R. Savery
DePaul University

Melissa Marie Grabner-Hagen
Indiana University

As the use of computer-mediated communication and collaboration is rapidly increasing in business, professional, and educational environments, educators and instructional designers are seeking to learn how to integrate it in an effective and efficient manner. This chapter provides guidance in this emerging field by reporting on the use of electronic mail (E-mail) in three graduate-level instructional systems technology courses: (a) an introductory project-based learning class, (b) an advanced seminar class, and (c) an advanced project-based learning class. In these three classes, E-mail served to continue the class content discussions, report individual and group activities to the instructor, and coordinate logistical and administrative issues. First of all, transaction analyses from a sociocultural perspective are used to indicate the presence of various means of assistance. Second, these analyses of electronic interactions are used to determine the nature of content discussions. Special attention is given to the overall analysis framework and the difficulties in analyzing E-mail discussions without the context of the face-to-face classroom interactions and the normal cues available in verbal interactions.

ELECTRONIC COLLABORATION

Electronic collaboration and computer-mediated communications are being touted as two of the main factors helping change the way in which we work and learn (Finholt, Sproull, & Kiesler, 1990; Kiesler, Siegel, & McGuire,

1988; Leslie, 1994; Riel, 1990; Stefik et al., 1988). One of the chief components of this new collaborative environment is E-mail. *Business Week* ("The Net Keeps," 1997) reports that 89% of Internet users use E-mail. One third of those consider themselves part of an online community. A report by Forrester Research, Inc. (1997) indicates that 15% of the U.S. population (40 million people) currently uses E-mail, up from 2% in 1992. By 2001 they estimate that 50% of the population (135 million people) will use it. According to a study published in the *Chronicle of Higher Education* (1996 Campus Computing, 1996), 25% of college courses used E-mail, up from 20% the previous year. The 5% increase was small in comparison to 1995, which saw a growth rate of about 12%.

Countless researchers are proclaiming E-mail's democratizing effects, citing substantial evidence that it flattens hierarchies, promotes teamwork, and increases involvement of peripheral workers within organizations (Leslie, 1994). For academia, it is spawning opportunities for developing collaborative networks and sharing information. Professors are no longer tied to working with the person down the hall or working with data from the same geographic location. For the student and instructor, learning no longer has to happen between the four walls of the classroom or in the same physical space. Instead, the learning environment can extend to anywhere a personal computer and telephone can be used. One resulting factor is that E-mail is now the predominant form of communication in many universities and businesses.

E-mail seems to be developing attributes more commonly associated with spoken language. According to Rob Kling, professor of library and information science at Indiana University, E-mail is different because it follows the norms and behaviors of both text and conversation (Leslie, 1994). In letter writing and many other forms of communications, language and sentence structure tends to be more formal and governed by a set of rules and standards. E-mail, however, often contains informal slang words (e.g., *gonna* and *gotta*), grammatical errors, and draws heavily on the form of spoken language. It also can have some of the immediacy of verbal communications because messages are usually delivered in a matter of seconds. This immediacy often leads to expectations of a prompt reply and frustration when it is not forthcoming (Leslie, 1994). In fact, we often find E-mail users "talking" continuously for hours via E-mail rather than talking on the phone. Not surprisingly, research also suggests that when E-mail use increases, other forms of communications decrease (Finholt et al., 1990).

Text-based communication is different from verbal communication in several important respects. These differences each have positive and negative ramifications. First is the lack of nonverbal cues found in face-to-face interactions. Though these cues are often necessary for ease of collaboration and understanding, they also reinforce social conventions such as hierarchies and dominant personalities. Of course, this is not always advantageous in a learning environment. Such cues "give speakers and listeners information they can use to regulate, modify, and control exchanges. Electronic communication may be inefficient for resolving such coordinating problems as telling another person you already have knowledge of something he or she is explaining" (Kraut, Lewis, & Swezey as cited in Kiesler et al., 1988, p. 1124). Second, as Kling indicated, E-mail may weaken some social influences by eliminating behavior such as taking the head of the table, speaking loudly, staring, touching, and gesturing (cited in Kiesler et al., 1984). This can be advantageous over face-to-face communications because it is easier to ignore or give minimal attention to an E-mail message than it is to ignore someone in person. Third, time efficiency is one of the key reasons administrators and others in leadership positions often prefer E-mail contact over face-to-face interactions. Some professors, for instance, have reported that students often seem to prefer communicating about problems and due dates via E-mail (Kiesler et al., 1984).

Studies of computer-mediated communication (CMC) usually focus on particular aspects of communication. In terms of E-mail, Komsky (1991) and D'Souza (1991) analyzed who sends messages to whom, when, and with what effect. Kiesler, Siegel, and McGuire (1984), in contrast, studied the social and psychological implications and effects of using CMC.

This chapter examines how E-mail was used to achieve instructional goals in three different classes. Specifically, it focuses on how E-mail helps to extend the conversation of the classroom and how various means of assistance can be achieved through the use of E-mail. Four primary issues addressed here include (a) the types of topics that were prevalent in the E-mail messages, (b) participation rates of different populations within a class, (c) how the content and volume of E-mail changed over time within a class and how it changed between classes, and (d) the perceived role E-mail played in establishing the overall characteristics of the learning environment. It is important to note that in these classes, E-mail correspondence was only one of several channels of communication between teacher and learner and among learners. Students and teachers were also able to communicate regularly in class and in individual face-to-face meetings. Thus, any concerns that E-mail correspondents can develop inaccurate or narrow views of each other because they have only written correspondence on which to base their views was not an issue with this study. However, these face-to-face interactions limit our conclusions about the impact of electronic social interactions on learning.

ANALYZING INTERACTIONS

This chapter reports the results of transaction analyses of the E-mail of three instructional technology graduate courses at a Midwest university. Two of these classes were part of a two-semester sequence and, therefore, were analyzed together. The other class was part of another two-semester sequence but was analyzed without its companion course. Each analysis is described later, followed by a discussion of the research findings.

Before exploring the data, however, it should be noted that students in this particular instructional technology program use E-mail heavily. Every student has an E-mail account and there are computer labs available 24 hours a day for their use. Not surprisingly, all students in this program are part of several large distribution lists, and most classes require them to access their accounts on a daily basis to monitor administrative matters and person-to-person messages on various topics. Therefore, issues of technology access and competence are only a minor concern here.

To better understand the role E-mail played in these classes, we conducted analyses of messages sent throughout the semester. As indicated throughout this book, analysis of E-mail transactions can take many forms. Fortunately, Meloth and Deering (1994) provide guidance into how verbal discourse might be analyzed. Because of the different nature of the courses analyzed and the role of E-mail dialogue, we analyzed the E-mail transactions using a different approach for each study. In the first study, we analyzed one class, examining the assistance provided by the instructors through the instructors' responses to a weekly report. In the other study, we looked at two classes holistically and conducted an analysis of all the E-mail transactions. Across the studies, we used a sociocultural framework to guide our thinking and instrument development. In both instances, we used the following categories to analyze E-mail transactions: means of assistance, content discussion, and classroom management and directions.

Means of Assistance: Providing Scaffolding and Support for Learning

All of our transaction analyses were adaptations of categories of the means of assistance developed by Gallimore and Tharp (1990) to understand teacher–student interactions. Assistance is most often provided by an instructor and in certain circumstances by a more capable peer. All of these categories are defined and described later (for further discussion see Sugar & Bonk, chap. 6 of this volume). Afterward, we indicate which of the categories were used for analyses in each particular study. Table 9.1 describes these categories.

Content Discussion

In examining the discussions in the second study holistically, we adapted categories from Meloth and Deering (1994) to describe the various forms of content discussion. Table 9.2 describes these categories.

TABLE 9.1
Means of Assistance Categories

Scaffolding	Refers to the help, guidance, assistance, suggestions, recommendations, advice, opinions, and comments that the instructor provides to help the learner master the materials and move to a higher level of understanding.
Feedback on Performance	It is used when the instructor or students provide information (positive or negative) on specific acts, performance, or situations or acknowledge a contribution in reference to a given standard or set of criteria. Often it includes grades.
Cognitive Structuring	It is a means of assistance whereby the teacher provides a structure for thinking and acting that helps the learner organize "raw" experience.
Modeling	This occurs when an instructor or more knowledgeable peer offers behavior for imitation.
Contingency Management	It is used by the instructor to reward desired behaviors through praise/encouragement, or to control undesirable behaviors through punishment in the form of reprimand/censure.
Instructing	This occurs when the instructor gives explicit information on specific acts (e.g., assignments, tasks, group processes, etc.) It is usually embedded in other means of assistance but is often identified when the teacher reassumes responsibility for learning.
Questioning	It calls for an active linguistic and cognitive response and is used as a prompt, to stimulate thinking and to provoke creations by the student. If the question is meant to provide assistance to the reader, then it is in this category.

Classroom Management and Directions

Classroom management was used in the second study to identify those issues involved in managing the activities of a class that were not directly related to content or assistance. In dealing with online support for classroom activities, we need to identify how to best use the tools to facilitate learning activities. Because the classes analyzed here allowed students to serve in leadership roles, E-mail was used by them for management as often as the instructor (e.g., coordinate, make assignments). Table 9.3 describes these categories.

PROVIDING LEARNING SUPPORT THROUGH E-MAIL

Introductory Production Class: Instructor to Student Assistance

In this instructional technology program, master's and doctoral students are required to take a two-semester sequence of core courses as a foundation for their program of studies. The course in this study was designed as an extended simulation in which student teams were "contracted" to produce

TABLE 9.2
Content Discussion Categories

Statement of an Opinion, Point of View, or linking	It is characterized by filtering and connecting ideas from various sources and statements that take a definite stand on the current content. The conversation ranges from definitive statements to playing with ideas.
Counterassertion	It is an alternate argument to someone's ideas or a correction to someone's factual statement. Closely tied to linking and statements of opinion, this category is generally a direct attack or response to someone else's claims or ideas. These counterassertions are usually conducted with scholarly respect for the other's point of view.
Questions Related to the Content	These ask for more discussion on, or clarification of discussion issues.
Product Evaluation	This describes messages in which homework assignments are being sent via E-mail (evaluations of specific software products) (note: it is separated out because it was a prevalent activity of one particular course here). It involves elements of linking and statements of opinion, but is different in nature from the rest of the free-flowing conversation in that it related more to assigned reports. Usually product evaluation messages are prompted by a group asking for the students to use the product and answer questions provided (i.e., list the two best authoring features).
Passing on Information	This describes those messages that are simply providing information, such as the name of a journal or the E-mail address of a listserv group.
Restatement of Previous Point	It is a clarification of one's previous statements or of another's point. It also includes conveying information found from nonclass discussions (i.e., abstract of a research report).
Discussion Tangential to the Subject Matter	This is a content issue generally not in the current discussion.
Off-Task Discussion	This has no relevance to the course content, the field being studied, or the tasks being worked on.
Metacognitive Statements	These are a reflection or self-appraisal of one's thinking and the learning process in which one is engaged.

TABLE 9.3
Classroom Management Categories

Assigning Tasks and Clarifying Tasks	It includes all the administrative messages dealing with task assignment, responsibilities, due dates, and miscellaneous management issues. This is the other part of "Instructing," which is described previously.
Requests for Clarification on Tasks	These are direct questions asking for clarification on task responsibilities and due dates from students.

an instructional product for a fictional company. These courses are taught by faculty teams who shared the responsibility for teaching the courses. This study analyzed the E-mail responses from the instructors to individual student reports in the second-semester introductory project-based learning class.

The students were part of a cohort that began the program together in the previous semester, with the addition of two new students. Forty-four master's and doctoral students were enrolled in the second-semester introductory project-based learning course. The class was heterogeneous in terms of age, race, gender, prior knowledge, and levels of skill. There were two instructors in the course, one male (e.g., Professor Y) and one female (e.g., Professor X). The instructors made the deliberate decision to allow the students to select their own four-person teams. Some teams formed on the basis of language preference (i.e., a group of Korean-speaking students formed a team, as did a group of Chinese-speaking students) or gender (i.e., two all-female groups formed as did three all-male groups). However, most teams self-selected on the basis of past friendships or shared interests. After teams were formed, they determined who would fill each of the four roles and areas of responsibility (animator, instructional designer, interface designer, and project manager; based, in part, on Myers–Briggs personality testing) required by the instructors for each group to mimic the real world of instructional product development.

The students and instructors were in core classes together three nights a week. In addition, each team met several times a week to work on their development project whereas instructors met with each team several times throughout the semester for consultations on work progress and team dynamics. Additional private meetings were held with individuals to address specific concerns. Beyond these face-to-face meetings, as indicated earlier, each student had an E-mail account. E-mail was used to coordinate schedules, collaborate and exchange work in progress, report to the instructors, and serve other logistical needs.

Weekly Reports

Each student was required to provide the instructor with a weekly report. The format of the weekly report was specified by the instructors and compliance to the format was rewarded with grades. The weekly report was also clearly designed to provide students with an opportunity to engage in some reflective thinking about the process they were experiencing. It contained the following categories: project and team responsibilities, action items, actions taken, decisions and group actions, and what is going well and what is not. The semester was 16 weeks long, but weekly reports were required for only 10 of those weeks. This study reports on a transaction analysis of the instructor's responses to these required weekly reports.

Analysis of Instructor Assistance. The analysis for these E-mail transactions was based on identifying the means of assistance provided by the instructors to the students. As indicated in Table 9.1, in conducting this analysis, we used the following six categories: modeling, contingency management, feedback, instructing, questioning, and cognitive structuring. Because the instructor responses averaged 200 words in length, the unit of analysis chosen was the instructional content of each individual sentence. However, different parts of the same sentences may have provided different forms of assistance. Table 9.4 represents the actual coding of a complete response by Professor Y to a student's weekly report. As is evident in Table 9.4, the instructor was heavily involved in instructing, feedback, and cognitive structuring when on E-mail.

TABLE 9.4
Analysis of an Instructor to Student Message

Means of Assistance	*An Example Correspondence to a Student*
a. Feedback	Three points.
b. Extraneous	I am giving the same feedback to each of your team members this week.
c. Feedback	After meeting with you and hearing what you have to say on how the project is going, I think you all have every reason to feel optimistic in moving forward.
d. Contingency Management	You have plenty of ability, a script and a design with potential, motivation that has seen you through a rocky beginning, and a good start on the kind of team communication that will get you through.
e. Extraneous	A few key points to remember—
f. Instruction	Talk more with each other, not less.
g. Cognitive Structuring	When you are not communicating with another person it's too easy to misunderstand what their actions imply, and it's not easy to coordinate your efforts toward getting the product done.
h. Instruction	Talk more about the way you're going to get things done and make fewer assumptions about it.
i. Cognitive Structuring	Clarifying the way in which each person will be working is a mark of respect for each other, and helps build trust between you.
j. Cognitive Structuring	Rethink what it means to work as a team.
k. Instruction	Team members teaching each other is not an unusual situation that you find only on substandard teams—it's a hallmark of the most successful and proficient teams.
l. Instruction	Don't panic over the product as much as the process.
m. Cognitive Structuring	Lack of coordination with each other ultimately loses more time and more points than it saves.
n. Feedback	I appreciate your willingness to talk with me and each other about the project this week.
o. Modeling	I invite any or all of you to seek me out or go to Professor Y as the semester progresses with technical, design, or process questions.

TABLE 9.5
Summary of the Three Cases

Categories	*Case #1* *N = 12*	*Case #2* *N = 59*	*Case #3* *N = 50*	*Totals* *N = 121*	*Avg.* *Total/N*	*Rank* *Order*
Modeling	2	4	18	24	.2	6
Contingency Management	20	50	51	121	1.0	4
Feeding Back	20	57	103	180	1.5	1
Assigning Grades	11	59	50	120	1.0	
Instructing	15	65	143	223	1.8	2
Questioning	10	12	34	56	.5	5
Cognitive Structuring	8	43	111	162	1.3	3
Total # Interactions	86	290	510	886		—

Table 9.5 provides a summary of three cases or analysis of this electronic data. Case 1 reports on the 11 responses by Professor X to three weekly reports from the members of one team. Case 2 tabulates the 59 responses provided by Professor Y to weekly reports submitted by students from each of the 11 teams. Case 3 reports on a stratified sample of responses from both instructors using one response from each team for each week. Each student is represented at least once, most are represented twice, but no one student is represented more than twice. The data set contained a total of 50 instructor responses.

Issues in Teacher Assistance via E-mail

The six means of assistance categories are intended to identify the various ways in which an instructor might provide a learner with electronic assistance. There is the implicit assumption that the instructor knows more about the product development process than the learner and that the instructional dialogue is intended to increase the learners' knowledge and skills in this area. This unequal teacher–student relationship is reflected in the structure of the weekly reports. The fixed format of the weekly report means that all students must present their information in a predetermined manner for teacher evaluation. In contrast, the response from the teacher is open-ended. The teacher can choose to respond to any, all, or none of the information provided by the learner in their weekly report. In this particular situation, instructors were receiving confidential reports from different members of the same team. This provided the instructors with multiple perspectives on the team dynamics. They were able to use insights gained from multiple group members in their comments back to the individual student. This reflection was presented to the student in various means of assistance as appropriate to the needs of that student. The next section examines each means of assistance in detail.

Modeling. The data summarized in Table 9.5 indicate that modeling (offering behavior for imitation) was the means of E-mail assistance used least frequently in this class. This finding was somewhat misleading because the modeling was often implicit rather than explicit. For example, the business world is rife with forms to be filled and formats to be followed. By establishing a format for the weekly reports and insisting on compliance, the instructors were modeling and shaping student behavior. At the same time, there were several instances when the instructor wrote: "Feel free to come to either of us at any time for assistance . . ." These statements were coded as modeling because they displayed the kind of behavior the students should adopt to be successful.

Contingency Management. This category was conceptually similar to classroom management. It captured instances of praise and encouragement as well as reprimands. For ease of display, these two different forms of contingency management were collapsed into one number. Of the 121 instances identified, 111 were positive, leaving only 10 of a reprimand nature. The key difficulty felt here was the lack of teacher voice, which can make the kindest comment sound severe, and the harshest rebuke seem friendly.

Feeding Back. Almost everything the instructors wrote to the students could be considered feeding back. The instructor was attempting to modify the functioning of the learner (their thinking process) by feeding back information based on the student's output (their weekly report). This feedback provided the students with new input to be processed and reflected on in their next weekly report. The 121 recorded instances of feedback, which is numerically the largest category, are directly related to the instructor assigning a grade to the weekly report. Student grades improved as they learned to complete the reports according to the predetermined criteria. This suggests that the instructors were effective in helping the students meet the required criteria. Feeding back comments were related to performance criteria, which were described in detail if the instructor felt the student was unaware of the criteria.

Instructing, Questioning, and Cognitive Structuring. These three categories are intended to capture those interactions concerned with developing higher order thinking skills. Due to their similarity, assigning interactions with one or the other of these categories was extremely context specific. The instructors were careful to treat the students as individuals and chose the means of assistance that was most appropriate to their personalities and needs. Some students benefited more from direct instruction, some benefited more from questions that helped them organize their thinking and test their depth of understanding, and others responded well to suggestions of a cognitive structuring nature.

Patterns in Computer-Mediated Communication

The instructors used the weekly report as a framework for starting a conversation with the individual student. As a means of identifying patterns in this complex data set, the total number of responses was divided into the total number counted for the particular means of assistance. A composite response from the instructor to the student would consist of the following pattern:

- A grade.
- At least one positive contingency management comment; that is, "Well done. . . ."
- One or two feedback comments; that is, "The lesson design is going well but the scope of the project is still too large . . ." or, "It seems as if your team members are not communicating with each other. . . ."
- At least two instructional statements; that is, "Changing the color images to black and white will save space . . ." and, "Provide more detail in the Responsibilities section of the report. . . ."
- A cognitive structuring comment; that is, "Focus on the process . . ." or, "Think about it this way. . . ."

In addition, every other instructor response would contain a question to help stretch the student's thinking; for example, "Why would the learner be puzzled at this point?" However, in only one of five cases would there be a comment that models behavior for the student to consider.

This pattern was evident only when a large number of the responses were averaged together. Of course, the preceding response was more the exception than the rule because responses often focused on a specific topic of interest at the time the weekly report was written.

Overall, this E-mail conversation was similar to ordinary classroom discourse between teacher and student. The students made observations and comments on their experiences, which were beneficial as an exercise in self-reflection and as a means of telling the teacher what was going on in their groups as well as individually. The teacher responded by addressing the student's stated needs with the most appropriate means of assistance as well as by addressing the unspoken needs that the experienced reader/teacher might perceive.

There is some evidence that the instructor selected a particular means of assistance to meet the learning needs of the individual student and that the use of cognitive structuring as a means of assistance increased as the relationship between the teacher and learner developed. For example, Professor Y provided a particular student (Mary) with direct instruction early in the semester. By the midpoint in the project (Week 6), the means of assistance had changed so that questioning and cognitive structuring were used more frequently. Further analysis is required to determine if this example was part of a larger pattern in which the instructors varied their means of assistance in general or in response to particular students. It is possible that greater familiarity and shared understandings made it easier for the instructor to suggest ways of thinking and learning that were appropriate to the particular learner. This hypothesis requires further investigation. The next investigation examines the use of E-mail to extend classroom dialogue. Whereas in the previous study we examined the E-mail assistance provided by the instructor, in the following study of two courses we sought to determine how whole-class discussions can be supported by E-mail in the areas of content discussion, means of assistance, classroom management, and the knowledge resources used.

Advanced Seminar and Project Development Class Sequence: Peer Discussions to Extend the Classroom Dialogue

The second study investigated the use of E-mail in a two-semester sequence of upper-level graduate courses. Although neither course was a prerequisite for the other, these courses were intended to be taken as a sequence. Only 30% of the participants were in both courses, however. One of these courses was an advanced seminar on the implications of instructional design for constructivism. This seminar utilized a learner-centered approach in which classroom activities were organized around whole-class discussions during the class meetings and an active E-mail distribution list for asynchronous communications between class meetings. Weekly assigned readings, class discussions, and a research-based, publishable paper (as determined by the instructor) were used for class assessment.

A key component of the course was the discussion of assigned readings. Students were expected to have completed the readings and were encouraged by the instructor to participate in the conversation about those readings and the implications of the theories presented. For a class participation grade, students were required to engage in discussions either in class meetings or by E-mail. Often the E-mail discussion was viewed as a mechanism to discuss new topics or to continue discussions not completed in class or deemed less important by either the instructor or the students.

The second course was an advanced project-based learning class that dealt with use of hypermedia for designing learning environments. This course revolved around two main tasks: (a) to review and evaluate existing hypermedia products within the framework of the current literature in the field, especially constructivism, and (b) to build a prototype of a hypermedia system that would train and support adult literacy tutors. Although readings were suggested, they were not assigned and classroom discussions were not dependent on them. Most class meetings consisted of group presentations of a particular hypermedia system, interviews with adult literacy subject matter experts, and discussions of the adult literacy project.

Altogether these classes consisted of 8 master's students, 21 doctoral students, 5 subject matter experts, and 1 faculty member. There were nearly equal numbers of native English speakers and non-native speakers, and male and female students. The instructor, Professor Z, had extensively published in the area of constructivist learning environments.

Analysis of a Learner-Centered Dialogue

The data[1] consisted of three components. First, there was a database of all 389 E-mail messages sent over the class distribution list for the two semesters. These messages were printed and coded for information deemed relevant to the coding scheme. Each message may have had content applicable to more than one area in the scheme. For instance, there could have been both scaffolding and content discussion in the same E-mail message. Unlike the analysis of the previous study, the coding of these messages was conducted at both the sentence and paragraph level. A final method of data collection was use of the researchers' observations and notes as a student in the class, which were used to fill in the gaps found in the E-mail transactions.

The instructor helped to create a learner-centered environment in which he was not the primary component of the discussion (i.e., a teacher as learner approach to instruction). Due to the collaborative nature of these classes, and the difficulty of separating teacher as learner and teacher as facilitator, most of the instructor content discussions were not categorized as using the means of assistance categories of the previous study. Although all the content discussion from the instructor, in fact, could have been seen as containing low levels of assistance.

Research Issues

The research issues investigated and the coding scheme for the E-mail interactions involved several components that were used to develop a rich picture of the different types of interactions that were occurring in the environment. The following is a list of issues we investigated and how the data were coded to answer the questions:

---

[1]Data were collected by one of the three authors, who also was a member of both classes. Attempts to limit bias were undertaken by having outside researchers validate analyses, conclusions and assertions.

1. *What demographic characteristics impact on a person's participation in E-mail dialogue?* It is often speculated that demographic characteristics are less important in E-mail dialogue. In order to determine how they impacted these discussions, we categorized messages to find out who was sending to whom (i.e., student to instructor, student to student, student to the whole class, instructor to student, instructor to whole class, and a message to or from a subject matter expert) and demographic subgroup information, that is, gender, nationality (U.S., Asian, European), student level (master's student, doctoral student), or instructor.

2. *Are there certain times in the semester when E-mail will be more prevalent? How many messages were typically exchanged as part of a thread?* The flow of E-mail was expected to change throughout the semester depending on topics being discussed and other class activities. To learn more about these patterns, each message was coded as to the week of the semester it was sent and categorized as being part of an interaction sequence or thread. A thread was considered any grouping of messages that followed a similar idea or topic. Therefore, a thread could last for a whole semester or be limited to only one message. For instance, in the advanced seminar class there was a thread on "viable knowledge constructions versus absolute knowledge constructions."

3. *What are the knowledge resources being used in the discussions?* In each message, the participants used prior knowledge as they worked through the issues. Whenever possible, a notation was made of the specific source of the information being conveyed. For instance, in the statement "In Miller and Miller they said . . . ," the knowledge resource is a journal article. Often more than one knowledge resource was used in a single message. The following resources were used for classification: an original idea or theory of a participant, case vignette, book, journal article, presentation, personal experience reflection or story, classroom discussion, and unknown or indeterminable (Bonk, personal communication, August 1994).

4. *What were the means of assistance, if any, being used to help the learners move through the zone of proximal development? What was the nature of the content discussions? Did E-mail lend itself to certain kinds of discussions? And, how could E-mail be used to support and manage the learning environment?* Of course, the purpose for the coding was not to provide a detailed, line-by-line analysis of each E-mail but rather to capture the flavor and intent of each message. Therefore, most coding was at the paragraph level and categories can cover multiple paragraphs (see earlier section for categories). For means of assistance we looked at scaffolding, feedback on performance (positive or negative), modeling, instructing, and questioning. Naturally, most of the interactions involved some sort of content discussion relevant to the class topic or tasks being completed as part of the course. We used the following categories to analyze this electronic discourse: (a) statement of

an opinion, point of view, or linking, (b) counterassertion, (c) questions related to the content, (d) turning in an assignment, (e) passing on information, (f) discussion tangential to the subject matter, (g) restatement of previous point, (h) off-task discussion, and (i) metacognitive statements. Finally, because many of the messages, especially in the hypermedia class, were of a logistical nature, the following categories were used to classify the management elements: assigning tasks, clarifying tasks, and requests for clarification on tasks.

RESULTS AND DISCUSSION

Nature of the Discussions

The purpose of E-mail in both of these classes was to carry on the conversation of the classroom. Both classes were implemented from a melding of constructivist and learner-centered approaches (as described in chap. 2 of this volume). The atmosphere of these classrooms was collaborative and was conducive to an open discussion of ideas. E-mail became an extension of that atmosphere. However, differences in the tasks of each class—theory discussion and development versus hands-on product evaluation and development—had a profound influence on the nature of the E-mail transactions.

A key difference in the two classes was the content of their electronic transactions. In the seminar class, E-mail was used primarily as a means to discuss, manipulate, and create theories of learning and knowing. Often the discussions revolved around abstract ideas and concepts and reflected the approach of a philosopher and a researcher, not that of the practitioner. Although the instances of direct contradiction or attack of another's statements were rare, the electronic interactions featured more subtle counterarguments. The informal, conversational style of the messages was a typical characteristic of the electronic transactions. This style featured grammatical structures associated with speech patterns, not written text. There also is an informality about the writing that conveys the message that the writer is more concerned with thoughts and ideas than with proper phrasing, spelling, or punctuation. The following excerpts are typical of an electronic debate and discussion here. (Note: Spelling and grammatical errors are from the original.)

> **Student #1 (Asian, female, doctoral):** In Bednar et al artcle [sic], you argue against being eclectic in the field of IST. Are you suggesting that becasue [sic] the supremacy of constructivism over objectivism in explaining the theory of knowing, or coming to know, thus, we should adopt the constuctivist [sic] theories or any new theories consistent with it. But how do constructivism [sic] evidence its supremacy over objectivism. . . .

Instructor (U.S., male): NO NO NO—THERE IS NEVER AN ISSUE OF SUPREMACY. REMEMBER THAT THESE ARE SIMPLY LENSES THROUGH WHICH WE VIEW THE WORLD (CONSTRUCTIVISM AND OBJECTIVISM). THEY ARE PHILOSOPHICAL VIEWS OF COMING TO KNOW. THE BEDNAR ET AL ARTICLE IS SIMPLY SAYING THAT.... [deleted text]

Student #2 (Asian, female, doctoral): I would like to talk about my perspective on the issue of "eclectic approaches of IST." I cannot make any value judge of whether eclectic appraoches [sic] are good or bad. [sic] but, at least the eclectic appraoches [sic] of IST do not violate any epistemological (or ontological) [sic] unity. In other words, the appraoche [sic] does not mean the mixture of different epistemology. . . . In a word, ID is eclectic in the sense of using various theories, but still not damaging the assumption that "it is inconceivabe [sic] to mix epistemoloies [sic]."

Likewise constructivism is also based upon diverse disciplines such as semiotics, connectionism, relativism, systems theory, etc. In this sense, constructivsm [sic] might also be eclectic. But still the above disciplines are sharing the same paradigm with constructivism.

In contrast, because the project-based course was dominated by the exchange of information on the course tasks, it reflected the discourse of the practitioner. As indicated, these tasks were projects that required the hands-on use and evaluation of products and the development of a prototype hypermedia product. Such tasks led to three primary forms of communication (note: a single message could contain more than one type of transaction): reporting and resolving logistical and administrative problems (24.7% of the messages contained this type of interaction), assigning tasks and reminding of due dates (12.5%), and reports by individuals of their evaluations of different hypermedia products (19.7%). Beyond the projects of the course, there was a considerable amount of linking and filtering of the issues being raised in the course readings and inclass discussions (20.1% of the messages). It should be noted that these interactions were typically sparked by the experiences with the projects or features of the projects. The following is a typical thread from the E-mail discussions:

Student #1 (U.S., male, doctoral): [Interface Design] How does the relationship between screen elements and real objects facilitate understanding the interface? For example, transferring or generalizing the relationship between the Macintosh trash can and a real trash can seems intuitive. The icon has the characteristics of a concrete object rather than an abstract one.

I suspect that the stronger the incon's [sic] relationship to something concrete that the learner already has experienced, the more transparent the interface and the easier it is to derive meaning from the icon or screen element.

Comments?

Student #2 (U.S., male, doctoral): I read in an article that one of the tough things about designing icons is designing icons for verbs. Nouns—trash cans—are easy. But verbs—linking, for example—are tough.

Student #2 (U.S., male, doctoral): Hello, Many of the issues we've been talking about in terms of interface issues—lack of modality, icons, etc.—are outlined in the Macintosh Interface Guidelines book. Can we just say that hypermedia designers in the Mac environment should simply follow the guidelines? Or are there things specific to hypermedia that require special thought and definition?

Student #2 (U.S., male, doctoral): You should not be looking at what the environment has to offer you and then design the system. Design the system first.

The implication of the above statement to me is that we should design the system in any way we want regardless of convention. This one reason why DOS software is so hard to use—e.g., everybody's windowing system works differently (GEM, AutoCad, GEOS, etc.).

Student #3 (European, female, doctoral): No, we cannot just say that hypermedia designers in the Mac environment should simply follow the guidelines in the Macintosh Interface book. You should not be looking at what the environment has to offer you and then design the system. Design the system first.

There are some rules about what constitutes a good interface design that apply to all kds [sic] of courseware. [deleted rules]

Student #2 (U.S., male, doctoral): Hi, Everything you mentioned in your 6 points falls squarely within the Macintosh Human Interface guidelines.

Student #3 (European, female, doctoral): Great, I wasn't familiar with the MHI guidelines. I thought you meant the very technical aspects (buttons, pull-down menus etc). [deleted text]

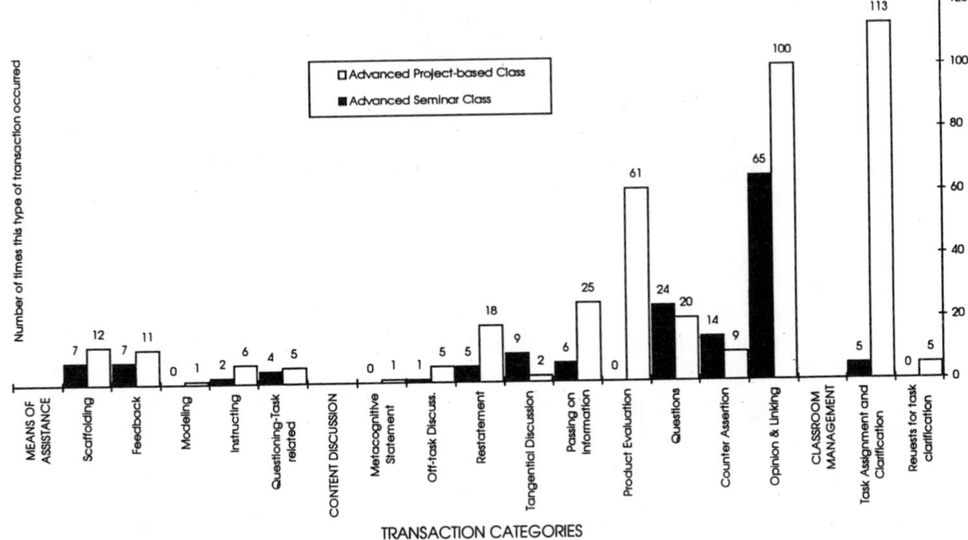

FIG. 9.1. Occurrences of content discussion, means of assistance, and classroom management transactions.

Figure 9.1 shows the total number of interactions that occurred for each of the transaction categories. It is evident from this chart that the seminar class was primarily centered around the following four discussion areas: linking (52.9%), questions on the content (28.2%), statements of opinion (23.5%), and counterassertions (16.5%). In contrast to the project-based class, there was virtually no administrative traffic on the list (5.9%).

In trying to promote a learner-centered environment, Professor Z set up an atmosphere in which he was just another member of the conversation, not the lecturer or dispenser of knowledge. When he engaged in discussion, he was attempting to carry on the conversation, not dominate it or overly direct it. This was not always successful because the leadership position of the instructor naturally caused the students to follow his lead. From this perspective, it is impossible to definitively categorize his contributions as either providing scaffolding, modeling his thinking processes, or sharing information as another discussant.

This issue led to the second problem. Because he was so central to the overall conversation of both classes (volume of messages), counting all of his messages as means of assistance would have skewed the content discussion results and been in opposition to the nature of the conversation he was trying to foster. Therefore, items were coded as being a type of assistance if it was clear that the instructor was attempting to provide support to the student beyond the normal conversation.

The analysis reveals that the number of messages strictly categorized as means of assistance is low in both courses (23.5% in the seminar, 11.5% in the project-based course, or 14.1% in both courses combined) when compared with content discussions and classroom management. This was unexpected considering the instructor was the dominant originator of all messages in both courses (30.6% in the seminar, 22.2% in the project-based course, or 24.2% in both courses combined) and that student group messages could also be counted as assistance. Although we expected the instructor to step outside his role as contributor more often and provide direct assistance, perhaps this would happen in other less learner-centered environments.

Frequency and Threads of Interactions

An analysis of the data reveals several interesting trends that can guide others in developing learning environments supported by E-mail interactions. Unlike the classroom interactions in which verbal exchanges tended to be directly from one person to another individual, the E-mail interactions featured very few one-to-one exchanges. Most of the time when something was addressed to a specific person, the response would return as a comment for the whole class. This probably was due to the list being a public forum and anything that needed to be said individually was done so off the list in a private transaction. Table 9.6 shows the frequency of each type of electronic message that was sent out in both courses over distribution lists.

TABLE 9.6
Sender and Intended Recipient of Each Message

	Number of Messages by Class			
	Advanced Seminar	*Advanced Project-based*	*Total/Percent*	
Student to the instructor	8	4	12	3.1%
Student to student	5	7	12	3.1%
Student to the whole class	44	224	268	68.9%
Instructor to a student	8	7	15	3.9%
Instructor to the whole class	16	58	74	19.0%
Message to/from an expert	4	4	8	2.1%

As is illustrated in Fig. 9.2, an analysis of the frequency of E-mail messages by week across both classes points out that the E-mail messages tend to increase from the second week of the term until the last 6 weeks when they taper off tremendously. In the advanced seminar, the first 6 weeks of class account for 68% of the transactions, and for the advanced project-based learning class, it was 66%. By the 12th week, 95.8% of all the messages had been sent by the advanced seminar class; for the advanced project-based class it was 87.5%. In part, this is indicative of students focusing on individual and group projects that were due at the end of the course, allowing them little time for E-mail activities. It may also have been affected by boredom or burnout with course content and discussion at the end of the semester, as well as the requirements of other courses.

Each message was coded as being part of a theme or thread. The threads in the advanced seminar class had a range of 1 to 11 individual messages in

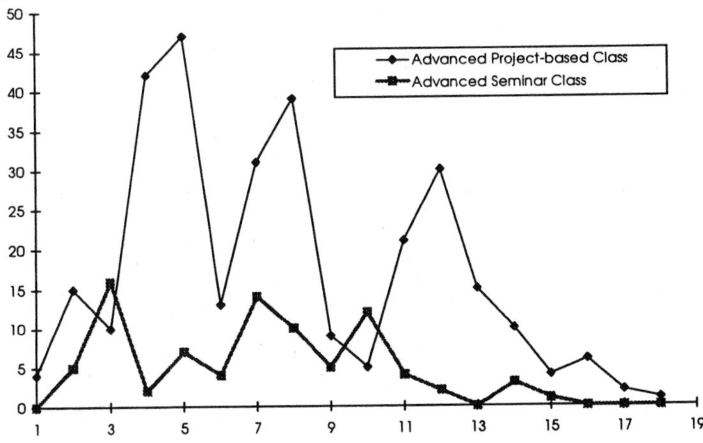

FIG. 9.2. Total E-mail transactions by week.

a sequence. In the advanced project-based class the range was 1 to 56. Most messages, however, were clustered in the one-to-five message range. The highly interactive threads in the advanced project-based course were all centered around a particular hypermedia software product. Whereas four of these threads reached 23, 27, 30, and 56 messages, the remainder were below 20. Many of these messages were of a logistical nature.

The participants were divided into demographic groups. As illustrated in Fig. 9.3, which illustrates the average number of messages sent by each member of the groups, we see that the instructor was the dominant contributor across both courses.

If we look at the groupings in a different way, several patterns emerge. It was predicted that the doctoral students would tend to dominate the volume of classroom discussions over the master's students. In the ratings (the scale was 3 = high-level participant, 2 = medium level participant, and 1 = low-level participant) of inclass face-to-face participation, the master's

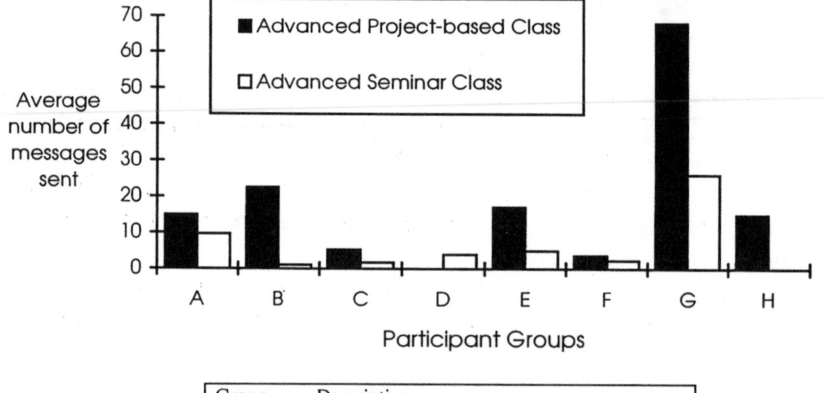

Group Letter	Description Native/ESL	Gender	Level
A	US	Male	Doctorate
B	US	Male	Master's
C	Asian	Male	Doctorate
D	US	Female	Doctorate
E	US	Female	Master's
F	Asian	Female	Doctorate
G	US	Male	Faculty
H	European	Female	Doctorate

FIG. 9.3. Average number of e-mail messages sent per person in each group. Note: There were no members of Group D in the advanced project-based course and none of Group H in the advanced seminar course.

student mean was 1.96 and the doctoral student average was 2.02. The same pattern was evident in the E-mail transactions for the advanced seminar class, wherein the average number of messages per person was slightly higher for the doctoral students. However, in the advanced project-based class, the master's students sent over a 2:1 ratio of messages when compared to doctoral students (see Fig. 9.4). This was in part due to leadership roles taken within the project teams that required administrative mailings to the distribution list. It also is due to the fact that all the Asian students, who were rated as low contributors, were doctoral students.

A comparison of the messages sent by the Asian and U.S. groups reveals over a 2:1 ratio of number of E-mail messages in the advanced seminar class and almost a 4:1 ratio in the advanced project-based class, both in favor of the U.S. students (see Fig. 9.4). Unlike the previous comparison of master's and doctoral students, the rankings of inclass face-to-face participation for these groups were also unequal, but to a much less degree. These rankings were determined by three members of these classes. The U.S. students had a median score of 2.30 and the Asians scored a median of 1.83 out of a possible 3 points. The reason for this discrepancy between classroom performance and E-mail transactions is unknown.

A comparison of male and female participation indicates that they kept about the same level of participation on E-mail as they did in class. The median scores for inclass face-to-face participation for men was 2.22 and for women it was 1.93. As shown in Fig. 9.4, the number of messages per person was roughly the same in the seminar class and the men sent slightly more in the project-based class.

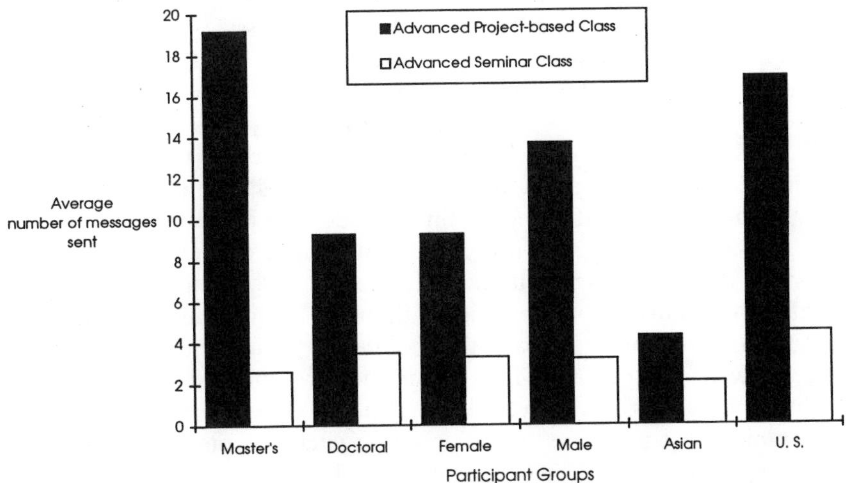

FIG. 9.4. Average number of e-mail messages sent per person by program, gender, and nationality.

Knowledge Resources Drawn On

Knowledge resources are what the writer draws from in order to carry out the discussion. As in any interaction, the writer draws on a lifetime of experience in determining what he or she chooses to say and how he or she chooses to express those thoughts. One of the key discoveries of this study was an inability to accurately determine the source of knowledge resources. However, the analyses did preliminarily indicate that for both classes the predominant identifiable source of information was from books, journals, and other primarily text-based sources.

IMPLICATIONS FOR PRACTITIONERS AND RESEARCHERS

The use of E-mail in these three courses provides a good example of how electronic communications can be used to support and enhance a face-to-face classroom environment. Not only did E-mail provide the opportunity for instructors to give individualized feedback and to extend classroom conversation, but it also enabled interactions that could never occur in the classroom because of time, conversation flow, interpersonal dynamics, cultural influences, and language barriers. Many of the threads that occurred on E-mail in the advanced seminar and the advanced project-based class were topics that were not part of the inclass discussion. These were usually generated by a student who had a thought, experience, or idea but did not have the opportunity to bring it up in class or who thought it was not important enough to take up class time. This extension of the classroom dialogue offered new opportunities for students to think through issues that the instructor, or a large majority of the class members, might have deemed less important to the group but that were, nonetheless, important to a subset of the class. E-mail also enables a more diverse set of content topics to be discussed in depth. Research investigating the impact these types of interactions have on the students' intellectual development, attitude, and performance could provide guidance to instructors using electronic course delivery mechanisms.

One of the key challenges in these studies was developing a coding scheme capable of capturing the meaning of the conversation and parsing it into categories that would indicate the fashion in which the instructors and students were using E-mail. This was particularly difficult because we were analyzing only part of the overall course instruction and interactions. Also, communication constraints can occur when switching from direct face-to-face communication to the E-mail environment. Experienced authors of E-mail messages make an effort to circumvent these constraints by adding the equivalent of nonverbal information to their messages. This includes the use of uppercase letters for emphasis and a conversational style of writing. These elements of style in electronic collaboration contribute to the clarity of the communication and relationship building. Further research needs to be conducted to capture the effects of the use of nonverbal cues within online dialogue.

The analyses of electronic interactions in these classes also pointed out some lingering problems, shortcomings, and constraints of this new instructional medium. A common belief is that E-mail provides the opportunity for everyone to contribute equally to the conversation, thereby eliminating nationality, race, gender, and status from the equation. However, in these two studies, there was evidence that many of these obstacles were not overcome. Men contributed more than women, and native speakers dominated the conversation. Those who were low-level participants in the face-to-face classroom interactions tended to stay low-level participants on E-mail. And the instructor was still the primary figure in the overall conversation. This may have been due, in part, to the participants knowing each other, and therefore, allowing personalities and physical attributes to be attached to the messages (i.e., different results may have occurred in anonymous and virtual environments). More research needs to be performed on the implications of gender, status, and cultural background on text-based interactions. For instance, does the language barrier or cultural traditions of ESL (English as a second language) students reduce their E-mail interactions? Based on our initial results, it does seem to impact their inclass participation.

In these classes, E-mail served as a conversation and administrative tool. In doing that, it was quite effective. However, many of the class members did not participate beyond receiving the information; in a way, they were "lurkers" (for a definition, see Zhu, chap. 10 in this volume). Guidance from E-mail research could inform the instructor about how to encourage these students to participate or determine even if that is a good idea.

Another element needing further investigation is how the electronic communications and collaborations can be integrated into different learning environments. In some courses, E-mail serves a purely administrative function; whereas in others, the entire course is delivered via E-mail and electronic forums wherein students never meet. Research into the roles that electronic communication plays in these situations, and those that use it for both, could provide valuable information to those attempting to integrate these capabilities into their learning environments.

A final area of investigation is how electronic collaboration impacts the overall learning environment. These studies focused on public distribution list collaborations. Although certainly important in the dialogue of the class, we did not have access to the private E-mail sent between individuals and within teams. How more private communication impacted this classroom environment, therefore, was impossible to determine. Future research might attempt to capture a more complete interaction pattern including public and private E-mail and the inclass interactions, thereby providing a rich picture of the whole learning environment.

Electronic communication is rapidly being integrated into the classrooms of the world. States are providing new moneys for various technologies and mandating that their schools become wired to the Internet. Universities are providing E-mail accounts to all students and faculty members on campus. Experts are touting the enormous benefits that these connections provide. As researchers, we need to provide the designers of learning environments with guidance on how to best position these technologies within the overall course and communication structure.

REFERENCES

D'Souza, P. (1991). The use of electronic mail as an instructional aid. *Journal of Computer-Based Instruction, 18*(3), 106–110.

Finholt, T., Sproull, L., & Kiesler, S. (1990). Communication and performance in ad hoc task groups. In J. Galegher, R. Kraut, & C. Egido (Eds.), *Intellectual teamwork: Social and technological foundations of cooperative work* (pp. 291–325). Hillsdale, NJ: Lawrence Erlbaum Associates.

Forrester Research, Inc. (1997). The e-mail explosion [On-line]. Available: http://www.forrester.com/pressrel/970107PT.htm

Gallimore, R., & Tharp, R. (1990). Teaching mind in society: Teaching, schooling, and literate discourse. In L. C. Moll (Ed.), *Vygotsky in education: Instructional implications of sociohistorical psychology* (pp. 175–205). New York: Cambridge University Press.

Kiesler, S., Siegel, J., & McGuire, T. (1984). Social psychological aspects of computer-mediated communication. *American Psychologist, 39*(10), 1123–1134.

Komsky, S. (1991). A profile of users of electronic mail in a university: Frequent vs. occasional users. *Management Communications Quarterly, 4*(3), 310–340.

Leslie, J. (1994). Mail bonding: E-mail is creating a new oral culture. *Wired Online* [On-line], *2.03*. Available: http://www.hotwired.com/wired/2.03/departments/electrosphere/e-mail.html

Meloth, M., & Deering, P. (1994). Task talk and task awareness under different cooperative learning conditions. *American Educational Research Journal, 31*(1), 138–165.

The Net keeps snagging'em. (1997, April 28). *Business Week*, pp. 22–24.

1996 Campus Computing Survey. (1996, November 22). *Chronicle of Higher Education*, pp. A21–A22.

Riel, M. (1990). Cooperative learning across classrooms in electronic learning circles. *Instructional Science, 19*, 445–466.

Stefik, M., Foster, G., Bobrow, D. G., Kahn, K., Lanning, S., & Suchman, L. (1988). Beyond the chalkboard: Computer support for collaboration and problem solving in meetings. In I. Greif (Ed.), *Computer-supported cooperative work: A book of readings* (pp. 335–393). San Mateo, CA: Morgan Kaufmann.

Tharp, R. G., & Gallimore, R. (1988). *Rousing minds to life: Teaching, learning and schooling in social context*. New York: Cambridge University Press.

10

Learning and Mentoring: Electronic Discussion in a Distance-Learning Course

Erping Zhu
Florida Gulf Coast University

Technology tools have been used in schools, corporations, and government agencies to extend or enhance individual physical and cognitive capabilities in both work and study. In education, they have been used to facilitate and revolutionize teaching and learning. Distance learning is one of many educational initiatives that have greatly benefited from the advent of recent technology tools, such as electronic conferencing systems, resource-sharing systems, and group-access support systems. The use of electronic conferencing not only promotes student-centered teaching but also active learning. In fact, electronic conferencing systems are proving to be powerful and increasingly popular mediums for totally "online" courses as well as more conventional classroom-based and distance-learning courses (Verdejo & Cerri, 1994). However, though most electronic conference software packages provide instructors with the technical information for structuring conference topics, pedagogical supports are seldom available.

The present study describes how VAX Notes—an electronic conference software tool—was used at a large Midwest university in a graduate distance-learning course entitled "Interactive Technologies for Learning." In this study, students' electronic discussions, knowledge construction, and instructors' methods for organizing the electronic conference in the distance-learning course were saved and analyzed to reveal patterns of students' electronic discussion and knowledge construction practices. Moreover, this research reviewed and analyzed various ways of organizing the electronic conferencing and mentoring in a distance-learning course. In effect, this study provided insights into how to employ electronic conferencing technology to facilitate teaching and learning. It is hoped that the study will be informative and perhaps inspire other instructors to employ social and cognitive learning theories in other electronic conferencing situations.

THEORETICAL FRAMEWORK

Vygotsky's (1978) sociocultural framework provides a good basis for understanding learning as a process of social negotiation or collaborative sense making, mentoring, and joint knowledge construction. One of the key concepts in Vygotsky's sociocultural theory is the zone of proximal development (ZPD). As indicated in earlier chapters, Vygotsky defined the ZPD as "the distance between the actual developmental level as determined by independent problem solving and the level of potential development as determined through problem solving under adult guidance or in collaboration with more capable peers" (p. 86). The term exemplifies Vygotsky's notion that what children can do with the assistance of others might be, in some sense, even more indicative of their mental development than what they can do alone (Meichenbaum, Burland, Gruson, & Cameron, 1985). As some electronic learning environments have shown, achievements in a supportive social environment contribute significantly to children's cognitive development (Fowler & Wheeler, 1995).

Another important concept in Vygotsky's theory is his idea that intellectual development takes place between people before internalization. From this perspective, instruction is most effective when it is in a form of discussions or dialogues wherein learners can interact with peers and adults or mentors who challenge and scaffold their learning. As sociological researchers point out, instruction should take place in an environment in which learners use socially mediated and intellectual tools to achieve cognitive development (Rogoff, 1990a; Salomon, 1993). Consequently, the instructor should design learning activities within the ZPD. This zone is a property of neither the child nor the interpsychological functioning alone, but is jointly determined by the child's level of development and the form of instruction involved. The challenge for educators is to develop forms of instruction so that interpsychological functioning can be structured to maximize the growth of intrapyschological functioning (Wertsch, 1990).

An electronic conference in distance education can be viewed as a sociocultural tool for student interaction and achievement. By using the electronic conference, students and instructors can voice their opinions and reflect on their learning, thereby increasing interpsychological and intrapsychological activities to promote individual's cognitive growth and development. The electronic conference provides a space for students to exchange ideas, discuss issues, and join efforts in searching for solutions to problems. The electronic conference therefore serves as a social context from which significant individual understanding can emerge. A number of researchers point out that an individual learner constructs his or her unique understanding of the world in a social context (Cunningham, Duffy, & Knuth, 1993). As indicated, the electronic conference not only enables interaction and collaboration but promotes self-regulated learning as well as reflective activities. When individuals examine and test their ideas, they are better equipped to use their knowledge in informed and self-directed ways. Reading and responding to peers' and instructors' notes forces students to think, form ideas, and articulate them in meaningful and sensible ways. In addition, reading peer and instructor thoughts and opinions urges students to compare these analyses with their own ideas and to reexamine their own understanding and interpretations. Reflective activities in the electronic conference cultivate individual learning and cognitive growth (Dewey, 1933).

The social aspect of learning and intellectual development guides the present study. Clearly, as theorists challenge the traditional role of the teacher and the student, learning is increasingly viewed as an active process of engaging in students' self-regulated, constructive, and reflective activities. The role of teaching and other instructional media is shifting from one that seeks to maximize the communication of fixed content and skills to one in which students are led to experience the knowledge construction process (Knuth & Cunningham, 1993). From this perspective, students are provided with multiple perspectives, guided to make sense of the world around them, and encouraged to develop and defend their own positions. That is, students are no longer passive recipients of bodies of knowledge, but are actively involved in the knowledge-building process, in which they discuss, elaborate upon, and devise relationships among concepts. Additionally, they view multiple perspectives on concepts and generate their understanding based on prior knowledge and current understanding (Jonassen, Mayes, & McAleese, 1993).

LEARNING AND MENTORING IN ELECTRONIC DISCUSSIONS

Distance-Learning Course

During the spring of 1995, a graduate seminar on interactive technologies for learning was cotaught by two instructors at a large midwestern university. The seminar discussion focused on the ideas related to uses of the computer as an educational tool. It incorporated an assortment of lectures, demonstrations, videos, and small- and large-group discussion activities as well as one class discussion with the actual authors of selected readings through CU-SeeMe and Picture-tel videoconferencing systems.

The students in the course were mainly master's and PhD students in such programs as instructional systems technology, educational psychology, and telecommunications. Students at two campus were connected via compressing videoconferencing technologies for 3 hours each week on Monday nights enabling them to see each other and their instructors at both ends. Each class period was usually devoted to a variety of activities such as the instructors summarizing weekly readings, class discussions of readings, and students or instructors demonstrating computer-mediated learning tools. An average of 80 pages was assigned for each week's reading. Because students were afforded insufficient time to voice their opinions, understandings, and questions about weekly readings during a session of 3 hours, most discussion of weekly readings and sharing of individual understandings, instead, took place in the form of computer-mediated communication (CMC). In this case, it was electronic mail (E-mail) and VAX Notes. E-mail was the primary communication channel for the first 2 weeks' discussions. Later class discussions gradually migrated into VAX Notes—an electronic conferencing tool for asynchronous discussion.

The student electronic discussion consisted of four major components: instructor's introductory questions and reading advice, weekly starter comments, participant comments, and weekly wrapper comments. The instructors designed the starter, the wrapper, and weekly participant roles for the students with participation in the electronic discussion worth 25% of the final grade. Though students assumed a starter or wrapper role just once during the semester, they were asked to participate in some manner each week.

As a starter of discussion, a student might (a) state reactions, questions, and suggestions for the upcoming readings, (b) point out the relationship of an upcoming topic or articles to past lectures or readings, (c) discuss the position of a pioneer in the field, or (d) attempt to relate student prior learning and discussion to the current week's readings. In effect, the starter role was intended to provide the class with key themes, issues, or questions leading to the upcoming week's readings.

A student in the wrapper role, on the other hand, was to bring some of the discussed issues and questions to some sense of closure. Summarizing and synthesizing key points and themes was within the wrapper's purview. Therefore, as a wrapper, a student might (a) react and reflect on any lectures, discussions, or demonstrations, (b) restate and reflect on the starter's initial points for that week, (c) point out questions and concerns that have yet to be answered, or (d) note any additional related reading.

As a weekly participant, one might (a) participate in the discussion, (b) answer questions and concerns of the other participants, (c) question or respond to a peer at another site, or (d) bring to everyone's attention related events (e.g., an upcoming conference) or issues.

In the middle of the semester, the instructors randomly assigned participants various thinking-related roles (e.g., optimist, pessimist, judge, connector, predictor, watchdog, critic, speculator, brainstormer, guesser, and summarizer) to assume during the following week's discussion. In most other weeks, participants' roles varied depending on their own expertise with each topic.

Student notes in the electronic discussion as a starter, wrapper, and participant were printed out at the end of the semester and attached to a summary paper each student wrote of his or her reflections regarding this new learning device. The students' electronic dialogues and reflections were then graded for insight, clarity/logic, originality, completeness, and feedback or responsiveness to one's peers.

Delayed Electronic Exchanges

Student electronic exchanges were collected from both E-mail and VAX Notes discussions. A total number of 408 notes were collected from E-mail and VAX Notes. Of these, 84 notes were contributed by the instructors. Quantitative analyses were performed on all these data; however, due to the vast amount of data, a more descriptive and detailed analysis was conducted on the discussion of only two randomly selected weeks (Week 9 and Week 12).

The collected E-mail and VAX Notes messages were coded into note categories (see Table 10.1) such as question, reflection, discussion, comment, and answer. Additionally, each student and instructor comment during the discussion was examined in light of four participant categories displayed or roles: contributor, wanderer, seeker, and mentor (see Table 10.2). Patterns of the student electronic discussion, interaction, and knowledge construction were detailed based on an analysis of participation and role categories. To further clarify this teaching and learning picture, the instructors' contributions were analyzed for planning, introductory questions, contributing toward discussions, commenting on students' responses, and guiding students' learning.

Horizontal Versus Vertical Interactions

Interesting relationships uncovered in students' and instructors' electronic conferencing notes provided insight into how students construct new knowledge and understanding and how electronic conferences can be efficiently organized to facilitate learning. The analyses required not only an understanding of how students contributed to the electronic conference but also a familiarity with the content area to help determine the role of each student, and the evolution and development of an idea or a topic.

No previous analytical framework or coding schemes, such as conversation analysis (Schegloff, 1993) or protocol analysis (Ericsson & Simon, 1984), could be readily applied to suit this interactive electronic discourse. Instead, a specific coding scheme was constructed for this study. The scheme incor-

TABLE 10.1
Note Categories and Interaction Types

	Note Categories	*Characteristics and Examples*	*Interaction Types*
1	Type 1 Question (Information seeking)	Ask for information or requesting an answer "What does hypermedia mean?"	VERTICAL
2	Type 2 Question (Discussion)	Inquire or start a dialogue "How can we resolve the control issues such as governing the shared space when using a collaborative tool?"	Horizontal
3	Answer	Provide answers to information-seeking questions "Hypermedia means . . ."	Horizontal
4	Information sharing	Share information "My colleague and I have done a lot of thinking about the nature and effect of simulations . . ."	Horizontal
5	Discussion	Elaborate, exchange, and express ideas or thoughts "What intrigues me from this week's readings is not how we define a tool, . . . but rather how tools change ourselves . . ."	Horizontal
6	Comment	Judgmental "I agree with A that Schorr's article was . . ."	Horizontal
7	Reflection	Evaluation, self-appraisal of learning "I found the class last night to be completely frustrating yet intellectually stimulating . . . it is what makes me think!"	Horizontal
8	Scaffolding	Provide guidance and suggestions to others ". . . let us not move our lives in this same 'scripted' direction. Use the tool as an idea generator, a place holder of ideas . . ."	Horizontal

porated both Hatano and Inagaki's (1991) theory of group interaction and Graesser and Person's (1994) theory of question analysis. According to Hatano and Inagaki, construction of knowledge through social interaction can be observed in two formats, *horizontal* and *vertical.* In the *vertical interaction*, some group members will concentrate on more capable members' answers rather than contributing and constructing their own knowledge. By contrast, in the *horizontal interaction*, members' desires to express their own ideas tend to be strong, because no correct answers are immediately forthcoming or expected. Therefore, the members often express a variety of ideas and exchange ideas that are likely to be examined and elaborated by peers and oneself (Hatano & Inagaki, 1991).

TABLE 10.2
Participant Category

Participant Category	*Note Categories (see Table 10.1)*
Contributor	Note categories 1–8
Mentor	Note categories 1–8
Wanderer	Mainly note categories 1 and 4
Seeker	Note category 1

Using this framework, it was important to keep track of the following variables: (a) participant categories, (b) types of interaction, and (c) note categories (see Tables 10.1 & 10.2). Within participant categories, the following four kinds of student roles were identified: contributor, wanderer, seeker, and mentor. Note categories included reflections, comments, discussions, answers, information-sharing notes, scaffolding notes, and questions.

The definition of each note category was established within the described theoretical framework and based on the note analysis. Reflective notes are defined as any reflective thoughts in participant notes. These can be (a) evaluation of the class and learning, (b) self-appraisal of learning and understanding, (c) instances of comparing and relating past readings or past experiences to current readings and understanding, and (d) instances of self-adjusting learning goals and objectives. The main characteristics of reflective notes here are evaluation, self-appraisal, and self-adjustment.

Discussion and information-sharing notes refer to general statements relevant to discussion topics. These may include (a) elaboration on discussion topics, (b) exchanges of thoughts or ideas on related concepts and issues, (c) personal understanding, and (d) topic-related discussion questions. Scaffolding notes here refer to those providing guidance or suggestion for discussions or readings. They can be notes from either instructors or students.

Note subcategories were also important in this study. For instance, two main types of questions are detected in the electronic conference. The first, Type 1, is information-seeking questions (Graesser & Person, 1994). When a genuine information-seeking question is asked, the questioner is missing information and believes the answerer can supply it (Graesser & Person, 1994). Van der Meiji (1987) identified several assumptions underlying a genuine information-seeking question: (a) The questioner does not know the information asked for in the question, (b) the questioner believes that an answer exists, (c) the questioner wants to know the answer, and (d) the questioner believes that the answer will not be given in absence of the question (Graesser & Person, 1994).

A Type 2 question was for prompting discussions. Assumptions underlying it are: (a) The questioner can provide some kind of explanation to the question, but he or she believes that it may not be complete or highly appropriate, (b) the questioner understands that there are no existing and ready answers to the question, (c) the questioner would like to seek opinions from peers or experts, and (d) the questioner intends to start a dialogue among peers rather than ask for answers.

Basically, then, while in vertical interaction, the individual concentrates on looking for answers rather than expressing or exchanging opinions. In contrast, in horizontal interaction, students express and exchange views, actively engaging in the discussion. Both interactions are important to constructive learning and contribute to meaning negotiation and individuals' knowledge construction.

Constructive Learning

Constructive learning is viewed as being active, cumulative, and goal oriented (Schuell, 1988). However, this does not mean that all constructive learning proceeds through or includes all these components (Simons, 1993). In reality, it may be that active learning periods and passive ones take turns, especially for learning that lasts for a long period of time. In essence, learning modes change in the process of learning. They could be very active, highly motivated, and reflective at one time, but less active, motivated, and reflective at another. To apply this perspective to the analyses of the present study, the discussion participant was identified as contributor, wanderer, seeker, and mentor according to the nature and the content of their notes (see Table 10.2). Keep in mind, however, each participant in the discussion was viewed as contributor no matter what type of note was contributed.

As indicated earlier, participants might furnish questions, reflections, opinions, information, prompts, and insights. Information-seeking questions, for instance, brought others' attention to questions that might otherwise have been ignored. The following quote discussing weekly readings was representative of a large number of participant notes in the electronic class discussion:

> The articles this week really made me think about the way people learn, especially the Envisioning Machine article. It is amazing that kids are able to go from not knowing anything about physics and eventually are able to make sense of it without a teacher in front of them telling them what to do. I think the key is that all of us want to make sense out of the world. We are wired from birth with the ability to take previous experiences and build upon them to discover new concepts. The important part here is that the learners did not do it on their own, but in order to make sense of the situation, they had to rely on each other and negotiate an understanding.

The student here expressed an opinion about learning and discussed how children rely on each other and collaboratively make sense of the world around them. By posting this note, the student brought to the class discussion a unique perspective on this important issue.

Wanderers are the ones who seem to be presently lost in the reading or discussion. Their notes usually address the weekly readings in general rather than specific terms. Wandering reflects a unique learning stage where learners are floundering, readjusting themselves, and striving for an understanding of the issue by relating and associating different pieces of information and knowledge. Of course, this stage is an important precedent to learning and understanding. The wanderer's notes contribute to the discussion from a different angle, that is, not through elaboration, but through creating perturbations and conflicts in the reader.

Seekers, on the other hand, are the ones who feel an information deficit and a need to seek information in order to gain a better or more appropriate understanding of concepts and issues. A seeker, for example, wrote: "I don't understand what they meant by shared space. I read the section more than once, but the idea doesn't want to sink in my mind. Can you help?" The seeker here apparently did not have enough knowledge and understanding about the concept—shared space. Without this, the seeker could not comprehend the meaning after reading the article and he was limited in the amount of shared space he could enjoy.

As stated earlier, a learner's learning modes change. A learner can be a wanderer, a seeker, or a mentor. Mentors in the electronic discussion read participant notes, trying to understand the participants' interpretation and knowledge levels in order to guide them in their reading or help them defend ideas and develop new understandings. A mentor in the discussion of Week 12, for instance, said: "Note A commented that the IdeaFisher could constrain one's creative thinking because you are using someone else's opinion of what things might be associated with other things. In fact, every piece of software you use could be considered an interpretive work at some level. . . ." Here, the mentor related a participant's note to a broader view and attempted this shift of the discussion.

Although students and instructors can fall into any of these categories in the electronic discussion, the period of time one is in the categories of seeker and wanderer is usually transitional and temporary. Because the constructive learning process involves both active and passive periods, a student's role in the electronic discussion naturally varies within a discussion topic or a discussion session.

Two Weeks in the Life of a Course

The quantitative analysis of this study consisted of reading every note, counting notes, note length, and contributors. In addition, each note was read and analyzed at the sentence and the paragraph level with a concentration on its meaning. Whereas these analyses examined the quantity and quality of the semester-long discussion, a more detailed analysis was conducted on

2 randomly selected weeks. It examined the pattern of electronic discussions and students' knowledge construction, the role of the instructor and the student, and ways of mentoring in the electronic discussion. The topics for these 2 weeks were "science tools for collaboration in a learning community" (Week 9) and "music, art, visualization, and animation tools for creativity and critical thinking" (Week 12).

General Analysis

Quantity. The electronic discussion of 15 weeks generated a total number of 408 notes (see Table 10.3) from 17 different discussion topics. The average number of notes each week was 27 and the average number of contributors was 14. These notes ranged in length from 8 lines in the first week to 55 lines in the fifth week, with an average note length of approximately 32 lines across the 17 topics. Because each line was roughly 10 words, the average note length was approximately 320 words. Of all the discussions in 15 weeks, only the first week had an average length under 20 lines. On average, 320 words filled one text page on screen or on paper, whereas 550 words amounted almost two pages, double-spaced. Though the quality of the electronic discussion is not solely determined by its quantity or note length, clearly these students were not simply raising information-seeking questions, but were really writing thoughtful reflections, discussions, and comments.

Students' Involvement. The number of contributors was steady across all the discussion topics and in appropriate proportion with the number of notes in each week, given the number of students taking the class. The smallest number of contributors was 7 (Week 1) and the largest was 19 (Weeks 11 & 13) in this class of 22 students. More than 73% of the students participated in the electronic discussion each week, with a participation rate ranging from 35% in the first week to 95% in Week 11 and Week 13. Excluding the first week, when students were relying on an initial class distribution list, the participation rate was fairly high. More important, the discussion space was not dominated by a few students, nor was it swamped with socializing statements, greetings, or information-seeking questions that might be used to earn a participation grade for this class. As indicated earlier, students mostly posted thought-provoking questions, discussions, and reflections.

Instructors' Involvement. Of the total number of notes, 86 notes were contributed by the instructors and accounted for an average of 20%. The percentage ranged from 7% in Week 15 to 50% in Week 1. Interesting to note, instructor scaffolding was high at the beginning of the semester. For instance, in the first week, the instructors' notes accounted for half of the class notes. Most of the initial notes were to suggest discussion parameters,

TABLE 10.3
General Analysis for a 15-Week Discussion

Week	*Topic*	*Notes (No.)*	*Contributors (No.)*	*Line Length (Avg.)*	*Instructors' Notes & Percentage*	
1	Introduction: Trends in computers as cognitive and sociomedia tools	10	7	7.68	5	(50%)
2	Linking tools to learner-centered psychological principles	17	13	20.5	3	(17%)
3	Learner-centered design	16	14	40.9	6	(37%)
4	Multimedia composition and knowledge construction	35	18	41.06	6	(17%)
5	Writing tools for idea generation and cognitive enhancement	24	16	54.6	5	(24%)
6	Distance-writing collaboration tools & computer-mediated communication	24	16	32.14	8	(33%)
7	Internet, Mosaic, WWW, & other information systems	29	16	30.2	6	(20%)
8	Science tools for conducting inquiry	40	18	30.8	4	(10%)
9	Science tools for collaboration in learning community	32	15	29.8	3	(9%)
10	Math tools for problem solving and problem representation	31	15	35.35	9	(29%)
11	Computer programming & CAD systems for designing knowledge	32	19	39.78	7	(21%)
12	Music, art, visualization, & animation tools for creativity & critical thinking	23	17	36.4	2	(9%)
13	Virtual reality, intelligent tools, & other dreams of reality	32	19	37.09	6	(18%)
14	Student self-selection week	21	18	28.5	2	(9%)
15	Cognitive and sociomedia tools revisited	14	12	44	1	(7%)
	Other creative reflections[a]	8	8	18.75	0	
	Tool taxonomy presentation[b]	20	12	16.35	8	(40%)
Total / Avg.		408 / 27	14	32 lines	19%	

[a]"Other creative reflections" was not a weekly discussion topic. This topic included notes contributed by students throughout the semester about their reflective thoughts.

[b]Tool taxonomy presentation was one of the class assignments and a discussion topic for the first half of the semester. Students asked questions and posted their discussion notes about the assignment under this topic exclusively.

call for students' participation, and ensure that the E-mail distribution list worked. As the semester progressed, instructors' notes gradually reduced to around 20% with the exception of Week 3 and Week 6 in which the instructors' notes reached over 30%. The discussion topic of Week 3 (learner-centered design) drew special interest from both students and instructors. The discussion topic of Week 6 (distance-writing, collaboration tools, and computer-mediated communication) was one of the instructor's special interest areas wherein he had vast research experiences to draw on. In that week's discussion, he shared his expertise and guided students to understand how to use computer tools to help generate ideas and enhance cognitive development.

Specific Analysis

Starter Notes. We were interested in how starter, wrapper, instructor, and student participant notes affected student discussions. Main ideas of each note for Weeks 9 and 12 were summarized and synthesized. These notes reflected each individual's unique understanding and represented the individual's unique contribution to the discussion. In both weeks, students tended to read the starter's note carefully and answer the questions or discuss the issues raised. The starter in Week 9 raised and discussed the issue of relevancy in using tools. The issue was then discussed and commented on by six other individuals during that week. The situation was similar in Week 12. During that week, the starter first discussed visuals used in daily life and education, and raised a number of questions about weekly readings. He wrote: "The art or visual has been disregarded in education for a long time. Now, we recognize that the information age is multidimensional and the computer is a way for us to grasp the enormous amount of usable information. We see computers as new ways of seeing. Some questions rise from here: How do we conceptualize with vision? How does the use of computational visual affect learner's cognitive development?" The starter's note initiated a heated discussion on visualization and learning. Several threads came out of the discussion: (a) visualization as a means to exchange information and ideas, (b) visualization as tool for learning, and (c) real-life experiences of using visualization in teaching and learning. During the discussion, students referred to the blackboards in the chemistry building on campus and commented that the blackboard served as a space for visualization and for exchanging ideas. One mentor here related visualization to tools and learning and reiterated the importance of visualization in learning. Mentors acquainted peers with some real-world practices for using visualization in teaching and learning. These notes, though falling into different categories such as comment, discussion, information sharing, and scaffolding, all centered around the discussion of how visualization was used in daily life as well as in instruction.

Wrapper Notes. The wrap-up for the weekly discussion typically failed to synthesize or summarize the group's discussion and understanding of the readings as was expected. In most weeks, wrappers simply expressed their personal feelings and then attempted to summarize their individual understandings of the topics discussed. For example, the wrapper for Week 9 wrote: "I particularly enjoyed the readings for this week. I am sure that part of the reason is that they were concerned with subject matter that I am familiar with, so my ability to envision the tools discussed was enhanced. . . . I agree with student B that the thrust of Lajoie's article is the 4 tools that assist learners to accomplish cognitive tasks. . . ." In some other weeks, the wrapper technically summarized each student's and instructor's notes, but failed to bring the discussion to a sense of closure or lead it toward the following week. For example, the wrapper for Week 12 wrote: "Student C raised a question of 'the chalk board in the Chemistry Building' which a couple of people replied that they will agree with this idea—gathering information from more than one source. . . ." In effect, wrappers read discussion notes, reflected on them, but often offered few insights or summaries.

Instructor Notes. In both weeks, the instructors' notes accounted for 9% of the total notes posted. During Week 9, one instructor contributed three notes (see Table 10.4). In these notes, his roles shifted between contributor and mentor. For example, he contributed to the discussion by making comments and suggestions, reading students' notes, joining the discussion, and reflecting on the reading. As a result, he was modeling all the activities he expected of his students. On the other hand, he concentrated on mentoring

TABLE 10.4
The Instructor's Notes During Week 9

Participant Category	*Note*	*Main Ideas*	*Note Category*
C/M	N. 9	• Reflect on the history of computing	Reflection
		• Reflect on tools evolution	Suggestion
		• Encourage debate and role play	
C/M	N. 14	• Comment on surfing the net and the related jobs	Comment
		• Comment on tools vs. theories	Scaffolding
C/M	N. 24	• Comment on learning in the class	Scaffolding
		• Share information about other available materials related to the class	Comment
		• Suggest students' writing proposals for conferences	Suggestion
		• Comment on the previous class (agree with Note 22)	Discussion
		• Discuss different kinds of tools and levels of learning	Scaffolding
		• Discuss four types of cognitive tools identified in one reading	Scaffolding

Note. C = Contributor; M = Mentor.

and scaffolding in his notes. By reflecting on the history of computing and evolution of computing tools and by commenting on the tools and theories guiding the development of tools, the instructor drew students' attention to the difference between the tools of the past and the present, while emphasizing the linkage between tools and underlying designing theories. Scaffolding assisted students' understanding the basic concept of computers as cognitive tools. Moreover, in the discussion, he shared with students his own experience and his understanding of various types of tools related to five distinct levels of learning and four types of cognitive tools identified in the readings. His experience and understanding further guided students' understanding of these important concepts. For instance, he wrote: "She (Lajoie) says that there are 4 types of cognitive tools that can be identified by the functions that they serve . . . they support my memory and strategic thinking, give me the facts so I don't have to waste my time, enable me to engage in new activities, and get me to test and explore new things. . . ." Such scaffolding and sharing of his expert understanding were frequently offered by the instructor after the weekly starter's comments and students' wandering or queries.

Participant Discussion for Week 9. During that week, students discussed differences between collaborative and cooperative learning and explored the role of reflective thinking in learning. The discussion also addressed the history and evolution of computing tools for instruction. The sharing and exchanging of opinions and ideas in the discussion shed light on students' understanding of technology tools and ways these tools can assist learning. The discussion also urged students to further explore issues of technology tools and their roles in instruction. The students interacted as contributors, mentors, and sometimes wanderers. They questioned whether these issues related to collaboration, virtual field trips, and other topics. If any of these issues were interconnected, the wanderers had yet to discover the associations among them. Wandering did not hinder learning. In fact wandering helped others learn, because the wanderers' notes added fuel to the discussion, created cognitive conflicts, and urged the reader to think. As Piaget (1977) would contend, their queries caused other participants to experience disequilibrium and cognitive dissonance that needed to be resolved through additional reflection, discussion, and negotiation. The following paragraph is a good example of a wandering note in Week 9. It said: "Transfer is important and depth is important. Students have to have opportunities to explore a concept in depth and make transfer from that depth. I think it's the teacher's job to stir that curiosity and that's when the learning becomes relevant, when from a constructionist's viewpoint, you start from the child's prior knowledge. From there you guide them to exploration and transfer and application." Although dwelling on general learning, critical-thinking skills, and knowledge transfer, this note did not address the theme of the week (distance-writing collaboration tools and computer-mediated communication); nor did it discuss or reference issues from the weekly readings. Instead, the note drew heavily from the student' prior experiences. This note, nevertheless, added much food for thought in the electronic class discussions.

Participant Discussion for Week 12. Several major topics of discussion and activities emerged from the discussion of Week 12. These notes included reflective activities, the issue of using computers with at-risk students, and the issue of software programs that help people think and plan. In addition, four individuals in Week 12 reflected on this distance-learning course and the weekly readings. For example, one student wrote: "Once again, I'm excited about the readings for this week. In the beginning of the semester I was intrigued with the technology of education and was at a point of believing that using technology could save our educational system. I really am understanding that technology alone really has no bearing on how someone is able to learn better. It's a very complicated process that I've become more aware of. . . ." Another student wrote: "I would like to say that I am REALLY getting the feeling of this distance thing. As you may not be aware, I am in Syracuse, New York for the rest of the semester. . . . I won't be in class, but I will be participating in the class discussion in VaxNotes. I can't think of a better class where this situation would be more suitable." (This student was in the hospital during the last month of the semester.) In these notes, both of the aforementioned students revealed their true feelings toward the course. They started from totally divergent routes but came to a converging point. That is, they felt they had learned a lot from reading and participating in the weekly electronic discussion.

The issue of using computers with at-risk students captured students' attention in that week. Students shared information and personal experiences regarding working with at-risk students, while discussing the ideas and approaches of one of the authors. Their notes analyzed the nature of software used with at-risk students and problems with at-risk students. These students also challenged the author's approach to at-risk students as well as the class by saying that ". . . at some time/different time we are all 'at risk.' " Some suggested that instead of emphasizing the use of computers with at-risk students, we should think about teaching general problem-solving skills with at-risk students because problem-solving skills are essential to all learners.

The design and the use of creative and effective thinking tools was another hot topic of the discussion for the week. Most students voiced their opinions about the issue. Their discussions revealed individual opinions as well as a common thread of the course—how can tools help people think creatively and plan. For example, one student wrote: "I thought that IdeaFisher would limit creativity more than increase it. Doesn't this tend to destroy our own creativity and turn us into lazy couch potatoes?" Another student voiced the opposite opinion: "You use this word (here it refers to 'potato') as a springboard to idea generation. This method sounds similar to the word list in IdeaFisher. It really doesn't limit you in terms of creative thinking any less than brainstorming. In fact, it opens you up because it forces you to find a way to use a word like 'potato' to generate ideas about a problem you'd like to solve." In response to a tool demonstration in class, one student noted that "I thought that Inspiration allowed for more creativity since the tool did not prod or lead the learner." Another student concurred: "I believe that everyone is in need of such a program—Inspiration. Everybody would like to find some sort of help when it comes to arranging ideas. The visual presentation of one's thoughts, rearranging them in order to create his/her own ideas, changing relationships and so forth makes this tool indeed impressive in my view."

Opinions on computer programs that help people think creatively and plan effectively were quite diverse. The electronic notes not only demonstrated personal preferences for certain programs, but also revealed excitement or doubts about tools that can help people think and plan. To further assist students' discussion about tools and understanding of how they worked, some of these tools were later demonstrated in class.

Summary of Discussions in Week 9 and Week 12

The analysis of electronic discussions from these 2 weeks revealed that almost all students were contributors and the instructors were primarily mentors. Their electronic notes were mostly in the categories of discussion, comment, reflection, information sharing, and scaffolding (see Table 10.5).

TABLE 10.5
Summary of Electronic Discussions for Weeks 9 and 12

Note/Participant Category[a]	*Week 9*	*Week 12*	*Interaction Type*
Type 1 question	1	1	Vertical
Type 2 question	4	10	Horizontal
Discussion	23	30	Horizontal
Answer	0	4	Horizontal
Information sharing	2	4	Horizontal
Comment	16	14	Horizontal
Reflection	6	2	Horizontal
Scaffolding	4	8	Horizontal
Contributor	46	43	Horizontal
Wanderer	1	4	Horizontal
Mentor	22	8	Horizontal
Seeker	0	1	Vertical

[a]Most notes were comprised of several paragraphs and each paragraph was usually devoted to discussion, commenting, and personal reflection. Thus, a note can fall into several participant categories.

Surprisingly, there were only two Type 1 questions (i.e., information-seeking questions). Also interesting, the interaction type during the two weeks of discussion analyzed was predominantly horizontal in nature with students exchanging ideas and elaborating on the issues of the week. In effect, students participated in a collaborative and democratic fashion when using this asynchronous conferencing tool.

Some Resulting Patterns of Electronic Discussion

The analysis has shown some interesting patterns in discussions. First of all, an electronic discussion usually centered around several major themes emerging from the weekly readings. For example, in Week 9, six notes discussed cognitive tools and the relevancy of tools used in learning. However, these analyses also revealed that a group of students' notes centering on one discussion topic does not eliminate the divergence and diversity of that discussion. Stated another way, even though quite a few notes were discussing the same topic, each perspective was quite idiosyncratic and based on each individual's previous understanding and experiences. To illustrate this point, consider Note 5 and Note 6 in Week 9. Both Note 5 and Note 6 were posted to respond to the first note in that week and discussed the issue of tool relevancy. Note 5 stated: "Anderson's article on Medical Center gives us the notion of how learning is facilitated by higher order of thinking. The issue that Student A brought forward regarding the concept of transferability of information and relevancy is good. In order for the software to be relevant, it has to set goals. One of the goals in designing Medical Center is to give learners the opportunity to build a schema and relate content knowledge to its application in clinical problem solving." In contrast, Note 6 stated: "I think relevancy is what the teacher's role is and also how teachers make the specific tools relevant to their course and learning in general. The process of problem solving is a very important goal in any course (just look at the Indiana standards for public education). I admit the context that the Medical Center program and the Envisioning Machine is not relevant to every subject, but the process of problem solving that these individual subjects teach can be applied to all areas." Student convergence on a few major discussion themes did not limit the depth of discussion or the understanding; on the contrary, it brought multiple perspectives to the topic under discussion, thereby providing an extremely rich context for students to construct an understanding of the issue.

Second, this electronic discussion supported both vertical and horizontal interactions. Participants were sometimes equal peers and other times guides or mentors for other students' learning. For example, one student in Week 6 wrote: "We all seem to be concerned with what technology will *do* to us. Will it improve our thought processes? Will it stunt our creativity? Will it augment or hinder our collaboration? I think there's a danger in giving so much agency to technology. We have to remember where tools come from. They come from our minds. So, tools might be catalysts for improvement of our thought processes, but the agent of change is ourselves." This student's note reminded the class of a central course idea that tools should be extensions of ourselves, not replacements or agents to direct our relationships to learners. Students were continually reminded to bear this in mind when they try to incorporate tools into instruction. When notes contributed immensely to the discussion due to their meaning and importance, the associated student contributor was more involved in that particular discussion topic than others. Across the weekly discussion, there were usually some participants who raised questions and asked for answers and others who actively shared, exchanged, and constructed new ideas and concepts. Both types of interaction in the discussion were conducive to knowledge construction.

Many researchers influenced by Vygotsky (Rogoff, 1990b; Wertsch, 1985) have studied vertical interaction (represented by adult–child interaction). Current learning models, cognitive apprenticeship, and situated learning (Collins, Brown, & Newman, 1989) also are concerned with social interaction and dialogue that is vertical in nature; however, other researchers argue that the construction of knowledge through social interaction can be observed more often in horizontal interaction (peer interaction) (Hatano & Inagaki, 1991). We observed the same phenomena in this distance-learning course. Actually, in the electronic class discussions, horizontal interaction appeared much more often than vertical interaction. The role each participant assumed in the discussion was not fixed or permanent, but could be easily switched and interchanged. Student and instructor electronic discussion moved naturally and smoothly on the interaction continuum rather than jumping from one end to the other. That is, the vertical–horizontal interaction can be seen as a continuum rather than a dichotomy (Hatano & Inagaki, 1991).

Third, the electronic discussion appeared to address everyone's ZPD. Everyone was engaged in the discussion, rather than just a few students. As the analyses have shown, while most students contributed once or twice each week, a few students contributed more than twice. Peers' thoughts and notes usually created cognitive conflicts or perturbations in the students that urged them to think and to act. VAX Notes provided a space for every student to engage in thinking, expressing ideas, and interacting with peers. Moreover, VAX Notes served as an excellent place for them to work within their ZPD with the assistance from peers and instructors. While working within their own ZPD with the help of the instructors and peers, the students settled many internal and external cognitive conflicts, thereby maximizing cognitive growth and development.

Pattern of Knowledge Construction in Electronic Discussion

The electronic class discussion is viewed as the zone of engagement and development (see Fig. 10.1) in which every member of the class can partici-

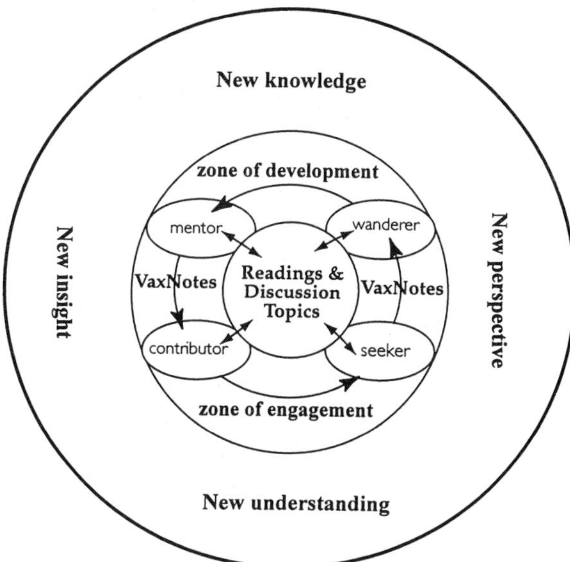

FIG. 10.1. Pattern of knowledge construction in the electronic discussion. The inner circle is the location of discussion topics. The middle circle is the zone of development and engagement. The outer circle is the place where students construct new knowledge, understanding, insight, and perspective.

pate, express or exchange views, and actively engage in constructing a better understanding of issues based on his or her prior knowledge and current understanding.

According to the revealed pattern, the construction of knowledge consisted of three stages here. It started from the core, that is, the inner circle—weekly discussion topics and readings—went through the middle circle representing the discussion space wherein each individual was involved and wherein engagement, interaction, and development activities took place, and finally arrived at the outer circle where new perspectives, insights, understandings, and knowledge reside.

In other words, students read weekly assignments and participated in discussion, interacting with peers in the electronic discussion space. As indicated by the bidirectional arrows between readings and discussion, students moved back and forth between readings and discussions and also between formulating ideas from readings and exchanging or sharing them with peers. The discussion space was also defined as the zone of engagement, interaction, and development. Multiple roles were assumed by participants in this electronic discussion. As indicated, these roles are by no means permanent or exclusive. In effect, the period of time one is in the position of a seeker or a wander is extremely temporary or transitional. The student can assume various roles and freely switch roles within one electronic note or one discussion topic. The circular arrows connecting various roles indicated the changing nature of roles in the electronic discussion.

Only after numerous trips between reading/rereading and discussing/re-discussing topics, and frequent interactions with peers and instructors, can a student finally arrive at the outer circle wherein he or she constructs new knowledge and understanding. In this process of learning and knowledge construction, social dialogue with and assistance from one's instructors and peers and the interaction among them are vital (Gallimore & Tharp, 1990).

While moving between readings and discussions, students were actually moving from the interpersonal plane to an intrapersonal one. The transformation from the interpersonal to the intrapersonal facilitates the student's generating new values, theories, and perspectives from the electronic discussion. In this process of knowledge construction, the activities of reading and discussion are highly integrated so that the student may read one article at one moment and in the next minute may post thoughts in the electronic conference or read notes from other students. Embedded in these electronic activities are a series of other learning activities such as sharing information, requesting answers, reflecting, and commenting. Thus, while engaging in asynchronous conferencing activities, the student also is assuming the responsibility to plan, monitor, motivate, and regulate learning—key metacognitive skills that have received increasing attention by educators and researchers (Paris & Winograd, 1990).

The formation of a plan, goal setting, and other activities are socially and cognitively regulated by the interaction with peers and instructors. From Vygotsky's (1981) point of view, the student is moving between the interpersonal plane (social plane) and the intrapersonal plane (psychological plane) in the electronic discussion, while activities such as planning, monitoring, and self-regulating become internalized. In other words, the individual's cognitive development is not attributed to the individual alone, but has its origins in social groups such as the large and small discussion groups in these asynchronous electronic discussions. The student has to adjust and redefine learning activities through interactions with peers and instructors. In the case presented here, the notes contributed by each individual urged other students to reexamine their learning goals and objectives. These notes in the discussion also created cognitive conflicts for any future reader and served as a stimulus for the cognitive growth in each individual.

Although knowledge acquisition and construction have common patterns in the asynchronous electronic discussion, differences do exist even among those who are actively involved in the discussion. Students' acquisition of new knowledge and understanding will not be equal. It depends on the amount of activities in which the individual is engaged, effort invested, and on his or her prior knowledge. Although the major pattern of knowledge construction in an electronic discussion is similar (i.e., starting from the inner circle and arriving at the outer circle as illustrated in Fig. 10.1), the subprocess in which each individual engages will likely differ. Two possible processes could be identified in the knowledge construction of the electronic discussion: (a) individual construction of knowledge motivated, influenced, and facilitated by the discussion and the interaction with peers, and (b) assimilation of information proposed by others with some individual editing. While more active students will more likely engage in the first process, the less active students will tend toward the latter.

Electronic Conference Organization

As indicated earlier, the organization of electronic discussion here consisted of four major components: the starter, the wrapper, the introductory questions and advice from the instructor, and participant comments. An effective discussion starter usually pointed to a few major themes for discussion and debate. However, using a wrapper for each week did not reveal many educational advantages. In fact, most students simply ignored the wrapper. The reason may be that summarizing one's learning can be quite individual. After a student has actively participated in a week's discussion, he or she needs to think or reflect about what and how is learned. There will be minimal or perhaps no commonality in the way each individual summarizes or concludes a weekly discussion. No individual's wrap-up can be so comprehensive and exhaustive as to include and represent the ideas of the entire class. From this perspective, the role of a wrapper does not function as successfully in the electronic discussion as anticipated.

The instructor's introductory questions, in contrast, served as exemplary guides to the discussion. However, the students usually did not focus the discussion around those questions, nor did the instructors endeavor to lead the discussion around those issues or questions. The reason for this could be that (a) students did not see any close relationships between the readings and the questions posted, (b) the students felt more restricted in the discussion if they followed these questions, (c) the questions were too broad to focus on, or (d) the instructors lacked adequate mechanisms to drive the discussion toward these questions. Questions in Week 7 and Week 10 could explain one point here. The instructor posted such introductory questions for Week 7 as: "Why is information access so important? Can we teach search skills?" For the discussion in Week 10, one introductory question was: "Is there any difference between tools, tutors, and multimedia word problems?" These questions were very broad and hard to focus on, providing no further guidance. Perhaps they were intended more as a guiding framework or discussion parameter, than as a specific set of focus questions.

Although the organization of the electronic conference was conducive to electronic discussions and effective in facilitating learning, much could be improved from a sociocultural viewpoint. First, after assigning the roles of starter and wrapper, mechanisms could be invented to constantly monitor the implementation of roles and to revise them if necessary. For instance, starter and wrapper comments might be required to have an instructor's approval prior to posting. Second, in addition to the role of the starter and the wrapper for the weekly discussion, volunteer students could be recruited each week to serve as additional facilitators and mentors during the discussion. In accordance with Vygotskian theories, the instructors could have paired up some advanced students with novice students (i.e., students who just stated their programs of study) and let them serve as mentors to the new students. When in a pair or a small group, advanced students could more accurately diagnose the new students' skill and understanding levels, thereby providing them with needed assistance and helping them reach adequate understandings of the issues. Although these students are still novices compared to instructors, they are perceived as experts by novice students. They could play dual roles—help themselves as well as fellow students learn the material. With the assistance of the advanced students, the novice could have achieved more than they would otherwise. Last, the introductory questions for the discussion could be more issue based, thereby allowing students more latitude in developing their own ideas and thoughts. Meanwhile, it could draw them to central issues and thus be easier for instructor guidance and scaffolding.

Roles of Students and Instructors

Students' Role

The use of VAX Notes and its discussion has reconfigured the role of the student and the instructor in this distance-learning course. Students in this class were actively involved in their own learning through such activities as planning, self-monitoring, and self-regulating. What the instructors provided here was reading materials, insights, and an electronic discussion tool. Students then chose how to take advantage of the tool, the electronic resources, and the assistance from the instructors. In addition, students decided how to participate in the discussion, how to learn, and what to learn. In effect, all learning was centered around and controlled by students. Some students enjoyed using VAX Notes as a tool to engage in the discussion because they believed the action of writing down their ideas encouraged them to think and reason more deeply and clearly. A survey indicated that students believed that by using this electronic discussion, they learned more about the course topics as well as their peers. Everyone was participating, even the most shy students whose perspectives and voices were usually absent in face-to-face discussions. For example, one student said: "Surely, using VAX Notes or news groups or even e-mail has a big advantage, that is, for shy and foreign students whose first language is not English, this is a very good place to express their opinions."

Instructors' Role

Like the student role, the instructor role has been reconfigured. The instructor was no longer a knowledge dispenser or a sage on the stage; rather, the instructor was a guide on the side, who attended to students' learning needs and guided them to achieve their own learning goals. The instructors of this course were the mentors and facilitators of students' learning. The instructors were actively engaged in the discussion, reading students' notes, interacting with them, assessing their understanding, and thus providing guidance for their understanding and learning. For example, in Week 6, one instructor explained the notion of shared space: "Shared space is the place where you can go to communicate and you and others can come back to it and review it. With technology, shared space makes thoughts and ideas visible through E-mail or a bulletin board system like VAX Notes. . . . If you and I were working on a paper and you left a copy of it on the network, then the file it is stored under is our shared space. It is a place we can go to when conversing and reflecting on that conversation."

Of course, the task of guiding students' learning was no easy job. In this course, the instructors invented several ways to guide students' learning. The methods of guidance used in this electronic discussion were quite successful on the whole. Most students expressed positive feelings toward the electronic discussion and their learning in the class. One student wrote:

> I admit that I dread coming to the lab to post notes and reflections about the articles and class discussion. However, like Julie, I recall times in class when there was something I wanted to discuss but for one reason or another, the point was forgotten. Using electronic classrooms as the primary means for discussion would allow us to explore ideas in depth and several ideas at the same time. Students who have a difficult time following the class discussions have a chance to catch up. The electronic classroom gives them a tool for reflection and clarification about class discussion. Students may not feel as apprehensive about discussing. That is a tool that benefited all of us.

Three methods of guidance have been invented and implemented here with varying successes and failures. First of all, the instructor designed the roles of the starter and wrapper to facilitate the electronic discussion. Although the introductory discussion questions were meant to guide students' discussion, most students disregarded the questions because "they are too hard, long, and difficult to follow."

A second method instructors employed to guide and scaffold students' learning was to build upon students' notes. During the discussion, the instructor added comments to generate more conversation, pushed students to defend their opinions, and answered students' information-seeking questions. Of course, due to the large number of students in this graduate class, it was extremely hard for the instructors to satisfy every student's learning needs and styles. Some students felt that the instructors could add more of their experiences and thoughts about the readings and could answer or comment more on the questions raised by students. Sometimes, they expected less. For example, one student wrote: "I'd like for the comments to be less all-encompassing. Just a nudge here or there would be fine. What the instructor says tends to be taken as the final word on an issue, thus it can stifle conversation." Another student disagreed: ". . . I think the instructor should pay more attention to lead the discussion and make sure everyone catches the points."

Finally, the instructors utilized the method of role play during a couple of weeks in the electronic discussion. Each student was given a role or could choose one. Some students assumed the role play very well and motivated other peers to contribute more. However, the role-play method was not well accepted by other students, because of their personal learning style. They simply felt that they could not discuss their unique thoughts and views and assume one of the roles simultaneously.

In a word, the starter role and the instructor's scaffolding in the discussion were quite successful. The role play would have been more beneficial to the discussion if the instructor had modeled its use and explained more about it in the discussion.

IMPLICATIONS

The methods of learning and mentoring exemplified in this distance-learning course should not be restricted to distance learning only. These techniques could be applied to a variety of learning activities in both academic and corporate worlds, because the learning environment and social context provided in this distance-learning course fostered the notion of learning as a constructive process with cumulative and goal-oriented activities and social interactions.

The pattern of knowledge construction as shown here reflects various relationships between learners and instructional materials, learners and technology, and learners and instructors. These knowledge construction relationships are the goals of many neo-Vygostkians (Collins et al., 1989; Knuth & Cunningham, 1993) and might be particularly salient when utilizing computer-conferencing tools. From the perspective of this pattern, real-world problems and issues are at the core of learning activities here. The instructor teaches skills and strategies and provides a range of tools. Instructors and students work together to solve problems and issues, using worldwide resources.

CONCLUSION

This study revealed a promising way of employing a piece of ordinary communication technology to successfully facilitate students' learning. In the electronic discussion, students selected topics, determined their goals, and shared experiences and understanding with peers. Meanwhile, these students tried to make sense of various issues and concepts through reading articles and working within their own ZPD with the assistance of instructors and peers. Clearly, VAX Notes is a shared space wherein students can engage in various collaborative learning activities. It is a social and intellectual tool for facilitating individual understanding and supporting the social construction of knowledge.

The study has reported some pioneering efforts in using CMC tools in instruction. Additional empirical research is now required to verify the participant- and note-coding schemes and models of analysis used here. More studies need to be conducted to establish practical guidelines for incorporating computer-mediated tools into classrooms. Though the field of electronic conference is promising and wide open to researchers from many disciplines, effective implementation of these emerging knowledge construction tools necessitates the understanding of the pedagogical strategies of use.

ACKNOWLEDGMENTS

I wish to thank Dr. Curtis J. Bonk for his tremendous efforts in helping me write and revise this chapter. His help, guidance, and encouragement were indispensable to the completion of this chapter.

REFERENCES

Collins, A., Brown, J. S., & Newman, S. E. (1989). Cognitive apprenticeship: Teaching the crafts of reading, writing, and mathematics. In L. B. Resnick (Ed.), *Knowing, learning, and instruction: Essays in honor of Robert Glasser* (pp. 453–494). Hillsdale, NJ: Lawrence Erlbaum Associates.

Cunningham, D. J., Duffy, T. M., & Knuth, R. A. (1993). The textbook of the future. In C. McKnight, A. Dillon, & J. Richardson (Eds.), *Hypertext: A psychological perspective* (pp. 19–50). New York: Ellis Horwood.

Dewey, J. (1933). *How we think: A restatement of the relation of reflective thinking to the educative process*. Boston: Heath.

Ericsson, K. A., & Simon, H. A. (1984). *Protocol analysis: Verbal reports as data*. Cambridge, MA: MIT Press.

Fowler, L. S., & Wheeler, D. D. (1995). Online from the K–12 classroom. In Z. L. Berge & M. P. Collins (Eds.), *Computer mediated communication and the online classroom* (pp. 83–100). Cresskill, NJ: Hampton Press.

Gallimore, R., & Tharp, R. (1990). Teaching mind in society: Teaching, schooling, and literate discourse. In L. C. Moll (Eds.), *Vygotsky and education: Instructional implications and applications of socio-historical psychology* (pp. 175–205). New York: Cambridge University Press.

Graesser, A. C., & Person, N. K. (1994). Question asking during tutoring. *American Educational Research Journal, 31*(1), 104–137.

Hatano, C., & Inagaki, K. (1991). Sharing cognition through collective comprehension activity. In L. Resnick, J. Levine, & S. D. Teasley (Eds.), *Perspectives on socially shared cognition* (pp. 331–349). Washington, DC: American Psychology Association.

Jonassen, D. H., Mayes, T., & McAleese, R. (1993). A manifesto for a constructivist approach to uses of technology in higher education. In T. M. Duffy, J. Lowyck, & D. H. Jonassen (Eds.), *Design environments for constructive learning* (pp. 231–247). New York: Springer-Verlag.

Knuth, R. A., & Cunningham, D. J. (1993). Tools for constructivism. In T. M. Duffy, J. Lowyck, & D. H. Jonassen (Eds.), *Design environments for constructive learning* (pp. 163–188). New York: Springer-Verlag.

Meichenbaum, D., Burland, S., Gruson, L., & Cameron, R. (1985). Metacognitive assessment. In S. R. Yussen (Ed.), *The growth of reflection in children* (pp. –). Orlando, FL: Academic Press.

Paris, S. G., & Winograd, P. (1990). How metacognition can promote academic learning and instruction. In B. F. Jones & L. Idol (Eds.), *Dimensions of thinking and cognitive instruction* (pp. 15–51). Hillsdale, NJ: Lawrence Erlbaum Associates.

Piaget, J. (1977). *The development of thought: Equilibration of cognitive structures*. New York: Viking.

Rogoff, B. (1990a). *Apprenticeship in thinking: Cognitive development in social context*. New York: Oxford University Press.

Rogoff, B. (1990b). Social interaction as apprenticeship in thinking: Guided participation in spatial planning. In L. Resnick, J. Levine, & S. D. Teasley (Eds.), *Perspectives on socially shared cognition* (pp. 349–365). Washington, DC: American Psychological Association.

Salomon, G. (1993). On the nature of pedagogic computer tools: The case of the writing partner. In S. P. Lajoie & S. J. Derry (Eds.), *Computers as cognitive tools* (pp. 179–186). Hillsdale, NJ: Lawrence Erlbaum Associates.

Schegloff, E. A. (1993). Reflection on quantification in the study of conversation. *Research on Language and Social Interaction, 26*(1), 99–128.

Schuell, T. J. (1988). The role of the student in learning from instruction. *Contemporary Educational Psychology, 12*, 276–295.

Simons, P. R. (1993). Constructive learning: The role of the learner. In T. M. Duffy, J. Lowyck, & D. H. Jonassen (Eds.), *Designing environments for constructive learning* (pp. 291–314). New York: Springer-Verlag.

Van der Meiji, M. H. (1987). Assumptions of information-seeking questions. *Questioning Exchange, 1*, 111–117.

Verdejo, M. F., & Cerri, S. A. (1994). *Collaborative dialogue technologies in distance learning*. New York: Springer-Verlag.

Vygotsky, L. S. (1978). *Mind in society: The development of higher psychological processes*. Cambridge, MA: Harvard University Press.

Vygotsky, L. S. (1981). The genesis of higher mental functions. In J. V. Wertsch (Ed.), *The concept of activity in Soviet psychology* (pp. 144–188). White Plains, NY: Sharpe.

Wertsch, J. V. (1985). *Vygotsky and the social formation of mind.* Cambridge, MA: Harvard University Press.

Wertsch, J. V. (1990). The voice of rationality in a sociocultural approach to mind. In L. C. Moll (Ed.), *Vygotsky and education: instructional implications and applications of sociohistorical psychology* (pp. 111–126). New York: Cambridge University Press.

MULTICONFERENCING: ASYNCHRONOUS AND SYNCHRONOUS CLASSROOMS

11

Sharing Aspects Within *Aspects*: Real-Time Collaboration in the High School English Classroom

Deborah H. Cooney
Park Tudor School

Society is witnessing an unprecedented phenomenon within the arena of telecommunications. Electronic global interconnectivity is growing at an exponential rate, and this worldwide network (i.e., the Internet) appears to be changing the face of communication within commerce, politics, academia, and the home. The explosive growth of the Internet leaves little doubt that communication is becoming a pervasive and powerful force in our society. In fact, in a keynote address to the 1995 Indiana Computer Educators conference, David Thornburg stated that we are no longer in the information age but are immersed in a communication age.

Schools and classrooms around the world are currently feeling the influence of this new phenomenon. Many educators have taken advantage of access to global communications by incorporating the use of electronic mail (E-mail) into their classrooms. Yet, we should not let the popularity of E-mail communications obscure other electronic communication tools from our view. Computer conferencing, Internet Relay Chats (IRCs), MUSEs, and other synchronous communication environments are proving to be dynamic tools for educators. Unlike the delayed exchange one experiences through E-mail, synchronous environments provide teachers and learners with a forum for an immediate and dynamic interchange of ideas. This real-time interactive exchange can be an exciting asset to collaborative learning environments. It was within this broad social framework that this investigation unfolded.

THEORETICAL FOUNDATION OF COLLABORATIVE LEARNING ENVIRONMENTS

The use of collaborative learning was built upon the foundation of social constructivist thought. Proponents of social constructivism view the individual primarily, and most important, as a social being. Vygotsky (1978) stated, "human learning presupposes a specific social nature and a process by which children grow into the intellectual life of those around them" (p. 88). Development of cognitive processes is not something that is innate or that originates within the individual; rather, it is a dialectical social process that originates outside of the individual on an interpsychological and social level and is gradually brought inside to the intrapsychological level (Vygotsky, 1978). The importance of social interactions in sparking learners' cognitive development, therefore, cannot be understated.

Collaborative learning is in many ways the practical embodiment of sociocultural theory. As a result, serious attention currently is being paid to collaborative learning environments both within education and nonacademic organizations. Collaborative learning is in direct contrast to the objectivist principle that knowledge is something "out there" that has to be given by an expert and memorized as truth. Participants in collaboration "learn when they challenge one another with questions, when they use the evidence and information available to them, when they develop relationships among issues, when they assume that knowledge is something *they can help create rather than something to be received whole from someone else*" (Gere, 1987, p. 68, italics added). Knowledge then is something that, through interactive discourse, is continually made and remade, shaped, and formed. Collaborative learning environments offer a vehicle for all members of the learning community to engage in substantive and authentic discourse (Newmann, 1991; Nystrand & Gamoran, 1990), instead of teachers pouring in facts and students immersed in trivial pursuits (Whipple, 1987).

Many studies in the last decade have suggested that peer-to-peer collaboration facilitates the learning process (Cazden, 1988; Golden, 1986; D. W. Johnson & R. T. Johnson, 1985; Nystrand, Gamoran, & Heck, 1991). Peer interaction gives the student the opportunity to exchange ideas and to hear different points of view that may not have surfaced in a more traditional teacher-directed setting. This exchange of multiple perspectives can create a conflict, or, following Piagetian thought, disequilibrium for the student. Conflict can be a powerful influence on group effectiveness and individual learning. Daiute and Dalton (1988) defined cognitive conflict as "the realization that one's perceptions, thoughts, or creations are inconsistent with new information or another person's point of view" (p. 251). This conflict, in turn, may offer the student a construct for considering other angles and changing one's own thoughts. Although ideas of the social aspect of learning seem to be gaining momentum in the past several years, they are not new. Over 30 years ago, Dewey (1963) recognized the importance of the social realm when he wrote ". . . all human experience is ultimately social: it involves contact and communication" (p. 38).

With the infusion of advanced technology into the schools in the last two decades, educators are recognizing that computer-supported collaborative learning environments can facilitate the interactive exchange of information and ideas among peers. Computer networks, in tandem with appropriate learning software, can support and enhance collaborative learning. In considering computer-mediated environments, there appears to be a cohesive relationship between collaborative learning and the advanced networked software tools. Many of the principles of collaborative learning, such as coconstructing of knowledge, participation by all learners, and shared authority in a community of learners, fit well with the elements of networked computer-mediated tools.

COMPUTER-MEDIATED CONVERSATIONS

The English classroom has been profoundly affected by the integration of computer-mediated tools. Word-processing software has radically affected writing instruction by supporting the three stages of the writing process: prewriting, writing, and revising. However, the process of writing was still a relatively solitary act with a written product at the end. With the advent of computer networks and software tools to support communication within collaborative environments, writing can now be viewed as a process that is less linear, less constant, and more social than the traditional writing process.

Contrasting this environment to common whole-class discussions in high school English, one begins to realize that the difference is not a cosmetic one, but one that is epistemological in nature. In a typical traditional discussion, the teacher is often the leader or a "sage on the stage." The teacher initiates the statements, the students respond, and the teacher evaluates. All of the information presented comes from or is filtered through the teacher, who passes judgment on the contributions made by the students. In linguistic terms, a "turn" is initiated and culminated by the teacher, with the student sandwiched in between. Only on rare exception are student-to-student turns taken, wherein students interact with one another without bouncing it to the teacher first.

Although there is disagreement as to how it will happen, it is clear that various writing and conferencing tools have the capability of changing the way we view text. Already, text has become a more fluid entity that can be shared more easily. When multiple collaborators can simultaneously view and change a shared document on connected computer monitors, the text truly becomes a shared and living entity. Such a shared space becomes a forum, a place where minds meet.

Kremers (1990) used synchronous cooperative networking tools with his college students when using role playing to create live scenarios. He reported that "by the sheer force of minds coming together, ideas emerge and are represented as text" (p. 41). He also found that students who were shy or reticent in traditional class discussions "wrote with enthusiasm" during the synchronous computer-mediated discussions.

Bump (1990) echoed these findings in his research on what he termed "computer assisted class discussion" (CACD). He examined classrooms using CACD and found that within this environment, participation was increased and conversation was more equally distributed. Furthermore, 84% of the students using CACD in his study reported that its primary advantage was that it gave every person an equal opportunity to contribute to the discussion.

Along these same lines, Mabrito (1992) analyzed the conversations of high- and low-apprehensive writers (as defined by the Writing Apprehension Test) in both face-to-face and computer-mediated settings. He found that high-apprehensive writers "participated more fully in the group discussion" (p. 29) and "assumed greater role of leadership by directing group conversations" (p. 29) in the computer-mediated mode than in face-to-face situations. Likewise, Hartman et al. (1991), in comparing various modes of communication, reported that computer-mediated communication, in general, provided a forum for a more equitable distribution of comments. In addition, teachers interacted more with their students over the network than in traditional classrooms, and students with lower verbal Scholastic Aptitude Test (SAT) scores communicated more with both their teachers and their peers electronically than did more able students.

ASPECTS RESEARCH

The purpose of this study was to contribute to the knowledge base of social interactions and the sharing of perspectives within computer-supported collaborative learning environments. Based on the theoretical positions of social constructivism and collaborative learning, the researcher conducted an ethnographic study using an embedded case study design (Yin, 1994). This approach was used to provide "an intensive, holistic description and analysis of a single phenomenon" (Merriam, 1988, p. 21). In this study, 10th-grade English students used computer conferencing during a fall semester to exchange ideas and analyze characters in their literature readings. The key resource here, *Aspects 1.03*, a prominent synchronous conference program, was used in various modes to give the students a "shared space" (Schrage, 1990) to negotiate meaning. This cooperative software falls under the highest category in Bonk, Medury, and Reynolds' (1994) five-level hierarchy of tools for collaborative writing and allows users to interact with each other in both a text mode (for simultaneous discussion of literary works or editing a shared document) and a graphics mode (for creation of character webbing and concept mapping). In the *Aspects* environment, students were placed in small groups to join in real-time conferences and carry out various tasks related to their study of literature.

Four principal analyses and corresponding research question guided the original study (Hoogstrate-Cooney, 1995). The initial unit of analysis, which focused on the *social interaction and participation patterns* within the class, asked whether social interaction patterns change when students communicate electronically. For instance, do traditional noncontributors continue to remain relatively disengaged? Similarly, do traditional discussion dominators maintain dominance in a networked setting? The second unit of analysis examined the *content* of the online discussions of the participants (e.g., substantive, procedural, off task). The third and fourth analyses focused on the *perceptions of the participants* of the process of using a computer network both to talk about text and in examining their own discourse as evident in the computer transcripts. Of these four units, only the first two are covered in the scope of this chapter.

SETTING

The student participants in this study were 10th-grade English students in a private college preparatory K–12 school in a midwestern city. The academic standards of the school are high as indicated by the policy to admit students with "average to above average academic capabilities." In fact, the school has the highest SAT scores in the state and 99% of its graduates attend college.

ASPECTS COMPUTER-CONFERENCING ENVIRONMENT

Aspects is a simultaneous computer-conferencing software package for use in a networked environment. The computers connected in an *Aspects* conference, regardless of location, all share the same screen. Furthermore, each participant has the capability of changing the information displayed on the screen. The participants in this study, therefore, interacted with one another through the computer screen as they shared and created documents.

Students in this study used three modes within the conferencing program *Aspects*: Free Mediation, the Painting application, and the Chat Box. They used the Free Mediation mode to record their thoughts and ideas in a textual format, as exemplified in initial brainstorming and freewriting tasks for a new topic. Students were encouraged to scroll up and down the screen to view their peers' contributions. Equally important, students could enter information at any place or any time within the conference.

Students used the Painting application to create character webs and concept maps in a graphic environment. Drawing from the material in the play, the students interacted in a graphic environment to connect their thoughts and ideas by drawing circles, lines, arrows, and other graphic characters as well as using text. For instance, one student might draw a circle with an adjective describing a character in the play, whereas another student might connect that circle to written examples cited from the play to support that characteristic.

Third, chat boxes, designed to foster highly interactive exchanges closely emulating face-to-face discussions, were used for student conversations and discussions. The Chat Box was used both as a stand-alone tool and as a supporting tool within the Painting application. Important to note, the time, date, and participant indicators and corresponding messages from this chat feature are savable. Figure 11.1 shows a student-generated character web within the Painting application with an accompanying Chat Box discussion on the same screen.

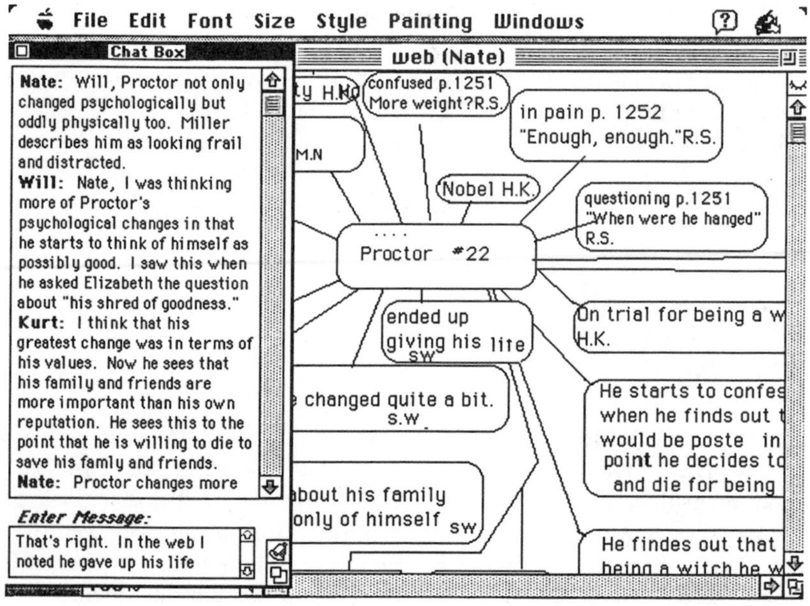

FIG. 11.1. Character web with accompanying Chat Box discussion.

PARTICIPANTS

There were four sections of sophomore English in the 1994 fall semester. Students were placed into sections without regard to academic level. Two of these sections (fourth period and sixth period) were chosen for the study. The fourth-period section consisted of 15 students: 12 boys and 3 girls. The sixth-period section consisted of nine students: six boys and three girls. It is interesting to note that the gender ratio in the composition of the classes was not balanced. Both the fourth and sixth sections were heavily weighted with boys. This gender imbalance, however, was atypical of most classes in the school.

The teacher for these two sections, referred to in this study as Barbara, was an experienced English teacher. She had a PhD degree in English and had been a language arts consultant for the State Department of Public Instruction. At the time of this study, she had used computer networking as a means for student collaboration for over 2 years within her English classes.

Barbara had firm ideas about learning through peer interaction and dialogue. She felt that if students constructed their own understanding of literary works from within themselves, and in collaboration with their peers, it would ultimately be more meaningful and helpful to them. Furthermore, she believed that by allowing the students to build their own meanings within the collaborative environments they would take responsibility for their own learning, thereby helping them to become independent learners. To facilitate these beliefs, she created a learning environment that engendered student talk and peer collaboration.

At the onset of the study, I had worked at this school for 2 years. My position involved both teaching computer classes and providing support to faculty using advanced technology in their teaching. I was, therefore, familiar to most of the students in the school. I had not had any of the participants of the present study in any of my previous computer classes.

STAGES OF DATA COLLECTION

There were three stages of data collection in this study. During Stage 1, *training*, students were trained on the various functions and applications within *Aspects*. During this stage, they also were asked to reflect on and rate their school-related participation in previous years in an online questionnaire and give reasons for their level of participation. During this stage, I observed the class in its regular classroom during traditional class discussions on *A Time to Kill* and *A Raisin in the Sun*, thereby enabling information to be gathered on participation patterns of members outside of the context of the computer environment.

Stage 2, *prereading collaboration*, consisted of reading preliminary materials and collaborative brainstorming within the Free Mediation mode of *Aspects* about the Salem witch hunts. After examining transcripts of their brainstorming sessions, students collaboratively discussed in the Chat Box the motives behind such persecutions, as well as other similar persecutions in history. Finally, students examined the content of the transcripts developed thus far and wrote personal reflections of their understanding.

Throughout Stage 3, *character, speech, and play analysis*, the students used the three modes of *Aspects* to analyze the play. During character analysis the students analyzed the main characters in the play by creating online graphic webs of characteristics using the Painting application (see Fig. 11.1). Students then analyzed the printed copies of the character webs, identifying and generating criteria for good webs. Likewise, students used the Chat Box to discuss character development. They analyzed the hard-copy transcripts of their chats and identified criteria for effective chats.

Through Free Mediation, students analyzed the speeches of *The Crucible* characters. After their electronic discussions, students analyzed the printed transcripts from all of the groups and underlined the "gem" statements to be included in a final essay. Students analyzed further development of the characters and webbed characteristics of all the main characters in the play.

Finally, the students analyzed the play on a global level using the Painting application to trace the character development throughout the four acts of the play. Using the Chat Box, they discussed the play in its entirety, choosing what they felt was one of the "burning issues" of the play.

Materials from each conference session were saved on a file server, printed out and distributed to the students for reflection and analysis. These transcripts were either text files (as generated in the *Aspects* Free Mediation mode from brainstorming and the Chat Box discussion sessions) or graphic files (as generated from *Aspects* Painting application from character-webbing sessions).

DATA SOURCES

Triangulation in this study (Lincoln & Guba, 1985; Stake, 1994) was sought by using the following multiple sources of data: (a) participation ratings from former ninth-grade teachers, the current English teacher, the student participants, and the researcher, (b) observation records from traditional class discussions, (c) computer transcripts of participant discussion and analysis of text, (d) prompted online participant journals, (e) researcher's observation field notes, and (f) informal discussions with the teacher.

PROCEDURES AND RESULTS OF THE STUDY

Research Question 1: Who Contributes to the Discussion and Analysis of the Play?

The intent of this question was to discover if and how the social interaction patterns change when students in a class are given the opportunity to work collaboratively in an electronic environment. The primary concern was to analyze who does the communicating in discussions within a computer-supported collaborative learning environment. It was of particular interest in this research to juxtapose that with who does the communicating in traditional classroom discussions.

To address these questions, both quantitative and qualitative data were used. Quantitatively, ratings scales and observation tallies were used to determine how the students contributed in traditional discussions. Additionally, computer transcripts were coded and a quantitative analysis of the coded results was conducted. Qualitatively, I observed and recorded my observations from all class sessions, both in the traditional setting and in the computer lab. I also read and analyzed all the transcripts numerous times, taking notes and summarizing each conference.

Measures of Participation in Traditional Settings. In order to establish baseline participation profiles, six separate ratings were gathered on each of the 24 participants within traditional discussion settings. First, a participation rating scale was given to three former teachers and to their current English teacher. On the rating form, teachers were asked to rate class participation for each student on a 5-point Likert-type scale, from (1) "Rarely, if ever, participated in class discussions" to (5) "Frequently, actively participated in every discussion." Before the students had started work on *The Crucible*, I also completed this scale for each of the students based on my several weeks of observations. Additionally, the students completed a self-rating of their own class participation in their online journals. Thus, up to six separate ratings were gathered for each of the 24 participants.

In order to triangulate these data, I also used a second measure by observing 18 class sessions (9 class sessions for each section) in which Barbara conducted a traditional class discussion. For each of these 18 class periods, I tallied who spoke in the discussion and who raised their hand but were not called on. High and low contributors across these settings became the primary focus in the subsequent data analysis for this research question. Table 11.1 presents the ordered lists of both the participation ratings and the traditional discussion observation tallies.

TABLE 11.1
Ordered Lists From Participation Ratings and Traditional Class Discussion Observation Tallies

Median Ratings From Teachers, Researcher, and Self			*Average Number of Observed Oral Contributions per Class*		
Fourth Period			*Fourth Period*		
High contributors	Stephen	4.0	High contributors	Neal	10.0
↕	Elizabeth	4.0	↕	Michael	8.7
Low contributors	Michael	3.5	Low contributors	Stephen	8.5
	Neal	3.5		Paul	7.4
	Elliott	3.5		Elliott	7.2
	Kurt	3.5		Hillary	6.9
	Paul	3.25		Will	5.1
	Will	3.0		Tim	4.5
	Hillary	3.0		Chris	4.0
	Chris	3.0		Elizabeth	3.7
	Nate	2.5		Nate	3.1
	Tim	2.5		Kurt	2.3
	Simon	2.5		Simon	1.3
	Holly	1.0		Holly	.9
	Janne	1.0		Janne	.7
Sixth Period			*Sixth Period*		
High contributors	Sam	4.5	High contributors	Frank	12.7
↕	Brendan	4.0	↕	Sam	11.4
Low contributors	Frank	3.0	Low contributors	Anne	11.4
	Floyd	3.0		Brendan	10.0
	Anne	3.0		Floyd	9.4
	Ben	2.5		Lawrence	6.6
	Lawrence	2.0		Ben	3.4
	Tina	1.5		Tina	1.7
	Heather	1.5		Heather	1.1

The bottom third of both lists (five students for fourth period and three students for sixth period) were considered the lower contributors in traditional class discussions. On the other end of the scale, the students from on the top third of the lists (five students for fourth period and three students for sixth period) were considered the higher contributors.

Measures of Participation in Electronic Settings. During the *Aspects* sessions, students joined a live conference with other students in the classroom. Activities typically involved whole-class brainstorming, or, more commonly, small-group activities such as the discussion of textual passages or the graphical webbing of characters. The computer transcripts for each online conference were analyzed and coded in numerous ways for the first two research questions. With respect to the first question regarding who was contributing to the online discussions, a count of written contributions was taken for each student. Each time the student entered a message or comment within the Chat Box or Free Mediation, or cited a characteristic within the character webs, it was considered one contribution.

Although oral contributions and written online contributions are different by their very nature, the written contributions, as defined previously, were roughly synonymous to the oral contributions, in that they were each

TABLE 11.2
Average Written Contributions Per Class Session
During Computer-Supported Conferences

	Total Mean	*SD*	*Free Med. Mean*	*SD*	*Webs Mean*	*SD*	*Chats Mean*	*SD*
Fourth Period	*n* = *12*		*n* = *3*		*n* = *4*		*n* = *5*	
Elliott	18.4	12.6	14.7	13.4	6.3	1.5	27.8	8.5
Paul	17.1	9.2	12.0	7.2	11.2	5.0	24.8	7.9
Chris	13.4	11.0	10.7	5.5	2.5	2.5	21.0	11.4
Simon	12.0	6.1	9.3	3.0	5.7	1.5	17.4	4.0
Kurt	11.1	8.5	7.0	5.6	4.7	3.9	17.8	7.4
Michael	11.0	12.2	5.0	0	3.0	1.0	21.0	13.5
Elizabeth	10.9	4.8	9.3	5.7	9.2	.9	13.2	5.9
Tim	10.8	6.0	11.3	9.0	5.7	.6	13.6	4.4
Will	10.7	7.0	18.0	12.7	4.7	1.7	12.6	3.8
Hillary	10.2	6.2	8.3	5.5	5.7	1.5	14.0	6.6
Nate	10.1	4.2	12.7	6.8	6.7	1.5	11.5	1.7
Neal	8.8	4.9	10.3	4.2	6.0	2.0	9.7	6.9
Holly	7.6	4.1	10.5	6.4	5.5	2.9	8.2	4.1
Janne	6.9	5.0	6.5	3.5	4.7	3.1	8.8	6.5
Stephen	6.9	3.6	5.0	4.0	6.7	2.5	8.2	4.0
Average	11.1	3.3	10.4	3.4	5.9	2.1	15.3	6.1
			6th Period					
Sam	19.2	21.2	6.0	5.2	3.5	1.7	40.4	16.9
Lawrence	17.4	9.9	13.0	2.8	7.7	4.5	27.0	3.5
Brendan	14.8	11.3	10.3	3.8	5.2	2.1	27.7	6.8
Ben	14.7	11.3	5.7	6.0	8.7	3.2	25.0	9.7
Frank	13.2	7.4	11.0	4.0	8.0	3.2	18.8	8.2
Tina	12.3	7.3	6.7	2.9	8.7	3.2	18.6	7.0
Floyd	10.8	7.3	5.7	3.0	6.0	2.6	16.8	6.6
Heather	10.2	8.7	9.3	9.4	3.5	1.7	16.2	8.4
Anne	9.4	4.3	5.5	3.5	6.7	.5	13.2	3.2
Average	13.5	3.3	8.1	2.8	6.4	2.0	22.6	8.4

Note. *n* = class sessions.

well-defined contributions, with clear a beginning and end. A contribution, be it oral or written, is a "spurt of consciousness" (Gere & Abott, 1985, p. 367) in which the student is offering an idea to the group. A summary of the averages of online written contributions for each student is presented in Table 11.2.

Although these data do not give us information about the *quality* of the students' input, they do indicate which students offered *most* of the online contributions and it is possible to determine who were the more dominant contributors, as well as the lesser contributors in these conferences. Table 11.2 reveals the average number of written contributions each individual member contributed per class to the online conferences over the course of the study. Column 1 indicates, in hierarchical order, the average of total written contributions, whereas columns 2, 3, and 4 denote the average number of written contributions as broken down into Free Mediation, Painting application, and Chat Box discussions. In surveying both higher and lower contributors we can begin to draw some comparisons to the ordered lists from traditional settings presented earlier (see Table 11.1).

Before doing so, it is imperative to discuss the intent of drawing such a comparison and to point out the limitations of doing so. First, the intent is one of generality rather than specificity. Basically, I sought to discover if the patterns of participation within a class changed or remained intact. The measures of both the participation ratings and the observation tallies of oral contributions provided some indication of the low and high contributors in traditional class discussions, whereas the measure of written online contributions indicated who entered the most messages in online conferences. By comparing these measures we can begin to examine the participation patterns both in traditional discussions and in online conferences. Limitations of making this comparison, however, include differences between oral and written contribution procedures, length of class sessions (i.e., sometimes technology set-up reduced class time), and student participation expectations favoring the networked class sessions.

A summary of the students' average daily oral and written contributions (in traditional discussions and computer-supported conferences, respectively) is presented in Table 11.3.

In comparing the two classes, it is apparent that in the fourth period, the overall mean contributions per class session increased from 4.9 contributions in the traditional setting to 11.1 contributions in the computer-supported environment. Likewise, in the sixth-period class, the overall mean contributions increased from 7.5 in the traditional setting to 13.5 in the computer-supported setting. Recognizing that the two settings *are* different constructs, one being the whole class (either 9 or 15 students *with* the teacher) and the other being primarily small groups (most typically three to five students, but up to seven or eight on some occasions) *without* the teacher, it is still interesting to point out that, overall, student contributions increased dramatically. Important to most collaborative learning and social constructivist

TABLE 11.3
Summary of Mean Oral and Written Contributions

	Oral (X) Contributions per Class Period	*Written (Y) Contributions per Class Period*	
	Traditional Discussions	*Computer-Supported Environment*	
	Mean	*Mean*	*Diff Y-X*
		Fourth Period	
Neal	10.0	8.8	−1.2
Michael	8.7	11.0	2.3
Stephen	8.5	6.9	−1.6
Paul	7.4	17.1	9.7
Elliott	7.2	18.4	11.2
Hillary	6.9	10.2	3.3
Will	5.1	10.7	7.5
Tim	4.5	10.8	6.3
Chris	4.0	13.4	9.4
Elizabeth	3.7	10.9	7.2
Nate	3.1	10.1	7.0
Kurt	2.3	11.1	8.8
Simon	1.3	12.0	10.7
Holly	.9	7.6	6.7
Janne	.7	6.9	6.2
	Mean 4.9	Mean 11.1	Mean 6.9
	SD 2.9	*SD* 3.3	*SD* 3.9
		Sixth Period	
Frank	12.7	19.2	6.5
Sam	11.4	17.4	6.0
Anne	11.4	14.8	3.4
Brendan	10.0	14.7	4.7
Floyd	9.4	13.2	3.8
Lawrence	6.6	12.3	5.7
Ben	3.4	10.8	7.4
Tina	1.7	10.2	8.5
Heather	1.1	9.4	8.3
	Mean 7.5	Mean 13.5	Mean 6.0
	SD 4.5	*SD* 3.3	*SD* 1.8

viewpoints, student contributions made within the computer-supported environment were *exclusively* peer to peer, whereas, nearly all student contributions within the traditional discussions were made directly to the teacher. Additionally, all but two students increased their contributions in the computer environment, some quite significantly.

From the previous measures of (a) teacher and self-ratings, as well as (b) observation tallies of traditional class discussions, four students from the fourth period and two students from the sixth period were found on the bottom third of both ordered lists. Subsequently, these students were considered the lower contributors. Of these six students, four remained in the bottom third in the measure of total written contributions within the computer setting: Nate, Holly, Janne, and Heather. One of the five students, Tina, moved to the middle range, and one of the five, Simon, moved to the top third range. Thus, it is interesting to note that whereas some of the traditional low contributors remained low contributors in the online environment, others moved to higher levels of contribution.

At the other end, previous measures showed six students as high contributors within traditional class discussions. Stephen, Michael, Neal, and Elliott, in the fourth-period class, were high contributors, whereas Sam and Frank were high contributors in the sixth-period class. In reviewing Table 11.3 once again, we see that only two of these five students, Elliott and Sam, remain as high contributors in the computer-conferencing environment. Two of the four, Michael and Frank, moved to the middle third, and two, Stephen and Neal, rotated down to the bottom third of the list.

Resulting Teaching and Learning Environment. In reviewing the data just presented, it becomes clear that students participated in the computer-supported collaborative learning environment in different ways than they did in the traditional classroom discussions. Some of the students who contributed minimally in traditional class discussions became higher contributors within the computer-supported environment. The inverse was also true, in that some of the dominant contributors in the traditional discussions became relatively low contributors in the computer-supported environment. Interestingly, some students maintained their position as the "quiet" ones or the dominant ones regardless of the environment. Furthermore, the *type of activity* within the computer-supported environment influenced the participation patterns as well. For instance, some of the traditionally quiet students were high contributors in the Painting application when creating character webs, but were low contributors in the Chat Box discussions.

In examining the classroom as a whole, we find a striking difference in the traditional and computer-supported environments. In the computer-supported collaborative learning environment, the students, rather than the teacher, did the "talking." Barbara skillfully created a scaffold on which the students sustained many weeks of peer communication and collaboration *with minimal direct teacher intervention.* Although Barbara helped shape the overall direction of the activities in the environment, the students decided what they would discuss, how long, and to what depth they would interact about certain issues. They analyzed, without substantial help from the teacher, all of the main characters of the play, following them through each act of the play.

Additionally, they chose speeches from within the play that were difficult for them to understand, wrote explanations of these speeches, and reacted to (and received reactions from) other students to better help them understand their "difficult speech." In the times in which Barbara did "talk" in the classroom, it was rarely about the content or analysis of the play; rather, it was to adjust or remove part of the scaffolding in the structure of the class. In accordance with sociocultural views on learning, she would continually mold and remold the environment by guiding the students in examining their own discourse and leading them in understanding how to communicate and collaborate with each other more effectively. Examples of this were when students generated criteria for good Chat Box discussions and good character webs. It is not surprising that toward the end of this study Barbara exclaimed, "They don't need me! They taught themselves the play!"

Throughout the 18 traditional discussion class periods observed in this study, only four instances of more than two consecutive student contributions without the teacher intervening were recorded (well under 1% of the time.) Within the computer-supported collaborative learning environment, this figure could be easily inversed. In fact, the computer-supported conferences were completely student driven and the teacher did not participate within the online conferences at all.

Although there were some vestiges of the traditional participation patterns evident in the computer-supported settings, the more important point is that within the new environment and without the teacher in front of the class, *everyone* participated. The teacher did not have to draw it out of the quiet ones; rather they were responding *within each and every activity*. Any teacher who has experienced the difficulty of engaging every member of the class in a discussion will recognize the power of this result.

Besides examining who was involved in the discourse we need to consider *what* the students talked about in the conferencing environment. Thus, the second research question focused on the content of the peer discourse within the electronic setting.

Research Question 2: What Types of Contributions (i.e., Talk About the Content, the Task, and Off-Task Talk) Shape the Discourse?

The intent of this question was to find out what students talk about when they are placed together in online conferences in an English class. Can they stay on task discussing literature? How long can they sustain a discussion without the input of the teacher? Is there collaboration within the group? Who decided what the topics of discussion will be and when to change topics?

To begin shedding light on these questions, a coding scheme was developed to analyze the make-up of the online discussions. Numerous coding schemes have been developed that have recognized the complexity of classroom discourse. Through an iterative process of reading, analyzing, and trial coding, a coding scheme emerged that was eventually used to code all online student interaction throughout the data collection period.

Coding of Electronic Discourse. The first consideration of a coding scheme was the basic unit of analysis to be used within the transcripts. Gere and Abbott (1985) considered these idea units a brief spurt of speech that reflect "the speaker's object of consciousness" (p. 84), roughly synonymous to the linguistic meaning of a phrase. The criteria used to decide if something could be considered an idea unit was whether or not it could stand alone as an idea. Each idea unit was individually coded according to a scheme that consisted of three broad categories: (a) discourse about the content, or substantive talk about *The Crucible*, (b) discourse about the task, or procedural talk about what they were supposed to do, and (c) off-task talk, or talk that was not substantive or procedural.

The "discourse about the content" category included anything that related to the readings (e.g., "He valued dignity and he eventually turned into a loyal man by Act IV."). The "discourse about the task" category included any statement about the procedural direction the group should take (e.g., "OK, let's get started" or "I think we should talk about the Proctor."). This category also included statements about their talk itself (e.g., "We have run out of things to say.") The "off-task talk" category included comments that did not have to do with the readings or the processes of the group (e.g., "Did you go to Leslie's party Friday night?").

Within these general categories, the idea units were analyzed for a more specific "focus of consciousness." For instance, within "discourse about content," the specific subcategories are statements (both supported and not supported), questions (for information, soliciting, challenging, clarifying), conjectures, agreements and disagreements, and answers to questions. "Discourse about the task" includes the subcategories of statements, questions, evaluations, and talk about talk. "Off-task talk" includes the subcategories of statements, questions, mechanics of the program, apologies and acceptance of apologies, and nonserious comments.

Once the coding scheme was set, some measure of stability for coding the idea units was obtained by coding the first set of Chat Box transcripts twice, 6 weeks apart. The congruence between the two coded Chat Box discussions was 97.6%. For every transcript, each idea unit was coded according to the coding scheme. Overall, within the online conferences, the students talked about the content of *The Crucible* about 75% of the time. They talked about the task or about their own talk, about 15% of the time. Finally, about 9% of the time the students were engaged in off-task talk or talk that had nothing to do with *The Crucible* or with the task.

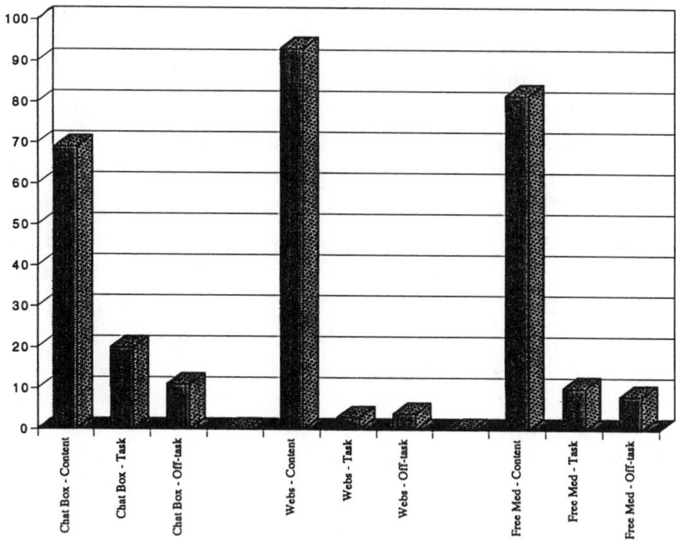

FIG. 11.2. Percentage of contributed idea units per types of discourse.

In examining this same breakdown within the three major types of *Aspects* conferences (i.e., Chat Box discussions, Free Mediation, and character webbing) it was found that different results were portrayed. Figure 11.2 illustrates these differences. The communication within each of these three activities was decidedly different in its scope and make-up. Likewise, the manner in which the students interacted within each of these "aspects" of the computer conferences was markedly different. The most extensive peer interaction took place within the discussion in the Chat Boxes. The Chat Box, because of its forced sequentiality, emulated face-to-face conversations more than the communication within Free Mediation or the Painting application.

CASE SUMMARY

The findings of this case study show us that the environment of the case is complex in nature, with many different factors influencing it. Not surprising, it was found that the communication patterns that emerged within the computer-supported environment were different from the patterns within the traditional teacher-led discussions. The manner in which these patterns changed was unpredictable. Whereas some of the students who contributed minimally in traditional discussions continued to be low contributors in online discussions, others became high contributors in the computer-supported environment. Conversely, whereas some of the students who contributed frequently in traditional discussions continued to be high contributors online, others contributed relatively infrequently in online discussions.

The findings also indicate that the types of activities, as well as features within the software applications, influence how the students interact with one another. Holly, for instance, was a low contributor in the traditional classroom and in the Chat Box of *Aspects*, but was a relatively high contributor in the Painting application. Interaction within the Chat Box, for instance, more closely emulated a face-to-face discussion than interaction within Free Mediation. Similarly, the Painting application seemed to elicit straightforward, almost factual information. As one student explained the difference between the Chat Box and the Painting application, "in the Chat box we talked and in Web we just put up facts."

Within the computer-supported collaborative learning environment, peer interaction in the Chat Box covered the full range of idea unit types such as statements, questions, agreements, and conjectures, whereas the variety of types used within the Painting application and Free Mediation was more limited in scope. Furthermore, the components that influenced the interaction also were interrelated. Problems with the technology influenced, or on some occasions, halted the peer discussions. The types of peer interaction (e.g., discussions, character webbing) and the members of the conferences influenced the outcome. Finally, previous types of discourse in which the students had engaged may have influenced subsequent interaction with similar conferences.

The first activity with the Free Mediation (i.e., cooperative word processing) mode was a brainstorming activity in which the students were asked to generate ideas about the Salem witch trials as well as other persecutions in history. Students used the entries of their peers to help them jog their own memories and thoughts on the topic. In observing the students as they communicated online and in reading the transcripts and journals entries, it appeared as though they did not interact in direct response to each other; rather, they read what their peers had written, or brainstormed, to give themselves additional insights and to add to their own brainstormed list. Subsequent activities within the Free Mediation mode in which Barbara wanted the students to react to one another, however, encountered more resistance than was expected. Students seemed to want to write their own explanations, and appeared reluctant to respond to others, in spite of their obvious ability to do so with the Chat Box discussions. A possible explanation for this was that the brainstorming activity "set" the students' perceptions about how they were to use Free Mediation, thereby subsequently limiting peer interaction within this mode of the program.

The availability of the printed transcripts gave the students a unique metacognitive opportunity to examine their own interactions with their peers. They used these transcripts with varying degrees of intensity. Whereas Barbara used the transcripts in class with the students to help them better understand their own collaborations in brainstorming, discussions, and graphic webbings, the students used them as reference materials in preparation for various assignments and for the final written essay. In spite of the positive uses the students found for the printed transcripts, the majority of the students found accessibility to peer and personal work more helpful *online*, during the interaction, rather than *later*, in the printed copies. The online accessibility to their peers' ideas gave them an opportunity to grow in and expand upon their own understanding of the play with peer challenges that encouraged students to stretch to higher level of analyses.

What became evident in the study is that the students jointly constructed their own understanding of the play, *The Crucible*. Given the relative freedom to do so, the students were able to discuss the content of the play at length. In their group discussions within the Chat Box, they spent considerable time delving into the plot, the development of the characters, and the social implications of this work. Figure 11.3 illustrates a typical conversation within the Chat Box. Overall, more than 75% of all interactions related to the content of the play.

What is encouraging about this is that, although only a few of the students had had any experience in a collaborative environment, and none of them had ever participated in online discussions prior to their experience in this study, they were able to immerse themselves in this new environment with minimal difficulty. In fact, one student in the study, Lawrence, who started the semester with a distaste for English class, became an active contributor during the computer conferencing *as well as in subsequent traditional English class instruction.*

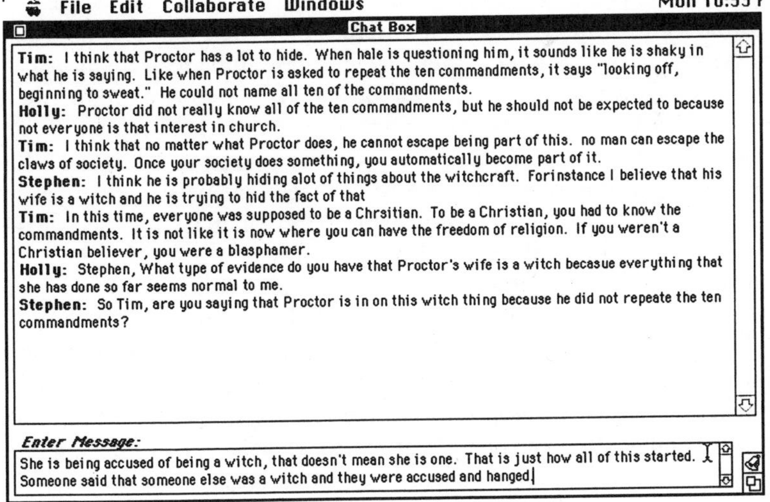

FIG. 11.3. Chat Box discussion text.

What these findings do not tell us is how well the students came to understand the play and at what level of literary comprehension the students interacted. In contrast to views of New Critical theorists (Anderson & Rubano, 1991; Garber, 1988), it was not the intent of the research to analyze the quality or "correctness" of their interpretations. In emphasizing process and student understanding over final products or analyses, Barbara sought to involve the students in a more transactional (Rosenblatt, 1978) analysis of the play, constructing their own meaning, through collaborative efforts with their peers. Although high level of Discussions were evident in many conferences, there is a need for a more in-depth study of the literary levels in which students are able to discuss and interact in online environments.

TEACHER REFLECTIONS

A few months after the students completed their study of *The Crucible*, I spoke with Barbara about what she felt were some of the benefits and drawbacks of using the computer-supported environment. She stated that the students knew the play more thoroughly than any of her previous classes, both on a specific and global level. She pointed out that, *in general*, the students' thesis statements in their final essays were "less superficial" than in her previous noncomputer English classes. She also claimed that perhaps the biggest benefit of using computer-supported collaboration was the students' ability to read the text for both the specifics and for the global intent and then draw appropriate inferences.

When asked for an example of evidence of this, she explained that students who had participated in the computer-networking case study were much more able to draw inferences on a different play (i.e., *Death of a Salesman*). Likewise, at the end of the semester, she felt these students were more capable of connecting evidence in text to support their statements about the play. She no longer had to ask for the source of their thinking because, as she put it, "The Chat Box discussions forced constant reference to books and notes, and in class students often are able to tell me what page number examples or points occur because they are in the habit of marking their texts and referring to them even during oral discussion."

On the affective side, Barbara witnessed a tremendous difference in self-confidence for many of her students as exhibited in "their willingness to contribute to class discussions." She noticed that students were much more willing to collaborate with others even off the computer, in contrast to classes in previous semesters. She found that the students appeared more "tolerant of others' viewpoints" and they "learned to be reflective about others' opinions by having to understand them in order to respond to them."

When reflecting on the downside of using the computer to collaborate, Barbara replied that in some ways the students had too much information about the play. They had worked with all of the transcripts from the Chat Box discussions and Free Mediation, as well as all of the Painting application webs. In essence, they were saturated with all aspects of the plot and character development. She felt that some students still had difficulty learning how to prioritize what was the most important. This phenomenon of "having too much information" ironically was echoed in statements made in Thornburg's (1995) address mentioned earlier. He too suggested that with the inundation of information available through the Internet, educators will soon have to teach students how to organize and select the best information for themselves. No longer will assignments for research papers carry with them the specification of *minimum* page length, but teachers may very well give students *maximum* page requirements. With the ease with which text and graphics can be generated and produced, evident even in this one case study, *managing* the amount of information may well become a serious educational, social, and political problem in the coming years.

Although at the end of the study Barbara wryly suggested that the "students taught themselves," a more accurate depiction is a statement she made much earlier in the study, when she stated, "They didn't know they had the information in their heads—enough to sustain forty minutes of conversation. It took a lot of preparation to get to the point where they could interact for that length of time." The preparation she spoke of was the scaffolding she had carefully constructed since the first day of the semester. Among other things, this scaffolding included (a) homework assignments that directly prepared the students for peer interaction, (b) eliciting information from the students and cycling it back to them in a form that facilitated their online interactions, and (c) using student-generated materials (e.g., transcripts of webs and chats) to guide the students in further understanding both their own discourse and the content and structure of the play.

IMPLICATIONS FOR COLLABORATIVE ENVIRONMENTS AND SOFTWARE DESIGN

The majority of the English literature classrooms in our country are still heavily influenced by the vestiges of the New Critical approach. Langer (1992) went so far as to state that our high school literature curriculum is "rudderless." Some teachers, influenced by reader-response theorists, however, have found ways to move beyond the teacher and text-centered philosophical stances of the New Critics. Reader response, built on a constructivist epistemology, implies that the understanding and the meaning will come from within the reader. Taking into consideration the difficult nature of the style of writing within *The Crucible*, it is not easy to imagine a single student constructing a well-rounded meaning of the play by herself. It would have been a daunting task for any individual in this study to do so. Collaborative learning theory, therefore, offers a practical foundation upon which literature classrooms can be built.

This study also has shown how a computer-conferencing tool can facilitate collaborative learning and student perspective taking (see also Sugar & Bonk, chap. 6 of this volume). The shared space of the computer screen made it possible for students to see what their peers were thinking and how they were interacting with each other. Perhaps more important, they were able to respond to multiple users without having to wait for their turn to speak. Clearly, this was an environment wherein students were more aware of each other and in which they could come up with new ideas and gain alternative insights with relative ease. This study indicates, moreover, that the students felt intellectually challenged by this close proximity to their peers' work. Without much difficulty, the students were able to use these tools to collaborate among themselves, to construct a meaning and understanding of *The Crucible*, and in doing so, also to learn about communicating with each other. It was not as individuals, therefore, that the students in this study "figured out" the play; rather, it was through the opportunity to amplify their intellectual activity as they collaborated in synchronous communication.

Along these same lines, there has been much attention paid to Vygotsky's zone of proximal development. Although his ideas were that of the social interaction between the teacher and the student, or in dyads with a more capable peer, Moll and Whitmore (1993) suggested that we extend this construct to include "collective, interrelated zones of proximal development as part of a transactive teaching system" (p. 21). In this study, the teacher created the scaffolding upon which the students worked within their own zone of proximal development. Although the students were not consciously coupled with "more capable peers," it became apparent that students were creating shared meanings of the play from the group interactions. As was the case in the analysis of *The Crucible*, literary works do not have *one* correct interpretation. Therefore, students, even when working with peers who were not necessarily known to the teacher as being *more* capable, were constructing viable meanings of the play. In light of this, the idea of the collective and interrelated zones of proximal development makes sense for a computer-conferencing environment.

In this study, the composition of the conference membership changed daily in that the same people were not always grouped together in various conferences. Thus, the entire class was involved with each other's work. As we look to the future in English literature classrooms, this idea of a more transactional view of collective zones may become a helpful concept in shaping the practical implementation of effective learning environments. Within this study of two English classrooms, the technological tool *Aspects* appeared to support the interrelated zones of proximal development both within and between conferences. This is not to suggest that all literature classrooms should use these tools exclusively. There is still an important and appropriate place for whole-class discussion, as well as for small-group face-to-face collaboration. Technology should not be integrated into every learning environment; rather, an appropriate balance must be found by the teacher and the school.

What we can learn from this study is that although interactive technologies can help us to create unique learning environments, and they can facilitate different means of communication within the classroom (as well as globally beyond the classroom walls), it is not the technologies themselves that create these unique learning environments, but how we choose to implement these technologies. As in the case with this study, the teacher used the hardware and the software to fit how she wanted the students to learn. She approached the technology with a plan, and she molded the technological environment to fit her plan. Her vision of learning, that of interactive collaborative constructivism, shaped how the technology was used. This is in contrast to the technology-driven classrooms found in most K–12 schools. Many educators, unfortunately, have allowed the technology to shape the manner in which they teach, rather than approaching technology with firm epistemological commitments.

BEYOND 2000

As we approach the end of the 20th century, we are witnessing a revolution in global communications. The impact of this revolution cannot be overemphasized. Computer-mediated communication is growing at an exponential rate, and communicating over the Internet (or whatever it might evolve into) could soon become the norm. As educators, we need to understand how these technological advancements will affect our schools, how learning environments might benefit from them, and how classrooms might be more integrally connected with the outside community. As educators are calling for complete restructuring of education at a systemic level (Banathy, 1973; Reigeluth, 1994), technological advancements of our time can help make this a possibility. If we allow technology to define our learning environments, however, then we may fail to utilize the potential it could offer. However, if we approach technology with a firm commitment to an epistemological ideal, we will then be able to create new educational environments based soundly on theoretical perspectives.

This research is just one piece of a much larger and ever expanding picture, that of technology and education. It is within this larger context that we must continually refine, reshape, and restructure for the future. As we leave the information age and become immersed in the communication age, technology will continue to become an increasingly integral part of our daily lives. As educators, we must use this timely opportunity to create, or re-create, an educational system that is ready for the 21st century.

ACKNOWLEDGMENTS

I wish to express gratitude to Diane Hamstra for putting into practice her vision of computer-supported collaborative learning environments. I wish also to thank Theodore Frick, Professor of Education, Instructional Systems Technology, Indiana University, for his guidance throughout this study.

REFERENCES

Anderson, P. M., & Rubano, G. (1991). *Enhancing aesthetic reading and response.* Urbana, IL: National Council of Teachers of English.

Banathy, B. H. (1973). *Developing a systems view of education: The systems-model approach.* Belmont, CA: Siegler/Fearon.

Bonk, C. J., Medury, P. V., & Reynolds, T. H. (1994). Cooperative hypermedia: The marriage of collaborative writing and mediated environments. In W. M. Reed, J. K. Burton, & M. Lui (Eds.), *Multimedia and megachange* (pp. 79–124). New York: Haworth.

Bump, J. (1990). Radical changes in class discussion using networked computers. *Computers and the Humanities, 24*, 49–65.

Cazden, C. B. (1988). *Classroom discourse: The language of teaching and learning.* Portsmouth, NH: Heinemann.

Daiute, C., & Dalton, B. (1988). "Let's brighten it up a bit": Collaboration and cognition in writing. In B. Rafoth & D. Rubin (Eds.), *Social construction of written communication* (pp. 249–272). Norwood, NJ: Ablex.

Dewey, J. (1963). *Experience and education.* New York: Macmillan.

Garber, E. K. (1988). "My kinsman, Major Molineux": Some interpretive and critical probes. In B. F. Nelms (Ed.), *Literature in the classroom* (pp. 83–104). Urbana, IL: National Council of Teachers of English.

Gere, A. R. (1987). *Writing groups: History, theory, and implications.* Carbondale: Southern Illinois University Press.

Gere, A. R., & Abbott, R. D. (1985). Talking about writing: The language of writing groups. *Research in the Teaching of English, 19*(4), 362–381.

Golden, J. M. (1986). Reader-text interaction. *Theory Into Practice, 25*, 92–96.

Hartman, K., Neuwirth, C. M., Kiesler, S., Sproull, L., Cochran, C., Palmquist, M., & Zubrow, D. (1991). Patterns of social interaction and learning to write. *Written Communication, 8*(1), 79–113.

Hoogstrate-Cooney, D. (1995). *Computer-supported collaborative learning: A case study of interactive written communication.* Doctoral dissertation, Indiana University, Bloomington.

Johnson, D. W., & Johnson, R. T. (1985). Student-student interaction: Ignored but powerful. *Journal of Teacher Education, 36*(4), 22–26.

Kremers, M. (1990). Sharing authority on a synchronous network: The case for riding the beast. *Computers and Composition, 7*, 33–44.

Langer, J. A. (1992). Rethinking literature instruction. In J. S. Langer (Ed.), *Literature instruction* (pp. 35–53). Urbana, IL: National Council of Teachers of English.

Lincoln, Y. S., & Guba, E. G. (1985). *Naturalistic inquiry*. Beverly Hills, CA: Sage.

Mabrito, M. (1992). Computer-mediated communication and high-apprehensive writers: Rethinking the collaborative process. *The Bulletin, 19*, 26–30.

Merriam, S. B. (1988). *Case study research in education*. San Francisco: Jossey-Bass.

Moll, L. C., & Whitmore, K. R. (1993). Vygotsky in classroom practice: Moving from individual transmission to social transaction. In E. A. Forman, N. Minick, & C. A. Stone (Eds.), *Contexts for learning: Sociocultural dynamics in children's development* (pp. 120–152). New York: Oxford University Press.

Newmann, F. M. (1991). Linking restructuring to authentic student achievement. *Phi Delta Kappan, 72*, 458–473.

Nystrand, M., & Gamoran, A. (1990). *Student engagement: When recitation becomes conversation*. Madison, WI: University of Wisconsin. (ERIC Document Reproduction Service No. ED 323 581)

Nystrand, M., Gamoran, A., & Heck, M. J. (1991). *Small groups in English: When do they help students and how are they best used?* Madison: University of Wisconsin–Madison, Center on the Organization and Restructuring of Schools.

Reigeluth, C. (1994). *Systemic change in education*. Englewood Cliffs, NJ: Educational Technology Publications.

Rosenblatt, L. M. (1978). *The reader, the text, the poem: The transactional theory of the literary work*. Carbondale: Southern Illinois University Press.

Schrage, M. (1990). *Shared minds: The new technology of collaboration*. New York: Random House.

Stake, R. E. (1994). Case studies. In N. K. Denzin & Y. S. Lincoln (Eds.), *Handbook of qualitative research* (pp. 236–247). Thousand Oaks, CA: Sage.

Thornburg, D. D. (1995, January). *Hitchhikers guide to cyberspace*. Keynote address given to the Indiana Computer Educators Association annual conference, Indianapolis.

Vygotsky, L. S. (1978). *Mind in society: The development of higher psychological processes* (M. Cole, V. John-Steiner, S. Scribner, & E. Souberman, Eds.). Cambridge, MA: Harvard University Press.

Whipple, W. R. (1987). Collaborative learning: Recognizing it when we see it. *Bulletin of the American Association for Higher Education, 40*(2), 3–7.

Yin, R. K. (1994). *Case study research: Design and methods*. Thousand Oaks, CA: Sage.

12

Time to "Connect": Synchronous and Asynchronous Case-Based Dialogue Among Preservice Teachers

Curtis Jay Bonk
Indiana University

Edmund J. Hansen
Emporia State University

Melissa Marie Grabner-Hagen
Indiana University

Shannon Ann Lazar
Indiana University

Christina Mirabelli
Harlan Elementary School

As higher education technologies have become more interactive and collaborative (Harasim, 1993; Koschmann, 1994), new opportunities for apprenticing preservice teachers in mentoring techniques, project-based learning, and global collaboration have emerged. In the midst of this technology proliferation, there is increasing attention on evaluating the impact of these tools on the learning process (Riel, 1993). Initial attempts to monitor social interaction and learning in traditional and electronic forms of communication have found that teachers in electronically networked classes assist and interact more with students, especially those less able, than do teachers in traditional learning situations (Hartman et al., 1991). However, comparisons among nontraditional electronic learning environments such as electronic mail (E-mail), bulletin boards, and groupware systems remain scant (Klemm & Snell, 1994). Because minimal direction exists for understanding how electronic communication and collaboration tools impact the learning process, there are calls to create new instruments for in-depth analyses of message content that can clarify the varied patterns of participation, interaction, and reflective processing fostered by these tools (Henri, 1992).

Electronic collaborative learning support currently includes E-mail discussion, delayed text collaboration and file sharing, real-time idea brainstorming, and real-time text and graphics collaboration (Bonk, Medury, & Reynolds, 1994). Research suggests that both the delayed and real-time conferencing support options tend to promote more frank discussion and equal opportunity among participants than traditional classroom instruction (Sproull & Kiesler, 1993). Harasim (1990), however, noted that delayed and real-time collaboration tools vary in terms of the timing of student feedback, tendency to foster competitiveness and communication anxiety, reflection opportunities, pace and place of learning, interaction control, consensus-building procedures, and overall learning results. With this multitude of issues surrounding the design and use of these new technologies, extensive field testing of collaboration tools is imperative.

Sociocultural Theory

During this evolution of new instructional technologies, educators and theorists have increasingly embraced Vygotskian sociocultural ideas of cognitive development to analyze the social context of learning (Gallimore & Tharp, 1990; Wells, 1996). Vygotsky's sociocultural views complement already popular constructivist ideas by informing researchers about the conditions of learning, activities leading to effective knowledge building, and mechanisms for skill internalization among participants (Bereiter, 1994; Cobb, 1994). According to neo-Vygotskian theorists (e.g., Cole, 1995; Wertsch, 1985), internalization occurs when those activities and processes first performed in conjunction with experts or more capable peers on the social plane later function as independent problem-solving skills (see Bonk & Cunningham, chap. 2 of this volume).

Learning is now best viewed as a generative, knowledge construction process rich in social interaction and dialogue (Chang-Wells & Wells, 1993). Fortunately, a myriad of collaborative technologies have emerged recently to support such generative learning with opportunities for student inquiry, social dialogue, problem finding, reflection, goal setting, and other mental efforts deemed essential for student learning (Koschmann, Myers, Feltovich, & Barrows, 1994). As groupware, hypermedia, and other innovative cultural tools support and guide students' sense-making activities (Cole, 1995), the educational focus shifts from individual knowledge growth to evaluating the impact of group collaboration and apprenticeship inherent in such interaction (Granott & Gardner, 1994). According to Pea (1994), properly designed computer-supported collaborative learning (CSCL) technologies foster a multitude of "collective learning" experiences (e.g., collaboratively presenting results from real-world experiments or conferring with distant scientists about text and interactive graphs), thereby making assessment an even more serious and difficult issue. Fortunately, electronic case collaboration provides a new assessment window for such collective experiences.

The Case Study Method

In realizing the importance of case-based knowledge, professional disciplines such as business, law, and medicine already ground their instructional techniques and ensuing apprenticeship programs within situationally based philosophical frameworks (Riesbeck, 1996). Williams (1992) pointed out that the case method approach typically supplies authentic problems that anchor classroom activities in complex situations that can be read, reflected on, and referred to. However, she also cautioned that cases vary in their complexity as well as their format, realism, engagement, and underlying assessment. Case formats include simple narratives, cases with alternatives scenarios, cases with expert reflection commentaries, and cases with embedded flaws (Kowalski, Weaver, & Henson, 1994; J. H. Shulman, 1991; Silverman, Welty, & Lyon, 1992). Of course, the variety of problem types and assessment practices makes their creation and use no simple matter (Merseth, 1991; Richert, 1992), while, in addition, such cases can be time consuming to produce, inefficient, and susceptible to student overgeneralization (L. S. Shulman, 1992).

Despite these potential problems, both written and videotaped case collections have been employed to provide novice teachers with flexible and pedagogically responsive skills unique to the teaching profession (Barnett, 1991; Livingston & Borko, 1989). Westerman's (1991) study of expert and novice teacher decision making, for instance, compared their lesson-planning interviews, videotaped lessons, stimulated recall of teaching, print materials used, and self-reports. She found that whereas expert teachers adapted their instruction to individual student needs, preservice teachers were more focused on their specific lesson objectives and structuring their lesson plans. Similarly, when students wrote sample cases, experienced teachers focused more on overall instructional situations, whereas preservice teachers wrote more often about specific disciplinary and motivational incidents (Kagan & Tippins, 1991). In general, these expert–novice studies suggest the need to restructure teacher education programs with case-related curricula.

Electronic cases offer time-independent opportunities for students to evaluate and communicate critical information about the case. During student electronic case reflections, college instructors might apprentice student learning into their chosen profession by modeling expertlike answers and providing feedback or instructional assistance on student misconceptions. More important, an instructor might draw learners into the problem-solving process by fostering idea sharing and resulting reflective commenting or debate (Grant, 1992; Wineburg, 1991).

Nearly a decade ago, Copeland (1989) argued for technology-mediated laboratory experiences to encourage preservice teacher reflection and clinical reasoning. Whereas he recommended using videodisc technologies because they were inexpensive, safe, and more controllable alternatives to actual K–12 field placements, a decade later, we find that cases located on a computer network or on the World Wide Web provide even cheaper, faster, and more extensive opportunities for preservice teacher reflection and discussion (Bonk, Malikowski, Angeli, & East, in press).

Cases From a Sociocultural Standpoint

Although electronic conferencing case collaboration is still in its infancy, Vygotsky's (1978) arguments about the social interaction mechanisms and developmental assistance students might receive from more capable peers to extend them beyond their independent reach certainly are applicable to electronic environments. In fact, electronic cases might allow students to jointly construct new knowledge under the tutelage of both the apprenticing case environment as well as the real-life stories and experiences of one's peers (Riesbeck, 1996). Such electronic collaboration might occur in chat or dialogue boxes, scratch pads, team-shared work spaces, peer commenting windows, or within jointly created text products or analyses (Bonk et al., 1994).

Research indicates that when individuals encounter new information in situations requiring meaningful processing like case dialogue, they tend to remember and apply it (Cognition and Technology Group at Vanderbilt, 1991). A sociocultural theorist, therefore, might view electronic case collaboration as an opportunity for preservice teachers to encounter and understand active learning situations and principles. Sociocultural principles might be applied through the creation of interactive computer case scenarios of actual or staged classroom situations that effectively pose questions within an individual's zone of proximal development (ZPD) (i.e., the area between the learner's actual unassisted performance on a task and his or her performance when given outside support or guidance; see Wertsch, 1985). Students brought into an electronic case dialogue might negotiate and debate points of view, thereby exposing each other to alternative strategies and contextual cues. During this time, teacher modeling, coaching, encouragement, feedback, and other support of students' cognitive abilities in those case discussions might be adjusted downward or withdrawn as student competence in the topic increases (Collins, J. S. Brown, & Newman, 1989; Palincsar & A. L. Brown, 1984).

With new electronic tools come new questions, however. For instance, does social interaction and collaborative problem solving differ in real-time and delayed interaction formats? Will electronic case-based learning make salient the importance of guided learning and meaning making to future teachers (DiPardo & Freedman, 1988; Rogoff, 1995)? Do shared experiences among participants on a computer screen stimulate interpersonal understanding (Riel, 1993), mutual knowledge (Krauss & Fussell, 1990), social cognition (Clements & Nastasi, 1988), intercultural awareness (Walls, 1993), and group cohesiveness (Sproull & Kiesler, 1993)? Exactly what types of electronic comments and suggestions do peers provide electronically to help others solve problems that are beyond their independent problem-solving level? Eventually, we hope to answer these questions as well as discover how strategic knowledge is socially displayed, reflected on, and abstracted and internalized by electronic learners. Like Henri (1992), we intend to understand how electronic collaborative learning tools can be used to foster student learning.

METHOD

Electronic Discourse and Research Questions

In this study, complete electronic discourse transcripts of preservice teachers solving problematic teaching scenarios were captured in computer log files. After acquiring this rich data set, a coding scheme, based on the small-group learning research from Meloth and Deering (1994), was designed to help analyze the impact of the social interaction on group problem solving and individual cognitive efforts. As Meloth and Deering's intensive analysis of discourse demonstrates, researchers are beginning to discover how collaborative interaction patterns and grouping structures impact student performance. Similarly, in this study, an intensive recording and analysis of preservice teacher problem-solving discourse provided insights into how social interaction and dialogue promoted new levels of understanding among participants.

The key research questions here were as follows:

1. What types of social interactions occur in real-time and delayed electronic case discussions among preservice teachers?
2. How might electronic social interaction patterns be coded to indicate the formats and types of interaction?
3. How do case size, complexity, and instructional guidance affect group processing?
4. Do real-time or delayed conferencing tools foster greater discussion depth and quality? Do students' interaction patterns vary from case to case?

5. Do shared experiences among participants on a computer screen stimulate group intersubjectivity and group cohesiveness?

Tools and Courses

This study investigated preservice teacher collaborative case diagnosis in real-time and delayed computer settings in a large midwestern university. During the fall of 1993, 32 secondary preservice teachers in one section of an educational psychology class electronically discussed four problematic teaching scenarios using a real-time or "synchronous" electronic conferencing tool called Connect. During the following spring of 1994, a delayed or "asynchronous" electronic conferencing system known as VAX Notes was used with 33 secondary majors enrolled in another section of this course. It is important to point out that the cases in the fall semester were briefer than those used during the spring, thereby limiting group comparisons and overall generalizability of the findings.

Context of Connect Task. During the fall semester, students interacted in real time on four occasions using a beta test version of the DOS-based Connect[1] software package during a designated 50-minute lab time. Connect originally was designed to foster social interaction and dialogue using (a) teacher prompts, (b) small-group tasks, (c) peer reviews and commenting, and (d) brainstorming or discussion sessions.

During this semester, students primarily used the commenting option after receiving one or more brief (i.e., 6–10 line) problematic teaching scenarios from the teacher for small-group processing. These small groups were organized by student major as follows: (a) physical education (PE), speech, and theater, (b) foreign language, (c) social studies, (d) English, and (e) math, science, and health. Case assignments were selected according to teaching issues that were recently discussed in class. As indicated, all students' written comments were chronologically saved in a computer log file.

Following group member introductions and a brief training session from the instructors, electronic case analyses were initiated. After reading the case and questions in one window, students were asked to answer these questions within their small, subject-matter specific groups. Student analyses were posted to other group members in an upper window labeled *Group Comments*, which peers could scroll through to read. An auditory cue was heard each

[1]Because this was a pilot version of Connect, currently marketed versions of the product may differ significantly from the one used here. Moreover, there were numerous Connect features not utilized in this study (e.g., one-to-one tutoring, paperless exams, electronically collecting and grading papers, student real-time group commenting on the instructor's posted assignments, and asynchronous reading and posting of comments). For more information on these options, see Tuman and Ann Arbor Software (1994).

time a new case comment from a peer had arrived. These new comments were accessible by switching to the peer commenting window.

The Context of the VAX Notes Task. As indicated, during the following spring, another section of students taking the same course interacted about similar cases using the asynchronous or time-independent electronic conferencing capabilities of VAX Notes. This simple conferencing program offered private course bulletin board capabilities on the university's central computing system. VAX Notes was designed to help the students and instructors communicate about classroom content between class meetings. Because students had access to this system from the many campus computer clusters as well as from their computers at home, they required only a brief training session to become familiar with the system.

As in the fall lab, students were clustered into five groups of six to eight group members, according to the subjects they were planning to teach (e.g., English or social studies). Each group had its own "electronic space" in the conferencing utility, although, unlike the Connect tool, VAX Notes allowed students to enter the discussions of other groups. After case descriptions were posted in the electronic conference by the instructor, students had about 10 days to finish their group discussion of the case and the four posted questions. In their electronic postings, students were instructed to aim for a total of two full text screens (about half a screen per question), while being thoughtful and specific in their remarks. In addition, they were asked to read and respond to one or two group members that they particularly agreed or disagreed with.

Using VAX Notes, students worked on four cases over the course of the semester. These cases were typically about two pages long and addressed an issue related to the key topic discussed that week in class or in the text. The four cases coincided with critical secondary teaching issues such as classroom management, cooperative learning, assessment, and individual differences. Case questions dealt with students' perceptions of the problems, how these problems related to concepts in the textbook, and how they thought these problems could be overcome.

Quantitative Results

Two raters individually coded all of the data using the coding scheme in Table 12.1. As mentioned earlier, this was a modified version of the task talk–coding scheme designed by Meloth and Deering (1994) for cooperative learning environments. This coding also was influenced by Gallimore and Tharp's (1990) ideas about the key forms of teaching assistance (e.g., questioning or modeling) available in most instructional settings. Main categories of the coding scheme were: (a) content answers, (b) questioning, (c) peer

TABLE 12.1
Electronic Dialogue Coding Scheme Categories and Examples

C = Content Answers—any unprompted statement about the task.
CAh = Help/scaffolding/guidance/assistance/information
Example: "Concepts from this class covered in this scenario are grouping, individual learning, at-risk students, and intelligence."
CAa = Appraisal/evaluation of the scenario/actors
Example: There are many elements in Karen's classroom that contribute to her problems. The first is that there were no set rules and procedures that were established and enforced from the beginning."
CAs = Suggestions/recommendations/advice/opinions/comments
Example: "The first thing I would suggest to Karen is to set some basic rules and make sure they understand them."
CAc = Linking/filtering/connecting ideas
CAr = Restatements or summaries of the original task
CApa = Pacing or concern about task completion or progress
CAsa = Self-appraisal/reflection/self-talk
Example: "I always hated it when the teacher went over the rules of the room, especially the first day of class."
CAg = General talk/tangentially related/other
Example: "I would first like to note that I had answered three of the questions but the phone rang so I was disconnected."
Q = Question—any unprompted question/request about the task.
Qt = Requests for task-related information/direct attention/other
Qr = Rhetorical/sarcastic/esoteric questions
Example: "Does he have a brain in his head?"
PR = Peer Response—any response to the Content Talk (C) or Question (Q).
PRh = Help/scaffolding/guidance/assistance/information
Example: "On the subject of unions, did you know that the NEA is now the country's largest union? 2.1 million members . . ."
PRd = Directive/request
PRc = Counter assertion/alternative argument/correction
Example: "One problem that I had with the response (to send the student to the principal) in case of disruptions . . . Many students see it as a privilege . . ."
PRf = General feedback/acknowledge/opinion/restate/recommendations/summary/suggest
Example: "By this time, I feel we've all expressed ourselves and there aren't any major disputes . . ."
PRp = Praise/positive appraisal of another or the task
Example: "I must give praise to _____ for his comments (they are a joy to read)."
PRn = Negative feedback or appraisal of another
Example: "We don't have enough information to assume any behavior, so this is useless anyway."
PRpa = Pacing/concern about task completion or progress
OT = Off Task—off-task talk or dialogue.
Example: "What you doing for break?"

feedback, and (d) off-task behaviors. Interrater reliability on these variables was approximately .71 for both the real-time (510 of 715 codes) and delayed data (1,050 of 1,472 codes). A third rater resolved differences. A summary of the types of interactions within each case for Connect and VAX Notes students is provided in Tables 12.2 and 12.3, respectively.

Whereas there are definite limitations in directly comparing the two groups here (e.g., differences in case length, response time, instruction, and software availability), the dialogue codings indicated vast differences in case processing and interaction when in these two modes. Although replication is required before any conclusive statements can be made, students in the real-time environment mainly contributed personal opinions and recommendations (i.e., content talk). In contrast, students using VAX Notes were much more responsive to their peers and elaborate in their remarks.

Tables 12.2 and 12.3 clearly show that students in the delayed collaboration group, as per their instructions, were more engaged in peer responses indicative of debate and interactive dialogue. For example, the categories for counterassertions and alternative arguments (PRc), general feedback,

TABLE 12.2
Breakdown of Real-Time Electronic Conferencing Group Dialogue by Case

	Case 1	*Case 2*	*Case 3*	*Case 4*	*Average*
C = Content Answers					
CAh	0	2	1	1	1
CAa	51	57	50	36	48
CAs	22	50	101	46	55
CAc	0	0	0	0	0
CAr	0	0	0	0	0
CApa	2	0	0	7	2
CAsa	4	5	7	42	15
CAg	1	4	7	5	4
Content Total	80	118	166	137	125
Q = Question					
Qt	4	6	7	8	6
Qr	0	1	2	0	1
Question Total	4	7	9	8	7
PR = Peer Response					
PRh	0	0	0	0	0
PRd	1	4	7	12	6
PRc	1	1	0	1	1
PRf	9	14	15	8	11
PRp	5	5	3	4	4
PRn	1	0	3	2	2
PRpa	0	1	2	1	1
Peer Response Total	17	25	30	28	25
OT = Off Task	2	25	17	42	22
Total E-mail Talk	103	175	222	215	179

TABLE 12.3
Breakdown of Delayed Electronic Conferencing Group Dialogue by Case

	Case #1	*Case #2*	*Case #3*	*Case #4*	*Average*
C = Content Answers					
CAh	0	0	1	2	1
CAa	108	91	125	70	99
CAs	95	80	109	81	91
CAc	0	0	1	1	1
CAr	0	0	4	0	1
CApa	0	0	1	0	0
CAsa	16	12	10	8	11
CAg	0	4	8	16	7
Content Total	219	187	259	177	211
Q = Question					
Qt	3	12	4	7	7
Qr	0	0	3	0	1
Question Total	3	12	7	7	8
PR = Peer Response					
PRh	0	0	0	0	0
PRd	1	3	1	4	3
PRc	0	21	15	9	11
PRf	5	121	88	76	73
PRp	0	60	18	17	24
PRn	0	7	8	4	5
PRpa	0	2	0	2	1
Peer Response Total	6	214	140	112	117
OT = Off Task	5	30	58	36	32
Total E-mail Talk	233	443	464	332	368

acknowledgments, and suggestions (PRf), and praise or positive appraisal of another or the task (PRp) were 6.7 times more frequent in the delayed collaboration groups than in real-time collaboration activities. (Specific dialogue examples for each of these categories can be found in Table 12.1.) Even though one third of student comments in VAX Notes involved peer responses, compared to 14% of the Connect interactions, this was a task requirement for the delayed group. It is interesting to note that students in both groups spent more than half their time writing content-related answers. Moreover, in both cases, there was minimal use of questioning tactics (less than 4%), and off-task behaviors occurred just 10% of the time (e.g., "My break was to[o] short, but only two more weeks and finals and I'm in Florida for Christmas.").

Whereas Tables 12.2 and 12.3 reflect totals across the five subject area groups, data also were available to examine individual or small-group changes over time. Consequently, to better understand the differences in the types of social interaction within the two electronic formats, the comments of the third participant within each of five small groups during the second case were tracked as well as the comments of the fifth participant within every group during the third case. Once these 20 particular individuals were identified (i.e., five students in both the synchronous and asynchronous groups on two different cases), their comments were tracked over that entire case.

This analysis illustrated that asynchronous communication facilitated more serious and lengthy interactions than those in real time over a local network. At the same time, students using the real-time software interacted more often during their case analyses (5.10 interactions per person) than students in the delayed mode (3.30 interactions per person). However, their comments were syntactically briefer (averaging 14.46 words per sentence) than VAX Notes' comments (17.04 words per sentence). In fact, the 10 students in the real-time mode (i.e., the Connect students) wrote and exchanged one tenth the words during each interaction the comparable delayed collaboration group using VAX Notes (i.e., 25.24 words per interaction or 1,287 total words in Connect mode compared to 266.00 words per interaction or 8,777 total words while in VAX Notes). Despite these enormous content differences, questions remained. For instance, although students in the delayed collaboration mode posted more comprehensive notes, did this result in more interactive discussions and common knowledge than students in real-time conferencing? Preliminary answers are presented in the following sections.

Microanalysis of Connect Transcripts

The strong content focus during real-time dialogue, as pointed out earlier, is apparent in the dialogue transcripts of Group 1: PE/speech/theater students when analyzing their third case about a PE teacher using videotapes of students' serves as an instructional tool. The reflections from Group 1 are rather extended considering the brevity of the case. However, as is evident in the following segments, few of the real-time collaboration comments directly address peer learning:

> By showing the students a video where they can see what a proper [tennis] serve looks like, the teacher is using a method of observational learning. . . . Instead of videotaping her students, she could have rented an instructional video about tennis and followed it by going through a serve in slow motion with the class . . . Just by watching a video and observing that you should follow through with your swing will not be as beneficial as watching the video and then practicing the technique. (October 26, 1993, Time: 11:11:24, Steffe Green, Group 1)

Like many of her peers, Steffe was most concerned about her voice and input to the situation, not about providing peer feedback or suggestions.

Whereas Steffe's first contribution (see preceding quotation) was coded as an appraisal of the situation (i.e., CAa), her next response was coded as a suggestion (i.e., CAs). In both cases, she was simply providing content-related answers and analyses.

A similar comment arrived just a few seconds later from a peer (i.e., Heather Stallings at 11:11:27) who discussed working backward, expert demonstrations, and peer tutoring. Other student suggestions here related to fostering positive early experiences, shaping behavior, comparing serves, and heterogeneously grouping students for instruction. Though these answers displayed a wealth of text-based learning, only 2 of this group's 37 coded responses included a question or a comment to a peer during this 50-minute electronic discussion. In addition, two students were totally off-task. The date and time indexing of student responses embedded in this group's messages, moreover, provided clear evidence that direct peer feedback and guidance was not provided in this particular discussion until just before the class ended. Students were so focused on presenting their thoughts and ideas that they were ignoring, or, at least downplaying, the comments of their peers. Notice that the example of peer feedback detailed next occurred with less than a minute left in class:

> To Stella:
> I just wanted to tell you that your comments are rather in depth. Great job. (October 26, 1993, 11:48:46, Chuck Hendrick, Group 1)
>
> Chuck, no doubt the statement would defin[i]tely rattle some minds, when I first read this, it really made me think about it, but I wasn't really sure how to take this. (October 26, 1993, 11:49:09, Stella Dunnick, Group 1)

To examine this puzzling issue further, the Case 3 transcripts for the remaining four groups were then reviewed. Here it was discovered that, although there were a few interesting comments about keeping peers on task ("Johnny needs to stay on task.") and timely questions (e.g., "What are examples of methods and cognitive principles?"), these students displayed few instances of personalized interactions addressing each others' ZPDs. Nevertheless, these students were making recommendations to use real-life approaches, role play, case-based learning, simulations, and cultural presentations that would address the language fluency and paragraph structure problems of the students described in this case. In effect, the real-time conferencing students were solving this problem situation as individuals, not as a group. The content focus of the social studies group (i.e., Group 3), for instance, was unmistakable in their initial Connect comments for Case 3, which mentioned providing background materials, lecture information, and connections among events, as well as in their final message, posted 5 minutes after class had ended: "By putting students in groups, he/she can have the students help each other. The students who understand better can help those that don't. The group can brainstorm together and come up with more conclusions. Between them, they can eliminate weaker points and build on the stronger ones" (October 26, 1993, Time: 11:55:42, Mark Lewis, Group 3). Mark Lewis was apparently so engaged in this task that he stayed after class to get this last comment in, although few of his social studies peers remained to read it. Such consistent task focus and engagement cannot be discounted, despite the limited direct student-student interactions. Perhaps that immediate focus on content and solving problems is the real utility of real-time tools.

Though there was consistency in student task focus and content-dumping behaviors, Group 5 (math/science/health) bucked this trend. Of the five Connect groups, this one was the most interactive during the real-time conferencing sessions in terms of their questioning and peer feedback as well as their interesting display of off-task behaviors. For example, the third case for this group was christened with the following comment from Ned before most students had arrived at lab: "Welcome back . . . group . . . are you ready for some wild and crazy fun in the ol' computer lab?" (October 26, 1993, Time: 10:58:35, Ned Mercle, Group 5).

This group also displayed more personalization, humor, positive feedback, and antagonism than the others. Here are a few other examples of their Case 3 dialogue:

> Come on Jaime!! You're a slacker. Just take a guess. (October 26, 1993, Time: 11:08:57, Ellen Lister, Group 5)
>
> How might he deal with these students? Well, he might flunk them. He might make them sit in the corner until they can get the problem correct . . . I don't know. (Um . . . hello . . . Jaime where is your valuable insight to these problems?) (October 26, 1993, Time: 11:19:37, Ellen Lister, Group 5)
>
> I agree with Ned to have the students compare their two answers. They can learn how to estimate better and that is useful in real life in shopping for groceries, etc. (October 26, 1995, Time: 11:20:23, Jaime Jones, Group 5)
>
> I'm impressed Jaime. Does this mean that you are too good for us? (October 26, 1995, Time: 11:34:08, Ned Mercle, Group 5)
>
> This is direct from Chapter 7 (I read it last night, p. 329). The teacher in this case is using attention getters . . . (this would be an example of a cognt[i]ive process). Okay . . . that's enough hard thinking for me today. I'm done. Write me a neat comment. (October 26, 1993, Time: 11:44:04, Ellen Lister, Group 5)

Clearly Group 5 was more interactive and responsive to fellow group members. They pushed and prodded each other to respond and then praised or critiqued those responses. Over time, this group also engaged in the most significant off-task behavior of the real-time sessions with comments such as Jaime's inquiry, "So—how about going out for some hot dogs and fish sometime?" Such off-task behavior, though still rather minimal, may have contributed to greater expectations for peer commenting and feedback, timely guidance in accordance with students' ZPDs, and the enhancement of intersubjectivity, common space, or sense of community.

Microanalysis of VAX Notes Transcripts

Student comments in the asynchronous group were more elaborate and thoughtful, in part, because their cases were more richly embedded with information about the teacher decision-making process than most of those used for the real-time conferencing. Quantitatively speaking, the delayed collaboration groups generated an average of 45 single-spaced pages of text per case or about three times the content of the real-time conferencing sessions. Stated another way, their hardcopy printouts were extremely thick!

The first case was more content centered because the instructor simply wanted students to become familiar with the system (see Table 12.2 for changes in focus for the VAX Notes class). The following is an abbreviated example of one of the numerous elaborate comments submitted by VAX Notes' students regarding the first case:

> Joyce's new system offers a wide variety of assessment forms. These different forms complement the diverse learning and test taking abilities of her students. Joyce seems to cover the two goals of classroom assessment with her final exam—to increase learning and increase motivation. Students will increase their learning because they will not just remember information to re[g]urgitate on an exam, but instead they will store these items in their long-term memory and later may be able to make a general transfer. Joyce will increase student motivation because she has deviated from the normal assessment method expected by her students.
>
> Joyce's test will probably be both reliable and valid considering that she implemented three different forms of tests. Joyce's test also might reduce test anxiety. If her students know what to expect on the test (they even wrote the questions) they more than likely will be less anxious on exam day. . . . (January 31, 1994, Time: 19:28, Sarah Fenway, Language Group)

Although Sarah's responses here were coded as a content appraisal or evaluation of the scenario (i.e., CAa), they reflected more insight and analysis than student content responses in the real-time format. Such analyses were indeed impressive for the third week of the semester, especially because they reflected a mere one third of her original evaluation. Additionally, this partial quote is representative of roughly half a typical VAX Notes' posting. Such thoughtfulness and depth is important to keep in mind as some of the examples provided later on may give the impression that the delayed conferencing discussion did not foster rich case analyses and resolutions.

The extremely focused case discussions generated by Sarah, though typical of both the real-time and delayed conferences, were definitely more prevalent and extended in the delayed VAX Notes format. During the four cases, students referred to key course concepts and theories such as observational learning, cooperative grouping, and individualizing instruction. Unfortunately, however, few student comments compared case situations or referenced their fieldwork. Though most case discussion was simply focused on responding to the scenario in question, some commenting, nevertheless, was clearly designed to spur one's peers into debate. It is this interchange and personal commenting to which we now turn.

During asynchronous case discussion sessions, students seemed to rely on classmates to start discussion, question ideas, and lend new insights into case solution with comments such as "Someone take me on and tell me my ideas on case study #1 are so much trash. Let's go! I'm waiting." In fact, invoking the "reply" command to respond to the comments of peers reinforced the sense that one is arguing with a peer or helping someone understand the problem, instead of simply adding one's perspective on a case. Just as the microanalysis of dialogue transcripts of the real-time student groups provided insights into the unusual social interaction patterns of the social studies group, the permanency of student discussion transcripts helped uncover peer groups' reactions to a member of the delayed electronic conference (i.e., Mr. Larry McConnely) who decided to be controversial. His arguments and debates focused group members on the task by provoking discussion, imitation, and deeper commenting. As pointed out next, a combination of opportunities promoted Larry to guide or leader[2] of the Social Studies Group.

Larry dominated the style in his social studies subgroup of six students, but was at least partially imitated by at least one other student in his group and two other students in the other groups. Whereas he was one of many elaborate responders during the first case, his two-page, single-spaced comments on the second case about Karen Lee, a replacement 10th-grade Spanish teacher experiencing extensive classroom management problems, begin with some choice words:

> From the start, I'd like to note that I've read several replies to this case. I just want to say—"withitness." There.
>
> Some damn fool's suggested group work for this poor beleaguered class. I'll attend to that in time. Don't think I'll let it drop, no sir.
>
> And, I've noticed several people writing and saying that they would have done this or that brilliant and intuitive thing. I personally am brilliant or

[2]In contrast, no students assumed such leadership roles in the earlier real-time (i.e., Connect) conferencing sessions.

> intuitive and I think others among us could use a little humility. This Karen's made some mistakes, but we all make mistakes, and when (dare I say if) we are in her shoes, we should expect to make some of the same ones that confound her . . .
>
> On to business. Karen's problems are legion. . . . The environment for learning in Karen's class is poor. She needs to re-establish order. She is not in a position to start anew . . .
>
> Jeff just strikes me as a pissy little slug. As others have suggested, he needs to be taken aside. His status as a leader doesn't necessarily make him someone who can be turned around and used for a positive purpose . . .
>
> That check mark business is dopey. There are a lot of dopey ideas in education today. That brings me to group work. Group work sucks. You should expect to find more information on that in the afore-mentioned alphabetized listing of things that suck, somewhere in the tenth volume I think. . . . (February 23, 1995, Time: 19:35, Larry McConnely, Social Studies Group)

Despite the negative and superficial tone regarding this task, Larry became extremely active on VAX Notes starting with this particular comment. Furthermore, this tirade startled his group into acknowledging his position and forced sides to be taken. Perhaps more importantly, other group members also became more passionate in their ideas and began to conjure up their own shrewd quips and humorous anecdotes. Whereas some students were cautious in how to respond, others in Larry's group actually thanked him for supporting their position.

Within about a week after Larry's first tantrum, he even received a message from someone in another group admitting that he liked peeking into the social studies group's notes and prodded Larry to "Seriously keep up the good work" and entertainment value; he referred to this group as an example of "Group Therapy" under Larry's supervision.[3] Those in the math/science group noted the "edgy" tone of this conference, whereas other groups blasted the social studies group for being so critical of one another and for its sexist tone. Fellow social studies group member, Jeremy Phillips, referred to Larry as a "pompous cynical twit," though he often agreed with Larry's views, as indicated by the following:

> Karen Lee. Man, did this girl get screwed or what? Put into an impossible situation that no veteran teacher wants to deal with, and her only recourse, understandably, is to resort to tricks learned in college. What to do . . .
>
> Tell the principal what kind of slime he really is! . . . Lay down the law from the beginning . . . You wouldn't ordinarily start out a reign as a teacher by being so hard-assed, but these kids aren't going to listen to anything else at this point.

[3]Unlike the Connect sessions, VAX Notes students were allowed to read the notes created by other groups, though this seemed to occur infrequently.

> I'm with Larry. Group work is right up there with dental surgery. . . . This is a foreign language class, however, and group work is vital here. Most of the techniques Karen is using are quite silly. Let's go through them. . . . (February 18, 1994, Time: 18:08, Jeremy Phillips, Social Studies Group)

Clearly, students began to understand that the second-grade management techniques were "a fatal mistake" with high school sophomores. The teacher's reliance on drills, assertive discipline, repetition, and rows of orderly students were dysfunctional. Although Larry was the discussion instigator on Case 2, the final comments from Jeremy on the first two cases served to close discussion. Perhaps these two were attempting to assume some control over their group, one as discussion starter and the other as the wrapper (see Zhu, chap. 10 of this volume).

As a returning adult student, Larry was very articulate, creative, entertaining, controversial, and domineering. Because he was aware that he was providing entertainment to his small group, he expanded his references to pop culture in his postings as the semester progressed (e.g., "I'm from Iowa, I only work in outer space"—Kirk; "Math is hard"—Barbie), teased or insulted fellow students (e.g., "Peace, dude, hop off the return key, save me some stress"), and displayed his contempt for current trends in education (e.g., "I am currently preparing my anti-groupwork support group"). He also added his own political concerns to the topic at hand (e.g., "Did you know that the NEA is now the country's largest union?"). He was such an articulate electronic debater and cynical writer that many of the younger students were probably too intimidated or bewildered to follow up on a host of thoughtful comments that Larry loosely interspersed ("One of the unique troubles in education is that its consumers aren't fully able to appreciate their interests. Children want short term satisfactions.").

Seen in this context, Larry shed some light on what roles might be helpful for electronic case discussions and what types of individuals might be assigned to these roles. As Piagetian developmental theory indicates (Cobb, 1994), having someone in each group who introduces controversy or provokes debate should foster students' joint composing practices and reflection within their shared text space. However, if this person has significantly outgrown the others' intellectual competence or ZPD, he or she may stimulate only superficial engagement or perhaps even frustration and intimidation. Larry's style seemed to encourage a number of other students to become more colloquial in their writing, but it failed to engage them in a debate of his substantive issues. By the end of the third case, Jeremy, for instance, started using quotes to reply to his peers from Humphrey Bogart ("Go away kid, you bother me.") and Madonna ("Hurt me, Baby"), while pointing out that he was waiting for Larry to "make someone feel like dirt." Larry responded that he did not want to try to humiliate Jeremy because he respected his intellect and would be "happier to massacre the masses." But he did offer the following comment: "You have all underestimated the nature of my diabolical intentions" (March 28, 1994, Time: 15:12, Larry McConnely, Social Studies Group).

Though these off-task quotes and criticisms were infrequent and were not indicative of students' understanding of the case situation, they shed light on the social context of electronic case collaboration. And although it is unclear how the humor and blunt criticism operated within a student's ZPD, it was an environment wherein this group jelled. If anything, it was controversial people (e.g., Larry) and topics (e.g., "groupwork") that fostered this group's most intense conversations, interactions, and badgerings.

Though the other four groups remained more focused on their solutions for the case, these groups also became more interactive, responsive, and even humorous over time. In solving the third case, the biology/PE group, for instance, used responsive phrases such as "I want to agree with Mark's analysis," "Tonya, I 100% agree with what you said about teachers needing to motivate students," and "I think Stan had a good point. . . ." Such feedback and praise was directed, genuine, and positive, thereby providing valuable peer performance appraisal.

The fourth case, which coincided with the final 3 weeks' course readings on special education and individual differences, provided a wide lens on the skills these students had internalized during the semester. In addressing the fourth research question, by providing answers and comments related to scaffolding, feedback, tutoring, guided learning pedagogy, assignment meaningfulness, and addressing student ZPDs, students were beginning to comprehend the range of learning supports available to teachers. Perhaps these cases really were making a difference!

Electronic Case Collaboration Reflections

Though Table 12.2 reveals that the VAX Notes group increased their total direct peer responding from just 6 times in Case 1 to 214 times in Case 2, instructor directions to respond to peers in Cases 2 to 4 were at least partially responsible for this shift in focus. In contrast, Connect students consistently engaged in task talk activities such as providing case-related suggestions, recommendations, comments, and personal appraisals of actors. At the same time, off-task behaviors were discovered somewhat more frequently in the real-time than delayed transcripts (see Fig. 12.1).

Why were real-time students off task or not responding diligently to each other? Student responses to questionnaires about the respective programs and tasks indicated that although this alternative environment could assist in their learning, it was less useful than anticipated. Several students in the real-time conferencing class suggested that a more traditional class discussion of problematic teaching scenarios would better foster their learning, whereas

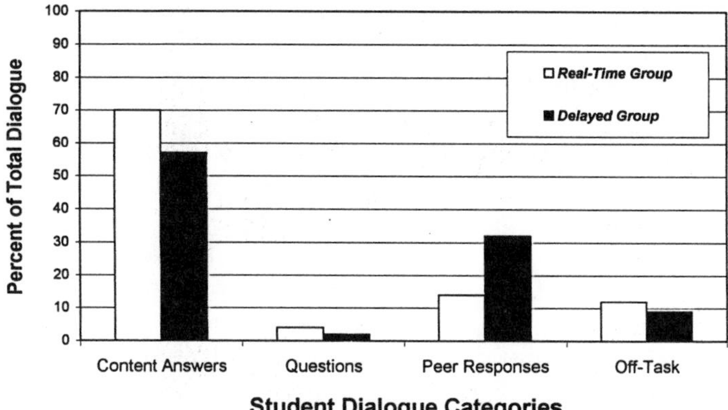

FIG. 12.1. Comparison of student dialogue in synchronous and asynchronous electronic collaborations.

many students using delayed collaboration were negative about adding work to their overloaded schedules. One insightful student, however, suggested that education schools could parallel the way the business school teaches its core courses; use real-time interactions for shorter cases and delayed formats for longer cases.

Despite lower than anticipated student ratings of the task across the two electronic conferencing formats, the electronic debates often were extremely intense and task focused. In reviewing the hundreds of pages of dialogue transcripts, it is clear that there was considerable learning going on here! *All* students, not just the most vocal, participated in solving the cases presented by reflecting on both personal experiences as well as the material learned in class. In fact, some Connect students arrived at the computer lab early or stayed late just to get additional comments in, whereas VAX Notes students were commenting on cases weeks after discussion had expected to be over. Across the two groups, most students spoke their minds more freely electronically than during class and many of them produced more entries than was required by the assignment.

In the VAX Notes interactions, new task structures were nurtured by the lively and provocative style of one slightly older student, whose articulate attacks at anything and anybody challenged others to respond. As Sproull and Kiesler (1993) found, students like Larry tend to express more extreme positions and vent their anger more often when in electronic discussions than in face-to-face settings. Although some irrelevant and off-task comments were featured in the previous quotes, on-task behaviors were amazingly high; ranging between 80% and 90% of coded activities in these two forums. Also, as the earlier quotes demonstrate, these tools intensified the learning experience and provided a group interaction setting with diminished instructor authority. Both tools, in fact, fostered a sense of student responsibility over classroom learning activities.

From an instructional design standpoint, brief as well as more detailed electronic case discussions were piloted, with advantages and disadvantages attributable to both. For successful group processing in electronic environments, the requirements appear to be: (a) few questions focused on course content linkages and problem solutions, (b) sufficient complexity for extended group disagreement, (c) an opportunity for fundamental pedagogical and philosophical debating, (d) cases organized by subject matter area in groups of five to eight members, (e) student responding to teacher questions prior to group interaction and processing, (f) guidelines for length of response (e.g., one to two screens), (g) more emphasis on performance assessment (i.e., depth of discussion, peer responsiveness, coherence, completeness, etc.), instead of traditional competitive grading, and (h) group member roles or participant structures. Hopefully, with guidelines such as these, electronic conferencing technologies can heighten classroom discussion and deepen student understanding of their field of study.

Sociocultural Reflections

Given the theoretical justification for this study, how well do the findings here mesh with Vygotsky's sociocultural theory? For instance, were there clear instances of scaffolding, internalization, or students addressing each other within their ZPDs?

The most important finding from a sociocultural perspective was that these two tools, VAX Notes and Connect, fostered vastly different dialogue and interaction patterns. In delayed collaboration, students witnessed not only more responses to their ideas, but these responses reflected more complex ideas and depth of thought. Keep in mind, however, that the VAX Notes tool was easier to use and more widely available than the Connect tool. Moreover, the VAX Notes response guidelines from their instructor helped students focus their feedback and praise. Students in the Connect environment, in contrast, spent more time spewing out content talk without much guidance. Our intense sampling of 20 students verified that Connect students interacted more frequently, but their participation also was more concise and egocentric. The focus for them was on specific content generation, not on extended peer interaction and dialogue.

Whereas content appraisal and frequent, concise responses dominated the real-time dialogue, students in the delayed mode shifted from extended content talk to greater peer responsiveness. Apparently, the confined writing time, shorter cases, and limited instructor guidance focused student real-time social interactions on case appraisal and forming case recommendations. In contrast, the delayed collaboration provided a framework for more balance in content and peer responding.

Though the two studies are not comparable, in both electronic case discussions there was high content-related talk exhibited by students, whereas direct peer responses were more limited and student questioning negligible. When electronic debates did occur, these were rather extended and frank discussions. Sometimes, however, such elaborate interactions resulted from unique individual prompting. In empowering students to take more responsibility for their own classroom learning, the software, both delayed and real time, facilitated and captured rich classroom conversations and stories that remain available for additional student, teacher, and researcher reflection. As found in Sproull and Kiesler's (1993) earlier work, over time, both groups began to experience greater group cohesiveness, peer scaffolding, and intersubjectivity, though this was definitely more pronounced in the delayed mode.

There are numerous explanations for group differences in peer responsiveness and content focus. Although length of session, task format, and particular tool used were all influential in student-learning outcomes, the teacher had a significant role in guiding the form of dialogue. Therefore, in order to enhance social interaction and dialogue, teachers may wish to model more of the questioning techniques students might use as well as spend time practicing these. Additionally, assigning students specific roles to provoke and summarize student interaction and debate (e.g., devil's advocates, protesters, idea generators, debaters, summarizers, critics, optimists, etc.) might spark controversy and enliven electronic discussion forums. Instructors in CSCL environments might further scaffold the activity through elaborate task instructions and timely and insightful feedback.

Limitations and Shortcomings

Given the diversity of the tasks and software tools, there are limitations in generalizing any of the results here to decisions about delayed or real-time collaborative tools or about their link to sociocultural theory. Differences in case length and response time make most comparisons between our Connect and VAX Notes data totally inappropriate. In either computer-conferencing situation, ferreting out critical incidents of scaffolded learning and then determining the proper coding designation was extremely difficult. Initial interrater agreement on these transcripts was lower than anticipated, in part, because more than one significant incident was often embedded in a single statement or paragraph. Such multidimensional problems highlight the need for continued coding scheme development.

Larry's case further illustrates the shortcomings of a formal categorization scheme such as the one used for this study. The more technical and narrow the categories, the less likely they will capture the mechanisms of cognitive change such as those described earlier. The purpose of categorizing different elements in an electronically mediated debate is to judge the quality of the learning activity. One should ask, therefore, how did the electronic medium contribute to student learning? Clearly, student "appraisal" of a case scenario can be extremely sophisticated and constructive or it can be as superficial as a thoughtless cliché. At the same time, praising a fellow student's posting may reflect simple politeness or it may actually elaborate on the insight generated by this comment. A categorization scheme that contributes to the analysis of the quality of student learning must permit such crucial distinctions. It cannot be neutral.

Future Questions and Implications

Both synchronous and asynchronous computer conferencing offer distinct advantages over live discussions of cases. For instance, electronic tools may facilitate greater student publishing of ideas as well as researcher understanding of how those ideas actually unfolded. More complex cases presented in asynchronous conferences foster elaborate analysis and interaction, whereas brief cases in real-time conferencing focus students directly on the case content. Across these two formats, students seem extremely motivated to impress their peers. But other questions remain regarding student appropriation of this new medium. For instance, how many new ideas are generated in each discussion group? How well are students picking up on each others' ideas and insights? And how does student intersubjectivity (as indicated by clichés, accolades, counterpoints, jokes, cryptic commenting, etc.) increase over time?

What apparently escaped our formal coding scheme was the fact that a number of students began to have fun working with written language while attempting to impress their peers with their ideas as well as with their writing style. In some cases, students spiced up their verbal exchanges with MTV generation jargon and antiauthoritarian attitudes, while rejecting the dryness of academic discourse. Resulting student comments may have lacked analytical or pedagogical correctness, but they did operate within common zones of development. The remarkable aspect of this interaction was that it was primarily directed at each other, not the instructor. In that sense, one could think of electronic conferencing and collaborative writing as a medium for peer tutoring and communication within students' ZPDs. Perhaps it is not surprising that writing for an authentic audience without the fear of failure (i.e., red ink and low grades), therefore, might so swiftly lead students to adapt a style that rebels against traditional classroom writing formats! College instructors should welcome this opportunity to assist students in connecting the written word to a fun and worthwhile event in the age of "writing across the curriculum." At the same time, composition researchers now have vast new data sources for documenting the impact of writing on thinking and for probing students' course understanding. If we continue to discover innovative ways of integrating emerging electronic media into academic environments without subjecting students to the same old rules that have made learning so colorless in the past, we may find an opportunity to refashion professional education, and learning in general, into a more energizing and authentic enterprise.

In addition to these energizing textual events, these two classes of preservice teachers were encouraged to discuss and debate problematic teaching scenarios similar to those they would soon face. By learning in a context, future teachers received a voice or pathway for generating future instructional decisions. Not only were these preservice teachers interacting with the technologies that they will encounter in the near future, but they also were learning about constructivist and sociocultural viewpoints firsthand. Although more limited than originally intended, they were debating, posing contradictions, discovering new relationships, reflecting on previous experiences, seeking peer elaboration, and sharing perspectives—all activities at the heart of the constructivist movement (Brooks, 1990).

As constructivistic tools transport students to new electronically shared spaces (Schrage, 1990) for conversation and collaboration, researchers should become concerned with how competent peers might scaffold their learning partners, how instructors might apprentice student tool use and problem analysis, and how discourse patterns could change according to task criteria, tool availability, and interaction timing. Clearly, delayed and real-time computer-conferencing tools are vehicles for traversing new learning highways of shared space and cognitive connections. Now is the time to connect. Safe travels!

ACKNOWLEDGMENTS

The research reported in this chapter was partially funded by a grant received from the Campuswide Writing Program at Indiana University. The authors would like to thank Ray Smith for this funding as well as for his encouragement. We also are greatly indebted to Fred McFarland and Steven R. King from W. W. Norton & Company for supplying a copy of *Norton Textra Connect* for this project and then supporting its use. Portions of this chapter were presented at the Mid-Western Educational Research Association annual meeting, 1994, Chicago, IL.

REFERENCES

Barnett, C. (1991). Building a case-based curriculum to enhance the pedagogical content knowledge of mathematics teachers. *Journal of Teacher Education*, *42*(4), 263–272.

Bereiter, C. (1994). Constructivism, socioculturalism, and Popper's World 3. *Educational Researcher*, *23*(7), 21–23.

Bonk, C. J., Malikowski, S., Angeli, C., & East, J. (in press). Case-based conferencing for preservice teaching education: Electronic discourse from the field. *Journal of Educational Computing Research.*

Bonk, C. J., Medury, P. V., & Reynolds, T. H. (1994). Cooperative hypermedia: The marriage of collaborative writing and mediated environments. *Computers in the Schools*, *10*(1/2), 79–124.

Brooks, J. G. (1990). Teachers and students: Constructivists forging new connections. *Educational Leadership*, *47*(5), 68–71.

Chang-Wells, G. M., & Wells, G. (1993). Dynamics of discourse: Literacy and the construction of knowledge. In E. A. Forman, N. Minnick, & C. A. Stone (Eds.), *Contexts for learning: Sociocultural dynamics in children's development* (pp. 58–90). New York: Oxford University Press.

Clements, D. H., & Nastasi, B. K. (1988). Social and cognitive interactions in educational computer environments. *American Educational Research Journal*, *25*(1), 87–106.

Cobb, P. (1994). Where is the mind? Constructivist and sociocultural perspectives on mathematical development. *Educational Researcher*, *23*(7), 13–20.

Cognition and Technology Group at Vanderbilt. (1991). Technology and the design of generative learning environments. *Educational Technology*, *31*(5), 34–40.

Cole, M. (1995). Socio-cultural-historical psychology: Some general remark and a proposal for a new kind of cultural-genetic methodology. In J. V. Wertsch, P. Del Rio, & A. Alvarez (Eds.), *Sociocultural studies of mind* (pp. 187–214). New York: Cambridge University Press.

Collins, A., Brown, J. S., & Newman, S. (1989). Cognitive apprenticeship: Teaching the crafts of reading, writing, and mathematics. In L. Resnick (Ed.), *Knowing, learning, and instruction: Essays in honor of Robert Glaser* (pp. 453–494). Hillsdale, NJ: Lawrence Erlbaum Associates.

Copeland, W. D. (1989). Technology-mediated laboratory experiences and the development of clinical reasoning in novice teachers. *Journal of Teacher Education*, *40*(3), 10–18.

DiPardo, A., & Freedman, S. W. (1988). Peer response groups in the writing classroom: Theoretical foundations and new directions. *Review of Educational Research*, *58*(2), 119–149.

Gallimore, R., & Tharp, R. (1990). Teaching mind in society: Teaching, schooling, and literate discourse. In L. C. Moll (Ed.), *Vygotsky in education: Instructional implications of sociohistorical psychology* (pp. 175–205). New York: Cambridge University Press.

Granott, N., & Gardner, H. (1994). When minds meet: Interactions, coincidence, and development in domains of ability. In R. J. Sternberg & R. K. Wagner (Eds.), *Mind in context: Interactionist perspectives in human intelligence* (pp. 171–201). New York: Cambridge University Press.

Grant, G. E. (1992). Using cases to develop teacher knowledge. In J. H. Shulman (Ed.), *Case methods in teacher education* (pp. 211–226). New York: Teachers College Press.

Harasim, L. M. (1990). Online education: An environment for collaboration and intellectual amplification. In L. M. Harasim (Ed.), *Online education: Perspectives on a new environment* (pp. 39–64). New York: Praeger.

Harasim, L. M. (1993). Networlds as social space. In L. M. Harasim (Ed.), *Global networks: Computers and international communication* (pp. 15–34). Cambridge, MA: MIT Press.

Hartman, K., Neuwirth, C. M., Sproull, L., Cochran, C., Palmquist, M., & Zubrow, D. (1991). Patterns of social interaction and learning to write: Some effect of network technologies. *Written Communication*, *8*(1), 79–113.

Henri, F. (1992). Computer conferencing and content analysis. In A. R. Kaye (Ed.), *Collaborative learning through computer conferencing: The Najaden papers* (pp. 117–135). New York: Springer-Verlag.

Kagan, D. M., & Tippins, D. J. (1991). How teachers' classroom cases express their pedagogical beliefs. *Journal of Teacher Education*, *42*(4), 263–272.

Klemm, W. R., & Snell, J. R. (1994). Teaching via networked PCs: What's the best medium? *Technological Horizons in Education*, *22*(3), 95–98.

Koschmann, T. D. (1994). Toward a theory of computer support for collaborative learning. *Journal of the Learning Sciences*, *3*(3), 219–225.

Koschmann, T. D., Myers, A. C., Feltovich, P. J., & Barrows, H. S. (1994). Using technology to assist in realizing effective learning and instruction: A principled approach to the use of computers in collaborative learning. *Journal of the Learning Sciences*, *3*(3), 219–225.

Kowalski, T. J., Weaver, R. A., & Henson, K. T. (1994). *Case studies of beginning teachers.* New York: Longman.

Krauss, R. M., & Fussell, S. R. (1990). Mutual knowledge and communicative effectiveness. In J. Galegher, R. E. Kraut, & C. Egido (Eds.), *Intellectual teamwork: Social and technological foundations of cooperative work* (pp. 111–145). Hillsdale, NJ: Lawrence Erlbaum Associates.

Livingston, C., & Borko, H. (1989). Expert-novice differences in teaching: A cognitive analysis and implications for teacher education. *Journal of Teacher Education*, *40*(3), 10–18.

Meloth, M., & Deering, P. (1994). Task talk and task awareness under different cooperative learning conditions. *American Educational Research Journal*, *31*(1), 138–165.

Merseth, K. K. (1991). The early history of case-based instruction: Insights from teacher education today. *Journal of Teacher Education*, *42*(4), 263–272.

Palincsar, A. S., & Brown, A. L. (1984). Reciprocal teaching of comprehension-fostering and comprehension-monitoring activities. *Cognition and Instruction*, *1*(2), 117–175.

Pea, R. D. (1994). Seeing what we build together: Distributed multimedia learning environments for transformative communications. *Journal of the Learning Sciences*, *3*(3), 219–225.

Richert, A. E. (1992). Writing cases: A vehicle for inquiry into the teaching process. In J. H. Shulman (Ed.), *Case methods in teacher education* (pp. 155–174). New York: Teachers College Press.

Riel, M. (1993). Global education through learning circles. In L. Harasim (Ed.), *Global networks: Computers and international communication* (pp. 221–236). Cambridge, MA: MIT Press.

Riesbeck, C. K. (1996). Case-based teaching and constructivism: Carpenters and tools. In B. G. Wilson (Ed.), *Constructivist learning environments: Case studies in instructional design* (pp. 49–61). Englewood Cliffs, NJ: Educational Technology Publications.

Rogoff, B. (1995). Observing sociocultural activity on three planes: Participatory appropriation, guided participation, and apprenticeship. In J. V. Wertsch, P. Del Rio, & A. Alvarez (Eds.), *Sociocultural studies of mind* (pp. 139–164). New York: Cambridge University Press.

Schrage, M. (1990). *Shared minds: The technologies of collaboration.* New York: Random House.

Shulman, J. H. (1991). Revealing the mysteries of teacher-written cases: Opening the black box. *Journal of Teacher Education*, *42*(4), 263–272.

Shulman, L. S. (1992). Toward a pedagogy of cases. In J. H. Shulman (Ed.), *Case methods in teacher education* (pp. 1–30). New York: Teachers College Press.

Silverman, R., Welty, W. M., & Lyon, S. (1992). *Case studies for teacher problem solving.* New York: McGraw-Hill.

Sproull, L., & Kiesler, S. (1993). Computers, networks, and work. In L. M. Harasim (Ed.), *Global networks: Computers and international communication* (pp. 105–119). Cambridge, MA: MIT Press.

Tuman, M. C., & Ann Arbor Software. (1994). *Instructor's guide for use with Norton Textra Connect: A networked writing environment.* New York: Norton.

Vygotsky, L. S. (1978). *Mind in society.* Cambridge, MA: Harvard University Press.

Walls, J. (1993). Global networking for local development: Task focus and relationship focus in cross-cultural communication. In L. M. Harasim (Ed.), *Global networks: Computers and international communication* (pp. 153–165). Cambridge, MA: MIT Press.

Wells, G. (1996). Using the tool-kit of discourse in the activity of learning and teaching. *Mind, Culture, and Activity*, *3*(2), 74–101.

Wertsch, J. V. (1985). *Vygotsky and the social formation of mind.* Cambridge, MA: Harvard University Press.

Westerman, D. A. (1991). Expert and novice teacher decision making. *Journal of Teacher Education*, *42*(4), 263–272.

Williams, S. M. (1992). Putting case-based instruction into context: Examples from legal and medical education. *Journal of the Learning Sciences*, *2*(4), 367–427.

Wineburg, S. S. (1991). A case of pedagogical failure: My own. *Journal of Teacher Education*, *42*(4), 263–272.

13

The Use of Computer-Mediated Communication: Electronic Collaboration and Interactivity

Inae Kang
Kyung Hee University

In Korea, a recent educational restructuring movement, called *open education*, emphasizes learner-centered instruction, interdisciplinary curriculum, and rich, authentic learning opportunities. As a direct result of this initiative, the Korean government as well as the corporate sector are beginning to support new opportunities for educational technology innovation and hands-on learning. Factors pushing Korea in this direction include rapid changes in information and knowledge, an educational restructuring movement, job-related reeducation and retraining, and the development of advanced information and communication technologies. In response to these trends, this study in a higher education environment attempted to marry innovative technologies with contemporary ideas about teaching and learning.

EDUCATIONAL PARADIGM SHIFT IN THE INFORMATION AGE

The relationships between society and education are dynamic and mutually influential such that a paradigm shift in society leads to similar changes in education (Banathy, 1991). For instance, as society progressed from the agricultural to the industrial age, education was transformed from home-based apprenticeship to mass education under centralized governmental control. In moving into the information age, both society and the field of education are once again affected by rapid and wide-scale change. Society now requires workers with new skills to work collaboratively, to think critically, and to solve problems as they work with vast amounts of information and knowledge.

The typical teaching and learning styles found in most current educational systems, unfortunately, are incompatible with these goals. Such educational institutions arose during the industrial age where a centralized curricula and results-centered approach with societal needs for uniformity, mechanization, standardization, and mass production was privileged (Reigeluth, 1994). The educational paradigm of the information age, in contrast, employs process-centered approaches to accommodate societal needs for diverse, creative, and flexible thinking. Such drastic changes from the results-oriented approach of memorizing a core body of information to the process-oriented approach of helping people learn how to learn in educational settings, have begun to transform public schools and universities from teacher-controlled to learner-centered pedagogical approaches. This shift, though seemingly simple, in fact, brings about holistic and radical changes in every aspect of education, a "paradigm shift" (Kuhn, 1962) as revolutionary as the Copernican movement of the 16th century.

There are currently two societal innovations in Korea and across the world supporting such revolutionary and paradigmatic ideas in education today. First, new educational methods can be created from sociocultural learning theories (Bonk & Kim, 1998; Duffy & Jonassen, 1991; Lave & Wenger, 1993; Rogoff, 1990). Since the 1980s, sociocultural learning theories have gained increasing attention as an alternative to current teacher-centered educational environments. Sociocultural goals and directions are closely aligned with the recent learner-centered movement in education (see the American Psychological Association, 1993; Wagner & McCombs, 1995), which advocates the design of effective learning experiences from the perspective of the learner, while also expanding the role of collaboration and peer mentoring in schooling (see Bonk & Cunningham, chap. 2, this volume). Not surprisingly, this departure from teacher-controlled education of the industrial society to learner-centered education of the information age has begun to confront and challenge Korean educators.

The second key variable affecting education is the rapid development of information and communication technology, in particular, computer-mediated communication (CMC) technologies. Advances in conferencing and collaboration systems provide practical tools to investigate the sociocultural implications of both corporate and school reforms (Hammer & Champy, 1993; Harasim, 1994; Senge, Roberts, Ross, Smith, & Kleiner, 1994).

SOCIOCULTURAL THEORY

As indicated, sociocultural theory has began to gain the attention of educational researchers and practitioners as problems of student motivation, lowered achievement, and inert knowledge are raised to a critical threshold

(Resnick, 1989). Traditionally, instructional approaches have analyzed learners and learning from the educator's perspective, not the students'. In effect, the teacher decides for learners what should be learned from the "outside" by defining specific learning objectives, instructional methods, and assessment. Learners, in turn, are expected to play the role of knowledge consumer rather than knowledge producer.

Given current expectations for lifelong and independent learning situations in the 21st century, however, it seems that traditional approaches to education are not appropriate for involving learners in lifelong skills like knowledge generation and evaluation. As an alternative to teacher-centered instructional approaches, therefore, learner-centered ideas and socioculturally based learning environments have emerged (Bonk & Cunningham, chap. 2 of this volume; Bonk, Hay, & Fischler, 1996).

Sociocultural theory, denying the traditional notion that we can arrive at the same ideas and knowledge, asserts that knowledge is constructed by the individual in terms of her own social experiences. From this viewpoint, when the learner socially interacts with others, she negotiates the meaning of the terms used and finds a common language to describe and discuss the problem at hand. The process of meaning negotiation is critical because it broadens students' understanding and moves them closer to full membership in a group of people who solve similar problems and speak a common language. As a result of continuous participation in the community of practice (see Lave & Wenger, 1993), the learner becomes acculturated to the community and acquires its unique ways of thinking, behaving, and discussing.

Sociocultural theory also supports individual learner's self-reflective activities. For instance, a learner might engage in questioning, idea analysis, and critical inquiry (Clift, Houston, & McCarthy, 1992; Ross, 1989; Schon, 1987). Such reflective skill can be exercised through electronic journals, discussion groups, and interactive debates.

CMC offers a chance to merge the technological aspect of computers with sociocultural theory. If, as Vygotsky (1978) contended, student learning and development cannot be understood without reference to the social context, then it becomes essential to study the role of CMC applications in authentic learning environments (Bonk & King, 1995). For instance, CMC might mediate student learning by encouraging student sharing of meaning and social dialogue (Tudge & Rogoff, 1989). Such technology might also offer new channels of communication and apprenticeship among students and learning participants of different cultural backgrounds, ability levels, and areas of expertise (Lave & Wenger, 1993). Therefore, in merging socioculturally based learning ideas with the unique capabilities of CMC technologies, we have an ideal opportunity to transcend our current educational paradigm and create the learner-centered environments desired by the information age.

With such a goal in mind, this chapter details one case wherein technology was used to create a learner-centered educational environment. Specifically, it analyzes a graduate course conducted in Korea that was designed to combine CMC technology with sociocultural practices related to collaborative learning, self-reflective activities, the teacher as a coach and colearner, electronic scaffolding, and student ownership over learning. Before detailing this study, however, the present state of CMC technology in Korea must be documented. In addition, a scheme for analyzing CMC is detailed.

PRESENT CMC USE IN KOREAN HIGHER EDUCATION

With competitive support and interest from the Korean government and mass media, concern about CMC use in education is rapidly expanding in Korea. According to May 1995 statistics from a commercial network company, "Dacom," more than 130 elementary schools and about 500 classes in 50 universities in Korea were adopting CMC using the company's network. And the number of schools adopting CMC was dramatically rising each semester.

Teaching and learning via CMC in Korea, nevertheless, is mainly restricted to local campus connections or a commercial network rather than the Internet. According to the taxonomy of collaborative writing tools from Bonk, Medury, and Reynolds (1994), most teachers and students in Korea are restricted to Level 1; that is, they use text-based electronic mail (E-mail) systems. Recently, however, there have been advances in both asynchronous (Level 2) and synchronous (Level 3) communication tools. Unlike the United States, in Korea educational uses of the Internet and the World Wide Web are uncommon and largely experimental. In fact, the majority of frustrations regarding CMC use in Korea are associated with technological limitations.

Another factor indicating the level of CMC use in Korean higher education is student attitudes toward learning with technology. Most Korean students, especially arts and humanities majors, are familiar only with word processing. Therefore, even though they may realize the current societal trend toward online education, they may feel intimidated about using CMC. Such student resistance usually stems from the additional time required to learn new computer software as well as the costs to actively participate in discussing, communicating, and writing. Consequently, compared with the strong interest in and concern about CMC use in education shown by the government and mass media, the reality in schools differs significantly.

Despite this lack of technological infrastructure, there is a recent educational restructuring movement called open education in Korea that emphasizes a more learner-centered, interdisciplinary, and authentic educational curriculum. Given this movement, CMC in education should not simply remain a temporary fad and curiosity, nor an exception communicated among a certain group of people; rather, it should develop as a norm for new "instructional and training contexts wherein learners are expected to function as self-motivated, self-directed, interactive, collaborative participants in their learning experiences" (Wagner & McCombs, 1995, p. 32). Before CMC can become a viable approach to learning in the 21st century in Korea, new evaluation tools must also arise to assess the utility of this approach to teaching and learning.

THE ELECTRONIC INTERACTION OF CMC

Every time a new medium has emerged since the 1950s, comparison studies between different media or between conventional classroom learning and the new media approaches have been conducted. Unfortunately, few studies discover actual differences favoring the new medium (Clark & Sugrue, 1991). Some consistent findings regarding this technology, however, have led to Walther's (1996) three-level matrix of the interpersonal effects of CMC. These three levels—impersonality, interpersonality, and hyperpersonality—are detailed in the following section.

Impersonal Effects of CMC

One of the most frequently raised questions about teaching and learning via CMC is whether user media dependency makes it dehumanistic or mechanistic. Early studies on the electronic interactions of CMC concluded it was impersonal, leading to its reputation as too task oriented and depersonalized.

The examination of the history and development of CMC indicates that it originally emerged as an unintended by-product of linking large computers to one another for security and information redundancy purposes. Initially, only text simple messages were exchanged among system operators. From there the notion grew that CMC could be used to coordinate tasks among geographically dispersed individuals (see Hiltz & Turoff, 1978; Rheingold, 1993), and CMC grew from simple relay systems into planned applications for group communication. After finding that coordination of tasks among geographically dispersed individuals could be achieved, researchers began to examine the effectiveness and social character of these interactions. The initial conclusion from CMC studies that it was impersonal, therefore, might have been affected by the inherent attribute of CMC as lacking in nonverbal signals and social context cues such as the hierarchical status among participants and the overall physical environment (Siegel, Dubrovsky, Kiesler, & McGuire, 1986).

Another reason that supports CMC's impersonality found in early studies on CMC use relates to the affordance of time. Instead of studying the effects of CMC use over time, most early studies of CMC use did not last long enough to develop extensive socioemotional communication. As a matter of fact, the early longitudinal studies on CMC (Hiltz, Johnson, & Angle, 1978; Rice & Love, 1987) resulted in conflicting findings regarding the impersonality of CMC use. These studies contended that users learn to adapt their verbal behavior to the restrictions of the textual medium and gradually develop their interaction to more interpersonal levels.

Even though CMC fosters less personal interaction than face-to-face (i.e., FTF) communication, its cognitively focused interactions and analyses might be advantageous. According to Dubrovsky (1985), computer conferences shift our focus from the affective component of communication to the exchange of content-related comments and thoughts. In fact, empirical research has identified an inverse relationship between the frequency of personal remarks and decision-making success in CMC (Smolensky, Carmody, & Halcomb, 1990). Similarly, the uninhibited and depersonalized effects of the use of E-mail and computer conferencing, as demonstrated in numerous empirical studies in the CMC literature (Garton & Wellman, 1995; Rice & Love, 1987; Rice & Shook, 1990; Walther, 1994), can be strategically used to foster group solidarity and efficient decision making in task-oriented situations.

Interpersonal Effects of CMC

Another framework for explaining the nature of CMC electronic interaction, in contrast to the impersonal effects shown in early studies on CMC, considers the development of interpersonal qualities among CMC users. Walther (1996) presented a model called a "social information-processing perspective" that addressed interpersonal CMC exchanges. According to this model, the key difference between CMC and FTF communication is found not in the amount of social information exchange, but in the rate of social information exchange. Thus, whereas the time-limited CMC use might lead to impersonal and task-oriented relations, longitudinal CMC studies would produce the opposite results (i.e., extensive interpersonal and social relations). In other words, the social information-processing perspective acknowledges that there is less social information per message in CMC due to the absence of nonverbal cues. Yet, given the accumulation of vast message exchanges over time (Slatin, 1993), increasing interpersonal effects are often found in computer-conferencing environments.

Another interesting feature supporting the interpersonality of CMC technologies is the anticipation of future interaction among users: Unlike one-shot experiments, where participants do not expect ongoing interaction, long-term electronic situations assume continuous partnerships among and between users, which, in turn, shapes their interpersonal interactions

(Walther, 1994). Additionally, according to social information-processing perspectives, CMC users adapt to their communication tools and create a number of nonverbal strategies for electronic communication (Walther, 1996). For example, there are many linguistic signs created by CMC users to express their emotional conditions such as the smile, the wink, crying, the sigh, and so on.

Hyperpersonal Effects of CMC

Quite different than the expected assumption of the interpersonal effects of CMC as dehumanizing, or impersonal, there are contrasting perspectives such "social identity-deindividuation (SIDE) theory" (Lea & Spears, 1991, 1992; Sproull & Faraj, in press; Walther, 1992), which advocate the "hyperpersonal effects of CMC." Of course, hyperpersonal phenomena already occur in CMC environments devoted primarily to "social," or "recreational" interactions such as bulletin boards, games, or chat systems. SIDE theories insist, however, that hyperpersonal relations can be generated even in task-oriented groups and business settings. According to SIDE theory, the attributes of CMC as media mediated tend to surpass the level of affection and emotion of FTF interaction, and hence, generate two mechanisms: (a) an "idealized perception" (Walther, 1996, p. 18) of the sender by the receiver, as well as (b) an "optimized self-presentation" of the sender (Walther, 1996, p. 19).

Regarding the idealized perception of the sender, Lea and Spears (1992) contended that in the absence of FTF cues and prior personal knowledge about one's partners, CMC users engage in building stereotypical impressions of their partners, often relying on minimal cues such as misspelling, typographical errors, and the like. When CMC users are in a group relationship, each tends to hold a "social self-categorization" rather than an "individual self-categorization"; in other words, it is a "deindividuated" (Walther, 1996, p.18) situation. Stated another way, due to limited social cues, CMC users tend to readily categorize and generalize their electronic partners into particular social categories with preset characteristics and features, rather than try to understand the individual qualities or personalities of each participant. In addition to this group relationship, geographic and physical isolation from other CMC communicators works in a positive way to affirm these categorizations. In fact, when CMC members are connected by similar concerns, expertise, or tasks, the tendency toward social self-categorization becomes even stronger (Baym, 1995; Rheingold, 1993). With common interests and shared social spaces, which usually arise quickly among members of electronic groups, participants, nonetheless, can transcend their limited knowledge of one another and develop productive friendships (Sproull & Faraj, in press).

In terms of one's optimized self-presentation, Bell and Daly (1984) maintained that people attempt to gain affection and interest from others by selecting and deploying favorable impressions in a thin context. Because CMC participants are not influenced by social cues such as physical appearance or vocalic attributes, especially when they have not previously met, they can focus their attention on self-censorship, constructing better messages, selecting more preferable terms, and becoming more objective and self-aware (Walther, 1996).

The point here is that the information one gives about oneself is more selective and subject to self-censorship in CMC than it is in FTF interaction because only verbal and linguistic cues are available. The lack of physical cues for the CMC sender might be helpful in devoting one's cognitive activities to message construction, management, and language selection, without being interrupted by unwanted cues or multiple conversational demands. CMC receivers, in turn, might make flattering constructions from those messages when a relationship or commonality is sensed.

Many studies on the interpersonal effects of CMC can be viewed from impersonal, interpersonal, and hyperpersonal perspectives. These seemingly contrasting results, nonetheless, indicate consistently positive utilization of these technologies in educational settings: Even impersonal effects can be utilized in enhancing group coherency and efficient decision making in task-oriented situations. Furthermore, with the reduced effects of social and physical cues, CMC can promote democratic and equal participation free of power relationships, thereby focusing participants on the content and process of tasks. What is important, in the end, is not whether this technology is impersonal or interpersonal, but rather how its various interpersonal effects can be utilized for educational purposes.

A CASE STUDY ON LEARNING AND TEACHING VIA CMC

Based on the theoretical frameworks of both the sociocultural theory and Walther's matrix on the electronic interactivity of CMC, a case study of a CMC class was conducted in an introductory educational technology course during the spring of 1995. Of the 20 graduate students in this study, half were inservice teachers with diverse majors. The students in the class were composed of both those who were familiar with computer networks and those who were unfamiliar with computers, yet, were taking this course as a degree requirement. To expand student perspectives with peer tutoring, student groups were heterogeneously mixed with the experts and nonexperienced computer users.

A commercial network called "Chollian" was used for this CMC class. The structure and activities of the class provided in the Chollian-networked class are detailed in Table 13.1.

TABLE 13.1
The Structure and Activities of the CMC Class

Activities	*Purpose*
• Bulletin Board	Faculty only: post assignment, class announcement
• Learning Resources	Faculty only: post supplementary learning resources
• Assignment Submission	Students: post assignment
• Computer Conferencing	Students and faculty: topic discussion (asynchronous participation)
• Lounge	Students and faculty: lounge
• Questions and Answers	Public posting of students questions and answers
• Chat	Synchronous discussion
• Electronic Mail	Personal message exchange
• Student List and Self-Introduction	Self-introduction to classmates

As shown in Table 13.1, course assignments and class announcements were posted in an electronic bulletin board. There were also supplementary learning resources (usually lecture materials) in the CMC system, whereas students' work (both group and individual) was posted in an electronic assignment submission section. Delayed- (i.e., asynchronous) conferencing tools were employed to foster peer commenting and feedback on the work of other groups (note: Each student was instructed to evaluate the work of the other groups). A real-time (i.e., synchronous) chat tool, on the other hand, was used by the students before posting their work in the assignment submission section. Whereas E-mail was used for personal message exchange between and among the students and the teacher, the students (as well as the teacher) could also publicly post their questions and answers. In addition, this CMC class had an electronic lounge for "pure" chat, and a section where students introduced themselves to other participants.

INSTRUCTIONAL DESIGN OF THE CMC CLASS

The course combined two different modes of instruction during the semester: CMC classes every 2 weeks followed by a live class during the third week. The first two classes were devoted to orientating the class with technical guides for students who were unfamiliar with the computer-conferencing system and the ways in which the class would be conducted. Just prior to this technical orientation, the class was divided into three groups and a leader for each group was chosen who was familiar with the system. This group leader was supposed to take responsibility for assisting his or her group members with any technical problems related to the CMC class.

Once the grouping of the students was completed, a group assignment for the next week was given to the students. As part of this task, all groups were required to engage in at least one synchronous conference prior to the dissemination of their ideas. Such synchronous group discussions were expected weekly. Asynchronous conferencing support, on the other hand, was used for student reflective journals and evaluation of the work of other groups. The journal reflections were intended to help students gain professional insights about their personal experiences, whereas the peer evaluations were meant to support critical-thinking skills.

In order to trace each student's progress and participation with respect to his or her assigned tasks, each team also had to submit all the dialogue transcripts captured during their chat sessions. Although there were no tests and few lectures, nearly every week the groups were required to turn in a solution to a problem posted on the electronic bulletin board during the previous session. Assessments of student achievement in this class included all materials such as group assignments, reflective journals, chat contents, and self- and peer evaluations within and among teams.

Compared with the students who directed the specific structure and contents of the class, the instructor's role was relatively subsidiary to course operations. She posted weekly assignments on the bulletin board, regularly responded to the students' E-mail submissions and questions, checked assignments, and, if possible, provided opportunities to electronically meet and interact with experts in related fields. Using ideas from sociocultural theory and learner-centeredness, students were clearly beginning to assume ownership for learning here. Whereas the students directed the specific structure and contents of the class and facilitated collaborative learning among themselves, the role of the faculty member was relatively decentralized as coach, scaffolder, and colearner (see Table 13.2).

The live classroom sessions were primarily devoted to follow-up or complementary discussion related to the previous 2-week CMC classes, and also for consolidating interpersonal relationships among students in the class as well as with the instructor.

DATA COLLECTION AND ANALYSIS

The methods of data collection and analysis employed in this study involved qualitative techniques such as interviews, observations, and document analysis

TABLE 13.2
Instructional Strategies of CMC Class

- short and limited lecture materials
- allot time for the CMC class every day
- foster collaborative learning environments facilitating group discussion and assignment
- practice the expected roles of teacher and student
- facilitate active and effective use of the bulletin board, asynchronous computer conferencing, and synchronous chat tools

(e.g., reflective journals, dialogue transcripts captured in the real-time chat tool, and other student work). The same questionnaire was distributed twice to the students in the first and last classes of the course to examine any changes in the students' attitudes, knowledge, and skills related to CMC usage.

The "constant comparison method" (Lincoln & Guba, 1985) of analysis was used as a guide for understanding the data collected. Important to note, this approach allowed for the simultaneous collection and processing of data, the verification and reconstruction of existing theoretical notions and categories, and the combination of a variety of data collection methods in analyzing the assumptions of a model or theory.

RESULTS AND DISCUSSION

Although Walther's matrix on electronic interaction in CMC served as the theoretical basis for sorting and categorizing the data, sociocultural theory was the overarching framework for this study. Among the sociocultural ideas evident in this study were collaborative learning, cognitive apprenticeship, new roles for both teacher and student, socially negotiated problem solving, and metacognitive self-reflection.

COLLABORATIVE LEARNING AND ACCULTURATION

The individual's cognitive development and functions, according to sociocultural theory, are the result of internalization of social interaction and dialogue within one's zone of proximal development (ZPD) (Vygotsky, 1978). From an apprenticeship standpoint, it is in the community of practice wherein one becomes acculturated (Lave & Wenger, 1993). Based on these tenets of sociocultural theory, this study promoted group projects and discussion to facilitate collaborative learning environments. For instance, amid the reflective journals and surveys, one student wrote about his experiences with group projects and discussions as follows:

> At the first time when I was told that every assignment proceeded with discussion among my team members in the chat tool, I thought it would be very much troublesome and extra work. Yet, while I was in the discussion with the members, I could be exposed to different and diverse ideas and thought of others, and also realized how limited my thought was. Even though we had difficulty in reaching at consensus after that discussion via the chat tool within that time constraints and technical problems, we came to learn how to tune our thoughts within diversity and differences, hence, to build consensus, which was really exciting to observe and experience.

Entry into a community of practice was examined through the analysis of dialogue transcripts, message postings, and reflective journals with a focus on the student problem-solving processes (i.e., searching for learning resources, making interpretations, engaging in negotiations, providing rationales, and reaching conclusions). In other words, the class activities were structured to apprentice students in more expertlike ways of thinking and acting.

As Vygotsky (1978) alluded to in his notion of the ZPD (see Bonk & Cunningham, chap. 2, this volume), selecting appropriate tasks for the students is critical in the sense that these activities should be not too easy nor too hard, but challenging enough to the students' cognitive activity and development. In the first few tasks, the students, in the middle of their electronic discussion, often suggested asking for instructor help in solving their problems. Most of the time, however, they proceeded without supplementary help from their professor. The lack of direct help from the instructor, in fact, did not affect the quality and direction of their assignments. Rather, students felt proud and more knowledgeable after completing their challenging assignments by themselves. In resonating with Lave and Wenger's (1993) notion of apprenticeship, student movement from novice to journeyperson to expert in this learning community helped them increase their confidence and involvement over the semester.

ROLE CHANGES BETWEEN TEACHER AND STUDENT

Slatin (1993) reported one CMC study wherein students in his English class dominated course activities using asynchronous and synchronous conferencing tools. According to Slatin, students in these computer conferences made new connections, persisted in their interactions, and were highly responsive to their peers. In fact, in "the single best experience [he] had in 15 years of teaching" (p. 49), Slatin's students authored more than 85% of the total class messages with most of those targeting another student or the entire class, not the instructor. And these messages were extremely focused on course content. In effect, electronic communication provided the forum for transforming the learning situation from teacher-centeredness to student-centeredness.

Similar to these results, the students in the present study made several attempts to control class activities by exploring and seeking learning resources, discussing topics among team members, posting both group and individual work, and evaluating the work of other groups. During this time, the faculty member was often engaged in replying to students' E-mail messages, posting weekly assignments, regularly checking students' posted messages, and continuously observing and tracing students' participation processes within their dialogue transcripts.

In fact, as the students pointed out in their surveys, they spent more than twice (in some cases four times) the time working on tasks for this class, compared with that in a regular classroom class. This might be attributed to the fact that the students were aware that their electronic dialogues and other work would be "permanently" recorded in an electronic database that was accessible by their peers. Another motivator was that the instructor was checking all electronic messages regularly and provided timely feedback and comments.

The instructor, while thoroughly tracing the students' progress and observing the contents of their discussions, was simultaneously a colearner as she became aware of new ways to interpret the issues students were electronically discussing. For example, in discussing the first topic of this class, "Educational Paradigm at the Information Age," the students raised some important and serious issues based on real problems they had witnessed in their classes (group-based discussion, team assignment, confidence, etc.). Important to note, this rich discussion lasted for a couple of weeks. Contrary to this topic, another topic, "Instructional Systems Design Models and Its Application in Classrooms," which was expected to be important and interesting to these students, did not get much discussion. These differences illustrate how comprehensive observation of the student activities and electronic discussions can help teachers better appreciate student ideas, prior knowledge, concerns, and problem-solving approaches.

REFLECTIVE THINKING AND PRACTICE

Along with collaborative effort among students, weekly reflective writing was also essential for constructing and examining personal beliefs and experiences. During these reflections, students gain empathetic insights about their experiences and everyday practice, while fostering professional growth in the community of practice to which they belong. One of the students pointed to the assumed roles and aims of reflective journals as follows:

> Students have been used to being passive learner acquiring and memorizing given knowledge from the teacher without any critical questionings so far. In this class, however, while writing this reflective journal, I could experience and observe transparently the whole process of how my thinking (and my team's) was raised, rejected, revised, negotiated, expanded, and finally reached a certain consensus or conclusion . . . Now, I think every class or learning environments should go to this way and direction.

Similarly, another student also showed her growing professional insights about her own learning practices in her journal: "[the fact that the students have to post their works in the CMC system] made me think more deeply and seriously about my thoughts, aware of that anyone can easily access and read my comments recorded in the computer screen."

ELECTRONIC INTERACTION IN THE CMC CLASS

Impersonal Effects of the CMC Class

According to Walther (1996), the impersonal effects of CMC can be used strategically to foster group cohesion, efficient decision making, and rationality in task-oriented situations. Yet, during the early stages of this course, group cohesion and decision making were difficult because the students were confronted with both technical and psychological problems. In terms of the technology, students experienced various problems accessing the real-time chat tool, and were frequently disconnected in the midst of their electronic discussions. Psychologically, the students were challenged by their feelings of confusion while handling unknown media, intense discomfort in communicating electronically with strangers, the stresses of gathering with team members late at night, and the pressures of reaching consensus under severe time constraints. Consequently, many of the students were unable to proceed with their tasks as planned. Such difficulties were often cited in previous studies on the interpersonality of CMC (Hiltz, Johnson, & Turoff, 1986; Rice, 1984; Siegel et al., 1986).

Starting from the third CMC class, the students began to suggest diverse strategies to help proceed efficiently, enhance discussion, and build a consensus within the given time constraints. For example, in the middle of real-time computer conferencing chats, a member of a group (usually the assigned team leader) would often interrupt their discussions and ask his or her team to concentrate on task-oriented conversations (i.e., the process and content of problem-solving discussions) and avoid extended electronic social conversation.

Related to the enhancement of group work, several students in this study pointed out in their reflective journals and interviews that CMC discussions feature more equal member participation than do comparable FTF discussion, and facilitate easier access to faculty members free of power relations. Furthermore, they mentioned in their journals that: "Early difficulties we [the group members] had to confront in leading electronic discussions as planned got reduced as we could build group cohesion—in fact, we met in an Internet cafe[1] near school to get to know each other better and learn more about computer networked communication systems before we had the

[1]An "Internet cafe" in Korea refers to a store providing facilities for Internet use to customers, while offering coffee or other beverages in the cafe.

electronic discussion—and we experienced the increased problem-solving skills related to CMC (technical things and efficient decision-making)." These effects might be an inherent feature of CMC interaction because it has the ability to promote "rationality," and "democratize" communication (Kiesler, Siegel, & McGuire, 1984). Such issues of "democratic" communication and "enhanced" discussion skills are extremely novel and exciting to Korean society where hierarchical relationship between the student and the teacher are so important and strict that a culture containing information exchanges, consensus building, and negotiation of conflicts and differences seems impossible. In other words, CMC interaction in Korea should help its citizens learn how to discuss, negotiate, and communicate.

Interpersonal Effects of CMC

The impersonal effects of CMC, according to Walther (1996), may be attributed mainly to time-limited studies that did not provide students with the chance to build interpersonal and sociable relations between themselves. In this semester-long study, however, the students were always grouped with the same members. As a result, this study included two aspects, disregarded in earlier studies of CMC, that provided the necessary support for the interpersonal potential of this technology: (a) It was a longitudinal study and (b) there were expectations of long-term partnerships with other students.

In early CMC studies, it was not easy to build interpersonal relationships and consensus within the limited time periods (Hiltz et al., 1986; Rice, 1984; Siegel et al., 1986). Overall, fewer messages were exchanged, and fewer statements of consensus were achieved. Additionally, students experienced a lack of leadership and a consequential difficulty in task organization. As some participants in the case study pointed out, CMC took two to three times longer in terms of preparation for class, discussion, and consensus building. However, as their interpersonal relationships developed over time, they acknowledged improvement in group cohesiveness and conflict-handling ability, and hence, consensus building. Time, therefore, appears to be a critical variable in CMC effectiveness and use.

Related to the matter of the duration of the study, the fact that the same students could work together as a group throughout the semester indicated that they could expect long-term partnerships among themselves over the semester. In fact, the students in this study were diverse in terms of their ages, backgrounds, majors, and jobs. Yet, the reason they all were there sharing interests and concerns was sufficient enough for them to build group cohesion.

As the number of electronic communications and messages accumulated, the use of unique signs and symbols to express thoughts and feelings escalated. Somewhat surprisingly, the assignment of roles within this real-time group chat (i.e., discussant, summarizer, note poster, transcript capturer, etc.) took place naturally among the students. More important, their electronic discussion included both task-oriented and socially oriented or casual exchanges, thereby endorsing the interpersonal and social effects of CMC.

This class seemed to facilitate similar interpersonal relationships as found in FTF communication. As many studies on CMC point out, these electronic communicators tended to build a "feeling of closeness," which was attributed not only to their social status, age, or gender, but rather to their shared concerns, interests, and electronic struggles.

Hyperpersonal Effects of CMC

Whereas the aforementioned interpersonal effects of CMC were extremely obvious and distinctive in this study, several hyperpersonal effects of this technology, as Walther (1996) insisted, could also be noticed here. The aspect of optimized self-presentation, which maintains the tendency to select and deploy favorable impressions free from physical appearance and voice attributes, was supported in this study when the participants attempted to use more formal and polite terms and expressions in their electronic discussions in both asynchronous and synchronous computer conferencing. For example, in synchronous conferencing, their discussions proceeded in systematic and organized ways. It was obvious that the students prepared their messages in advance so that they could develop their discussions more effectively within the course time constraints. At the same time, these students realized that all their dialogue transcripts were being evaluated by their instructor, thereby increasing the possibility for self-censorship.

In fact, in participant interviews and surveys, students commonly pointed out that the CMC class required two to four times more preparation time than did the regular classroom class. This may be partly attributed to the fact that all their dialogues would be recorded in the computer-conferencing system, and hence, anyone, including the faculty member, could read the transcripts. As a result of more time for message construction and less stress of ongoing interaction, the students may have selected and transmitted preferable cues and content while engaging in more objective self-reflection during their electronic discussions.

On the other hand, the aspect of idealized perception of the message sender by the receiver was sensed in the asynchronous computer conferencing among the students in which the students were supposed to post their individual comments as well as an evaluation of another groups' work. Interestingly, their overall comments and evaluations were extremely favorable rather than critical. Even when the students encountered different ideas from students outside of their groups, they did not perceive them as wrong. Instead, they viewed these instances as opportunities to learn about other viewpoints and ask for further explanation and elaboration from team members. This kind of favorable or flattering attitude in evaluating peer work and ideas directly corresponds to the notion of idealized perception of others' messages.

An informal party held by the students after the class ended also illustrated this hyperpersonal behavior. Students at this party were eager to discuss their experiences and thoughts related to the interpersonal effects of the CMC class. They mentioned, for example, "how exciting [it was] to get to know each other intensely within that short period of time among people whose majors and backgrounds were so different from each other." Many noted they would recommend or take similar courses in the future. Thus, the CMC class, unlike what people vaguely suspect about the impersonality and mechanical qualities of such classes, provided opportunities to build the interpersonal interactions typically expected in a traditional classroom as well as hyperpersonal instances rarely witnessed.

Though any CMC class can be depersonalized and mechanical in some senses, it is important to note how this technology can be utilized for emerging educational purposes. The impersonal effects of CMC shown in initial studies can be rather strategically used to foster group cohesion, efficient decision making, rationality, and democratic practice in education (i.e., equal participation). Nevertheless, numerous interpersonal and even hyperpersonal effects of CMC here supported the SIDE theory notions of involving idealized perception and optimized self-presentation in designing CMC classes.

Table 13.3 succinctly summarizes the findings of this study using Walther's (1996) CMC matrix.

CHALLENGES TO THE CMC CLASS

This study provides "concrete" support for the sociotechnical nature of CMC as advocated by Walther and also presents a palette of instructional design strategies for CMC classes. This support does not mean that there were no challenges and unresolved issues, however. First, there were numerous technical problems that the students frequently pointed out. For example, it took time for students to access the synchronous chat tool for electronic class discussion, and when they were online, their electronic discussions were frequently disconnected in midstream. Second, these students had to pay a fee to use this commercial CMC system. Such time and money, moreover, were spent to use systems that were still somewhat primitive compared to collaborative tools found in other countries (Bonk et al., 1994).

Another key challenge that emerged during this study was the lack of student preparation for CMC classes. Half of the students lacked confidence in their work because of minimal technology experience. In contrast, the students who were familiar with the CMC system expressed confidence and personal interests here, while displaying leadership in their teams. Not surprisingly, the overall grades of the expert users in this course were better

TABLE 13.3
The Findings of This Study Using Walther's Matrix

	Impersonal	*Interpersonal*	*Hyperpersonal*
Conclusions	• reduced interpersonal affect • depersonalized • inhibited • task oriented	• social relationships as much as FTF	• more socially desirable • personal & relational optimization
Reasons	• cues-filtered-out approach • reduced social cues • increased anonymity • short-term studies	• social information-processing perspectives • longitudinal study • anticipation for future interaction • adaptation to the linguistic code	• social identity deindividuation • reduced social cue • the receiver: idealized perception • the sender: optimized self-presentation
Strategic Use	• enhanced group work • promoted rationality • focus on the content & process • brainstorming • equal participation • fair criticism	• more time and amount of message exchange • leadership emergence • role assignments	• objective self-awareness • more reflection • increased cognitive resources to message construction • message management & coordination, and language selection
Findings From This Study	• focused attention on the problem-solving process & discussion • hard to reach consensus at the early stages	• creations of signs or linguistic codes to express feelings & emotions • easily building consensus	• refined, reflective, & thoughtful message content

than those of the less experienced students. However, it remains unclear whether their good grades were directly attributable to their confidence about this course, familiarity with the CMC system, effort, or other knowledge and expertise. Fortunately, most fears displayed in the early stages of this course were reduced over the semester. Many students in this class, in fact, were extremely satisfied with this experience and were proud of themselves as "pioneers leading the information age."

Still another challenge that the CMC class had to consider was that the students in this class tended to be concerned more with the class as technology-mediated, rather than with the introductory educational technology course content. In fact, the students' reflective journals were dominated by their comments and thoughts about the strengths and weaknesses of electronic conferencing. Finally, the additional time required by students to prepare for discussion, conduct assignments, and write down one's ideas is also a problem with CMC and a barrier to CMC course success. Although such challenges should not be disregarded, additional support from the Korean government and the business sector should help resolve some of them.

CMC AS AN ALTERNATIVE EDUCATIONAL MODE IN THE INFORMATION AGE

As gradual changes of the industrial age give way to more radical and holistic ones in the information age, there is an associated shift in teaching and learning via media from reactivity (e.g., print, slide, overhead projector, cassette tape, radio, TV) to interactivity (e.g., programmed instruction, computer-assisted instruction, interactive video, video-teleconferencing systems) to proactivity (e.g., hypermedia, World Wide Web, computer conferencing) (Bates, 1995). Whereas reactive media were welcomed in educational settings represented by a banking metaphor, the interactive paradigm appeared late in the industrial age wherein individualized learning was popular. Currently, the proactive paradigm seems to be appropriate for the information age where active learners, critical thinking, and collaborative modes of learning are more valued. This shift and adaptation toward the proactive paradigm is supported by sociocultural theory and the learner-centered movement, on the one hand, and advances in information and communication technologies for online education, on the other.

Studies such as this one indicate that online educational activities are well suited for graduate-level education, reporting higher satisfaction and higher levels of critical thinking and problem solving with online courses than with traditional classes (Kearsley, Lynch, & Wizer, 1995). Also, as proved in this particular study, instructors can now electronically track student progress in a detailed way and better understand what students are learning as well as what they are struggling with. Finally, online educational environments can become a concrete way of entering the open education movement in Korea. Now there are increased opportunities for student choice in terms of courses and professors as well as unique possibilities for students to communicate with other educational professionals and experts during these courses.

CONCLUDING REMARKS

In this study of electronic collaboration and dialogue, CMC turned out to be an appropriate alternative for student learning. The data collected supported Walther's (1996) three-level matrix of electronic interaction by showing that CMC environments provided more chances for increasing collaboration and social interaction among and between the teacher and students. By using this electronic evaluation scheme, common viewpoints on CMC as impersonal have been retorted. Students expressed a "feeling of closeness" that was attributed to shared concerns and experiences. In addition, CMC lowered the stress of social interaction by affording participants greater opportunity to self-censor comments and be selective in language use. Many comments and messages by students in the CMC class also contained instances of close (i.e., hyperpersonal) relationships and intersubjectivity that had developed with each other during the semester.

CMC is a new instructional approach that endorses both task-oriented and socially oriented exchanges without the limitation of time and geographical location. Equally important, CMC uses learner-centered educational environments in a concrete and feasible form, thereby increasing the possibility and potential of actualizing educational paradigms required in the information age as well as the open educational practices advocated in Korea today. Though caution is needed regarding both student and teacher resistance to this new teaching and learning technology, it is vitally important to consider how CMC can be utilized for educational purposes. Although the technical nature of CMC as a distribution system has been heavily discussed in the literature for a couple of decades, it is finally time to discuss the practical kinds of information and interactions that can be fostered and disseminated through such a system.

A key accomplishment here was the merging of a number of CMC tools in one teaching situation. Using a mix of electronic conferencing tools, this study presents a palette of instructional design possibilities for CMC classes. These instructional considerations relate to proper task structuring, group interaction, teacher scaffolding, student training, fostering of multiple perspectives, expert mentorship, and institutional support. Not only is this study unique in simultaneously exploring both synchronous and asynchronous tools as well as live and electronic learning, this may be the first educational study in Korea based on a sociocultural perspective.

This study illustrates that it is not important whether CMC is impersonal or not, but, rather, how to utilize CMC for the purpose of learner-centered educational environments. Clearly, CMC is an instructional approach that endorses both task-oriented and socially oriented exchanges without the limitations of time and geographic location. By fostering collaborative learning, student negotiation of meaning, and significant teacher scaffolding, CMC may be an ideal instructional approach for applying sociocultural theory within technology-enhanced educational settings, thereby moving Korea into the global learning community of the 21st century.

ACKNOWLEDGMENTS

I want to thank Curt Bonk for his apprenticeship into the sociocultural field back when I was a doctoral student at Indiana University as well as his help with this particular manuscript. Not only did he provide timely guidance, extensive feedback, and consistent encouragement on this manuscript, but he spent endless hours personally revising significant portions of it to expedite production efforts. In addition to being an excellent mentor, he has become a wonderful colleague and friend as well.

REFERENCES

American Psychological Association. (1993). *Learner centered psychological principles: Guidelines for school redesign and reform*. Washington, DC: Author and the Mid-continent Regional Educational Laboratory.

Banathy, B. (1991). *Systems design of education: A journey to create the future*. Englewood Cliffs, NJ: Educational Technology Publications.

Bates, A. (1995). *Technology, open learning, and distance education*. New York: Routledge.

Baym, N. (1995). The emergence of community in computer-mediated interaction. In S. Jones (Ed.), *Cybersociety: Computer-mediated communication and community* (pp. 138–163). Thousand Oaks, CA: Sage.

Bell, R., & Daly, J. (1984). The affinity-seeking function of communication. *Communication Monographs, 51*, 91–115.

Bonk, C., Hay, K., & Fischler, R. (1996). Five key resources for an electronic community of elementary student weather forecasters. *Journal of Computing in Childhood Education, 7*(1/2), 93–118.

Bonk, C., & Kim, K. A. (1998). Extending sociocultural theory to adult learning. In M. C. Smith & T. Pourcot (Eds.), *Adult learning and development: Perspectives from educational psychology*. Mahwah, NJ: Lawrence Erlbaum Associates.

Bonk, C., & King, K. (1995). Computer conferencing and collaborative writing tools: Starting a dialogue about student dialogue. In *CSCL '95: The first international conference on computer support for collaborative learning* (pp. 22–26). Mahwah, NJ: Lawrence Erlbaum Associates.

Bonk, C., Medury, P., & Reynolds, T. (1994). Cooperative hypermedia: The marriage of collaborative writing and mediated environments. *Computers in the Schools, 10*(1/2), 79–124.

Clark, R., & Sugrue, B. (1991). Research on instructional media, 1978–1988. In G. Anglin (Ed.), *Instructional technology: Past, present and the future* (pp. 327–347). Englewood, CO: Libraries Unlimited, Inc.

Clift, R., Houston, R., & McCarthy, J. (1992). Getting it RITE: A case of negotiated curriculum in teacher preparation at the University of Houston. In L. Valli (Ed.), *Reflective teacher education: Cases and critiques* (pp. 116–138). Albany: State University of New York Press.

Dubrovsky, V. (1985). Real-time computer conferencing versus electronic mail. In *Proceedings of the Human Factors Society* (Vol. 29, pp. 380–384). Santa Monica, CA: Human Factors Society.

Duffy, T. M., & Jonassen, D. H. (1991). New implications for instructional technology. *Instructional Technology, 31*(5), 7–12.

Garton, L., & Wellman, B. (1995). Social impacts of electronic mail in organizations: A review of the research literature. In B. Burleson (Ed.), *Communication yearbook, 18* (pp. 434–453). Thousand Oaks, CA: Sage.

Hammer, M., & Champy, J. (1993). *Reengineering the corporation*. New York: HarperCollins.

Harasim, L. (1994). *Global networks: Computers and international communication*. Cambridge, MA: MIT Press.

Hiltz, S., Johnson, K., & Angle, G. (1978). *Replicating Bales' problem solving experiments on a computerized conference: A pilot study* (Research Rep. No. 8). Newark: New Jersey Institute of Technology, Computerized Conferencing and Communications Center.

Hiltz, S., Johnson, K., & Turoff, M. (1986). Experiments in group decision making: Communication process and outcome in face-to-face versus computerized conferences. *Human Communication Research*, *13*, 225–252.

Hiltz, S., & Turoff, M. (1978). *The network nation*. Reading, MA: Addison-Wesley.

Kearsley, G., Lynch, W., & Wizer, D. (1995). The effectiveness and impact of online learning in graduate education. *Educational Technology*, *35*(6), 37–42.

Kiesler, S., Siegel, J., McGuire, T. (1984). Social psychological aspects of computer-mediated communication. *American Psychologist*, *39*, 1123–1134.

Kuhn, T. S. (1962). *The structure of scientific revolutions*. Chicago: University of Chicago Press.

Lave, J., & Wenger, E. (1993). *Situated learning: Legitimate peripheral participation*. New York: Cambridge University Press.

Lea, M., & Spears, R. (1991). Computer-mediated communication, de-individuation and group decision making. *International Journal of Man-Machine Studies*, *34*, 283–301.

Lea, M., & Spears, R. (1992). Paralanguage and social perception in computer-mediated communication. *Journal of Organizational Computing*, *2*, 321–341.

Lincoln, Y. S., & Guba, E. G. (1985). *Naturalistic inquiry*. Beverly Hills, CA: Sage.

Reigeluth, C. (1994). Introduction: The imperative for systemic chance. In C. Reigeluth & R. Garfinkle (Eds.), *Systemic chance in education* (pp. 3–11). Englewood Cliffs, NJ: Educational Technology Publications.

Resnick, L. B. (1989). Introduction. In L. B. Resnick (Ed.), *Knowing, learning, and instruction: Essays in honor of Robert Glaser* (pp. 1–24). Hillsdale, NJ: Lawrence Erlbaum Associates.

Rheingold, H. (1993). *The virtual community: Homesteading on the electronic frontier*. Reading, MA: Addison-Wesley.

Rice, R. (Ed.). (1984). *The new media: Communication, research, and technology*. Beverly Hills, CA: Sage.

Rice, R., & Love, G. (1987). Electronic emotion: Socioemotional content in a computer-mediated network. *Communication Research*, *14*, 85–108.

Rice, R., & Shook, D. (1990). Relationships of job categories and organizational levels to use of communication channels, including electronic mail: A meta-analysis and extension. *Journal of Management Studies*, *27*, 195–229.

Rogoff, B. (1990). *Apprenticeship in thinking: Cognitive development in social context*. New York: Oxford University Press.

Ross, D. (1989). First steps in developing a reflective approach. *Journal of Teacher Education*, *40*(2), 22–30.

Schon, D. (1987). *Educating the reflective practitioner*. San Francisco: Jossey-Bass.

Senge, P., Roberts, C., Ross, R., Smith, B., & Kleiner, A. (1994). *The fifth discipline fieldbook: Strategies and tools for building a learning organization*. London: Nicholas Brealey Publishing.

Siegel, J., Dubrovsky, V., Kiesler, S., & McGuire, T. (1986). Group processes in computer-mediated communication. *Organizational Behavior and Human Decision Processes*, *37*, 157–187.

Slatin, J. M. (1993). Is there a class in this text? Creating knowledge in an electronic classroom. In E. Barrett (Ed.), *Sociomedia: Multimedia, hypermedia, and the social construction of knowledge* (pp. 27–51). Cambridge, MA: MIT Press.

Smolensky, M., Carmody, M., & Halcomb, C. (1990). The influence of task type, group structure and extroversion on uninhibited speech in computer-mediated communication. *Computers in Human Behavior*, *6*, 261–272.

Sproull, L., & Faraj, S. (in press). Atheism, sex, and databases: The Net as a social technology. In B. Kahin & J. Keller (Eds.), *Public access to the Internet*. Cambridge, MA: MIT Press.

Tudge, J., & Rogoff, B. (1989). Peer influences on cognitive development: Piagetian and Vygotskian perspectives. In M. Bornstein & J. Bruner (Eds.), *Interaction in human development* (pp. 17–40). Hillsdale. NJ: Lawrence Erlbaum Associates.

Vygotsky, L. (1978). *Mind in society: The development of higher psychological processes.* Cambridge, MA: Harvard University Press.

Wagner, E., & McCombs, B. (1995). Learner centered psychological principles in practice: Designs for distance education. *Educational Technology*, *35*(2), 32–35.

Walther, J. (1992). A longitudinal experiment on relational tone in computer-mediated and face to face interaction. *Proceedings of the Hawaii International Conference on System Sciences*, *4*, 220–231.

Walther, J. (1994). Anticipated ongoing interaction versus channel effects on relational communication in computer-mediated interaction. *Human Communication Research*, *40*, 473–501.

Walther, J. (1996). Computer-mediated communication: Impersonal, interpersonal, and hyperpersonal interaction. *Communication Research*, *23*(1), 3–43.

V

LOOKING BACK AND GLANCING AHEAD

14

▼▼▼▼▼▼▼▼▼

Adventure Learning as a Vision of the Digital Learning Environment

Martin A. Siegel
Sonny E. Kirkley
Indiana University

> Now and then one foot falls through a soft spot as we maneuver over a low ridge formed last fall and covered with hard-packed snow until this week's thaw. After some tugging, huffing and puffing and straining against our harnesses, we manage to "lurch" the canoe over the top. Thud! The bow of the canoe hits the hard smooth ice on the other side. We take a few trotting steps to regain our balance, then lean into the harnesses when the canoe bogs down again in soft snow. Sometimes we "march" fast and smoothly across flat pans of ice, and our boots and ski poles sound like soldiers or horses' hooves if we're not in step. Occasionally, we find open leads, so we have to jump across. I think everybody likes the challenge of jumping across even a small part of the Arctic Ocean!

During the spring 1995 expedition, Arctic explorer Will Steger communicated this message to thousands of students across the globe. His polar adventure inspired multidisciplinary, multiple perspective, problem-based classroom study. Internet and satellite-based communications supported this study, connecting clusters of learning communities to each other, the explorers, and the subject matter experts. Some of the learning communities developed adventures of their own, and in time, the work of these learning communities overshadowed the importance and focus of Steger's original catalytic event. For the students, the adventure became local and personal.

Since 1991, the Center for Excellence in Education (CEE) at Indiana University has participated in the creation of three independent projects

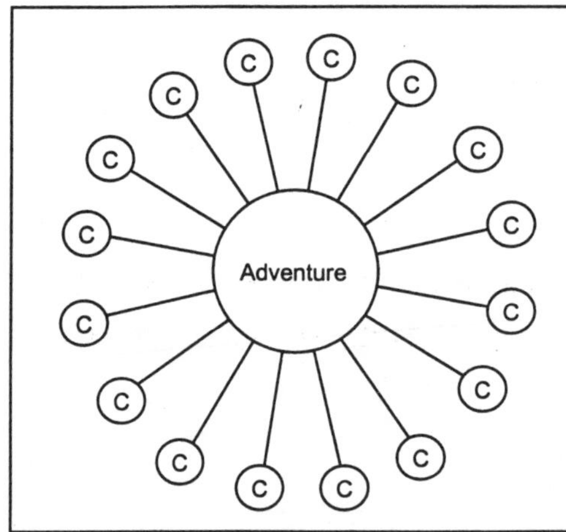

FIG. 14.1. An inspiring adventure for multiple classrooms.

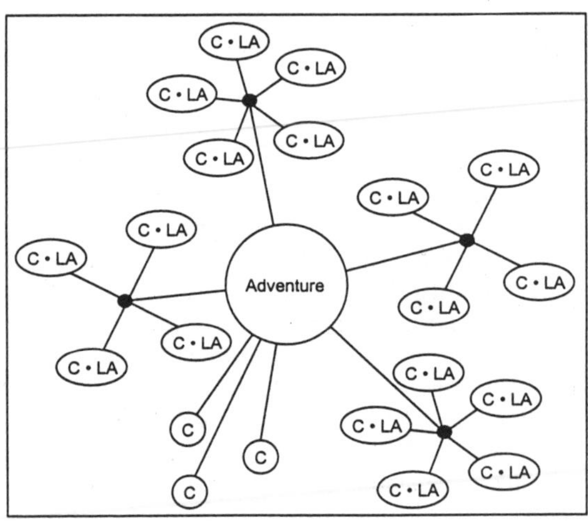

FIG. 14.2. Learning circles tied to common themes.

ized around the theme of adventure learning.[1] Figures 14.1 and 14.2 show how an idealized adventure-learning configuration evolves. In Fig. 14.1, the original adventure is the catalytic event. Electronic communications allow a myriad of classrooms (C) to track the adventure. In Fig. 14.2, as classrooms gain experience with adventure learning, they create local adventures (LA). Classrooms with similar subthemes form learning communities, again linked

[1]This should not be confused with "adventure education" and outward bound programs that have students learn in wilderness and backcountry settings, and that involve physically active activities. For more information on these programs, see Hattie, Marsh, Neill, and Richards (1997).

again linked through electronic communications. Over time, these learning communities obtain the participation of external experts and the interest in the local adventures dominate the students' time and interest.

This chapter describes each of the CEE's adventure-learning projects and then shows how they contribute to a learner-centered vision we call the *digital learning environment* (DLE). Finally, we speculate on some future forms of adventure learning that take advantage of emerging technologies and represent the highest level of interactions—real-time multimedia and hypermedia collaboration (see Bonk & King, chap. 1, this volume).

WORLD SCHOOL FOR ADVENTURE LEARNING

Program Overview

The World School for Adventure Learning (WSAL) found its origins in the International Arctic Project (IAP), an environmental education program that began in 1992 and culminated in an international dog sled and canoe expedition across the Arctic Ocean from Siberia to the North Pole to Alaska. In 1995, students from 17 countries followed the spring training missions of the IAP, via telecommunications, and when the expedition team reached the North Pole, thousands of children followed their footsteps and, even better, took adventurous footsteps of their own (for program and learning evaluations, see Sugar & Bonk, chap. 6, this volume).

Explorer, teacher, and author Will Steger conceived of the IAP after the successful 1990 Trans-Antarctica Expedition. Several million students, worldwide, followed the expedition by computer telecommunications or through a variety of print material, almost all impromptu. Students' excitement about Trans-Antarctica helped build public support for the addition of an environmental protocol to the 1959 Antarctica Treaty. In all, the success of the expedition provided the vision for a deliberate environmental education program and an accompanying multimedia network that tied school-based studies to inspiring, global events.

The Trans-Antarctica education program was responsible for a new genre of distance learning, called adventure learning or expedition learning, whereby students take "electronic field trips" with explorers and field researchers. But unlike similar adventure-learning examples that focus solely on an event, the IAP recognized that the true adventurers are the students it attracts.

The CEE inherited the organization that produced the education programs for the Trans-Antarctica Expedition. In cooperation with the University of St. Thomas, Hamline University, and the University of Michigan, the IAP and the CEE created what became known as the WSAL. Its purpose was to engage students, Grades 4–12 worldwide, in an adventurous study of the global environment.[2]

The primary components of the WSAL included:

- Expedition/adventure as the impetus for all other aspects of the program.
- Daily expedition communications including satellite positioning, scientific observations, personal journals from the explorers, and response to student-directed questions (selected through IAP headquarters in St. Paul, MN).
- Teacher-developed, school-based projects and study circles (coordinated exercises, activities, experiments, compositions, and communications) that emphasized multidisciplinary learning, comparative studies, and interschool cooperation. An international design team of teachers established and coordinated these activities and plans. Though this team gathered once a year in Bloomington, IN, or St. Paul, MN, throughout the year they communicated via listserv technology.
- Interactive communications with expedition teams and with faculty of host universities and environmental centers.
- Three increasing levels of school participation—the global common study, the World Forum, and the study circles.

Global Common Study. There was a common area of global investigation with a new study theme provided each year. The 1994 theme, for example, focused on the spring migration throughout the North American continent, culminating in the Mackenzie Watershed where the IAP conducted its third training expedition. Each common study included teacher and student resource materials, online discussion of the study themes, and access to daily expedition communications.

World Forum. Sponsored by the Interactive Communications and Simulations group at the University of Michigan, students role played highly diverse groups of distinguished world figures—authors, politicians, religious leaders, scientists, and so forth—articulating views and opinions on a set of environmental issues relating to the IAP and from the point of view of the figure the student portrayed. A final phase of simulation allowed the students to express their own views and opinions. The forum was conducted using electronic mail (E-mail) and listserv communications and included university

---

[2]The authors wish to acknowledge the contributions of others to these adventure-learning projects. David Duffee was the principal architect of the WSAL's philosophy and design. The WonderLab Online Project team includes Julie Moore, Shana Weber, Chris Borland, Christine Mathews, and Jennifer Borse.

mentors to model appropriate levels of practice (see Sugar & Bonk, chap. 6, this volume).

Study Circles. Each study circle (students, teachers, advisors, and explorers) was connected by listserv technology. Themes included waterway ecosystems, wildlife migration and habitat protection, land reclamation, transboundary pollution, and beliefs about environmental protection, particularly among the native peoples of the Circumpolar Region. The schools that participated in the comprehensive problem-based program were also enrolled in the global common study and, of course, the expedition communications mentioned earlier.

Example of Program Implementation

In one example of full program implementation, sixth-grade students at a middle school in Wisconsin worked to recover a lake near the school property, reclaiming it chemically and biologically from a century of agricultural run-off. The WSAL sponsored the design of the project as students enlisted city leaders, community groups, and government and university advisors to build a wildlife preserve at one end of the lake—a preserve that successive sixth-graders now maintain.

The WSAL connected these sixth-graders to students elsewhere in the Upper Midwest, in Missouri and South Carolina, in Khabarovsk, Russia, and in Inuvik and Igloolik in the Arctic Northwest Territories; all conducted similar waterway studies. This study circle on waterways was one of many in the program. All of the study circles were guided by persons from the Arctic—researchers, scientists, scholars, artists, writers, and others—who also conducted professional work similar to the students. These experts were linked electronically (principally through E-mail and listserv technologies) to help students stretch what they learned locally to a region of the world particularly sensitive to global environmental change.

To show how their lives affect the Arctic, students were finally connected to the IAP expedition team through interactive satellite and Internet communications. The expedition team acted as another school in each of the study circles—reporting on water quality in the Arctic, land use issues, wildlife migration, and the beliefs of native peoples.

During both the 1994 training expedition and on the last leg of the final ocean crossing in 1995, the team members crossed the Beaufort Sea during the spring breakup of the winter's ice. To provide a global context for that time and place, all schools joined a global common study with a network of scientists, scholars, and volunteers to monitor the coming of spring to midcontinent America. For example, as spring moved northward, students were linked to university researchers using satellite tracking devices to moni-

FIG. 14.3. The exploration team at the North Pole. Photograph by Gordon Wiltsie. Reprinted with permission.

tor the migration of wildlife into the barrens and out on the sea ice of the High Arctic.

Figure 14.3 is a picture taken of the exploration team at the North Pole. Will Steger, standing in the middle, and his fellow explorers are displaying Indiana University's flag.

Example Interactions

The following are sample communications from the expedition team on their final 1995 journey across the Arctic Ocean:

DAY: 111, 1:40 Z, April 21, 1995
Position: 89 degrees 56 minutes N, 145 degrees 18 minutes E
Temperature: –20 to –25 C
Weather: partly cloudy
Wind speed: 3–6 meters per second
Wind direction: SE
Barometric pressure: 1020–1025
Percentage of multi-year ice: 90
Width of leads: less than 1 meter
Snow cover: 10–20 centimeters
Height of pressure ridges: 2–3 meters
Drift of team: 11.5 kilometers NW during a 24 hour period

Today we relished an easier day of travel, with smooth ice most of the day. We continue to see sun dogs, and today saw a condition called "diamond dust." It was a beautiful, sunny day and we are energized by the challenge of reaching the North Pole. The schedule switch we tried yesterday worked pretty well, but we were all yawning by 4:30 PM!

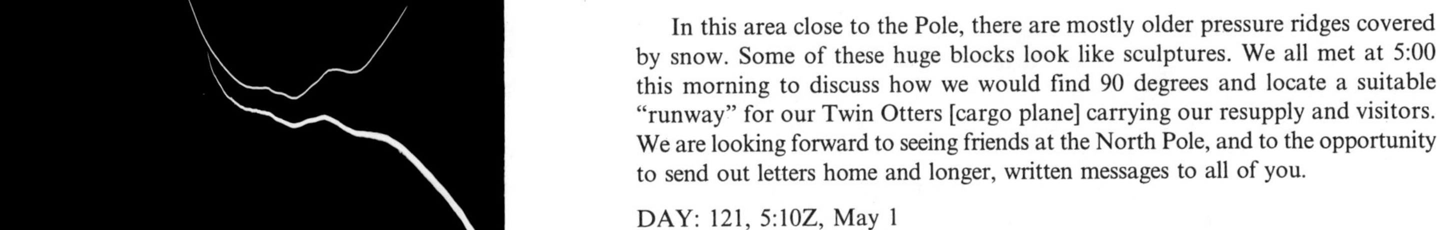

In this area close to the Pole, there are mostly older pressure ridges covered by snow. Some of these huge blocks look like sculptures. We all met at 5:00 this morning to discuss how we would find 90 degrees and locate a suitable "runway" for our Twin Otters [cargo plane] carrying our resupply and visitors. We are looking forward to seeing friends at the North Pole, and to the opportunity to send out letters home and longer, written messages to all of you.

DAY: 121, 5:10Z, May 1
Position: 89 degrees 12 minutes N, 71 degrees 11 minutes W
Temperature: –15 to –20 C
Weather: whiteout
Wind speed: 3–6 meters per second
Wind direction: NE
Barometric pressure: 1010–1015
Percentage of multi-year ice: 90
Width of leads: 100–200 meters!
Depth of snow coverage: 30–40 centimeters
Height of pressure ridges: 3–4 meters
Drift of team during the night: 1.9 km SW

Due to the whiteout conditions, navigation today was very difficult! The black open water seemed to cause a cloud to form a ring around us. We found it necessary to travel east for almost an hour in order to avoid a large open lead. Our general bearing is southwest. Right before dinner, as we were setting up camp, the same lead changed rapidly and opened from 20 meters to 100 meters! The ice around it is blue and green striped colors and is in many chunks.

May 1 message from Will Steger to teachers: On Earth Day we made history at the North Pole. For the first time, we were able to send out, via satellite, detailed descriptions of our surroundings and how we felt. We even were able to send a photograph! In return, we received information from the outside as well. The ability to interact with students around the world from the confines of my tent in the polar regions was a personal dream come true. . . . As teachers and educators, we are no longer isolated. Telecommunications and computers are revolutionizing the way we communicate and teach. And what a fantastic tool these are for increasing awareness of the world around us. They have the ability to bring awe into the classroom. The greatest gift you can give children is to provide them with sparks of inspiration that give them direction and may be remembered the rest of their lives. To follow dreams means to tap into what is "you" and, if we as educators can shepherd this process, we can foster life-long processes in the individual . . .

The learning experience is a pleasure. It is comforting, hopeful and durable. Discovery of oneself is true and lasting joy. It doesn't fluctuate with luck or outside influences—it is permanent learning. If you inspire a child, it is forever. If we can now organize through the catalyst of telecommunications, it is possible to show or "spark" the awareness of the whole. This is the heart of environmental education.

Greetings from Will Steger and the IAP team on the Arctic Ocean!

Steger's message exemplifies the inspiring catalytic nature of adventure learning. It is difficult to imagine any teacher unmoved by these words. The challenge for teachers, of course, is to make these words personal, to guide their students in the creation of local adventures, and to use the Steger adventure as a metaphor for learning.

The following is a sample communication that occurred during one study circle focused on water quality. It is from an elementary school in British Columbia:

> Look what we've done!
>
> Our experiment was to give one plant every week ¼ cup of water, a second plant ¼ cup water and a teaspoon of vinegar, a third plant ¼ cup of water and a teaspoon of salt. We started April 4/95. The next day we found our salt plant practically dead. After we made our drastic discovery Mrs. Couch bought us 2 new plants. We decided to give one plant ½ a teaspoon of salt and ¼ cup of water, the other plant we gave ¼ cup salt and ¼ cup water.
>
> Twice a week we took pictures of each plant. Every time our group meets we predict, water and observe our plants.
>
> Our Conclusions
>
> We found out that too much salt is bad for living things. Acid rain didn't effect the plant at first but after about a week it started to droop. The plant that only had fresh water is green and healthy. Fresh water evaporates more than salt water for we had to supply water more often than the other plants. Therefore salt water and acid rain are bad for all living things.

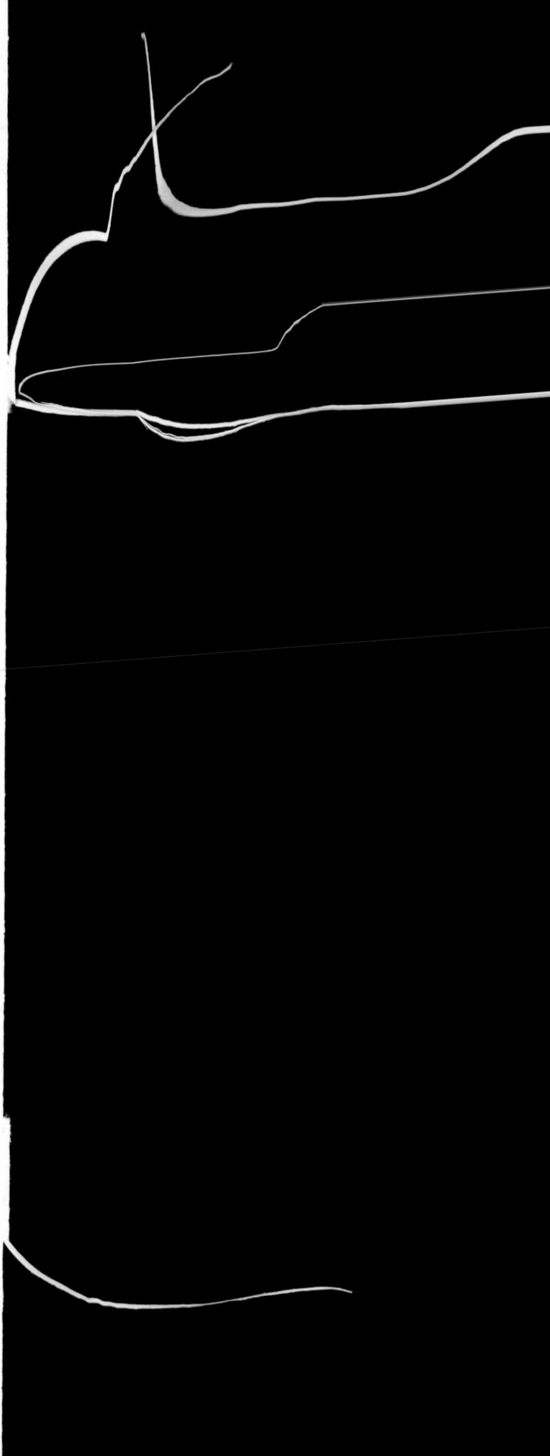

It is clear that this study circle moved beyond the personalities and exploits of the Arctic explorers. Nevertheless, the Arctic still functions as a catalyst for scientific exploration of local issues that parallel Arctic concerns, namely acid rain. Other examples were evident in the study circles. For example, one class investigated the cultural impact of their local river—in much the same way that the Arctic region reflects Inuvik tradition.

The following is a sample communication that occurred among the international design team of teachers:

> Thanks for the words of encouragement!
>
> . . . I was also wondering if our "yellow book" from last summer is current with e-mail addresses. It might be a good idea for all of us to take a look and post changes here. Also, I THINK I know which project circles are going to continue on with a life of their own, but am not absolutely sure. The following are the ones I thought were going on. Is this correct?:
>
> - Water Fit to Drink—Justin
> - Poison From Above—Becky—plus you are doing other things too, including involvement in the wolves—what else are you doing?
> - River Connection—Greg and Paula?—I wasn't sure about this one

[remainder of list deleted]

Do any of you object to my giving your e-mail addresses to interested teachers who may want to join your circles? By the way—please DO give mine to anyone interested in joining the wolf study. My group was very active, but very small. Several classes who were supposed to be active participants just "lurked." This year should be better than ever. We hope to have Becky's advanced biology students doing research at the Ely Center and then mentoring the younger students on-line. I have two biology teachers at the high school level here who want to be involved this year, so it could be very interesting. One of those teachers lived with and studied the wolves on the Upper Peninsula, so he is very much an "expert" and can act as such on-line.

Throughout the program, these teachers "met" on a daily basis planning all aspects of the WSAL. With little guidance from project staff, these teachers designed the scope and sequence of the adventure-learning curriculum, a unique example of teacher self-empowerment.

Three fundamental conclusions emerged from these student to student, teacher to student, student to teacher, and teacher to teacher communications, namely:

1. *Successful communications require structure.* Simply grouping people with no particular purpose or direction is a recipe for failure. Participants need to understand clearly why they are joining a study circle, what is expected of their participation, and what procedures will be followed. Communications to and from the expedition team must follow a fixed format so that participants can easily track that part of the communication that is of interest to them. And conversation among teachers must be on-task and directed toward some goal or participation wanes.

2. *Successful communications require leadership.* Within a communications study circle or teacher dialogue, a leader must be appointed or must emerge. This person undertakes the responsibility for ensuring ongoing discussion and direction.

3. *Successful communications transform the traditional roles of teachers and students.* Teachers function less like lecturers and more like advisors and tutors. Students function less like memorizers and more like problem solvers and cooperative learners; they take increasing responsibility for their own learning.

Program Design Trade-Offs

The WSAL had two goals: (a) to create a permanent international telecommunications network of schools for the purpose of ongoing, interactive environmental studies, and (b) to create a program model that can be replicated for a variety of adventure projects, supporting students as active inquirers and vital contributors to their home communities and to the world community. In both goals, the program fell short and ultimately ended.

There were two primary reasons why the WSAL ended. First, there was a lack of continued funding. Adventure learning, particularly on an international scale, is expensive and requires significant financial backing. In the case of the WSAL, both the expedition and the educational program required funding, and attempts to create a self-supporting nonprofit organization through the sponsoring universities were unsuccessful. Second, conflict of goals arose between the WSAL-sponsoring institutions and the expedition team's sponsors. Commercial sponsors for the expedition wanted to promote the team of explorers; associating explorer names with company merchandise sells products. In contrast, university sponsors of the WSAL wanted to emphasize teacher and student adventures. This fundamental conflict of commercial and educational goals was never fully resolved during the course of the project.

Nevertheless, the WSAL was successful in several ways. First, the WSAL demonstrated the power of adventure learning as a viable learner-centered model of instruction, providing the first examples of student collaborative communications around an adventure theme. Second, the WSAL laid the foundation for other adventure-learning projects, including the one described later, Turner Adventure Learning. Third, the WSAL empowered the middle school and high school teachers that participated on the international design team. Most WSAL teachers became leader/advocates of problem-centered learning in their districts. Some of these teachers became leaders in new national efforts for adventure learning. All of the teachers reported that the WSAL transformed their personal and professional lives, as in the following example:

> Our involvement in this project brought a new lease on life to us, a new lease on how we look at educating children. It has given us a chance to meet such wonderful people, to share with educators who have the most tremendous ideas! This project provided the impetus to change the way we teach, the way we look at the world, and the way we involve kids in learning. (Jan Wee, Teacher, West Salem, Wisconsin)

Although the WSAL formally ended at the conclusion of the cross–Arctic Ocean expedition in 1995, the international design team continues to communicate on a daily basis by way of the group's listserv, sharing their ongoing professional and personal adventures. Aspects of the WSAL continue in the Journey North program (see the Web site <http://www.learner.org/jnorth/>).

TURNER ADVENTURE LEARNING

Program Overview

On May 18, 1994, Turner Educational Services, Inc. in collaboration with the CEE launched a new commercial product for schools, Turner Adventure Learning (TAL). TAL was a series of electronic field trips with the following characteristics:

- Three consecutive days of telepresence directed to the classroom. Multiple 1-hour feeds were accessible each day for different time zones and grade levels. During an electronic field trip, students "traveled" via live cablecast to visit people and places they might otherwise never encounter. The first field trip was to the battlefields of Gettysburg; succeeding trips included the Okefenokee National Wildlife Refuge; CNN Newsroom; Lake Nakuru National Park in Kenya, Africa; Ellis Island, New York, New York; and Germany, England, and Russia for the 50th celebration of V-E Day.
- Teacher training via live satellite and cable broadcast in advance of the trip (later ones were by videotape).
- Comprehensive teaching guides with pre- and postevent curricula—one edition for primary grades and one for secondary. These guides provided a learner-centered, problem-based curriculum rather than a mere presentation of facts and ideas (see Appendix for some example activities).
- Online resources specifically planned for the trips: real-time text-based chat conferences with subject experts (via America Online); special forums for participants; call-in polls; digital primary resources accessed through the TAL Web site or through America Online; real-time questions to experts during the telecasts by calling an 800 number, sending a FAX, or sending an electronic mail (E-mail) message. Selected 800-number callers were put on the air live and interacted with the expert. Certain E-mail and FAX questions were also read and answered live. All questions were answered within a few days of the event by E-mail.

Example of Program Implementation

"Time Machine to Gettysburg" was the first electronic field trip implemented. The Battle of Gettysburg was a turning point in the Civil War, a point at which issues of federal and states' rights, sectionalism, and economic differences could no longer be resolved by compromise or discussion.

The Gettysburg field trip was a case study that allowed students to apply lessons of the past to concepts studied in history, geography, civics, government, and current events classes. It supplied resources for critical-thinking and problem-solving skills, issues for debate and analysis, and topics for creative writing and research. For 3 days, students traveled via satellite to Gettysburg National Park. To enhance the meaningfulness of the event, each of these 1-hour telecasts followed the daily chronology of the battle. Moreover, each day addressed a broad, major theme: The *social context* of the Civil War presented the personal motivations of Confederate and Union soldiers, the role of civilians and the social impact of the war in history; the *technology* of war demonstrated the advances in weapons, communications, medicine, and transportation during the Civil War and the impact of these changes; and *reporting and recording history* provided a view of war through journalism, film, and photography, and compared points of view and historical analysis. Throughout the telecasts and the supporting curricular materials, the field trip emphasized conflict resolution—its role in wars and society both past and present—and the sociopolitical impact of the Civil War and the continuing struggle to resolve the issue of diversity in American society.

Primary digital resources were made available through America Online, the TAL Web site, and computer diskettes. These included brief biographical sketches, descriptions of battle sites, graphic images of maps and illustrations, letters, diaries (of Civil War–era people and soldiers in the more recent Gulf War), news clippings, and bibliographical references for further research.

In addition, America Online offered synchronous and asynchronous forums before, during, and after the trip. These online conferences enabled elementary students, high school students, and teachers to speak with Civil War historians, reenactors, and other specialists. Through E-mail, participants shared their own expertise, resources, and research with other field trip travelers.

Prior to the field trip, participants could access by cable television a series of special broadcasts that prepared the students for the field trip to come. These included two CNN Newsroom special reports. One segment, called "Our World," discussed the social change initiated by the Civil War and continuing today. Another segment coincided with the 40th anniversary of the historic Supreme Court decision, *Brown v. the Board of Education*. It reviewed this important decision and examined desegregation and diversity efforts in schools today.

Underlying the electronic field trip perspective as well as the pre- and posttrip curricula activities, was a theoretical model of problem-centered, constructivist instruction called the PES/C model (Siegel & Sousa, 1994): *P* stands for presentation of the problem; *E* stands for exploration of the problem, using resources and system-provided tools; and *S/C* stands for synthesis and competence, where the student resolves the cognitive dissonance created in the *P* section, and, in effect, demonstrates deep conceptual understandings or powerful ideas of the content. Competent performance and understanding may be evaluated with traditional testing means, but more powerfully with portfolio assessments.

Example Interactions

Online communication and collaboration played a central role in TAL learning activities. Many interactions occurred in E-mail dialogue between individual classes and teachers, and thus were not available for our analysis. However, we analyzed the TAL live chats on America Online to gain a better understanding of the nature of the online discussions and how the modifications in format effected the quality of the interactions.

The forums most often involved students talking to other students or experts. However, special discussions were arranged for participating teachers to interact with master teachers, experts, and each other. The early model for chat interaction were of two types: an open forum with no moderation in which anyone could discuss issues, and semimoderated discussions with experts in which a TAL master teacher or staff person was online to facilitate the discussions and keep students on track. Because of problems and frustrations in a "free for all" environment, more recent forums with experts have become controlled events in which questions are submitted to a moderator who screens them for appropriateness and passes them on to the expert.

The following excerpt illustrates the problems and frustrations in an open, unfacilitated discussion environment:

Participant 1: sweden, have you ever seen american woman?
Participant 2: }:-(
Sweden: you've gotta be kidding
Participant 2: :-)
Participant 3: WE ARE FROM N.H.
Participant 4: Dave stop asking pointless questions!
Participant 5: What are BBS programs, networks of what—TV, computers, elephants
Participant 6: :-8
Participant 2: Where in NH?
Participant 1: what does that mean?
Participant 3: TAMWORTH
Participant 2: <|:-)
Participant 6: Key codes?
Participant 2: Faces sideways

Participant 6: |:-()>

Participant 7: We knew that!!!

Participant 6: Good . . .

TAL online: Finland, do you have race problems like the ones in the U.S.?

Participant 2: (*-(

Participant 4: so, about VE Day . . .

Participant 8: we would like to know if you guys are going to talk about VE day!

As seen from the transaction, there was frustration being expressed by several participants in this short excerpt, which represented less than 1% of the discussion. Later in the forum, TAL online (the moderator) had to be stronger in trying to keep the forum focused with phrases such as: "This is [name deleted], the moderator from Turner Adventure Learning. It is important that you read the forum guidelines in the conference schedule" and "NO CHATTING PLEASE" and "Go [Participant 9], then [Participant 10], then [Participant 11]." Although one could argue that such off-task discussions can help people understand each other better and build common knowledge, from a strict learning point of view it was chaotic and not as effective as possible. That is not to say learning and meaningful discussion did not occur, because it did as the following excerpt (minus the off-task discussion) illustrates:

Participant 12: New research says that Kruschev wanted american missiles out of turkey

Participant 13: to [Participant 12]: right. Kennedy had promised Khrushchev that we would remove our nuclear

Participant 14: ? [indicating the desire to ask a question]

Participant 13: missiles from Turkey; during the Cuban crisis, Kennedy was furious to learn we hadn't.

Participant 12: intimidate us, then establish a sphere of domination in the Pacific region.

TAL online: Go [Participant 15], then [Participant 11], Then [Participant 14], then [Participant 16], then [Participant 17].

Participant 14: How long did it take to destroy the wall?

As TAL became better at controlling these forums, new procedures were implemented. The primary change was the control of interactions through a moderator. The following interactions from a recent trip illustrate some of these changes:

Message: This room is moderated.

Moderator: Hello [deleted name], are you here for the chat?

Moderator:	This is a moderated chat room so you must select "to" and type in "moderator" to send a question.
Moderator:	Our guest will be online shortly. Where are you located?
Moderator:	Welcome everyone!
Moderator:	We'll be starting in about 5 minutes.
Moderator:	This is a moderated chatroom. If you would like to ask a question do the following: [deleted instructions]
Moderator:	We have [Expert] from the [a Company], a Republican polling company online to discuss Dole's stand on the issues and how they do polling.
Moderator:	[Expert], would you tell our students a little about yourself.
Expert:	I'm president of the largest Republican polling firm in the US! we currently represent 61 members of the US house of Representatives. Im 44 years old, Ive been working in politics since I was twelve. I started off in 1964 working in the Lyndon Johnson campaign passing out flyers. My dad was in the Vietnam War, that's what got me involved. In 1974 I changed parties, I went from a democrat to a REPUBLICAN.
Moderator:	[Participant 1]> to <moderator>: Why do you (republicans) want to get rid of the Department of Education?
Expert:	It's not necessarily the dept of ed we want to get rid of, it's that 8 % of the total funding of education comes from federal dollars. Most of that $ goes to the bureaucracy and not to schools. So our basic philosophy is LET THE STATES DO WHAT THEY DO BEST, and don't let the federal govt. tie them up with a lot of rules and regulations!

With this new moderated format, the off-task discussion was eliminated and the thread of discussion was easy to follow. Those wishing to engage in off-topic discussions could move to other public chat rooms or engage in private chats.

Program Design Trade-Offs

TAL had many advocates in the educational community because it provided inspirational events that served as a motivational source for learning. It also provided curriculum materials and online events for teachers and students to use with this event. This one-stop approach for delivering adventures to the classroom saved the teachers planning time, which allowed them to concentrate on developing the learning environment. However, we were not able to provide materials appropriate to every learning approach a teacher might want to use. Instead, we provided a *traditional* path and a problem-based learning path from which the teacher could select and customize. This excluded other instructional approaches and activities. It forced the teachers to adapt to the TAL approach or to create their own activities to accompany the event.

The most important lesson learned about live conferencing was the need for more structured dialogues in the online forums. As in the WSAL, we learned that guided discussion and cognitive prompting was often necessary for meaningful and ongoing dialogues. This is not to suggest that it always has to be this way. With a group of students who are task oriented and understand the rules of appropriate behavior in online discourse (as they do with classroom actions), we can conduct meaningful and insightful learning events. In the case of TAL, the participants were often new to each other and the medium. This led to some of the problems and the need for facilitator moderation. Over time, as students learned how to act in these environments and were committed to the learning outcomes or the dialogue, less moderation of the chat forums was needed. This is not to imply that the forums were not effective learning tools. To the contrary, many excellent conversations occurred. The discussion here is intended to point out problems that had to be overcome to create the most efficient and effective learning environment.

For More Information. For more information on TAL, see the Web site <http://learning.turner.com/tal/index.html>.

WETLANDS EXPLORATION THINKSHOP

Program Overview

In 1995, the CEE joined an effort to create a museum of science, health, and technology called the WonderLab. Our role is to help the organization establish an online component for WonderLab's outreach program, traveling exhibits in schools, shopping malls, and other local venues. A central theme of this online effort is an adventure-learning focus at the local level (i.e., school, individual classroom, and community groups). Our first effort is called the Wetlands Exploration ThinkShop.

Although adventure learning focuses on vicarious participation in a national or international adventure, often a local adventure component is included as well. When using the WonderLab, most of the adventures will be local or classroom based. However, a single teacher or group of teachers may develop their own adventures—local adventure learning. Local adventure learning has the following components:

- Using out-of-classroom events or settings as a means to inspire interest and guide learning activities (i.e., local, national, and international current events, news stories, and documentaries). Although these events may derive from any source, they must be exciting and interesting to the learners. These are the rallying points around which the larger learning activities occur.

- Utilizing authentic, multidisciplinary learning materials and a problem-based learning approach.
- Joining students, teachers, experts, information resources, and the community together into a learning community.
- Recognizing that the students and the teachers are the "adventurers," even if you are following a national or international event.

The Internet and Internet tools can be used in five primary ways: (a) as a library of static and interactive items (i.e., documents, simulations, animations), (b) as a place to publish and make available your work, (c) as a communications network, (d) as a collaboration environment, and (e) as a vehicle to build community. In support of local adventure learning, the WonderLab seeks to effectively exploit each of these uses. Of particular interest is our long-term goal of creating a community of adventures around various learning themes. Figure 14.4 illustrates the continuum along which we want our users to progress from communicating with each other to collaborating on projects to establishing a community connected by online tools.

The WonderLab Web site has one unique feature that differentiates technologically from most museum Web sites, a program called the "Profiler." The Profiler allows us to gather information about interests, technological capabilities, and other demographic information about an individual user or group and to customize the Web site accordingly. For an individual user, therefore, we can direct them to exhibits that are relevant to their interests

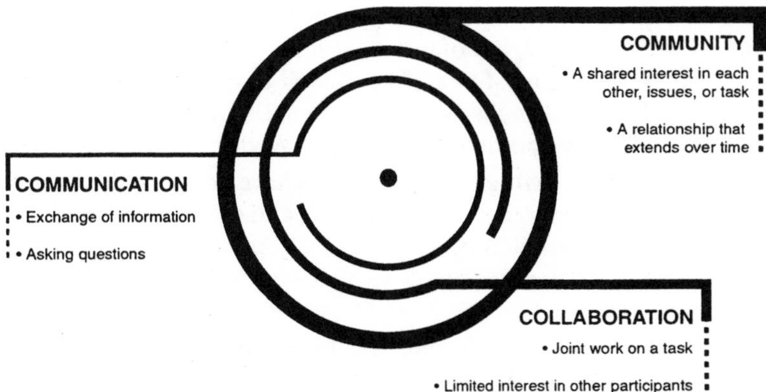

FIG. 14.4. The concentric relationship between communication, collaboration, and community.

or skill level. For instance, a third-grader may not see a document or discussion forum created for high school students. A teacher or group leader can complete a profile for a particular class and design a class "homepage" for a particular unit or adventure. These tools allow the group leader to develop private forums and chats available only to a select group.

Example of Program Implementation

The "Wetlands Exploration ThinkShop" (WET) is the first virtual exhibit hall of the WonderLab Online Web site. Wetlands are part of the landscape we call home. No matter where you live in the landscape you live in a watershed, the land that contributes water to a lake or river system. Because wetlands are all around us and the study of them can link to every curriculum area, the study of wetlands fits perfectly in an adventure-learning framework—they are easily accessible, there are many adventure-type activities that can be designed, and they support a multidisciplinary approach.

The WET project seeks to provide resources needed for the successful completion of an adventure-learning project. The major components of the site are as follows:

1. *Information Resources:* WonderLab developed background information (i.e., overviews, case studies, and definitions and terms), links to Wetlands in the news Web sites, and links to other Web sites with wetland information or activities. These resources can serve as stimulus materials for the project or background data for research.

2. *Online Interactive Exhibits:* These offer students the chance to interact with computer simulations, interactive quizzes, and to contribute their work to the Web site for others to use. The main idea behind the latter is to get students off the computer, out of the classroom, and into the field to conduct research, experiments, and studies. The student or class can then report their data back to others through the Web site by completing Web forms. In this way, the students eventually contribute more of the Web site content than we do.

3. *Print-and-Do Activities:* Many activities have no computer component; that is, we describe how to conduct an activity and how it links into curricular frameworks, but all activities occur off of the computer. We call these print-and-do because the computer serves as merely a delivery mechanism for the activity description.

4. *Electronic Forums:* Our forums are of two types: synchronous, real-time chat; and asynchronous Web-based text conferencing. These conferences serve several purposes. For instance, for teachers there are forums for general discussions, exchanging project ideas and finding partners, and working on

specific topic areas like the wetlands. For students there are general and specific topic discussions.

5. *Access to Experts:* One of our key beliefs is that experts must be part of both the development of exhibits and in the implementation of different activities. It is only through an expert's experience that we can ensure that we are designing activities that are authentic in nature. When learners are engaged in our activities, it is often important to have the guiding hand or perspective of an expert to make those critical connections that give insight into a subject or way of thinking. The use of online forums, E-mail questions, and occasional on-site visits enables us to provide that access. Monitoring the forums and teacher exchange areas helps us to see when a particular expert might be needed and to try and connect up local adventurers with the best expert available.

Program Design Trade-Offs

Although more expensive and time consuming, it is easier to develop and implement a large-scale, single-theme adventure-learning event than it is to develop a resource center to support local adventure learning. In the former, we were able to decide on the stimulus events, develop a single set of curriculum materials, decide on the best experts to interact with online, and set a calendar that others followed. In developing local adventure learning resources for WET, we must serve as a resource that is responsive to the designs and plans of every classroom, group, or individual that uses our resources. To get around this, we have attempted to link up several classrooms in a learning circle so that when we work with them, or when we provide experts online, our resources are maximized.

Another key trade-off is that it is often harder to find the stimulus event that moves this particular activity beyond normal classroom activity to "adventure" learning. It is not that we have to be like Indiana Jones, seeking the Holy Grail, but there needs to be a critical event or activity that excites and motivates students and teachers. Although we can provide the resources needed for an adventure, it is usually up to the creativity of the teacher and the students to take it that extra step.

For More Information. For more information on the WonderLab go to the Web site <http://www.wonderlab.org>.

MOVING TOWARD THE DIGITAL LEARNING ENVIRONMENT

Each of the three projects—the WSAL, TAL, and the WET—represents an emerging vision of networked, learner-centered instruction. We call this model the DLE (defined earlier) and it incorporates the following features (Siegel & Kirkley, 1997):

- A learner-centered and problem-based (rather than content-centered) instructional support system, in which learning is based on analysis of a series of complex, real-world issues rather than on memorization of facts and principles (Brown, Collins, & Duguid, 1989; Duffy & Jonassen, 1992).
- Safe settings for learning, in which making mistakes becomes as powerful a learning heuristic as employing successful problem-solving strategies in real-world contexts (Schank, 1994).
- A blurring of teacher and student roles, such that teachers model and demonstrate learning in problem-based settings, whereas students facilitate and manage their own learning environments (Duffy & Cunningham, 1996).
- Access to an integrated package of navigational, productivity, communication, collaboration, and knowledge/wisdom creation tools (Edelson, Pea, & Gomez, 1996; Harasim, Hiltz, Teles, & Turoff, 1995; Soloway, Guzdial, & Hay, 1994).
- Management tools that facilitate the development of student goals and activities as a collaboration between students, parents, and teachers, of which key components are alternative and traditional assessment practices (Farr & Tone, 1994; Reeves & Okey, 1996).
- Independence of any particular hardware or delivery system configuration (Siegel & Sousa, 1994).
- An open, ever-changing, and ever-expanding information architecture (Siegel & Sousa, 1994), which has access to a global information network like the Internet, in contrast to a closed information architecture (e.g., book, diskette, video disk, or a CD-ROM), which is finite and frozen in time.

Taken together, these features are designed to facilitate big-concept, multidisciplinary learning, and the development of authentic, cooperative problem-solving strategies. Learning how to learn in a domain is as important as accumulating facts and decontextualized information (Oshima, Bereiter, & Scardamalia, 1995; Riel, 1994). Moreover, changes in teacher and student behavior are promoted by direct training and collaboration embedded in tools that foster self-regulated behavior, metacognition, and the development of a community of learners and teachers (Harasim, 1993).

Although adventure learning is not the only metaphor for the DLE, it coalesces DLE features in a powerful way to create imaginative examples of learner-centered learning. In the final section, we speculate on the future of adventure learning given emerging technologies.

FUTURE OF ADVENTURE LEARNING

In a field where the cycles of change are accelerating beyond what most of us can comprehend, it is difficult to project how these changes will impact new designs for learner-centered instruction and communications. Nevertheless, we examine some of the trends shaping the future of computing and speculate how these trends might change our models of adventure learning.

Over the next decade, we expect the following trends to continue (Association of Computing Machinery, 1992): (a) decreasing hardware costs leading to larger memories and faster systems, (b) miniaturization of hardware leading to portability, (c) reduction in power requirements leading to prolonged portability, (d) new display technologies leading to the packaging of computational devices in new forms, (e) assimilation of computation into the environment, (f) specialized hardware leading to new functions (e.g., rapid searches and agent data mining), (g) increased development of fast network communication and distributed computing, (h) increasing innovation in input techniques (e.g., voice, gesture, pen), (i) decreasing costs of computers, approaching the "less than $100 range," and (j) increasing use of global positioning satellites and local infrared and wireless technologies to locate the position of any stationary or moving object.

Computers will become inexpensive, miniaturized, and embedded in common objects, moving away from the "computer as desktop" view we have today. Worldwide and local networks will become very fast and commonplace. Global and local positioning systems will be able to locate the position of any object within 0.5 centimeters! Three-dimensional virtual worlds will be the state of multimedia. Display devices will be inexpensive flat screen devices (of almost any size), whereas small display devices will be embedded in eyewear. All of these features exist today in the research laboratory. In 10 years, they will be commonplace.

In 2008, we will view the mid-1990s as the start of a World Wide Web that was viewed through workstations. By 2008, reality will become our web! Virtual reality and the real world will be merged in unique and innovative ways. To provide a simple example, it should be possible for a student with a computing device to walk through a real forest, point to a tree, and "post" a virtual note on the tree asking for information about it. A future hiker through the same forest, wearing special eyewear (similar in size and weight to normal glasses), will see the virtual note, respond to it, and her response will be automatically v-mailed (video mailed) to the first person.

In another example, imagine a group of students in a farm field near a river wearing their virtual eyewear. Standing with them in virtual space is an environmental specialist (who is really 500 miles away at the university). Working with the expert, the students plan various possible landscapes to reclaim the land and attract different animals. Through realistic animations, the students watch the plants and animals at various stages of development over the next 20 years and physically walk through the virtual landscape looking at real objects such as the river and associated virtual objects. After trying several different experiments, the students select the best landscape and embark on a year-long project to plant the field and provide shelter for the wildlife they want to attract.

Such "just in place" computing will impact every aspect of our lives: how we learn, how we play, how we work, and how we communicate and relate to one another. Daniel Burrus, a futurist and author of *Technotrends*, predicts that we will see more change in the next 5 years than we have seen in the last 50. He compares the impact of these changes to that of the introduction of the automobile and the telephone. This convergence of computing, communication, and media will impact our learning environments in significant ways.

How can we relate the future changes to the adventure-learning environments of today? On a global scale, the future of adventure learning will allow students to stand virtually at the North Pole with the explorers, to virtually inspect an ancient artifact on an archaeological dig, or to "fly" virtually with a flock of birds as they migrate North for the summer. On a local scale, students will be able to visit a science museum with each other and perform experiments collaboratively although they are on opposite sides of the globe. Or, as Gene Roddenberry (1966) has prompted us to do:

> To explore strange new worlds,
> to seek out new life and new civilizations,
> to boldly go where no one has gone before.

APPENDIX: Sample Curriculum Activities From Turner Adventure Learning

The following are brief descriptions of the critical components of several activities in the field trip "Time Machine to Gettysburg."

Public Opinion Poll

Students state and compare their opinions on civil conflict and war.
Students role play someone of 1861.
Students tally and correlate results and lead a discussion.

A Profile of the Nation, 1863

Students create a profile of their local area during the Civil War and share it with others online.

Taking a Role at Gettysburg

Using roles provided with the curriculum kit, or ones they choose, students research a person from that era and assume the persona for the 3 days of the trip in class discussions. These roles include generals, soldiers, and average people in the area such as farmers. Students keep diaries of how they perceive that person's life.

Parents' Page

Students survey their parents on war and its impact on their family past, present, and future. From this, class creates a profile of conflict and its impact. Parents and community members then come to class or join discussions online.

Soldier Equipment

Students research, create lists, make illustrations, and justify why soldiers needed certain equipment in the Civil War.

REFERENCES

Association of Computing Machinery. (1992). *Curricula for human-computer interaction.* Reading, MA: Addisson-Wesley.

Brown, J. S., Collins, A., & Duguid, P. (1989). Situated cognition and the culture of learning. *Educational Researcher, 18*(1), 32–41.

Duffy, T. M., & Cunningham, D. J. (1996). Constructivism: Implications for the design and delivery of instruction. In D. H. Jonassen (Ed.), *Handbook of research on educational communications and technology* (pp. 170–198). New York: Scholastic.

Duffy, T. M., & Jonassen, D. H. (Eds.). (1992). *Constructivism and the technology of instruction: A conversation.* Hillsdale, NJ: Lawrence Erlbaum Associates.

Edelson, D. C., Pea, R. D., & Gomez, L. M. (1996). Constructivism in the collaboratory. In B. G. Wilson (Ed.), *Constructivist learning environments: Case studies in instructional design* (pp. 151–164). Englewood Cliffs, NJ: Educational Technology Publications.

Farr, R., & Tone, B. (1994). *Portfolio and performance assessment: Helping students evaluate their progress as readers and writers.* Fort Worth, TX: Harcourt Brace College Publishers.

Harasim, L. (1993). Collaborating in cyberspace: Using computer conferences as a group. *Interactive Learning Environments, 3*(2), 199–230.

Harasim, L., Hiltz, S. R., Teles, L., & Turoff, M. (1995). *Learning networks: A field guide to teaching and learning online.* Cambridge, MA: MIT Press.

Hattie, J., Marsh, H. W., Neill, J. T., & Richards, G. E. (1997). Adventure education and Outward Bound: Out-of-class experiences that make a lasting difference. *Review of Educational Research, 67*(1), 43–87.

Oshima, J., Bereiter, C., & Scardamalia, M. (1995). Information-access characteristics for high conceptual progress in a computer-networked learning environment. In J. L. Schnase & E. L. Cunnis (Eds.), *Proceedings of CSCL '95: The first international conference on computer support for collaborative learning* (pp. 259–267). Mahwah, NJ: Lawrence Erlbaum Associates.

Reeves, T. C., & Okey, J. R. (1996). Alternative assessment for constructivist learning environments. In B. G. Wilson (Ed.), *Constructivist learning environments: Case studies in instructional design* (pp. 191–202). Englewood Cliffs, NJ: Educational Technology Publications.

Riel, M. (1994). Educational change in a technology-rich environment. *Journal of Research on Computing, 26*(4), 452–474.

Roddenberry, G. (1966). *Star trek* (television series).

Schank, R. C. (1994). Why hitchhikers on the Information Highway are going to have to wait a long time for a ride. *The Aspen Institute Quarterly, 6*(2), 28–58.

Siegel, M. A., & Kirkley, S. E. (1997). Moving toward the digital learning environment: The future of Web-based instruction. In B. H. Khan (Ed.), *Web-based instruction.* Englewood Cliffs, NJ: Educational Technology Publications.

Siegel, M. A., & Sousa, G. A. (1994). Inventing the virtual textbook: Changing the nature of schooling. *Educational Technology, 34*(7), 49–54.

Soloway, E., Guzdial, M., & Hay, K. (1994). Learner-centered design: The challenge for HCI in the 21st century. *Interactions, 1*(2), 36–48.

15

Designing 21st-Century Educational Networlds: Structuring Electronic Social Spaces

Kira S. King
Indiana University

THE COMMUNICATION AGE: COMPUTER CONFERENCING, SOCIAL CHANGE, AND THE KNOWLEDGE WORKER

As the preceding chapters indicate, we are at the threshold of an exciting new era for education, instructional technology, and society at large. With the approach of the 21st century, we find ourselves in the midst of the information age, and at the dawn of a new time period that some researchers are calling the communication age (Cooney, chap. 11, this volume; Thornburg, 1995). These new time periods, no matter how we label them, are associated with an unparalleled pace of social change that is requiring the fundamental redesign of most of our social systems—including our schools. As Drucker (1994) stated, society has experienced more social transformation during this century than in any other century in recorded history. Furthermore, he argued that the shift from the industrial to the information age represented more than social change; rather, it was a shift in the human condition. For the first time in history, the average person does not earn a living through manual labor on the farm or in the factory. Rather, by the end of this century, one third of our workforce will consist of "knowledge workers" (Drucker, 1994) who are skilled in learning, collaboration, and problem solving. With so much information available, we need people who can synthesize meaning from large bodies of diverse knowledge; and with the arrival of the communication age, we are beginning to realize that this meaning-making activity is a highly collaborative process. Learning, thinking, and working are no longer solitary activities. Therefore, it should come as no surprise to us that our traditional notions of schooling must be redesigned in order to enable our children to excel in these new living and working environments.

Perhaps one of the most revolutionary changes enabling global communication and collaboration is the use of computer conferencing to extend the virtual boundaries of our schools and businesses. Many researchers are even predicting that computer-networking and -conferencing technologies will have a social impact rivaling the inventions of human language and the printing press (Harasim, 1993a; Provenzo, 1986). No matter what our field of specialty, the tools for telecommunications are changing the way we work, study, research, and socialize.

In fact, as Blumenfeld, Marx, Soloway, and Krajcik (1996) argued, computer-supported collaborative learning (CSCL) tools can provide us with powerful new educational environments:

> The newest generation of collaborative environments supports conversations but goes substantially further, providing a "place" to which students can go. This new generation of environments, provides tools to accumulate and integrate a range of communications functions. Such a software will constitute a suite of virtual Internet rooms where students can go to collaborate. Conversations can take place in the context of digital artifacts. Students can view the same drawing, text document, or interactive program in one window as their conversations go on in another window, or students can drop output from their simulation program into a collaborator's visualization program, all the while chatting synchronously. (p. 39)

Thus, for the first time in history, we have the opportunity to create virtual subcultures where our students and teachers can assemble electronically, across time and space, to engage in and extend the powerful dialogue of learning. Harasim (1993b) identified these virtual spaces as "educational networlds," in which educators and learners ". . . can access virtual classrooms, on-line work groups, learning circles, peer networks, electronic campuses, and on-line libraries in a shared space . . . that connects people all over the globe" (p. 21). Such educational networlds promote the creation of lifelong learners who collaborate with peers and experts within the classroom and across the globe to build and share knowledge (Harasim, 1993b).

As the authors within this text caution us, however, computer-networking and -communications tools themselves cannot ensure the realization of such ambitious goals. Technology itself—no matter how glitzy—can be used either to our benefit or to our disadvantage; it can foster the creation of innovative new social interactions, or can cause further abstraction and individualization. The choice is up to us. Therefore, embedded within the opportunity to harness new CSCL technologies, is the responsibility to design its effective implementation, with the goal of developing knowledge-building virtual communities.

INSTRUCTIONAL TECHNOLOGY: PAST CHALLENGES INFORM FUTURE PRACTICE

One way of ensuring the effective design and implementation of CSCL is to learn from the challenges we faced with previous instructional technology; that is, to plan the future we must begin by looking at our past.

A brief examination of the history of instructional technology reveals a discouraging pattern of high expectations for new media followed by disillusionment (Cuban, 1986; Saettler, 1990). Beginning in the early 1900s, researchers looked toward film, radio, television, and early computer applications (i.e., computer-assisted instruction) to increase teacher efficiency. For example, in the following quote, Thomas Edison predicted that film would make textbooks obsolete:

> I believe that the motion picture is destined to revolutionize our educational system and that in a few years it will supplant largely, if not entirely, the use of textbooks. I should say that on the average we get about two percent efficiency out of schoolbooks as they are written today. The education of the future, as I see it, will be conducted through the medium of the motion picture . . . where it should be possible to obtain one hundred percent efficiency. (Thomas Edison, 1922, cited in Cuban, 1986, p. 9)

As we now know, such optimistic predictions were shattered when subsequent surveys indicated limited teacher adoption of these technologies, whereas media comparison studies failed to prove that any one medium is superior to another (Clark, 1985, 1991; Cuban, 1986; Saettler, 1990).

By the 1980s, researchers such as Seymour Papert shifted our focus away from using technology to increase educational efficiency toward using it as a catalyst for educational reform. To achieve his goal of changing our schools, Papert purposefully blended current learning philosophy with computer technology. For instance, his hope for the resulting mathematical microworld, Logo, was that it would so extensively revolutionize our educational system, that ". . . schools as we know them today will have no place in the future" (Papert, 1980, p. 8). However, more than 10 years later, Papert (1993) himself stated that these optimistic predictions had failed to come true. Instead of helping us revolutionize our schools, computer technology has most often been used to fit the traditional drill-and-practice model of education. Rather than being a catalyst for change, in many ways, early computer usage merely supported the dominant instructional approaches of knowledge dissemination. Such reification of traditional practice has been true of each new medium encountered and is still prevalent in many classrooms (Cuban, 1986; Papert, 1993). Without due care, this trend will continue into the 21st century. No matter how high our expectations are for CSCL technology, only the careful development and implementation of these tools will help us realize their full potential.

DESIGNING AND IMPLEMENTING CSCL TECHNOLOGIES

Whereas the 1980s prompted concern over the alienating context of human–computer interaction inherent in drill and practice, computer-assisted instruction, computer programming, and simulation software applications (Cuban, 1986; Lauzon & Moore, 1993; Sloan, 1984), the 1990s offer us the opportunity to explore the social ramifications of human–human interaction via computer networking. With CSCL technology, educators have the chance to create new forms of collaboration and dialogue that augment and redefine classroom interaction, and that unite peers and colleagues across time and space. Although this is an exciting opportunity, there is still concern that rather than elevating the quality and intensity of our social discourse, computer-conferencing technology may actually increase human alienation as some face-to-face communication is supplanted by computer-mediated interaction. As previously discussed, this is certainly a possibility; the effect of implementing these technologies is dependent on the ways in which we utilize them. One of the major goals of this final chapter is to suggest two strategies for ensuring effective design, development, and implementation: the pursuit of systemic educational redesign, and the use of educational philosophy to structure the social spaces of educational networlds.

Embedding CSCL Implementation Within Educational Systems Design

There is no doubt that sociocultural learning theory and CSCL technology are powerful tools enabling us to break the traditional mold of education. They challenge us to create innovative learning communities that promote active learning, collaboration, problem solving, and the use of real-world contexts (Brown, Collins, & Duguid, 1989; Cognition and Technology Group at Vanderbilt, 1991; Honebein, Duffy, & Fishman, 1991; Ruopp, Gal, Drayton, & Pfister, 1993). Not only is this a more effective way to learn, but it is also essential to providing our children with the skills they will need to become the future workers of the 21st century—employees who can work collaboratively, think critically, solve problems, and pursue lifelong learning

(Drucker, 1994). However, recent advances in educational systems design indicate that to use these tools effectively we must embed their use in large-scale efforts to redesign our schools, because our current industrial age school model cannot be adequately adapted (Banathy, 1991; Jenlink, Reigeluth, Carr, & Nelson, 1998; Reigeluth & Garfinkle, 1994; Salisbury, 1992).

As a society, we are becoming painfully aware that we have outgrown the current educational model, which was designed to produce factory workers, rather than the knowledge workers who will be so prevalent in the communication age (Branson, 1987; Darling-Hammond, 1990; Kozol, 1991). Research in educational systems design maintains that recent efforts to change education through instructional technology adoption and school reform have failed largely because they were wedded to outdated, mechanistic, industrial age thinking (Ackoff, 1981; Jenlink et al., 1998; Reigeluth, 1994).

As a result of this mechanistic thinking, most educational change and reform efforts have been guided by the belief that our schools are broken and need to be "fixed." Such attempts focus on piecemeal reform that involve the modification of several system components, such as adding new computer technology tools, increasing teacher–student ratios, and extending the school year (Reigeluth, 1994). When used in isolation, these approaches are inadequate bandages for our outdated industrial age educational model. Due to the very nature of human activity systems, attempts to change only one component at a time typically end in failure. That is, because human beings have a fundamental need for maintaining order and control in their lives, rather than quickly adopting a new innovation, many will unconsciously alter it to fit into the structure of the existing system (Conner, 1993; Dormant, in press; Reigeluth, 1994; Rogers, 1983). This is what most likely happened with past efforts to realize change through the introduction of instructional technology.

Therefore, the addition of CSCL technology by itself cannot dramatically alter our schools. Concurrent with the implementation of CSCL technologies, we need to transcend our current educational paradigm, create an entirely new image of school, teacher, student, and learning, and completely redesign every component of our current educational model (Banathy, 1991, 1992; Jenlink et al., 1998; Reigeluth, 1994; Reigeluth & Garfinkle, 1994). This involves redesigning not only the learning environment, but also the administrative and governance systems. Such a task, although essential to the development of effective schooling, is beyond the scope of this text. However, our emphasis on transforming the learning environment is an essential first step because, while designing new educational models, we need to place learning as the primary focus—developing all other subsystems to support the desired learning system (Banathy, 1991). In this way, we can move from teacher-directed, dissemination-based instruction to more learner-centered, constructivist learning environments. Consequently, as we discuss the use of learning theory to shape CSCL technologies, we must remember that, in order to realize educational change, such efforts must be embedded within systemic, redesign efforts.

Using Educational Philosophy to Design and Implement CSCL Technology

In chapter 2, Bonk and Cunningham outline three innovations in learning theory and philosophy that must guide our use of CSCL technology: constructivism, learner-centered principles, and sociocultural theory.

First, in the constructivist viewpoint, the educator's goal becomes that of helping students construct their own knowledge, through active learning, inquiry, reflection, and student-generated, relevant learning activities. This requires that the focus shift from knowledge transmission to knowledge creation. Rather than presenting prediscovered information to be memorized, teachers must guide learners in the creation of their own body of knowledge (Wells & Chang-Wells, 1992).

Second, the concept of learner-centered principles (LCPs) fosters the creation of new interaction patterns and learning communities—shifting the attention away from the teacher and toward the learner. In this approach, teachers no longer dominate classroom discourse and deliver standard instruction for all students. Instead, LCPs suggest that instruction should be geared toward the individual learner's needs, addressing cognitive, affective, developmental and social issues (American Psychological Association, 1993).

And finally, the development of sociocultural theory has called our attention to the social context of learning (Vygotsky, 1978). With this viewpoint, learning is no longer seen as a solitary activity, but is described as occurring through social interaction with peers, mentors, and experts. Because learning cannot be separated from context, sociocultural theory encourages the practice of situating instruction within real-world apprenticeships. As discussed in chapter 2, sociocultural theory involves such concepts as cognitive apprenticeship, problem-based learning, scaffolded instruction, distributed intelligence, zones of proximal development, internalization, and intersubjectivity.

In summary, these three innovations in learning philosophy challenge educators to create learning communities that utilize authentic problem-solving activities that are learner centered, and that require scaffolded instruction, intersubjectivity, and new forms of learning assistance. Scardamalia and Bereiter (1994) succinctly synthesized these educational reform efforts by suggesting that the new goal of schooling is to create "knowledge-building communities" that are modeled after the process researchers undergo in journal publication. This involves embedding learning within a real-world context of creating new knowledge that is subject to peer review, and that is shared with a wider audience for reflection and synthesis.

A critical component of such instruction is collaborative learning, because it promotes the process of knowledge creation, and new patterns of social discourse and interaction (Koschmann, 1994). As researchers indicate, what is most unique about collaborative learning is that it requires and supports alternative communication patterns. Indeed, dialogue is at the very heart of collaborative learning (Koschmann, Myers, Feltovich, & Barrows, 1994; Pea, 1994; Scardamalia & Bereiter, 1994).

However, collaborative learning and knowledge-building communities require a form of dialogue that is drastically different from the discourse that most commonly occurs in traditional schools. In chapter 3, Duffy, Deuber, and Hawley begin to characterize this dialogue by exploring the role of two different types of communication—exploratory conversation and issue-based discussion—that enable critical thinking in collaborative inquiry. Furthermore, Pea (1994) referred to the new form of discourse as "transformative dialogue," which has the following characteristics: (a) high levels of interactivity, (b) real-world problem solving, (c) questioning, hypothesizing, explaining, and (d) building collective understanding (Scardamalia & Bereiter, 1994).

As we have seen, CSCL technology offers us a unique opportunity to help build this new form of transformative dialogue. For example, CSCL can be used to dramatically alter interaction patterns, connecting learners and their teachers with peers, collaborators, and experts from around the world. Additionally, it fosters new communication patterns such as student–teacher, student–student, student–peers, and student–expert. And finally, CSCL can alter the roles of student and teachers within the classroom, by empowering students to initiate questions, debate, and reflect, and by helping teachers in guiding, modeling, questioning, and scaffolding their students' learning. Therefore, CSCL can be used to develop transformative dialogue which, in turn, helps educators create knowledge-building communities.

Structuring Electronic Social Spaces

As many of the chapters within this text indicate, rather than creating dramatically different social interaction, poorly structured CSCL can actually impede learning and the development of knowledge-building communities. Computer conferencing can easily be reduced to worthless busywork where students enter their gossip-related entries for minimal credit (Bonk et al., chap. 12; Chong, chap. 11; Duffy et al., chap. 3; Siegel & Kirkley, chap. 14, all this volume).

One of our guiding principles to prevent such occurrences relates to Harasim's (1993b) statement that educational networlds are open spaces requiring social shaping for effective dialogue. To achieve this goal, CSCL must be embedded within an alternative educational system that employs an appropriate learning philosophy. A primary goal of this text, therefore, is to create a variety of sociocultural methods and models to structure electronic social spaces that will ensure the creation of challenging, effective, and exciting online learning communities.

Findings from our research indicate that, when we do structure social spaces, CSCL enables students and teachers to dramatically change their roles and interaction patterns (Cooney, chap. 11; Kang, chap. 13; Siegel & Kirkley, chap. 14, all this volume), and to extend the learning dialogue beyond the traditional boundaries of the classroom. In emerging educational networlds, teachers become coaches and mentors who guide student dialogue, while allowing them to build critical-thinking and collaborative learning skills by reflecting, responding, socializing, and challenging their classmates, peers, mentors, and teachers online. The very existence of computer conferencing changes communication by removing nonverbal social cues, and by forcing students to reflect upon and challenge their own comments, and those of their peers, in more depth than in traditional classroom discussions (see the following chapters: Angeli & Cunningham, chap. 4; Bonk et al., chap. 12; Chong, chap. 7; Kang, chap. 13; Kirkley et al., chap. 9; Sugar & Bonk, chap. 6, all this volume). For instance, Chong demonstrates that instructors of large college classes can use CSCL to develop the social support and cognitive debate usually only possible in small seminars. Furthermore, as Cooney discovered, some of the electronic interaction patterns and skills are even carried back into the face-to-face interactions of classroom discussions. In fact, a teacher in Cooney's study reported that her students showed an increased willingness to participate in classroom dialogue, and to collaborate on noncomputer activities. Additionally, several of the works presented within this volume (i.e., Cooney, chap. 11; Sugar & Bonk, chap. 6; Zhu, chap. 10, all this volume) maintain that CSCL supports high levels of perspective taking and interpersonal understanding.

With such initial success, sociocultural theory is providing clues into how educational networlds can become powerful catalysts for change as well as tools for redesigning our learning and instructional systems. In an effort to guide future efforts, this chapter reviews the models and approaches presented within this volume to structure the social space of educational networlds, while also presenting several strategies for conducting research within this arena.

CSCL Design Models and Strategies

In chapter 3, Duffy et al. call our attention to the importance of beginning our efforts to structure electronic social spaces at the software design level. With the goal of supporting effective communication and minimizing off-task electronic dialogue, this research group is currently designing an asynchronous conferencing environment, ACT, that builds four separate spaces for the following types of dialogue: class-wide chat, class-wide administrative issue postings, team-based exploratory conversation, and team-based issue-based discussion. Additionally, student reflection is encouraged through requirements that students categorize their comments and complete periodic summary entries. Although this conferencing system is still under development, it serves as a strong model to guide future design efforts. As Duffy et al. state, most computer-based conferencing systems fail to distinguish dialogue beyond whether it is real time or time independent. By assuming that all dialogue is the same, software designers are failing to build the types of tools that will enable teachers and students to effectively structure electronic social spaces.

After focusing on the development of appropriate networking technology, our focus moves to the curricular level—designing the classroom environment. Working from a learning philosophy and learning goals, the structure of instructional systems must be developed so that the activities and assignments within both the classroom and the educational networld are interrelated and complementary. This may include assigning letter grades to both types of activities, thereby ensuring that participation in the online community is taken seriously by students.

Early on in this design process, we must grapple with the technical concerns of CSCL. Namely, what software should be used? How user friendly is it? Can we secure sufficient training and easy access? Although these concerns seem quite rudimentary, they are essential because many authors within this text encountered technical difficulties that severely interfered with the learning activities. Further, the tools we choose will affect the possible communication interactions, and set the dialogue boundaries by determining who will be participating. Koschmann (1994) helped frame the issue by identifying the following three types of usage:

- intra-classroom (between you and your students),
- inter-classroom (between two or more classrooms),
- extra-classroom (between your classroom and peers/mentors outside of academia).

Another key issue to consider while choosing the CSCL tool is whether synchronous or asynchronous conferencing is preferred. Bonk, Medury, and Reynold's (1994) taxonomy of CSCL tools mentioned in chapter 1 of this text provides further discussion of such options.

Once the overall course structure has been determined, and the CSCL tools have been chosen, learning activities must be designed. For large college classrooms using asynchronous computer conferencing, Chong (chap. 7, this volume) presents four different models that strive to extend the limited interaction and collaboration opportunities typically available within such large lecture halls. These models explore the following four types of activities: ongoing discussion topics, collaborative test preparation, case study work, and group projects. Zhu (chap. 10, this volume) reviews another approach that attempts to structure participation through the assignment of the student dialogue roles: starter, wrapper, and participant.

Perhaps the most critical, time-consuming, and delicate task is that of guiding the student dialogue while the instruction is being implemented. The central goal here is to foster student ownership, and active, self-regulated learning, which requires that the teacher relinquish the traditional role of director. As teachers electronically guide and coach learners, they are enabling students to navigate through the dialogue. Research within this text offers several sociocultural techniques for such electronic dialogue guidance.

Althauser and Matuga (chap. 8, this volume) suggest the use of scaffolding (Rogoff, 1990) in both the educational networld and the accompanying noncomputer classroom. This requires three major phases: initial cognitive support from the teacher, active engagement from the students, and finally, the gradual fading of teacher support as learners reach mastery. Under this model, the teacher's role includes a more visible presence initially, with the gradual withdrawal as students assume primary responsibility for the dialogue.

Several authors (Chong, chap. 7; Kirkley et al., chap. 9; Sugar & Bonk, chap. 6, all this volume) examine teachers' use of Tharp and Gallimore's (1990) seven means of assistance, suggesting that during the initial stages of scaffolding, it is essential to provide students with instances of modeling, questioning, and feedback. This assistance helps ensure that students understand the type of dialogue the teacher expects them to engage in, while diminishing the occurrence of gossipy chat rooms and unfocused discussions.

As the students gain competence, the teacher must fade into the background of the discussion, and can focus more closely on monitoring student participation and dialogue. One of the areas educators and researchers must monitor and better understand is the predominance of social or off-task behavior. Whereas too many comments unrelated to the topic can degrade the dialogue to the level of a chat room, it appears that some off-task chatter may be a necessary component of the online subculture that builds the camaraderie or intersubjectivity needed to sustain the challenging debate required in a learning community (Bonk et al., chap. 12; Duffy et al., chap. 3; Kang, chap. 13; Savery, chap. 5, all this volume). In fact, as Chong (chap. 7, this volume) indicates, it is through these comments that the teacher is offered a unique window on students' social, emotional experiences, and cognitive development.

It is interesting to note that our findings regarding social comments in electronic dialogue are corroborated by other research. In a study on computer-mediated communication, Henri (1992) also indicated that high levels of socially oriented messages can have diverse implications. For example, although extensive social chatter may be distracting and disruptive, it may also indicate a learning group that is socially cohesive, or it may reflect the affective component of the learning process.

IMPLICATIONS FOR RESEARCH, DESIGN, AND IMPLEMENTATION

The findings presented within this text regarding the design and implementation of CSCL are only a beginning. As Blumenfeld et al. (1996) stated, there is a tremendous dearth of literature regarding the marriage of collaborative learning and computer-conferencing tools. Further research is critical to ensure our successful use of these technologies. Perhaps one of the key impediments is the limited expertise available for documenting, analyzing, and evaluating online discourse within a sociocultural perspective. Such knowledge is needed not only for researchers, but also for educators who are using CSCL in their classrooms. After all, in order to guide computer-supported collaborative learning, teachers must be able to understand the resulting electronic student dialogue as it reflects the cognitive, social, and affective processes of learning (Henri, 1992). With the goal of facilitating future development, this chapter continues with a synthesis of the diverse research and implementation methods discussed within the text.

Although the preceding chapters cover a range of settings and research designs, they all follow recent trends in inquiry (Guba, 1987; Merriam, 1988; Miles & Huberman, 1994), and in computer-conferencing research (Henri, 1992), by combining a variety of data collection methods—quantitative, qualitative, and survey. In doing so, they provide the systemic, open-ended portraits characteristic of qualitative research, while simultaneously providing a more detailed picture through the use of surveys and numerical analyses. As Miles and Huberman stated, ". . . we have to face the fact that numbers and words are *both* needed if we are to understand the world" (p. 40). The trick is in knowing when and in what way to use those numbers or words, and how to do so (Gherardi & Turner, 1987; Miles & Huberman, 1994; Salomon, 1991, 1996) while remaining firmly entrenched within a single research paradigm—quantitative or qualitative.

In distilling the various methods used by our authors, I am embedding the discussion within a three-stage research design approach. These phases involve: creating a preliminary sketch of the instructional system, developing a detailed portrait of the educational networld, and synthesizing key learnings. In the first stage, researchers should develop a quick sketch of the educational system and its participants, primarily using observation, interviews, and document analysis as their tools. Some of the questions pursued within this stage are listed as follows:

- What learning theory and pedagogy does the instructor espouse?
- What are the learning and discourse activities?
- What computer software is being used?
- To what extent are the software tools and learning pedagogy integrated?

Second, once researchers become familiar with the context, they should create a more detailed portrait by focusing on the educational networld. As previously discussed, the networld has two primary components, the technical and the social domains. Thus, we begin with a look at the way in which computer technology is being used. Some guiding questions are listed next:

- Does the software facilitate collaboration?
- Does the software facilitate the creation of a community of learners?
- Is the software easy to use?
- Is there adequate training?
- Do the participants have frequent and easy access to the computer technology?

Painting a portrait of the social aspect of CSCL is the primary activity of this research. After all, learning dialogues and meaning-making activities are the units of analysis. Through the analysis of dialogue transcripts, we attempt to identify models and activities that help create an online community of learners, and promote active, self-regulated, and collaborative learning.

To sketch the patterns of social interaction, several researchers within this volume found it helpful to begin with a quantitative description of the dialogue transcripts. For example, we might determine the number of comments entered by teachers, learners, and experts from outside the classroom. In particular, the following calculations were helpful to our authors:

- total number and type of comments per week, topic, session, and tool feature,
- the ratio of learner–teacher, learner–learner, and learner–expert comments,
- the average number of comments by all learners, experts, and teachers,
- the average number of comments for each learner, expert, and teacher.

It may also be informative to determine the type of interactions and their frequency; that is, were the comments one-to-one, one-to-many, or many-to-many? Was there a pattern involved with these interactions, and did that (or any other) pattern change over time?

Although quantitative analysis provides a numerical portrait of the dialogue, it tells us nothing about the quality and flavor of the discourse. For this, qualitative methods of data collection and analysis are needed. That is, the electronic transcripts need to be analyzed for the words themselves, with researchers searching for emergent patterns. Additionally, the participants' perceptions should be sought through observation, interviews, and surveys, if possible.

With respect to analyzing the transcripts, authors within this text utilized several combinations of the following approaches, which are listed in Table 15.1. In the first approach, lenses for analyzing dialogue transcripts included:

- Tharp and Gallimore's (1990) seven means of assistance (Kirkley et al., chap. 9; Savory, chap. 5; Sugar & Bonk, chap. 6, all this volume),
- Selman's (1980) degree of perspective taking (Sugar, & Bonk, chap. 6, this volume),
- Bloom's (1956) taxonomy (Sugar & Bonk, chap. 6, this volume),
- Rogoff's (1990) ideas about scaffolding (Althauser & Matuga, chap. 8, this volume),
- Walther's (1996) matrix on electronic interactivity (Kang, chap. 13, this volume).

While choosing this strategy, it may be wise to follow Sugar and Bonk's (chap. 6, all this volume) use of several lenses, which helps build theoretical triangulation (Yin, 1994). That is, although the use of a sociocultural model can be helpful to focus the researcher's attention on salient issues in the discourse, it may also bias his or her observations, data collection, and analyses. By using more than one lens to filter material, researchers can build a stronger case for the authenticity of their findings.

In the second approach, several authors have used existing sociocultural theory to create a model through which to analyze data. For example, Savery

TABLE 15.1
Transcript Analysis Approaches

Transcript Analysis Approach	*Chapter/Author*
Using one or more sociocultural perspectives or coding schemes to sort dialogue.	Althauser & Matuga; Bonk et al.; Cooney; Kang; Kirkley et al.; Sugar & Bonk
Sorting dialogue for levels of interactivity.	Kang
Creating new sociocultural models to guide analysis.	Angeli & Cunningham; Savery; Zhu
Creating new coding schemes by searching for emergent comment categories and participant roles.	Althauser & Matuga; Bonk et al.; Kirkley et al.; Zhu

(chap. 5) created a model to determine to what extent students had ownership of their learning. All of the data were sifted through this four-quadrant model covering the cognitive, affective, and sociocultural domains. In chapter 10, Zhu presents a powerful model that portrays knowledge construction as a process in which learners assume a variety of dialogue participant roles (contributor, wanderer, mentor, seeker) while moving back and forth between the discussion space and the zones of engagement and development. In chapter 4, Angeli and Cunningham discuss their system of continuous assessment for literacy development in young children as they utilize computer-supported collaborative writing tools. In addition to the research presented within this volume, Henri (1992) proposed another useful method for electronic transcript analysis, which uses a three-level process to examine both the product and the process of learning dialogue. While focusing on both what was said and how it was said, Henri analyzed dialogue transcripts regarding the following five characteristics: participation, social presence, interactivity, cognition, and metacognition.

In the third approach of analyzing electronic dialogue, several authors created their own sociocultural coding schemes of emergent comment categories and participant roles. Table 15.2 summarizes the resulting coding schemes. Although all three approaches have been presented separately, in many instances, the researchers used a combination of them.

The third stage of CSCL research is to create a final portrait that is a composite of the first two sketches. The intent is to synthesize key learnings regarding how the instructional system utilized CSCL to further student cognitive, social, and cultural development. Typically, it will culminate in a final report or journal article.

In summary, while researching CSCL educational systems, our approach is to embed the study design into a detailed depiction of the phenomena. The preceding three-step process suggests beginning the study by creating a

TABLE 15.2
Comment Categorization and Role Coding Schemes

Coding Scheme	*Chapter Authors*
Comment Categorization	
Content talk, questions, peer feedback, off-task.	Althauser & Matuga; Bonk et al.; Kirkley et al.
Question, reflection, comment, answer, discussion, information sharing, scaffolding.	Althauser & Matuga; Bonk et al.; Zhu
Role Categorization	
Wanderer, lurker, contributor, mentor.	Zhu
Starter, wrapper, participant.	Zhu

rough, preliminary sketch of the foundational elements of the system, such as describing the learning theory and activities, and the software utilized. In the second step, the researcher focuses more closely on describing and analyzing the educational networld, examining both its technical and social aspects. With regard to the latter, the online dialogue can be analyzed through a variety of approaches, such as using existing sociocultural perspectives to sort discourse entries, creating a new sociocultural model to guide analysis, or creating new coding schemes by searching for emergent comment categories and participant roles. The last stage involves crystallizing key learnings through a final data analysis and synthesis, which may culminate in a written report, journal article, or dissertation.

CONCLUDING REMARKS

As this volume comes to a close, we are reminded of the tremendous challenges and opportunities that lie on the horizon of our near and distant futures. The information age has already accelerated our rate of change beyond anything we have ever experienced in recorded history. As a result, we are struggling to transform the social systems we have outgrown. Perhaps the most crucial challenge is to redesign our school systems, because they will be responsible for preparing our children as the knowledge workers of tomorrow.

Recent innovations in educational design, instructional technology, and learning theory not only provide us with new tools to help us transform our schools, but are also contributing to the impetus for such change. Computer-conferencing and collaboration technologies are altering the focus of instructional technology from human–computer communication to human–human communication, and are thereby pushing society out of the information and into the communication age. With the use of the Internet, it is now commonplace for people to collaborate, research, and socialize with peers and colleagues from across the world. Simultaneously, learning theory is stressing the importance of collaboration and dialogue as essential components of the learning process. Both activities are essential for the learning process, and are necessary foundational skills for the current and future workforce.

In fact, it is through dialogue that our learners and our workers can collaboratively synthesize meaning out of the vast amounts of information and complex problems they encounter. In the workplace, dialogue is being seen as a critical technique for building consensus, improving communication, and solving complex problems (Isaacs, 1994). Most important, dialogue is described as helping "... people learn how to think together—not just in the sense of analyzing a shared problem or creating new pieces of shared knowledge, but in the sense of occupying a collective sensibility, in which the thoughts, emotions and resulting actions belong not to one individual, but to all of them together" (Isaacs, 1994, p. 358). In the field of education, students and researchers can use dialogue for similar goals. For example, currently the annual Asilomar systems thinking conference is designed to build knowledge and understanding by engaging a select group of researchers, scholars, and students with 4 full days of dialogue. As we have demonstrated in this text, CSCL can be used to extend these dialogues across time and space, with the goal of fostering reflection, multiple perspectives, debate, questioning, and learner-generated discourse.

In order to realize the full potential of CSCL, however, we must engage in systemic design efforts that encompass all of the component subsystems. One of the first steps is to focus our primary activity on creating alternative learning systems around which all other subsystems will be developed. While designing these new learning systems, we must use current learning philosophy to structure the social spaces of our educational networlds. That is, without proper integration, guidance, and scaffolding, online discourse can easily degenerate into wasteful busy work, which will only perpetuate past failures of instructional technology implementations. Thus, we must lead CSCL design, implementation, and evaluation with holistic and systemic approaches.

The task ahead of us is awe inspiring. Rather than simply adding a new innovation to our existing systems, we are challenged to transcend our very notions of school and to redefine what it means to be a student, a teacher, or an administrator (Banathy, 1992; Jenlink et al., 1998; Reigeluth, 1994). As Siegel and Kirkley (chap. 14, this volume) discuss, being a student and teacher in this new form of schooling may involve such real-world projects as working with community officials and university experts to reclaim a polluted lake, while simultaneously communicating with peers from around the globe who are engaged in similar projects.

Although the primary impetus for such alternative learning environments is that they will prepare our children for the future, there is an even greater purpose that we may choose for ourselves. Banathy (1991) described the opportunity by using a boating metaphor. Our society is currently experiencing several waves of change, and we are sitting in a boat along the shore, struggling for survival. One response, the "preactive strategy," is to look toward the horizon, and try to determine the direction of the wave and to steer toward it. This is the approach we currently follow when we attempt to anticipate the skills our children will need in the future workplace, and attempt to design a school that will provide them with the necessary skills. Though this is certainly an effective approach, we should simultaneously consider an "interactionist" response (Banathy, 1991). Rather than simply following the pathway appearing on the horizon, we should also be attempting to steer our boat in the direction we desire—to create the society we envision. What is the future we want for ourselves and for our children? Once we have that image in our minds, we must ask ourselves what type of school can help create the individuals who will be capable of realizing that image.

Therefore, as we realize that the communication age is a wave moving in the direction of increased human–human interaction, we must ask ourselves what forms of communication we want to create. Siegel and Kirkley discuss the exciting possibilities of new dialogue opportunities with virtual reality that—through the use of special eyewear—will allow students to post virtual notes on actual objects, such as trees in a forest, and wait for another hiker to post a virtual response. Alternatively, a group of environmental experts and community representatives might assemble virtually with students and teachers to plan a new ecological project. Clearly, this new form of interaction will also require transformative patterns of discourse. By helping our students become experts in dialogue, we can foster the development of a future society where people gather, whether in person or through technology, to ponder, think, learn, and create meaning out of the vast sources of knowledge, problems, and mysteries of the world.

ACKNOWLEDGMENTS

I wish to thank Dr. Curtis J. Bonk for being a supportive and insightful collaborator on this book. Additionally, I want to express my gratitude to both Dr. Bonk and Dr. Laurie Miller Nelson for their editorial assistance on this final chapter.

REFERENCES

Ackoff, R. L. (1981). *Creating the corporate future*. New York: Wiley.

American Psychological Association. (1993). *Learner-centered psychological principles: Guidelines for school reform and restructuring*. Washington, DC: Author and Mid-continent Regional Educational Laboratory.

Banathy, B. H. (1991). *Systems design of education: A journey to create the future*. Englewood Cliffs, NJ: Educational Technology Publications.

Banathy, B. H. (1992). *A systems view of education: Concepts and principles of effective practice*. Englewood Cliffs, NJ: Educational Technology Publications.

Bloom, B. (1956). *Taxonomy of educational objectives: The classification of educational goals, by a committee of college and university examiners*. New York: Longmans, Green.

Blumenfeld, P. C., Marx, R. W., Soloway, E., & Krajcik, J. (1996). Learning with peers: From small group cooperation to collaborative communities. *Educational Researcher, 25*(8), 37–40.

Bonk, C. J., Medury, P. V., & Reynolds, T. H. (1994). Cooperative hypermedia: The marriage of collaborative writing and mediated environments. *Computers in the Schools, 10*(1/2), 79–124.

Branson, R. K. (1987). Why the schools can't improve: The upper limit hypothesis. *Journal of Instructional Development, 10*(4), 15–26.

Brown, J. S., Collins, A., & Duguid, P. (1989). Situated cognition and the culture of learning. *Educational Researcher, 18*, 32–42.

Clark, R. E. (1985). Confounding in educational computing research. *Journal of Educational Computing Research, 1*, 137–148.

Clark, R. E. (1991). When researchers swim upstream: Reflections on an unpopular argument about learning from media. *Educational Technology, 31*(2), 34–40.

Cognition and Technology Group at Vanderbilt. (1991). Designing learning environments that support thinking: The Jasper Series as a case study. In T. M. Duffy, J. Lowyck, D. H. Jonassen, & T. M. Welsh (Eds.), *Designing environments for constructivist learning* (pp. 9–36). New York: Springer-Verlag.

Conner, D. R. (1993). *Managing at the speed of change*. New York: Villard Books.

Cuban, L. (1986). *Teachers and machines: The classroom use of technology since 1920*. New York: Teachers College Press.

Darling-Hammond, L. (1990, December). Achieving your goals: Superficial or structure reforms? *Phi Delta Kappan*, pp. 286–295.

Dormant, D. (in press). The ABCD's of managing change. In H. Stolovitch (Ed.), *Handbook for human performance technology* (2nd ed.). San Francisco: Jossey-Bass.

Drucker, P. F. (1994, November). The age of social transformation. *The Atlantic Monthly*, pp. 53–80.

Gherardi, S., & Turner, B. A. (1987). Real men don't collect soft data. *Quaderno 13*, Dipartimento di Politica Sociale, Universita di Trento, Italy.

Guba, E. G. (1987). What have we learned about naturalistic evaluation? *Evaluation Practice, 8*(1), 23–43.

Harasim, L. M. (1993a). Global networks: An introduction. In L. M. Harasim (Ed.), *Global networks: Computers and international communications* (pp. 3–14). Cambridge, MA: MIT Press.

Harasim, L. M. (1993b). Networlds: Networks as social space. In L. M. Harasim (Ed.), *Global networks: Computers and international communications* (pp. 15–34). Cambridge, MA: MIT Press.

Henri, F. (1992). Computer conferencing and content analysis. In A. R. Kaye (Ed.), *Collaborative learning through computer conferencing: The Najaden papers* (pp. 117–135). New York: Springer-Verlag.

Honebein, P. C., Duffy, T. M., & Fishman, B. J. (1991). Constructivism and the design of learning environments: Context and authentic activities for learning. In T. M. Duffy, J. Lowyck, D. H. Jonassen, & T. M. Welsh (Eds.), *Designing environments for constructivist learning* (pp. 88–108). New York: Springer-Verlag.

Isaacs, W. (1994). Dialogue. In P. M. Senge, A. Kleiner, C. Roberts, R. B. Ross, & B. J. Smith (Eds.), *The fifth discipline fieldbook: Strategies and tools for building a learning organization* (pp. 357–364). New York: Doubleday.

Jenlink, P. M., Reigeluth, C. M., Carr, A. A., & Nelson, L. M. (1998). *Facilitating systemic change in school districts: A guidebook*. Manuscript in preparation.

Koschmann, T. D. (1994). Toward a theory of computer support for collaborative learning. *The Journal of the Learning Sciences, 3*(3), 219–225.

Koschmann, T. D., Myers, A. C., Feltovich, P. J., & Barrows, H. S. (1994). Using technology to assist in realizing effective learning and instruction: A principled approach to the use of computers in collaborative learning. *The Journal of the Learning Sciences, 3*(3), 227–264.

Kozol, J. (1991). *Savage inequalities: Children in American schools*. New York: Crown Publishers.

Lauzon, A., & Moore, G. (1989). A fourth generation distance education system: Integrating computer-assisted learning and computer conferencing. *The American Journal of Distance Education, 3*(1), 38–49.

Merriam, S. B. (1988). *Case study research in education: A qualitative approach*. San Francisco: Jossey-Bass.

Miles, M. B., & Huberman, A. M. (1994). *Qualitative data analysis: An expanded sourcebook* (2nd ed.). Beverly Hills, CA: Sage.

Papert, S. (1980). *Mindstorms: Children, computers and powerful ideas*. New York: Basic Books.

Papert, S. (1993). *The children's machine: Rethinking school in the age of the computer*. New York: Basic Books.

Pea, R. D. (1994). Seeing what we build together: Distributed multimedia learning environments for transformative communications. *The Journal of the Learning Sciences, 3*(3), 285–299.

Provenzo, E. F. (1986). *Beyond the Gutenberg galaxy: Microcomputers and the emergence of post-typographic culture*. New York: Teachers College Press.

Reigeluth, C. M. (1994). Introduction: The imperative for systemic change. In C. M. Reigeluth & R. J. Garfinkle (Eds.), *Systemic change in education* (pp. 3–11). Englewood Cliffs, NJ: Educational Technology Publications.

Reigeluth, C. M., & Garfinkle, R. J. (Eds.). (1994). *Systemic change in education*. Englewood Cliffs, NJ: Educational Technology Publications.

Rogers, E. (1983). *Diffusion of innovations* (3rd ed.). New York: The Free Press.

Rogoff, B. (1990). *Apprenticeship in thinking: Cognitive development in social context*. New York: Oxford University Press.

Ruopp, R., Gal, S., Drayton, B., & Pfister, M. (1993). *LabNet: Toward a community of practice*. Hillsdale, NJ: Lawrence Erlbaum Associates.

Saettler, P. (1990). *The evolution of American educational technology*. Englewood, CO: Libraries Unlimited.

Salisbury, D. F. (1992, July). Toward a new generation of schools: The Florida Schoolyear 2000 Initiative. *Educational Technology*, pp. 7–12.

Salomon, G. (1991). Transcending the qualitative-quantitative debate: The analytic and systematic approaches to educational research. *Educational Researcher, 20*(6), 10–18.

Salomon, G. (1996). Studying novel learning environments as patterns of change. In S. Vosniados, E. DeCorte, R. Glaser, & H. Mandl (Eds.), *International perspectives on the design of technology supported learning environments* (pp. 363–377). Mahwah, NJ: Lawrence Erlbaum Associates.

Scardamalia, M., & Bereiter, C. (1994). Computer support for knowledge-building communities. *The Journal of the Learning Sciences, 3*(3), 265–283.

Selman, R. (1980). *The growth of interpersonal understanding: Developmental and clinical analysis*. New York: Academic Press.

Sloan, D. (Ed.). (1984). *The computer in education: A critical perspective*. New York: Teachers College Press.

Tharp, R., & Gallimore, R. (1990). Teaching mind in society: Teaching, schooling, and literate discourse. In L. C. Moll (Ed.), *Vygotsky in education: Instructional implications of sociohistorical psychology* (pp. 175–205). New York: Cambridge University Press.

Thornburg, D. D. (1995, January). *Hitchhikers' guide to cyberspace*. Keynote address given to Indiana Computer Educators' Association annual conference, Indianapolis.

Vygotsky, L. S. (1978). *Mind in society: The development of higher psychological processes* (M. Cole, V. John-Steiner, S. Scribner, & E. Souberman, Eds.). Cambridge, MA: Harvard University Press.

Walther, J. B. (1996). Computer-mediated communication: Impersonal, interpersonal and hyperpersonal interaction. *Communication Researcher, 23*(1), 3–43.

Wells, G., & Chang-Wells, G. L. (1992). *Constructing knowledge together: Classrooms as centers of inquiry and literacy*. Portsmouth, NH: Heinemann.

Yin, R. K. (1994). *Case study research design and methods* (2nd ed.). Beverly Hills, CA: Sage.

Author Index

H

I

J

K

L

M

N

O

P

Q

R

S

T

V

W

Y

Z

Subject Index

A

B

C

D

E

F

G

H

I

K

L

M

T

U

V

W

Z